"Custome Is an Idiot"

"Custome Is an Idiot"

JACOBEAN PAMPHLET LITERATURE ON WOMEN

Edited by *Susan Gushee O'Malley*

Afterword by *Ann Rosalind Jones*

UNIVERSITY OF ILLINOIS PRESS

URBANA AND CHICAGO

∞ This book is printed on acid-free paper.

Library of Congress Cataloging-in-Publication Data
Custome is an idiot : Jacobean pamphlet literature on women /
edited by Susan Gushee O'Malley ; afterword by Ann Rosalind Jones.
p. cm.
Includes bibliographical references and index.
ISBN 0-252-02842-2 (cloth : alk. paper)
ISBN 0-252-07128-X (pbk. : alk. paper)
1. Women—England—History—17th century.
2. Women in literature.
I. O'Malley, Susan Gushee, 1942– .
HQ1599.E5C87 2004
305.4'0942—dc21 2002155571

For Barbara Bowen,

friend, scholar, and union leader

and

Calla, Aedan Grace, and Liam Hastings,

the next generation

Contents

Acknowledgments

"Custome Is an Idiot" would not have been possible without the patience of my family and the support of friends and numerous grants. Several graduate students were also essential to its completion.

Foremost thanks go to my children, Ragan and Brendan O'Malley; my partner, Will Saunders; my father, who always read everything I wrote; my son-in-law, Calvin Hastings; and my grandchildren: Calla, who often politely inquired when I expected to finish, and Aedan Grace and Liam Henry, who were too young to ask.

Many friends read sections of the manuscript or encouraged me in numerous conversations and e-mails about the importance of the project. Barbara Bowen worked with me on earlier stages of the manuscript before she was elected president of the City University of New York union; Jean Howard, Margaret Ferguson, Pamela Brown, Valerie Wayne, Betty Travitsky, Natasha Korda, Suzanne Gossett, Melinda Gough, Berenice Fisher, Kennie Lyman, Patricia Lennox, Joseph Wittriech, and Gerald Bray read my proposal, helped me with obscure annotations, or provided sane conversation and support over the years. Special thanks go to Cristina Malcolmson and Mihoko Suzuki for their Shakespeare Association of America seminar on early modern women writers and the pamphlet debate on gender; to the Society for the Study of Renaissance Women, for which I presented several talks based on the pamphlets; and to Ann Rosalind Jones, for writing the afterword.

Grant support allowed me to spend time at the Folger, Huntington, Bodleian, and British libraries. The Office of Academic Affairs of the City University of New York provided me with a generous CUNY Collaborative Grant that permitted me to work at the Folger and British libraries. I also received several Professional Staff Congress/CUNY grants that provided release time from teaching and library research support. In addition, I received two National Endowment for the Humanities travel grants, a Huntington Library Fellowship, and several Folger Seminar Grants, one of which allowed me to participate in Ann Rosalind Jones's seminar on the polemics of gender.

Several current and former graduate students were instrumental in the completion of *"Custome Is an Idiot."* Two classicists, Anthony Austin and Georgia Tsouvala, helped translate the Greek and Latin passages. Christine Hutchins, Ian Moulton, and Michael Rothberg, all of whom now have tenure-track jobs, helped annotate the pamphlets (including some that were cut in the final version of the manuscript). Erin Hendrikson, a recent Ph.D. recipient, and Desma Polydorou, a current graduate student, helped research the chapters. Thanks also go to Jeptha Evans, who taught some of my classes, supported by the CUNY Collaborative Grant. Peter Saunders and Charles Labita provided much-needed computer support.

Final thanks go to the librarians and editors without whom my work would not be possible. Georgianna Ziegler at the Folger Library and Robert Scott at the Columbia University Library led me to resources that I would not have found otherwise. To Ann Lowry, my editor at the University of Illinois Press, many thanks for your patience and belief in *"Custome Is an Idiot."*

I am grateful to the following libraries for providing the illustrations that appear in this book:

Title page of *Well met Gossip* (1619). C.57.b.47. Reproduced by permission of the British Library.

Title page of *Well met gossip* (1627). Reproduced by permission of the Henry W. and Albert A. Berg Collection of English and American Literature, New York Public Library, Astor, Lenox, and Tilden Foundations.

Title page of *Tis Merry when Gossips meet* (1609). Mal 299(10). Reproduced by permission of the Bodleian Library, University of Oxford.

Title page of *A whole crew of kind Gossips, all met to be merry* (1609). Mal 717(4). Reproduced by permission of the Bodleian Library, University of Oxford.

Title page of Christopher Newstead's *Apology For Women* (1620). RB62767. Reproduced by permission of the Huntington Library, San Marino, California.

Title page of William Heale's *Apologie For Women* (1609). 8415e46. Reproduced by permission of the British Library.

Page 30 [E2v] of William Heale's *Apologie For Women* (1609). 8415e46. Reproduced by permission of the British Library.

Title page of *Hic Mulier* (1620). RB61256. Reproduced by permission of the Huntington Library, San Marino, California.

Title page of *Haec-Vir* (1620). RB61257. Reproduced by permission of the Huntington Library, San Marino, California.

"Custome Is an Idiot"

Introduction

Were women thought to be superior to men in the early seventeenth century? Was it lawful for a man to beat his wife? Were women allowed to wear men's clothing? *"Custome Is an Idiot": Jacobean Pamphlet Literature on Women,* an annotated edition of six pamphlets written between 1609 and 1620, attempts to answer such questions. These "gender pamphlets" voice competing positions on the urgent seventeenth-century question about the nature of women: How much was ordained by God and how much was custom, and therefore subject to change?

The title of this book comes from *Haec-Vir; or, The Womanish-Man,* an anonymous pamphlet written in 1620. Hic-Mulier (The Man-Woman), dressed in male attire, answers the accusation of "unnaturalnesse" by Haec-Vir (The Womanish Man) by asserting that "Custome is an Idiot." Haec-Vir condemns Hic-Mulier because he believes that the deformity of her dress has caused her "to forsake the Creation of God, and Customes of the Kingdome." Hic-Mulier responds by deconstructing the idea of custom: she argues that in England it is the fashion for mourners to wear black, in Rome, white; in England men may shave their mustaches, in other countries this is considered immodest. Therefore, to Hic-Mulier, "whosoever dependeth wholey upon [Custome], without the discourse of Reason, . . . will become a slave indeed to contempt and censure." What Hic-Mulier objects to, I suggest, is the transformation of custom into the so-called natural, or that which is God-given.[1]

The writers of the pamphlets reprinted in this collection typically put forth arguments that contest custom, specifically regarding what was considered acceptable behavior or treatment of women in the seventeenth century. Dressed in masculine clothing, Hic-Mulier asserts that women "are as free-borne as Men." In *An Apology For Women; or, Women's Defence,* Christopher Newstead argues for the superiority of women. William Heale argues against wife beating in *An Apologie For Women,* and Samuel Rowlands's gossips drink together in a tavern and proclaim "Weele have a Wench shall be our Poet" in *Tis Merry when Gossips meet.* These protestations of equality and sometimes female superiority are what led me to choose these pamphlets from among the many other polemics on women in the Jacobean period.

Although these six pamphlets flout custom, they ultimately reinscribe it. At the end of *Haec-Vir,* the man-woman and the womanish man exchange clothes. Hic-Mulier agrees to assume feminine garb and act like a woman if Haec-Vir will be less effeminate. In his *Apology,* Newstead argues that women are more virtuous primarily because they were created inferior to men. He also excludes "the dregges and scumme . . . of woman kinde" from "the shield" of his defense. These women, whom seventeenth-century misogynists labeled "necessary evils," are the focus of antiwomen pamphlets. In addition, Newstead claims that "the Sexe feminine [is] to govern the house" and be a comfort to her husband. Heale may argue against wife beating, but his pamphlet was written in response to the assertion that "'it was lawfull for husbands to beate their wives,'" which was part of a formal disputation at Oxford; in fact, at the time it *was* legal for husbands to beat their wives. Although in his defense against wife beating Heale sounds like Hic-Mulier in proclaiming women's equality with men, he also describes how a woman should behave to be true to her "nature." In his chapter on civil and canon law, he states that wives are "in the law free burgesses of the same citie whereof their husbands are free . . . both participating the same rightes, both injoying the same liberties." But women, according to Heale, are by nature "milde, loving, gentle & faire." Rowlands ends his gossip pamphlet, *A whole crew,* with the sixth husband's bitter desire that his wife and those of the other husbands die:

> But let us hope they'le shortly to their grave,
> And then we quyet lives a peece shall have:
> And he to whom kind *Death* this freedome gives,
> Let him take heed of wiving while he lives."

It is impossible to say how these pamphlets were received by those who read or heard them,[2] but we can assume that not all readers responded alike. Certainly an educated reader would have responded differently from an uneducated one, and female readers probably read the pamphlets differently from male readers. In his introduction to *Popular Culture in England, c. 1500–1850,* Tim Harris suggests that "men and women experienced popular culture in very different ways and . . . did not occupy the culture of their class in the same way."[3] In her edition of Shakespeare's *Taming of the Shrew,* Frances E. Dolan speculates on possible responses to Thomas Heywood's *Curtain Lecture.* She suggests that "it is possible to imagine a female reader who finds encouragement in all this female complaint or who picks up tips about things she might resent or insults she could level."[4] Pamela Brown echoes this contention when she writes that some "satire [of women] raises to view scenes and pleasures that some might prefer to imitate rather than scorn."[5] Might not some women, particularly those like Rachel Speght and Aemelia Lanyer, who would publish under their own names,[6] have gained sustenance from Rowlands's *Whole crew,* in which the gossips insist that "Weele have a Wench shall be our Poet"? Or perhaps they were encouraged by *Tis Merry,* in which a woman sings a ballad "Pen'd by a Mayde her selfe" and the husbands complain that their wives have slandered them "in print." Or might not women who were beaten by their husbands have found in Heale's pamphlet the courage to protest against abuse? Some of the pamphlets may have been written as rhetorical exercises, but for readers not trained in rhetoric, perhaps their content was more important than their form.

Several of these pamphlets were published in multiple editions, so it is likely that they circulated widely among seventeenth-century readers. There were seven editions of Rowlands's *Tis Merry* between 1602 and 1675—rivaling in popularity Joseph Swetnam's antiwoman tract *The Araignment of Lewd, idle, froward, and unconstant women,* which had ten editions between 1615 and 1637— three of *A whole crew* between 1609 and 1663, and two of Heale's *Apologie For Women* (the second edition of which was significantly revised). Female readership may be indicated by the fact that some of the pamphlets are dedicated to women: Heale's *Apologie For Women* (1609) to Lady M.H. and Newstead's *Apology For Women* (1620) to Mary Beaumont, the Countess of Buckingham. Studies by Margaret Ferguson, Jacqueline Pearson, and Eve Sanders suggest that the literacy rate for women, particularly in London, was higher than previously thought.[7] Given the strictures on their time, women who could read may have been more likely to read a short pamphlet than a longer book, and the brevity of the pamphlets also might have made it more likely for them to be read aloud in household circles.[8] I think we may safely assume that the pamphlets in *"Custome Is an Idiot"* were read or at least heard by many women and that the reception of these pamphlets by some of these women may have differed from the dominant readings.

The pamphlet form itself also resisted custom, or at least what was considered acceptable. Sir Thomas Bodley wanted no pamphlets to defile the library he founded at Oxford in 1603. He wrote to the librarian at the Bodleian that "'the benefit therof will nothing neere contervaile, the harme that the scandal will bring unto the Librarie, when it shalbe given out, that we stuffe it full of baggage books.'"[9] (Despite its founder's wishes, the six pamphlets included in *"Custome Is an Idiot"* found their way into the Bodleian Library.) Pamphlets were also described as ephemeral or as having to do with gossip. Several of the pamphlets in this volume were published in octavo, which meant that they were small enough to be carried in the reader's pocket. In a preface to *Tis Merry,* the Apprentice persuades the Gentleman to buy the pamphlet because he can put it in his pocket when he tires of hearing the voices of the Maid, the Wife, and the Widow and take it out when he is ready to listen to more. In this case the pamphlet becomes a female commodity for gentlemen to own and listen to at their leisure.[10]

What exactly is a pamphlet? It is unclear what Jacobean writers meant by the word, but the *Oxford English Dictionary* defines it as "a small treatise occupying fewer pages or sheets than would make a book, composed and (a) written, or (b, since c. 1500) printed, and issued as a separate work; always (at least in later use) unbound, with or without paper covers." In his dedication to the Earl of Southampton, Shakespeare describes his narrative poem *The Rape of Lucrece* (1594) as a pamphlet: "The love I dedicate to your Lordship is without end: wherof this Pamphlet without beginning is but a superfluous Moity."[11] William Gouge describes his sermon *The Extent of God's Providence* (1623) as "a little Pamphlet" because "of the smalnesse of it."[12] Modern scholars, too, have not reached a consensus on the definiton of "pamphlet." Marie Helen Davies writes that the term derives from the French *palme-feuillet,* which means what can be held in the hand; therefore, a pamphlet is a small, thin book that is never bound because of its insignificance.[13] In *Women and the English Renaissance,* Linda Woodbridge dispenses with the term "pamphlet," labeling it "insidious" and arguing that it denotes "hasty composition, ephemerality, a popular and undiscriminating readership, and hack work."[14] After admitting the difficulty of defining "pamphlet," George Orwell, in volume 1 of *British Pamphleteers from the Sixteenth Century to the*

French Revolution, describes it as a "special literary form," a "short piece of polemical writing, printed in the form of a booklet and aimed at a large public . . . that is never written to give entertainment or to make money."[15]

Unlike Woodbridge, I prefer to retain the term "pamphlet," but I define it less restrictedly than Orwell. In my view, a pamphlet is simply a short unbound book. It may be in prose or verse (Rowlands's two gossip pamphlets in *"Custome Is an Idiot"* are in verse); it may have been written to inform and instruct as well as entertain; and it may have been written to make money. (I suspect—but cannot prove—that some of the authors of the pamphlets in this volume hoped eventually to realize a profit from their writing.) Although I will not argue that the pamphlet is a literary genre, I suggest that it has literary value and is a critical part of the early modern print culture, hence the term "literature" in my subtitle: *Jacobean Pamphlet Literature on Women.*

Other than ballads and broadsides, pamphlets were the least expensive printed matter available at seventeenth-century bookstalls. A pamphlet cost two to six pence, depending on the number of pages;[16] the sixpence that the Gentleman in the preface to *Tis Merry* pays would have been considered a very high price. Although pamphlets were disparaged, they were necessary for the survival of printing houses. Printers, particularly those who were not booksellers or publishers, did not fare well financially because there was neither enough work nor enough capital to finance new work. Pamphlet printing was necessary for their survival because the turnaround time for printing a pamphlet was short. Printers could set the type, print a pamphlet, and realize a quick profit at the same time they were setting the type and correcting the proofs for a longer work. Because one of the major costs of production was paper,[17] which was bought in great quantity, the quick returns on pamphlets helped solve the printing houses' frequent cash flow problems. William Jaggard, printer of the 1609 edition of Rowlands's two gossip pamphlets, produced many pamphlets and other small texts while his compositors were working on Shakespeare's first folio, published in 1623.

The authors represented in *"Custome Is an Idiot"* probably made little money writing their pamphlets. Payments generally ranged from a small fee (plus a certain number of copies of the pamphlet to sell themselves) to about two pounds for one pamphlet. Because there was no copyright law, writers made no extra money for subsequent editions unless they wrote additional material; instead, the publisher profited from the reprintings. If a press run was 1250–1500 copies and a pamphlet sold for three pence, the publisher made about seventeen pounds minus printing costs if he paid the writer the top price of two pounds.[18]

Although pamphlets were necessary for the survival of print shops and probably were more widely read in the early seventeenth century than the writings of Edmund Spenser or Philip Sidney, they were also an anomalous, disruptive form. Alexandra Halasz suggests that the most interesting features of pamphlets are "the ways in which they trouble categories within the discursive field and the distinctions between economic and cultural forms of value, in short, their dissolving effect on systems of classification or opposition."[19] If pamphlets were in some sense indefinable, they might also have been considered uncontrollable, although attempts were made to control them. In 1559, many pamphlets were burned by the Stationers Company at the command of John Whitgift, Archbishop of Canterbury, and Richard Bancroft, Bishop of London, the official censors of the press.[20] *A Mery Meetinge; or, 'Tis Merry when Knaves mete* and *The Letting of Humours Blood in the Head-Vaine,* two pamphlets by Rowlands that are not included here, were deemed so offensive that they were publicly burned by order of the censors in the kitchen of the Stationers Company on 26 October 1600.

The burning of pamphlets on controversial subjects indicates an anxiety about their disruptiveness that is similar to the patriarchal anxiety many pamphlet writers expressed about the lack of control of women. Printed texts were often likened to women's bodies, whether improperly on public display or as a means of reproduction. *Tis Merry* was marketed by the Apprentice as a female commodity to be pocketed at will by the Gentleman. Wendy Wall cites other examples of published books represented as bodies, particularly women's bodies, in *The Imprint of Gender Authorship and Publication in the English Renaissance.* For example, in the 1570 edition of *Gorboduc,* written by Thomas Sackville and Thomas Norton and retitled *The Tragidie of Ferrix and Porrex,* the preface describes the former edition as a virgin ravished by a printer and then abandoned.[21] Pamphlets, in particular, might be described as being female due to their changeable form, their doubtful reputation as literary works, and the way in which they were handed from reader to reader.

What cultural work did the six pamphlets included in *"Custome Is an Idiot"* do? As Stuart Hall argues, meaning is not inscribed within a cultural text but is the result of articulation within a specific context that varies according to the education, politics, and class, among many characteristics, of those who receive the text. "'Meaning,'" according to Hall, "'is therefore a social production. . . . And because different meanings can be ascribed to the same text or practice or event, meaning is always a potential site of conflict. . . . a terrain of "incorporation" and "resistance"; one of the sites where hegemony is to be won or lost.'"[22] The polemics in *"Custome Is an Idiot"* participate in this "potential site of conflict" and provide a context for understanding more canonical texts. After reading Heale's *Apologie For Women* on wife beating, one might read or view Shakespeare's *Taming of the Shrew* or *Othello* differently. In their use of classical, religious, literary, and legal references, Newstead, Heale, and the anonymous authors of *Hic Mulier* and *Haec-Vir* reveal the texts that educated people read and the issues they debated. The five authors of the pamphlets in *"Custome Is an Idiot"* participated in the contestation over women's bodies, tongues, and minds and in the naturalization of women's subjugation. In some ways their pamphlets pushed against the strictures defining women—for example, there are significant moments in which women may have found space for their speech, camaraderie, and agency—but ultimately they reinscribed women's nature as chaste, silent, and obedient. Yet it is important not to forget the statements in the pamphlets that support the idea of "custome" as an "Idiot" in understanding early modern women's culture.

Methodology

We have come a long way since the pioneering book *Half Humankind: Contexts and Texts of the Controversy about Women in England, 1540–1640.*[23] Much of the pamphlet literature on the controversy about women and on the construction of woman's "nature" is now available in excerpted form for classroom use. The new Bedford editions of Shakespeare's plays include pamphlet literature among the historical documents that accompany each play. Dolan's edition of *The Taming of the Shrew* excerpts pamphlets that discuss marriage, shrews, and wife- and servant-beating, which could change how students read the play. Also, several complete editions of pamphlets focus on single writers: Barbara Kiefer Lewalski's edition of Speght's *Mouzell for Melastomus* (1617) and Valerie Wayne's edition of Edmund Tilney's *Flower of Friendship: A Renaissance Dialogue Contesting Marriage* (1568). Facsimile editions, such as my *Defences of Women: Jane Anger, Rachel Speght, Ester Sowernam, and Constantia Munda,* are also available.[24]

"Custome Is an Idiot" differs from previous editions of pamphlets because it presents six complete texts that, if available at all, have been found only in excerpted form. Instead of presenting one text in a critical edition, this collection provides a range of the pamphlet literature on women that was circulating in England in the early seventeenth century. The copy text chosen is always the first complete printed edition. Any additions or deletions in later editions (or, in the case of Rowlands's *Tis Merry,* a previous incomplete edition) are included at the end of the main text so that the reader may understand how a text changed over time. I have chosen not to collate different editions because I want to give a sense of what actual readers encountered in varying editions. Today's readers can better understand the historical transmission of these texts by observing how dedications or prefatory material changed or what new ballads were appended to later editions. This editing decision is evident in the two Rowlands pamphlets (only one edition existed of the Newstead pamphlet and of *Hic Mulier* and *Haec-Vir*). The second edition of the Heale pamphlet is so different from the first that I did not include the changes.

For greater authenticity and to keep the sense of play and punning in the pamphlets' language, the original spelling has been retained. (Examples of puns that would be lost with modernized spelling are "malecontent" for "malcontent" and "wonderfool" for "wonderful.") I have, however, silently replaced *i* with *j* and *u* with *v* where necessary and regularized uneven spacing. Any other changes appear in square brackets after the word in question.

Four of the six pamphlets contain marginalia, whereby the author shows off his learning, using the strength of his erudition to prove that his argument is superior. Moses à Vauts, in *The Husband's Authority Unvail'd; Wherein It is moderately discussed whether it be fit or lawfull for a good Man, to beat his bad Wife,* states that the margin presents "the Meat, the *Page* but the *Sauce.*"[25] Marginal citations are occasionally incorrect, perhaps because the authors wrote them from memory or changed them to fit their arguments. For example, Newstead refers to the wrong book by Aristotle and points to a discussion in *Diogenes Laertius* that does not exist; Heale falsely cites Aerodius and claims that Nero appears in Plutarch's *Advice to Bride and Groom,* which he does not. Such errors are frustrating but have been retained so that readers can see how these authors substantiated their arguments. In my view, the number of references cited is more important than the accuracy of the citations because most seventeenth-century readers would not have had access to the books in any event, nor would they have considered accurate citation to be important.

Because the marginalia in the Heale and Newstead pamphlets is extensive and difficult to read, given the use of Latin and, occasionally, Greek abbreviations, I have moved it to the endnotes, where it is enclosed in angle brackets. So that readers can see the importance of the marginalia to the text, I have included a photograph of one page of Heale's *Apologie For Women.* The marginalia in *Hic Mulier* and *Haec-Vir* has been retained and should prove useful in locating the various arguments of the pamphlet. It offers a playful dialectic with the text that will help readers understand the humor of the anonymous authors. When Hic Mulier in the pamphlet of that name harangues women for painting their faces, the author writes in the margin, "Where the best painting is sold." When Hic Mulier in *Haec-Vir* explains how customs vary in different countries, a comment in the margin reads, "Foolish Customes."

I make extensive use of endnotes in the pamphlets to define words and explain mythical, historical, literary, legal, and religious allusions. The nature and extent of this information varies with each pamphlet. In the gossip pamphlets, the endnotes primarily provide readings of confusing lines and explain topical references to London, contemporary ballads, tavern culture, proverbs, women's clothing, and work. The endnotes in Newstead's *Apology For Women* deal with classical literature and religious history as well as references to the contemporary poets Philip Sidney and Michael Drayton. In Heale's *Apologie For Women* I provide many endnotes on canon and civil law, classical literature, church history, commentaries on the Bible, and literary references to Petrarch and Sidney. The endnotes for *Hic Mulier* and *Haec-Vir* address fashion, contemporary history, and classical literature and include references to Sidney, Spenser, Michel de Montaigne, Miguel de Cervantes, Guillame de Salluste Du Bartas, and Ludovico Ariosto. I also pay particular attention to issues concerning women, such as women's work, dress, marriage, and courtship. Of course, the pamphlets may be read without the endnotes, but the endnotes do provide a grounding in the cultural history of the early seventeenth century that it would be unfortunate for readers to miss. I suppose the endnotes are my "sauce" to the pamphlets' "meat."

NOTES

1. My views on how ideology works to naturalize subjugation are influenced by Louis Althusser's conception of culture as an ideological state apparatus. See his "Ideology and Ideological State Apparatuses (Notes towards an Investigation)," in *"Lenin and Philosophy" and Other Essays* (New York: Monthly Review Press, 1971), 127–86.

2. See Barry Reay, "Orality, Literacy, and Print," in *Popular Cultures in England, 1550–1750* (London: Longman, 1998), 36–70.

3. Tim Harris, ed., *Popular Culture in England, c. 1500–1850* (London: MacMillan, 1995).

4. Frances E. Dolan, "Texts and Contexts," in *The Taming of the Shrew* by William Shakespeare, ed. Frances E. Dolan (Boston: Bedford Books of St. Martin's Press, 1996), 325.

5. Pamela Allen Brown, *Better a Shrew Than a Sheep: Jesting Women in Early Modern Drama and Culture* (Ithaca, N.Y.: Cornell University Press, 2003).

6. In 1617, Rachel Speght wrote *A Mouzell for Melastomus,* a response to Joseph Swetnam's *Araignment of Lewde, idle, froward and unconstant women.* In 1611 Aemelia Lanyer wrote *Salve Deus Rex Judarorum,* a poem on Christ's passion that includes nine dedications to women as well as the country-house poem "Cooke-ham."

7. Margaret Ferguson, "Renaissance Concepts of the 'Woman Writer,'" in *Women and Literature,* ed. Helen Wilcox (New York: Cambridge University Press, 1996), 147–50; and Jacqueline Pearson, "Women Reading, Reading Women," in *Women and Literature,* ed. Wilcox, 80–81. Eve Rachele Sanders includes a brief survey of articles on women and literacy in *Gender and Literacy on Stage in Early Modern England* (Cambridge: Cambridge University Press, 1988), 197n.3.

8. See "Women's Household Circles as a Gendered Reading Formation: Whitney, Tyler, and Lanyer" in Louise Schleiner's *Tudor and Stuart Women Writers* (Bloomington: Indiana University Press, 1994), 1–29.

9. *Letters of Sir Thomas Bodley to Thomas James. First Keeper of the Bodleian Library,* ed. G. W. Wheeler, 222, quoted in Alexandra Halasz, *The Marketplace of Print: Pamphlets and the Public Sphere in Early Modern England* (Cambridge: Cambridge University Press, 1997), 1.

10. In *The Imprint of Gender: Authorship and Publication in the English Renaissance* (Ithaca, N.Y.: Cornell University Press, 1993), Wendy Wall uses "A Conference between a Gentleman and a Prentice" to suggest "the conflation of [pamphlet] text and woman" (204). Halasz discusses the preface to *Tis Merry* in her section on commodity pamphlets in *Marketplace of Print,* 171–74.

11. William Shakespeare, *The Rape of Lucrece,* in *The Riverside Shakespeare,* 2d ed. (Boston: Houghton Mifflin, 1997), 1816. All references to Shakespeare's works are from this edition.

12. William Gouge, *The Extent of God's Providence* (1623; London, 1631).

13. Marie Helen Davies, *Reflections of Renaissance England: Thought and Religion Mirrored in Illustrated Pamphlets, 1535–1640* (Allison Park, Pa.: Pickwick Press, 1986), 2.

14. Linda Woodbridge, *Women and the English Renaissance: Literature and the Nature of Women, 1549–1620* (Urbana: University of Illinois Press, 1986), 7.

15. George Orwell and Reginald Reynolds, eds., *British Pamphleteers,* vol. 1: *From the Sixteenth Century to the French Revolution* (London: Wingatc, 1948), 7.

16. Edwin Miller Haviland, *The Professional Writer in Elizabethan England: A Study of Nondramatic Literature* (Cambridge, Mass.: Harvard University Press, 1959), 151–64; Sandra Clark, *The Elizabethan Moralistic Pamphlets, 1580–1640* (London: Athlone Press, 1983), 25; H. S. Bennett, *English Books and Readers, 1603–1640,* vol. 2 (New York: Cambridge University Press, 1965), 228; Davies, *Reflections of Renaissance England,* 2.

17. Halasz, *Marketplace of Print,* 15. In *Cheap Print and Popular Piety, 1550–1540* (Cambridge: Cambridge University Press, 1991), 262, Tessa Watt states that paper was often 75 percent of the cost of production of a book, depending on length and whether or not it was the first edition.

18. See Phoebe Sheavyn, *The Literary Profession in the Elizabethan Age* (1909; rpt., New York: Haskell House, 1964); and Colin Clair, *A History of Printing in Britain* (London: Cassell, 1965).

19. Halasz, *Marketplace of Print,* 7.

20. *Records of the Court of the Stationers Co. from Register B.,* ed. W. W. Greg and Eleanor Boswell (London: Bibliographical Society, 1930), 79. The pamphlets and books burned by the Stationers Company in 1599 were written by Thomas Nashe, John Marston, Christopher Marlowe, Gabriel Harvey, Robert Tofte, Sir John Davies, and Thomas Middleton, among others. See Lynda E. Boose, "The 1599 Bishops' Ban, Elizabethan Pornography, and the Sexualization of the Jacobean Stage," in *Enclosure Acts,* ed. Richard Burt and John Michael Archer (Ithaca, N.Y.: Cornell University Press, 1994), 185–87.

21. Wall, *Imprint of Gender,* 181–88.

22. Stuart Hall, quoted in Richard Johnson, "What Is Cultural Studies Anyway?" in *What Is Cultural Studies? A Reader,* ed. John Stray (London: Arnold, 1996), 4.

23. *Half Humankind: Contexts and Texts of the Controversy about Women in England, 1540–1640,* ed. Katherine Usher Henderson and Barbara F. McManus (Urbana: University of Illinois Press, 1985).

24. *The Polemics and Poems of Rachel Speght,* ed. Barbara Kiefer Lewalski (New York: Oxford University Press, 1996); Edmund Tilney, *The Flower of Friendship: A Renaissance Dialogue Contesting Marriage,* ed. Valerie Wayne (Ithaca, N.Y.: Cornell University Press, 1992); *Defences of Women: Jane Anger, Rachel Speght, Ester Sowernam, and Constantia Munda,* ed. Susan Gushee O'Malley, vol. 4 of *The Early Modern Englishwoman: A Facsimile Library of Essential Works,* pt. 1: *Printed Works, 1500–1640,* ed. Betty S. Travitsky and Patrick Cullen (Aldershot, England: Scolar Press, 1996).

25. Moses à Vauts, *The Husband's Authority Unvail'd; Wherein It is moderately discussed whether it be fit or lawfull for a good Man, to beat his bad Wife* (London, 1650), A2r.

1 "A Shroe is ten times better then a sheepe": Samuel Rowlands's Gossip Pamphlets

ALTHOUGH "gossip" was not necessarily a derogatory term in the early 1600s, it was sometimes used as such. In the fifteenth and sixteenth centuries, "gossip" or "godsip" was used to describe godparents of either gender; in the sixteenth and seventeenth centuries, the definition was expanded to include any close male or female friend. Gossip, or the exchange of stories, opinion, or rumor, was useful to a community in maintaining order and neighborliness.[1] In the eighteenth century, as the term began to apply only to women, it took on a negative connotation. For example, Samuel Johnson's *Dictionary* (1755) defines "gossip" as "one who runs about tattling like women in a lying in."

The gossips in *Tis Merry when Gossips meet* and *A whole crew of kind Gossips,* are drinking wine in a tavern, and evidence exists that this was not an unusual occurrence in the early modern period. In 1599, Thomas Platter of Switzerland commented in an account of his travels in England that "women as well as the men, in fact more often than they will frequent the taverns or ale-houses for enjoyment. They count it a great honour to be taken there and given wine with sugar to drink; and if one woman only is invited, then she will bring three or four other women along and they gaily toast each other; the husband afterwards thanks him who has given his wife such pleasure, for they deem it a real kindness."[2] But Platter missed the anxiety expressed by male authors of gossip literature about women drinking together in the taverns.[3] The women in Rowlands's gossip pamphlets enter the tavern without men and, in *Tis Merry,* drink "like men"—at least six pints of claret or sack until the bells of St. Mary-le-Bow ring at 9 P.M.

The fact that the gossips are drinking in a tavern, not an alehouse, may indicate their class aspirations. Taverns generally sold wine to more prosperous individuals while alehouses sold beer and ale to the less prosperous. In a dialogue entitled *Wine, Beere, Ale, and Tobacco,*[4] written in 1630, wine is said to be the drink of courtiers, gentlemen, and poetical wits; beer, the drink of citizens; and ale, the drink of those who live in the country. The women in Rowlands's pamphlets are proud that they can pay their own drinking bills; in the preface to *Tis Merry,* the Wife, the Maid, and the Widow assert that "there was no man charg'd with our expence." In the early modern period, patrons of alehouses often ran up large debts. In *The Taming of the Shrew* (1593–94), Christopher Sly tells the hostess that he will pay "not a denier" for the glasses he has broken in the alehouse (Induction 1.9), while in *I Henry IV* (1596–97), Mistress Quickly of the Boar's Head tells Falstaff, "You owe money here besides, Sir John, for your diet and by-drinkings, and money lent you, four and twenty pound" (3.3.72–74). The Widow in *Tis Merry* tells the Vintner's Boy, "Weele pay your Maister for the Wine we have." The first wife in *A whole crew,* according to the narrator, "spend[s] her Crowne [in the tavern] / With any he that durst . . . / That never plaide the Mizer in her life." These are women with some means. In *Tis Merry,* the Widow was previously in domestic service, and the Wife tends her husband's shop. In *A whole crew,* the husbands complain that their wives do not earn money but spend their days gadding about, playing with their lapdogs and spending their husbands' money, a common complaint in gossip literature.

Both pamphlets emphasize the social status of the women. In *Tis Merry,* the Widow and the Wife assert that they are "London-Gentlewomen," and they are referred to as gentlewomen by the Fiddler and the Vintner, although technically they would not have been considered gentlewomen because their husbands were not landowners.[5] The emphasis on gentlewomen by the Vintner and the Fiddler may be simple flattery or else mockery. The women in the pamphlet are the new middling sort, the wives and daughters of the merchant class, not the landed gentry. Rowlands also describes the women, again probably mockingly, as "citizens" in the 1602 preface dedicated to "Gentlemen"; what it meant to be a "citizen" was not clearly defined for men (and certainly not for women) in the early seventeenth century.[6] The wives in *A whole crew* are not described as gentlewomen or citizens but, according to their husbands, live a life of comfort, spending more money than they can afford.

Rowlands does make clear that the women in his gossip pamphlets are residents of London, for the settings are insistently localized. The Wife, the Maid, and the Widow drink London's best claret in a London tavern, hear the bells of St. Mary-le-Bow, refer to London streets, and make fun of "clowns" from the countyside who do not know how to drink like Londoners. *A whole crew* is dedicated "To the Maids of LONDON," the first wife states that "London doth not yeeld a kinder man" than her sister Sara's husband, and the sixth wife laments that "Ther's not a Whore in *London* nor about, / But he [her husband] hath all the haunts to find her out."

The writing in *Tis Merry* is more sophisticated than much of Rowlands's work. The dialogue, written in iambic pentameter and worked into six-line stanzas rhyming a-b-a-b-c-c, is skillfully individuated, such that each of the three women has a distinct voice that changes as the evening progresses: the Maid and the Wife become more garrulous, while the Widow becomes more assertive. All three abandon their pretensions because they are in a private room away from the judgment of men. The Widow tells the Maid and the Wife

> fill your Cup,
> Wee'le have no pingling now we are alone,
> If heere were men, I would not drinke it up
> For twenty pounds my selfe.

The choice of words and specific details of London and everyday life are also carefully crafted. The women complain of the stink of tobacco ("Fough, what a filthy smell? / as sure as death *I* am e'ne like to choke, / Methinkes *I* feele my selfe not very well. / Now out upon't it is *Tobacco* smoke"); they talk about eating dagger pie, pigeon, and goose flesh as well as burning and sugaring sack; and they reminisce about courtship, pregnancy, husbands, and good times had when the Widow's mistress, who had taken ill, was away in Kent one midsummer. The Widow and the Wife also instruct the Maid on how to find a husband and how to get what she wants from him. When the Maid says, "I thought mens love must still be fed with kindnesse," the Widow responds,

> God helpe thee *Besse,* not one among a score,
> That poore opinion is but Maidens blindnesse
> . . . .
> So best in strangenesse we our meanings hide,
> Which makes them love, & give good words beside.

The language of *Tis Merry* is marvelously bawdy: the Widow asserts that "Wine and Virginity kept stale, drinke flat" and that yellow-haired men are unfaithful because they hope "From every wench to gaine a golden Fleece";

the Wife talks about putting "errors in a Maydens head." John Manningham, a young law student of the Middle Temple, was so taken with the language of *Tis Merry* that a month after the first edition was printed he copied into his diary thirteen lines or passages that had to do with drinking or were particularly bawdy, such as "A Drapers man and shee were mighty in" or the description of the man "Whose fore-frunt lookes like *J*acke-an-Apes behind."[7]

In *A whole crew,* the less popular (in terms of the number of editions) of the two Rowlands pamphlets in this collection, six women drink at a tavern and complain about their husbands. Instead of a dialogue, each woman speaks at length of her situation.[8] The fourth wife berates her husband's impotence, asserting that although her husband is a "Gamester" and "up at Dice and Cards all night," he is "no Cocke of game" and "doth his busines lame, / In things (you know my meaning) scant worth praise, / But fast and welcome as a number sayes." The women also deplore their husbands' infidelity and miserliness ("His mind's of Money bags, to fill them full: / Ther's nothing that comes from him with good will"); their gaming; their incessant smoking ("With filthy leaves he smoakes his head with all, / Such Weeds, as *Indians* do *Tobacco* call: / But sure as *Black-amores* looke outward skin, / So Collier-like are English-men within, / That take such trash"); their infidelity; and their lack of prowess in lovemaking. The second wife complains that when her husband crosses her "many a way" when she would have her "humour," they often end up "at the fist" having "a bout" or hitting each other. The six gossips also describe how they control their husbands: the second hit her husband with a faggot until his head bled; the third tripped her husband with a stool when he was drunk; and the first asserts that she gets what she wants by being difficult, for "a Shroe [shrew] is ten times better than a sheepe."

In the second half of the pamphlet, the husbands respond to their wives in a much less inspired fashion as they relate their tales of "the civill warres of marriage." They charge their wives with being lazy, wearing the "breeches" or asserting mastery over them, and cuckolding them. The tone is much more somber: the fourth husband says he will "not be a Wittoll and an asse, / But even next Summer turne my wife to grasse," and the sixth husband prays that the wives will die soon: "But let us hope they'le shortly to their grave, / And then we quyet lives a peece shall have."

Rowlands consciously positioned his gossip pamphlets to be read by the newly emerging and increasingly literate middle class. In the preface to *Tis*

Merry, "In Commendation of this Booke," I.S. advertises the pamphlet as a suitable work for the middling sort, "not seated in a sumptuous Chaire, / Nor do thy Lines import of Majesty," but instead "*A Gossips friendly meeting,* art thou named." Rowlands's gossip pamphlets were also probably read aloud in gatherings or "friendly meeting[s]." Recent work in early modern reading practices suggests that people who could read often read aloud in groups consisting of many people who could not read, and it was not the usual practice for one person to read alone.[9] In *A whole crew,* the narrator warns the husbands that because their wives' complaints are flying "about the Towne," they must respond. In "A Conference betweene a Gentleman and a Prentice," appended to the 1602 edition of *Tis Merry,* the men discuss the latest popular pamphlets by Robert Greene, Nicholas Breton, and Thomas Nashe.

Rowlands most likely wrote these two pamphlets to satirize the gossips and to instruct young women how *not* to behave. In one of the dedications to *A whole crew,* addressed "To the Maids of LONDON" and signed by Rowlands, the women are warned not to act like the six gossips when they marry:

> *Consider how their* HUSBANDS *they abuse*
> . . . .
> *When you are* WIVES *do you the like refraine:*
> *Abuse not* HUSBANDS *at each Gossips feast,*
> *When they (good harmelesse men) offend you least:*
> *For if with any fault you can them touch,*
> *It onely is, their loving you too much.*

In "*Their Husbands Resolution,*" the speaker hopes that the gossips will be proved "lying huswives to their faces." Other evidence that Rowlands intended to satirize the gossips is in one of the prefaces to *Tis Merry.* The Apprentice persuades the Gentleman to buy *Tis Merry* by assuring him that he can "carry *Wife, Mayde,* and / *Widdow* in [his] pocket, when [he] may as it were / conferre and heare them talke togither." When the Gentleman tires of the female voices, the Apprentice says, he can repocket them, listening to them only at his leisure. In other words, by possessing the pamphlet, he can control the Wife, the Maid, the Widow, and their voices. There is also ample evidence in the two pamphlets that Rowlands is praising neither the six wives nor the Maid, the Wife, and the Widow: the Wife has just come from the pawnshop where a man who is not her husband promised to give her some cloth; the Wife and the Widow tell the Maid how they feign illness to get what they want from their husbands; and the Wife schools the Maid on how to marry without her parents' permission.

Rowlands's gossip pamphlets contain several comments about women and literacy that are startling in light of the pamphlets' misogyny. In the 1619 preface to *Tis Merry,* the Wife, the Maid, and the Widow contend that men drink but have "no Bookes in Rime to show it." By writing a pamphlet and asserting that "*a Wench shall be our* Poet," the three women will "pay them home, because they doe provoke." This is a joke, of course, but Rowlands does include a ballad, "pen'd by a Mayde her selfe," in the 1615 and 1619 editions entitled "The Maydes bad choyce." The Maid ends up "not *Widow, Wife,* nor *Mayde,* But of another size"—or, in other words, pregnant. Finally, in *A whole crew,* the first husband rallies his drinking mates by asserting, "We have beene slandered by our wives in print, / Yet have bin silent it appeares too long." This curiously reverses the norm of chaste, silent women who did not publish and men who did. Few texts by women were in print in 1609, so it is remarkable that the first husband uses the wives' committing their criticisms to print as a serious offense against the husbands. Although Rowlands probably assumed that these printed works by women would be read as egregious instances of unchaste shrews, it seems unlikely that all women who read or heard these lines would have interpreted them as jokes. Perhaps some women missed his intent and instead thought of the possibilities for women's work in print.

In a number of places in *Tis Merry* and *A whole crew,* women readers, or women who heard the pamphlets read aloud, may have gained some sustenance or read against the probable dominant reading. Both pamphlets have dedications to women and thus, apparently, women readers: *Tis Merry* is dedicated "To all the Pleasaunt Conceited [clever, intelligent] LONDON Gentle-women," and *A whole crew* "To the Maids of LONDON." Current research indicates that the literacy rate for London women was higher than previously thought.[10] Perhaps these two pamphlets offered a space for women's speech, camaraderie, and agency. How might seventeenth-century women writers, such as Rachel Speght, Aemilia Lanyer, and Dorothy Leigh, have read the references to women's work in print?[11] Might not some women have quietly applauded the independence of the Wife, the Maid, and the Widow, who drank together, shared gossip, and paid their own drinking bills? Might not some women have reveled in the antimasculinist humor and taken pleasure in the women's bawdiness?

Rowlands makes extravagant literary claims for *Tis Merry.* In his dedication in the 1602 edition he states, perhaps facetiously, that the pamphlet is an improvement on Geoffrey Chaucer's *Canterbury Tales.* He compares Chaucer's pilgrims at the Taberd Inn to his own pamphlet's wife, maid, and widow at a London tavern. He also claims to fill the imaginative gap he identifies in Chaucer and at the same time inserts himself as a corrective to the literary tradition. Unlike Chaucer, who "of blithe Wenches scarcitie he hath / Of all that Crue none but the wife of Bathe," Rowlands gives us all-woman scenes except for brief appearances by the Fiddler, the Vintner, and the Vintner's Boy. In both pamphlets he imagines what women talk about when they are in a tavern, away from their homes and out of the control of men. Although the women mention childbearing, tending a shop, and deceiving a mistress, in Rowlands's representation the gossips primarily talk about men: how to deceive them, which men make better lovers, how the possibility of many gifts from numerous men makes maidenhood the best state for women, and how inadequate most husbands are. In giving voice to the three women in *Tis Merry* and the six women in *A whole crew,* Rowlands controls their speech by speaking for them, expressing an anxiety shared by other male writers of the early modern period: What happens when women congregate out of the earshot of men?

Modern critical opinion of Rowlands's two gossip pamphlets has been mixed, with *Tis Merry* receiving better reviews. In an excellent discussion of the pamphlets in *Women and the English Renaissance,* Linda Woodbridge describes *Tis Merry* as Rowlands's "best poem," one that "fails to accomplish its satiric objectives and bumbles instead into being a work of art," making Rowlands "England's laureate of gossip verse."[12] Edmund W. Gosse, in *The Complete Works of Samuel Rowlands, 1598–1628,* describes *Tis Merry* as "one of the best studies of *genre* we possess in all Elizabethan literature."[13] Both, however, are critical of *A whole crew:* Woodbridge terms it "a lifeless, mean-spirited piece of work" and Gosse describes it as "one of Rowlands's failures."[14] Woodbridge's and Gosse's dismissal of *A whole crew* is, I think, unfair. *A whole crew* is part of a tradition, similar to ballads or jests, that deals with wife beating and female revenge more directly than other literature.[15] My hope is that, with the publication of *"Custome Is an Idiot,"* Rowlands's gossip pamphlets will be reassessed and viewed more positively.

Little is known of Samuel Rowlands. The *Dictionary of National Biography* (1959–60, vol. 17) gives his dates as 1570?–1630?, while Gosse assigns 1573 as Rowlands's year of birth, the same year in which John Donne and Ben Jonson were born.[16] It is not known if Rowlands attended university, married, or worked at other employment to supplement the income he received from writing the thirty-two pamphlets attributed to him. In a letter to George Gaywood written in 1602, quoted in the *DNB,* Rowlands states, "'My pen never was and never shall be mercenary,'" which may mean that he had another profession, that he was professing modesty at having his work printed, or that he did not write only to make money. In an advertisement for Rowlands's *Letting of Humours Blood in the Head Vaine,* Sir Walter Scott observes, "It has been remarked, that his muse is seldom found in the best company; and, to have become so well acquainted with the bullies, drunkards, gamesters, and cheats, whom he describes, he must have frequented the haunts of dissipation."[17] A note later appended by Thomas Campbell states that such an accusation is unjust.[18]

Tis Merry was the fifth of Rowlands's pamphlets to be published. Although his first pamphlet, *The Betraying of Christ* (1598), was religious, his second and third pamphlets, *A Mery Meetinge; or, 'Tis Merry when Knaves mete* (1600) and *The Letting of Humours Blood in the Head Vaine* (1600), were deemed so offensive that they were publicly burned in the kitchen of the Stationers Company on 26 October 1600. In March 1601, twenty-eight booksellers were fined 2s 6d for selling *The Letting,* and a twenty-ninth was fined the following March.[19] When William White entered *Tis Merry* in the Stationers Register on 15 September 1602,[20] Samuel Rowlands had become, if not a famous writer, then at least a notorious one. *A whole crew* was printed in 1609 with a second edition of *Tis Merry* and is believed to be a rewriting of the 1607 *Six London Gossips,* all copies of which have disappeared.[21]

Textual Introduction

The copy texts (text on which an edition is based) for *Tis Merry* and *A whole crew* are the 1609 editions, the first complete edition that survives of *Tis Merry* and the first edition of *A whole crew.* Any changes to the copy text are indicated in brackets. In *Tis Merry,* when the first letter of a speech heading was lowercased, it has been capitalized silently. On page 32, the Widow speech heading was moved from "For this" to "Nay, but I pray." In *A whole crew,* the capitalization has been regularized at the beginning of each section (e.g., "MY" is now "My"). There were seven editions of *Tis Merry* (in 1602, 1609,

1613/1615?,[22] 1619, 1627, 1656, and 1675) and three of *A whole crew* (in 1609, 1613, and 1663). Each edition is different from the previous: material that may have been considered out-of-date was deleted in subsequent editions, and new material, such as ballads and new prefaces, was added to encourage readers to buy the newest edition. In preparing this edition, I decided against collating all of the additional material into one edition because the result would not reflect how the text was printed or received in the seventeenth century. Instead, the additional verses are now appended at the conclusion of the 1609 copy texts; also included, from the 1619 and 1627 editions of *Tis Merry,* are two reproductions of woodcuts that reflect seventeenth-century women's fashions. The references to Chaucer and the dialogue between the Apprentice and the Gentleman appear only in the earliest edition of *Tis Merry;* perhaps the publisher of later editions believed that the dialogue's references to the writers Greene and Nashe were out-of-date and that using Chaucer's name[23] was unnecessary to sell the pamphlet. The 1613 edition of *A whole crew* concludes with an additional dialogue between a bachelor and a maid who censure the complaints of the gossips and speak of the possibilities of marriage, thus ending the pamphlet more positively than the 1609 edition, which ends with the sixth husband hoping the wives "will shortly to their grave."

Tis Merry when Gossips meet (*STC* 21409) was entered to W. White in the Stationers Register on 15 September 1602. The Huntington Library possesses the only known remaining copy of the first edition, but it is missing signature E. The survival of only one incomplete copy may be due to the censoring and burning of two of Rowlands's pamphlets, *A Mery Meetinge; or, 'Tis Merry when Knaves mete* and *The Letting of Humours in the Head Vaine,* in 1602. The similarity of the titles, *Tis Merry* and *A Mery Metinge,* may have led to the destruction of the first.

The earliest complete copy of *Tis Merry* that survives is the 1609 edition (*STC* 21410), printed by W. Jaggard for John Deane. The Bodleian Library possesses the only existing copy of this edition (Malone 299 [10]). The 1609 edition of *Tis Merry* is bound with and follows *A whole crew of kind Gossips* (*STC* 21413). The running head on each page of the two pamphlets reads "A Crew of kind Gossips."

W. Jaggard, the printer for the 1609 combined edition of the two pamphlets, became printer to the City of London in 1608. He was also the printer for Shakespeare's first folio, although it was entered in the Stationers Register in his son Isaac's name. The publisher John Deane had previously com-

Well met Goſsip:

OR,

Tis merrie when

Goſsips meete

NEWLY ENLARGED WITH
diuers merrie Songs.

LONDON,
Printed by *I. W.* for *Iohn Deane*, and are to be ſold at his
Shop iuſt vnder *Temple-barre.* 1619.

missioned pamphlets by Breton, several of which are mentioned in "A Conference betweene a Gentleman and a Prentice." The 1609 edition of *Tis Merry* differs from the 1602 edition in many places in substantives, spelling, capitalization, accidentals, and italics as well as in the deletion and addition of material.

The only copy of the 1615? edition of *Tis Merry* (*STC* 21410.5), printed by W. White for J. Deane, is an imperfect quarto located at the Folger Library. It contains, for the first time, the woodcut of the "Widdow," the "Wif," and the "Mayde." This edition also differs from the previous two editions in deletions and additions of new material and in spelling, substantives, italics, capitalization, and accidentals. The 1619 edition, entitled *Well met gossip; or, Tis merrie when gossips meete. Newly Enlarged With divers merrie Songs,* was printed for John Deane by John White, the son of William White. It includes the same woodcut as the 1615? edition but has different prefatory material and several additional stanzas in the dialogue. The British Library and the Bodleian Library own the only two copies of the 1619 edition.

The 1627 edition, printed by Augustine Mathews for Michael Sparkes, is similar to the 1619 edition. The woodcut differs in that, in the latter edition, all three women wear hats, with those of the Widow and the Wife considerably larger than in the 1619 woodcut. Also, the Maid no longer wears a ruff, reflecting contemporary fashion, and the women are larger in comparison to the serving man, who has become smaller. The only copy of the 1627 edition is in the New York Public Library. The 1656 edition, which can be found in the British Library, was printed for William Gilbertson and is in black letter (a heavy typeface that resembles early European handlettering); it is otherwise similar in content to the two earlier editions. The 1675 edition, also owned by the British Library, was printed by Thomas Vere. It has the same material as the 1656 edition but is not in black letter. The two most recent editions of *Tis Merry* are the 1818 reprint of the 1609 edition by C. Whittingham for the Chiswick Press and the 1880 edition of *The Complete Works of Samuel Rowlands, 1598–1628,* published by the Hunterian Club, which uses the 1602 text but interpolates a signature from the 1609 edition.

The printing history of *A whole crew* is much simpler. In addition to the 1609 edition, editions were published in 1613, 1663, and 1880. The 1613 edition, entitled *A crew of kind gossips, all met to be merrie. Newly enlarged,* was printed by William White for John Deane and is owned by the British

VVell met Goſsip:

OR,

Tis merrie when *Goſsips meete.*

Now Newly enlarged, with diuers merry Songes.

LONDON,

Printed by *Auguſtine Mathewes*, and are to be ſold by *Michael Sparkes*. 1627.

Library. Unlike the 1609 edition in which the six wives speak followed by the six husbands, in the 1613 edition the speeches of the husbands and wives alternate. Additional material (specifically, "The Censure of the Batcheler and the Mayde") is appended to the end of the pamphlet. The 1663 edition is an octavo entitled *A Crew of kind London Gossips All met to be Merry. Complaining of their Husbands. With their Husbands Answer in their own Defence To which is Added Ingenious Poems. Or Wit and Drollery. Written and newly enlarged by S.R.* (It is more likely that the printer, not "S.R.," added new material at the time of publication since it is believed that Rowlands died ca. 1630.) The British Library and the Folger Library have copies of this edition. *A whole crew* as it appears in *The Complete Works* is based on the 1609 edition.

NOTES

1. Sara Mendelson and Patricia Crawford, *Women in Early Modern England, 1550–1720* (Oxford: Clarendon Press, 1998), 215.

2. *Thomas Platter's Travels in England 1599,* trans. Clare Williams (London: Jonathan Cape, 1937), 170.

3. Linda Woodbridge discusses the genre of gossip literature in *Women and the English Renaissance* (Urbana: University of Illinois Press, 1986), 224–43. Some of the characteristics of gossip literature are an emphasis on drinking; experienced women schooling maids on husband management; debate about whether being a wife, a maid, or a widow is the preferred state; and wives complaining about the faults of their husbands. Among the works Woodbridge cites are: Anon., *The proude wyves Pater noster that would go gaye* (1560); Edward Gosynhyll, *The Scole house of women* (ca. 1542); William Dunbar, *The Twa marrit wemen and the wedo* (The two married women and the widow [ca. 1508]); Henry Parrot, *The Gossips Greeting* (1620); *The Batchelars Banquet* (1603); and John Davies, *A contention betwixt a Wife, a Widdow and a Maide* (1608), which was probably influenced by *Tis Merry.* On the latter speculation, see John Manningham, *The Diary of John Manningham of the Middle Temple, 1602–1603,* ed. Robert Parker Sorlien (Hanover, N.H.: University Press of New England, 1976), 333.

4. [Gallobelgious (pseud.)], *Wine, Beere, Ale, and Tobacco* (1630), C2.

5. Landed wealth was most important in determining gentleman status, but the category "gentleman" (or "gentlewoman") was not legally defined. See Keith Wrightson, *English Society, 1580–1680* (New Brunswick, N.J.: Rutgers University Press, 1982), 17–38.

6. See Mendelson and Crawford's discussion of citizenship in *Women in Early Modern England,* 49–58.

7. Manningham, *Diary,* 98–99 (folio 45).

8. In the 1613 edition of *A whole crew,* the wives and husbands alternate comments; in the 1609 and 1663 editions, the husbands' comments follow the wives'.

9. See Barry Reay, "Orality, Literacy, and Print," *Popular Cultures in England, 1550–1750* (London: Longman, 1998), 36–70.

10. For a brief survey of articles on women's literacy in early modern England, see Eve Rachele Sanders, *Gender and Literacy on Stage in Early Modern England* (Cambridge: Cambridge University Press, 1998), 197n.3.

11. Rachel Speght wrote *Mouzell for Melastomus* (1617), a response to Swetnam's *Araignment of Lewde, idle, froward, and unconstant women* (1615); Aemilia Lanyer wrote *Salve Deus Rex Judaeorum* (1611); and Dorothy Leigh wrote *The Mothers Blessing* (1616), which did not appear until shortly after her death.

12. Woodbridge, *Women and the English Renaissance,* 224, 229.

13. Edmund W. Gosse, "Memoir on Samuel Rowlands," in *The Complete Works of Samuel Rowlands, 1598–1628* (Glasgow: Printed for the Hunterian Club, 1880), 1:17.

14. Woodbridge, *Women and the English Renaissance,* 229; Gosse, "Memoir," 1:17.

15. On jesting, see Pamela Brown, *Better a Shrew Than a Sheep: Women, Drama, and the Culture of Jest in Early Modern England* (Ithaca, N.Y.: Cornell University Press, 2003), esp. chap. 2.

16. Gosse, "Memoir," 1:4.

17. Walter Scott, "Advertisement" for *The Letting of Humours Blood in the Head Vaine* & by Samuel Rowlands, in *The Complete Works of Samuel Rowlands, 1598–1628,* 1:7.

18. See Scott, "Advertisement," 1:7n.2.

19. *Records of the Court of the Stationers Co. from Register B,* ed. W. W. Greg and Eleanor Boswell (London: Bibliographical Society, 1930), 79; *A Transcript of the Register of the Company of the Stationers of London, 1554–1640 A.D.,* ed. Edward Arber (London: 1875), 2:832–33. *A Mery Meetinge* was reissued in 1609 as *The knave of clubbes.* There are three surviving copies of the 1600 edition of *The Letting of Humours Blood in the Head Vaine.*

20. Arber, *Transcript of the Register,* 3:216.

21. Gosse, "Memoir," 1:14–17.

22. The *STC*'s 1613 date is unverified because the bottom right-hand corner of the title page, where the date was located, is missing. See A. W. Pollard and G. R. Redgrave, eds., *A Short-Title Catalogue of Books Printed in England, Scotland, and Ireland and of English Books Printed Abroad, 1475–1640,* 2d ed. revised and enlarged by W. A. Jackson and F. S. Ferguson, completed by Katherine F. Pantzer (London: Bibliographical Society, 1976), 2:290. The Folger Library assigns 1615? to the *STC* 1613 edition. I have used 1615? instead of 1613? because the Folger Library possesses the only copy of this edition. *University Microfilms of Early Printed Books* states that it includes a 1620 edition of *Tis Merry* (reel 665); however, I can find no extant 1620 copy, nor is one listed in the *STC.* The microfilm indicates that it was photographed from the 1620 edition at the Folger Library; this must be a reference to the library's 1615? edition.

23. New editions of Chaucer's work were edited by Thomas Speght in 1598 and 1602.

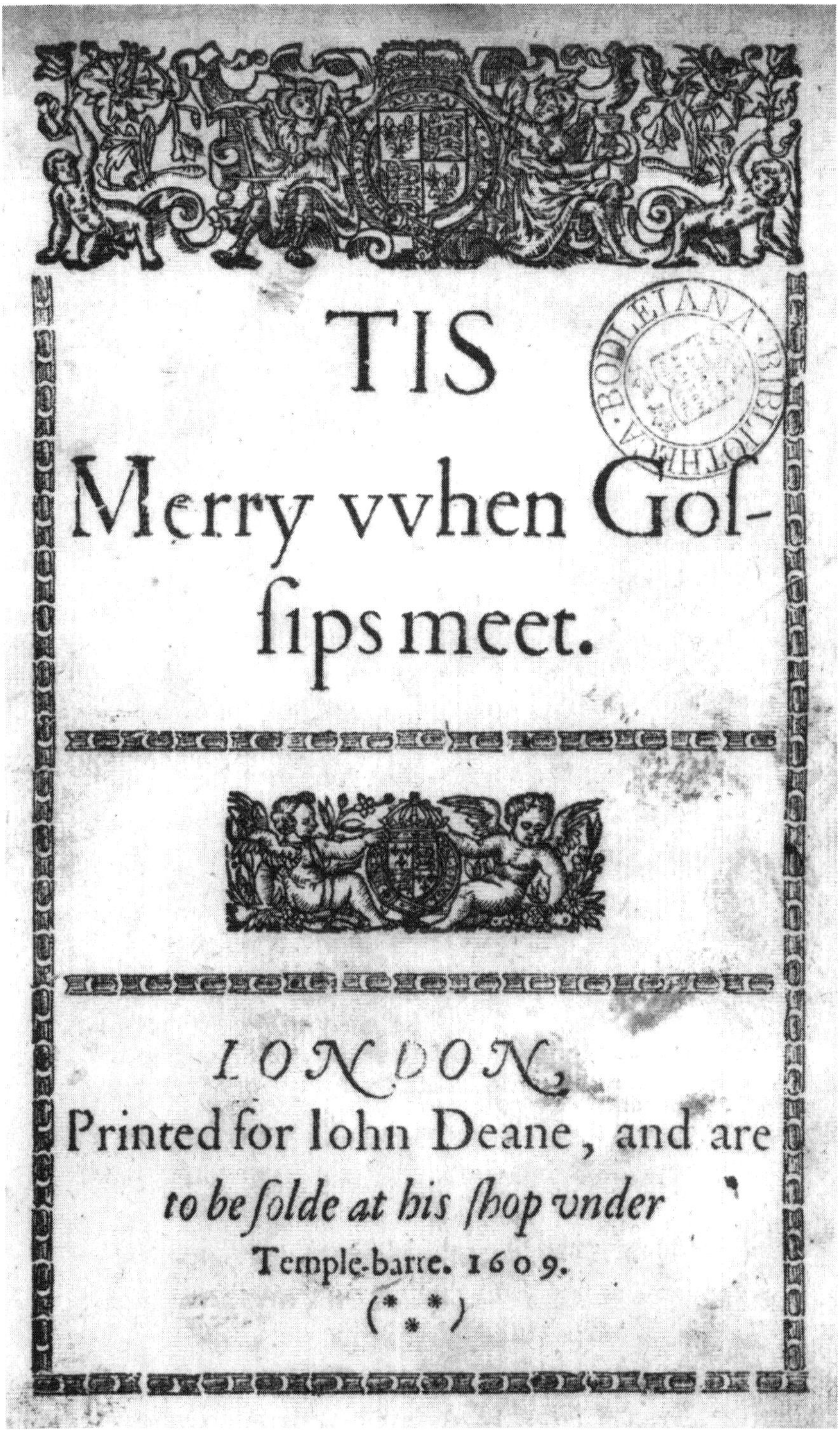

TIS

Merry vvhen Gos-
ſips meet.

LONDON,
Printed for Iohn Deane, and are
to be ſolde at his ſhop vnder
Temple-barre. 1609.
(*.*)

Tis Merry when Gossips meet. London, Printed for John Deane,[1] and are to be solde at his shop under Temple-barre, 1609.

In Commendations of this Booke.[2]

I cannot tell how others will thee like,
But my conceit is, thou art passing wittie:
No viperous tongue thy pleasant vaine will strike?
And if they should (infaith) the more t'were pittie.
Thou medlest not with *Wives* which civill bee,
But *Widdowes* wanton; *Maydes* of mean'st degree:
What reason then have Envious, envie thee?

Thou[3] art not seated in a sumptuous Chaire,
Nor do thy Lines import of Majesty:
Thy Table is not deck't with costly faire:
Thy Servants at a call, Anon will crie.
Indeed thy drinke is (Spirit, Vigor, Life,
No spurre to Envy, nor no prop for Strife)
Good Wine, which cheare's a *Widdow, Maide, or Wife.*

Thou art not thwack't[4] with Bawdy riball stuffe,
Nor doost thou touch in ought a Vertuous creature:
Thou need'st not care though Vice at thee do snuffe,[5]
A vicious man is like a fiery Meature,[6]
Which shewes farre off a terror to the eye,
Yet as a flash of Lightning soone doth dye:
But thou of Myrth, and not of Hate, art framed.
A Gossips friendly meeting, art thou named.

I.S.[7]

Tis merry when Gossips meet.

The Conference.

Widdow Good den good Coussen; Jesu, how de'e do?
When shall we eate another *Dagger Pie*?[8]
You are a stranger, Christ when met we two?
I Muse you do not call as you go by:
What lucky businesse pra'y hath brought you hither,
That we should meet at *Taverne*[9]-doore togither?

Wife In truth (kind Cousse) my comming's from the *Pawne,*[10]
But *I* protest I lost my labour there:
A *Gentleman* promist to give me *Lawne,*[11]
And did not meet me, which he well shall heare.
Widdow Some lets may happen in the way unknowne:[12]
Wife He hath been hindred, that's to bide upon.

Widdow Why how now *Besse?*[13] to passe unseene doost thinke?
Where go'st my wench? *Bes:* To see my brother *Steven*
Widdow Heere's *Widdow, Wife,* and *Maid:* Efayth[14] let's drinke
A parting Pint, and so God make us even:
Slip in good Coussen, you are next the dore,
Won pinte of kindnesse and away, no more.

Wife No in good faith: Introth I must away,
My husbands forth, our shop must needs be tended,
Mayde My Mother's gone to Church, I cannot stay,
If I be found from home, shee'le be offended:
Widdow Ile lead the way my selfe: Lord, heere's alife,
I know these shifts[15] since I was Maid and Wife.

Where shall we be? (*Vint:*) I pray go up the staires,
Wife Good Coussen no, let's take it standing heere,

Widdow Beshrew me then, where every one repaires,
Ile none of that, weele have a roome my deere:
Come, you looke that I should be your leader,
Wife Cousse, that's because you are a nimble treader.

Vintner Y're welcome Gentle-women; what Wine drinke ye?
Widdow Al's one to me: what say you Mistris *Besse,*
Wife What wine's the best for our complexions thinke ye?
Vintner I have no Physicke, (*wife*) yet good Brother gesse;[16]
Widdow Why ha'st good Clarret?[17] (*Vint.*) the best in London,
Wife Either fill good; be briefe, or leav't undon.

Vintner Heere *Gentlewomen* this is neat and pure,
Wife Pray tast it Couz, you know good Wine and Beere,
Widdow Good Lord, good Lord, that you grow so demure:
Let's drinke familiar, wherefore come we heere?
This to you both, Couz, *Grace,* and Mistris *Besse,*
A full Carouse, Ile have you pledge no lesse.

T'is pretty wine in truth: nay fill your Cup,
Wee'le have no pingling[18] now we are alone,
If heere were men, I would not drinke it up
For twenty pounds my selfe; but now al's one:
Sometime wet lip, and smell the Wine's enuffe,
And leese[19] a kisse, rather then marre our Ruffe.[20]

But now let's barre dissembling to be merry,
And in good earnest entertaine our Wine;
This touch, and taste, makes the sences weary,
What reason now we should be foolish fine?
No Lovers nor no Suter's heere, that sees it,
We have good time and liquor, let's not leese it.

Wife Content (say I) nay *Besse* Ile be thy skinker,[21]
Mayde Intruth (forsooth) a full Cup doth excell:
Good Lord, I am become a might drinker.
Widdow Another Pint; the fellow us'd us well:

Wife I by my troth, the wine is good in truth:
Fill tother Pint, (*wid.*) Prethee go right sweet youth[.]

Widdow Now Cousse, heere's to our friends in *Soperlane,*[22]
Wife Let come sweet Couzen, I will pledge them all,
Widdow But Jesu Christ! what is become of *Jane*?
Wife Oh, she is gone to dwell by *London-wall:*[23]
Widdow Good God (insooth) I never was more merry,
Then when we both did dwell in *Bucklers-berry.*[24]

Now heavenly Christ, how pleasant we have bin,
But yet one time we had a cruell stirre,
A Drapers man[25] and she were mighty in.
I pra'y, whats she with him, or he with her?
Wife Faith both in love: Well, *Jane's* an honest Mayd:
Widdow But Lord the prankes that we mad Wenches playd.

My Mistresse got my Maister to consent[26]
One Midsommer, shee being very ill,
To leave the Citty, and go lye in *Kent,*
By which good hap, we had the house at will:
There *Roger, Jane,* and I, met every night;
Wife Heere *Besse:* good Brother fil's a quart of White.

Widdow No Musique in the Evening we did lacke,
Such dauncing Coussen you would hardly thinke it;
Whole pottles of the daintiest burned Sack,[27]
T'would do a wench good at the heart to drinke it.
Such store of tickling Galliards,[28] *I* do vow,
Not an old Dance, but *John come kisse me now.*[29]

And let them talke, and praise the marriage life
To be so ful of pleasure, as they say:
I that have liv'd both Widdow, Maide, and Wife,[30]
And try'd all pleasures every kind of way,
Know what to do, and will maintaine this still,
That of the three, Maides have the world at will.

Wife Efayth they have and have not; for you know,
(Put to[31] the doore, heere's none but friends you see)
They say, Love creepeth where it cannot go:
Maids must be married,[32] least they mar'd should bee:
I will be sworne, before I saw fifteene,
I wisht that I my wedding day had seene.

[*Widdow*] Tush tittle tattle: *Besse,* it must be done,
My Coussen thinkes not as her words import,
I could not for a world have liv'd a Nunne:
Oh, flesh is fraile,[33] we are a sinfull sort,
I know that beautious wenches are inclinde
To harbour handsome men within their minde.

[*Wife*] Coussen, you meane because a Mayd is free,
Having no head to keepe her body under,[34]
She lives a life not bound so much as we:
The *J*est is simple, and it makes me wonder,
That you which have with *Venus* sports bin fed,
Should put such errors in a Maydens head.[35]

Widdow Nay, but I pray you understand my reason,
The youthfull favours that they do attaine,
For this you know, that all the wooing season,
Sutors with Gifts continuall seeke to gaine
Their Mistresse love, to joyne with their affection,
With words and Lives, humbled in subjection.

Wife That's very true, the bounty of their loves,
Are lib'rall still with many a kind respect;
In conscience I had twenty paire of Gloves
When I was Maid, given to that effect:
Garters, Knives, Purses, Girdles,[36] store of Rings,
And many a hundred dainty pretty things.

Widdow Well Cozen well, those daies in date be past,
Wife T'is very true, with us that world doth change,
Heere stands a cup of Wine, pray who dranke last?
Widdow Why that did *I* to *Besse:* Lord, Maids be strange:
They looke for thousand words of Sweet, and Pray,
And take few things, to which they say not nay.

Mayde T'is Maidens modesty to use deniall,
A willing offer commeth twice or thice,
Widdow But heere's a cup of Wine doth stand for triall,
Your Maiden-ship takes liquor in too nice:
Pray mend your fault kind Besse, wee'l none of that,
Wine and Virginity kept stale, drinke flat.

Mayde You are to blame, in truth, we drinke like men,
Now by my truely I am e'ne ashamed,
Widdow Tut wench, God knowes when we shall meet agen:
Nor need we feare of husbands to be blamed;
Our cent of wine shall not by them be felt,
The married wife in kissing will be smelt.

Wife Oh Couz, if that be all the worst, I care not,
Ile take allowance even with the best:
This Cup to you, you shall not say I dare not:
My husband smell? Oh Jesu! there's a jest,
I care as little for my husbands smelling,
As any wench this houre in London dwelling.

Widdow T'is well you need not, sure I take him kinde,
Wife As kind a man as woman need to lye with,
Mayde Would I as well were fitted to my minde,
A loving man who would not live and die with:
Widdow My husband did to other Loves incline,
Wife Nay mine is constant, by this cup of Wine.

Mayde Now Christ, how *wives* and *widdowes* take occasions
T'inlarge their husband credits, or dispraise:
Some harbour jelous thoughts, some kind perswasions:
In some match men, in some the women straies:
And when they meet, they so discourse and scan
About whose choyce hath got the kindest man.

Wife Alas (good *Besse*) thou speak'st thou know'st not what,
Thy judgemeu[n]t is not worth a Walnut-shell:
There's an old grave Proverbe tel's us, that
Such as dye Mayds, do all lead Apes in Hell:[37]
I rather whiles I live, would yearely marry,
Then waighting-maide on such preferment tarry.

Mayd That *P*roverbes proofe can do you little stead,
But married Wives oft gives, and takes such claps,
Taurus so rules and guides their husbands head,
That every night they sleepe in Horn-worke caps:[38]
I pray what Proverbe is it that allowes
The Divels picture on your Husbands browes.[39]

Widdow Enough you wrangling Wenches, fie for shame,
Take me in drinke, leave out your disputation:
Pray Brother fill a pinte more of the same,
Wife Coussen belike you meane to drinke in fashion,
We shall be trim'd, and have our wits refinde,
Efaith we shail, if you may have your minde.

Widdow Now to your Husband Cousse, this full carouse,
Wife In truth I pledge you, and I thanke you truely:
To all our friends *Besse* at your Mother house.
Mayde Thankes gentle Mistris *Grace,* I dranke but newly.
Wife Beshrew my heart, this wine is not the worst.
Widdow Good-faith methinkes tis better then the first.

Wife But Coussen, pre'thee art not yet towarde marriage?
Widdow Truly I am, and am not, as it standes:

A Gentleman of passing gallant carr'age,
Doth ply me hard; one that has prettie Lands:
Handsomer man never in shoo did tread,
By this good drinke, a kinder ne're broke bread.

To try his love, sometimes I faigne me sicke,
And (by this Candle) he will sit and weepe.
Wife Now by my troth, that's ene my Good-mans tricke,
Let me complaine; Christ what a quoile[40] hee'le keepe:
Asking what ayles my sweet-hart, tell me honny,
My Love, my Dove, my Lamb, my pretty Conny?[41]

Widdow See see, how say: But sirra Coussen, than
I force a sigh with halfe a dozen grones;
This comes (sayes he) to lye without a man,
Wife My husband sayes, kind Love, thou breedst yong bones[42]
Well *John* (say I) you jest to see my paine,
Then (by this Wine) the foole will weepe againe.

Widdow Cousse you are happy you have such a one,
Make much of him, a Jewell Wench thou hast,
But I had one would let me grunt and grone,
The veriest Clowne; but well, tis gone and past,
If he had liv'd Coussen, I do protest,
I would have done a thing: well, let that rest.

Ile never trust a Red-hair'd man againe,[43]
If I should live a hundred yeares that's flat:
His turne cannot be serv'd with one or twaine,
And how can any woman suffer that?
I know tis better to take wrong then do it,
But yet in such a case flesh leads us to it.

Mayde Why is a red-hair'd man so bad of life?
What say you to a yellow flaxen haire?

Widdow Not one among a hundred true t'his wife,
That constant loyall-harted thoughts doth beare.
They love, but how? as did the youth of *Greece,*
From every wench to gaine a golden Fleece.[44]

And they whose minds have this corrupt infection,
(Because I would have *Besse* to take good heed)
Are such as are cal'd *Sanguine* of complection,
I prethee Girle, let no such Sutor speed:
I speake it by experience and good triall,
Of all haire-cullours give that haire deniall.

A *Nut-browne* colour, or an *Aburne* either,
May both do well, and are to be alow'd:
A *Waxen*-colour hath no great fault neither:
But for a ragged chin I firme have vow'd,
It shall by me perpetuall be abhord,
And with my heeles *I* scorne it by the Lord.

A man whose beard seems scar'd with spirits t' have bin,
That wants the worthiest grace length, bredth & thicknes,
And hath no difference twixt his nose and chin,
But all his haires have got the falling sicknes,
Whose fore-frunt lookes like *J*acke-an-Apes behind,[45]
Shee that can love him, beares a scurvy minde.

Wife I pray you, what say you to my Husband then?
Widdow The rar'st complexion that you can devise,
The Golden sentence proves blacke-bearded-men,
Are precious Pearles in beautious womens eyes:[46]
Their loyall hearts none justly can controule,
I love a blacke man[47] Couzen, with my soule.

Wife Let *Besse* note this; for when *I* was a Maide,
and to the love of men began to bow,
I gave great eare to that which women said,

When they were merry met, as we are now:
    Yea and my mother did perswade me too,
    Wench (would she say) note what your Elders doo.

That lesson without Booke was straight mine owne,
She need not to repeat it over twice,
I quickly smelt what t'was to live alone,
What to be kind in love, what to be nice:
Vintner A nan, a nan,[48] what i'st (forsooth) you lacke?
Widdow Sauceages Brother, and a pint of Sack.

Mayde No more in sadnesse, now t'is time to part,
*I*n conscience it is sixe a clocke at least,
Widdow Wee'le have a reckoning after t'other quart,
Mayde They say enough's as good as any feast:[49]
Widdow In deed my Wench, enough's a feast, that's right,
    But we want that, which lye alone all night.

Wife You both may mend that matter when you will,
Whose fault i'st but your owne you do not marrie?
God made not *Besse* to live a Mayden still,
Mayde Faith t'is my Mothers counsel that I tarrie,
    She alwayes sayes, when youngmen come a woing,
    Stay daughter stay, you must not yet be doing.

Widdow Now in good faith your mother is too blame,
To wish so womanly a wench to stay;
She knowes fifteene, may Hu[s]bands justly claime.
Mayde Fifteene, why I was that last Lady-day:[50]
    You are deceiv'd, for I am no such youth,
    I am sixteene when next March comes in truth.

Widdow Beshrew my heart but thats a goodly time,
I would to Christ that I could say so too,
I would not linger out my youthfull prime,
Nor stand and aske my Mother what to doo,
    No, I could tell I trow, as well as she,
    Toward *Batchelers* how Maidens ought to be.

Mayde I, I know somet[h]ing too: but what of that?
Our Parents wils you know must be obay'd.
Wife Well, say they must: yet shall I tell you what
A Scholler told me when I was a Mayd,
Of Marriage knot, they have no power to break it,
Now by this Sacke, a Learned man did speake it.

Widdow T'was nothing but sound truth which he did tell,
For husbands, we our Parents must forsake,
Wife Were this wine burn'd Coussen, it would do well,
Mayde Faith I was thinking on it when you spake;
My Mother sayes burnt Sacke is good at night,
Wife A'my word *Besse,* your Mother's in the right.

[*Widdow*] Brother, I prethee let this wine be burn'd,
And see (good youth) the Sauceages be ready:
To one good meaning our three minds be turn'd,
When Sacke is sugered[51] t'will not be so heady,
Mayde We drinke so much, my cheeks are passing warme,
Wife Sweet *Elsabeth,* good Wine can do no harme.

Yet trust me Coussen, when I was a Girle,
For Taverne, no young-man could get me to it,
Neither for Love, Gold, precious Stones, or Pearle:
My tongue deny'd, when heart inclin'd to do it:
For (by my faith) I ever lov'd good Wine,
But oft refrain'd, I was so Mayden fine.

Widdow Well, wot[52] you *Besse* to whom Ile drinke to now?
Sure as I live, unto your Sister *Sisse,*
And to the Youth that did the Angell bow,
And sent it for a token:[53] truth halfe this:
He loves you both, upon my word he doth,
Resolve it, or you wrong him *Besse,* in soth.

Mayde His love to me I little do regard,
Perhaps my sister doth respect it more,

Widdow Then *Elsabeth,* in truth you use him hard.
Mayde How hard? he had his answere long before?
I will not love him whatsoere befall,
Ile have a handsome man, or none at all.

Widdow Go to, go to, his riches doth excell,
Mayde A Figge for wealth, tis person *I* affect,
Widdow You are a foole, he will maintaine you well,
Mayde *I* tell you, I a propper man respect:
De'e thinke that I with such a dwarffe[54] will store me,
That shall disgrace me when he goes before me.

Ile have a comely man from head to foot,
*I*n whose neat limbes no blemish can be spide:
Whose Legge shall grace his stocking or his Boot,
and weare his Rapier manly by his side:
With such a one my humour doth agree,
He shall be welcome to my bed and mee.

[*Wife*] *Besse,* and[55] th'art wise, hold that opinion still,
For were *I* to begin the world to morrow,
In such a choice, *I* would my minde fulfill:
And so *I* drinke to thee: come on, hang sorrow:
Wench, let it be thy rule at any hand,
To make thy choyce even as thy mind doth stand.

Many do match (as true as this is Wine)
With some Dunce, Clown, or Gul, they care not who,
For no cause but to be maintained fine,
and have their wils in what they please to do:
When their hearts loves as much in other things,
As there is Vertue in mine Apron-strings.

Widdow Faith tis too true. Fough, what a filthy smell?
as sure as death *I* am e'ne like to choke,
Mayde Methinkes *I* feele my selfe not very well.

Wife Now out upon't it is *Tobacco*[56] smoke:
Knocke Cozen knocke, heere is a filthy smother,
For Gods love quicke: some Juniper[57] sweet Brother.

Widdow There cannot be a more detested stinke,
And yet you see how dainty many make it.
Mayde As true as this is Wine that I do drinke,
I would not for a Crowne kisse one that takes it:
Wife My Husband is so kind an honest man,
That heele touch none, if I say, Do not *Ian.*

Widdow His commendations certaine is the more,
With one another we are bound to beare,
He beares with you, favour you him therefore.
Wife Surely I do, as both of you shall heare:
T'is death to him to smell but a Goose-pye,
and therefore Goose-flesh never do I buy.

Widdow That's a strange matter sure; I love a Goose,
But for a Wood-cocke I did never care,
Wife When I eat Pigge it makes my body loose,
Mayde I love a tender Rabbet, or a Hare,
A Turkey-pie, or Pigion for a need:
But on grosse Butchers[58] flesh I cannot feed.

Wife Coussen, when I lay in[59] of my first Boy,
Lord how I long'd to eate a Partridge wing,
And when it came, my stomacke had no joy,
But all my minde was of another thing.
Thou shalt lacke nought (quoth *John*) that gold will buy,
Why then (sweet-hart) lets have a Cherry-pye.

If *London* yeeld it (*Love*) thou shalt not lacke,
So kind, methinkes I heare him still repeat it.
But hasting downe the staires, I cald him backe,

Tis full of stones (quoth I) I cannot eat it:
    With that he kist me, and began to weepe,
    And I being somewhat heavy fell asleepe.

But then I fell into the strangest dreame
Of fire and water, that you ever heard:
And *I* was troubled Cousse the most extreame
With one all night, that had a yellow beard:
    And with a Cocke had neither spurres nor combe,
    And with the little Bitch you have at home.

Widdow Why surely now you talke of dreames in sadnesse,
I dream't last night two Cattes[60] did leape and skip,
Playing together with great sport and gladnesse,
Untill one came to part them with a whip:
    I laughed that my heart did ake thereat,
    To see the foolish fellow whip the Cat.

Wife A pretty jest: But *Besse* to whom de'e drinke?
I spy a fault, you do your selfe forget:
The Wine stands waiting in the cup me thinke,
Prethee my Wench, lets have our lips kept wet.
    I pledge thee my Girle: nay sweet now drinke it up,
    A *Gossips* round, that's every one a Cup.

Widdow Next house to mine a *Gentlewoman* lies,
Fidler Wilt please you *Gentlewomen* heare a song?
Wife Good fellow, now we are about to rise:
Where stayes the *Vintners* service Boy so long?
    Shut dore pray Cossen after that base groome,
    Weele have no fidling Knave disgrace our roome.

Widdow Well, go to Cousse, go forward with the rest,
Wife What rest I pray? I know not what you meane:
Widdow No, why of her that is your neighbours guest?

Wife T'is true, t'is true, my gallant silken Queane:[61]
I had forgot the talke I was about,
The Fidler comes me in, and puts me out.

Why she forsooth (an't please you) is so fine,
She never drinkes unlesse she dine or sup,
And then she hath her penny pot of wine:
Marry and gip,[62] some body take her up:
Some Doctors wench a'my word for her skill,
That takes in Diet by the dram and pill.

My Husband doth alow me Ile be sworne,
A pint a meale as true as we sit heere:
I tell you (as my friends) I would e'ne scorne
To dine or sup without it in a yeere:
He knowes (efaith) to please me in my diet,
Or for a month I shall be out of quiet.

Then if he sees me out of patience once,
Oh Christ, how we will seeke to amends,
Then do I sigh to grieve him for the nonce,
Wherewith, hee'le kisse and say, Sweet love be frends:
I let him kisse, and speake me faire a while,
And when the sullen humor's past, I smile.

Widdow I cannot chuse but praise thy pretty wit,
It is the very course that I would take,
Thou entertain'st his humour passing fit.
Mayde Why, I thought men had lov'd for kindnesse sake?
Wife Alas plaine wench, God knowes thou art not in it,[63]
She that will settle love, must this way win it.

Mayde Indeed I never heard that tricke before,
I thought mens love must still be fed with kindnesse,

Wife God helpe thee *Besse,* not one among a score,
That poore opinion is but Maidens blindnesse:
In these things thou knowest little, it appeares,
But it will come, for now thou com'st to yeares.

Why woman, if we seeme not in behaviour
As though we car'd not greatly to consort,
They'le thinke forsooth they do us mighty favour,
And we must seeme beholden for our sport:
So best in strangenesse we our meanings hide,
which makes them love, & give good words beside.

This for instruction *Besse,* I have disclosed,
Mayde Intruth I yeeld more thankes then may be told,
Widdow Heere's to you both against you are disposed.
Lord, while you talke the Sauceages wax cold,
Come draw your knives: fall to, I pray begin,
You know cold Puddings[64] are not worth a pin.

Wife How pretty salt they tast: but tis the better,
Widdow Most rare efayth to drinke Sacke withall,
Besse, pray go too, will you remaine my detter?
Why de'e not pledge me? troth and fayth you shall,
Mayde Nay sure all this: trust me t'is more then need,
In truth, in sadnesse, now in very deed.

Widdow Well, if you do not *Besse* you do me wrong,
You shall not be forsworne[65] for twenty pound.
Mayde How't burnes my belly as it goes along,
Wife My turne is next, and so it passeth round:
Looke *Gentlewomen* is it full de'e thinke?
I scorne to be intreated take my drinke.

Widdow Why laugh you Cossen? sweet lets know,
Mayde An odde conceite *I* thinke on, makes me smile:
When I am forth in company, or so,

How by the dram I take in Wine that while,
  Kissing the Cup, upon the Wine I frowne,
  And so with smelling it, *I* set it downe.

Some simple fooles (all manners for his wit)
Comes on me with the French salute[66] most quaintly,
And sayes, Sweet, mend your draft,[67] you drink no whit,
Introth you shew your selfe too mayden-dainty,
  Drinke better Lady at my kind request,
  I say sweet Sir, *I* can no wine digest.

Widdow Marry wee'le beare you witnesse when you will,
Ile take my oath on twenty Table-bookes,[68]
The last full cup hath made you mighty ill:
Some *Rosa-solis,*[69] see how pale she lookes,
  Another pinte of that she tasted last,
  To breake wind with, and then the worst is past.

Wife Good (efaith) good, my Cousse is in the vaine,
*I*le match you for it Wench, I hold a Crowne:
Fill none, unlesse you'le drinke about againe,
Widdow Content say I, you cannot put me downe:
  How say'st thou *Besse,* shall it be so Girle, speake?
Mayde If *I* make one, pray God my girdle breake.

Wife Talke not so loud, what will folke thinke that heare?
The very *Vintners* Boy laugh't when you spake,
Widdow Had *I* seene that, *I* would have found his eares,
Why Maister Boy, weele pay for that we take,
  Base groome, I say, although thou tak'st me mellow,
  Know smooth-facst knave, *I* am your Mistris fellow.[70]

Wife Good Lord, what ayles my Coussen be so hot?
Tush let it passe, you know Boyes sawcy be,
Widdow It shall not be forgiven nor forgot:

Your Maisters lives you slave by such as we:[71]
Call for a reck'ning; let's know what's to pay?
By heaven *I* scorne a minute more to stay.

Brother, *I* pray is it your Maisters minde,
Your fellow Boy should flout guests when they drinke?
Vintner My Maisters will is for to use you kinde,
Widdow T'will scath[72] him more my friend, then he doth thinke:
What is thy name? *Vint.* Forsooth my name is *Will,*
Widdow What country man? *Vin:* Forsooth at Fish-street hill.[73]

william, we come not heere to be abused,
There are more Tavernes besides your's in towne,
We can go where we might be curteous used,
Vintner Intruth forsooth my fellow's but a Clowne:
Widdow *william,* we have some credit where we dwell,
And *william,* Boyes should use their betters well.

For *William,*[74] say the case were but your owne,
And that you were as we are at this season,
With friends a drinking where you are unknowne,
Would you be flouted? (*Vint.*) By my faith no reason,
Widdow *William,* thou answer'st like a youth of sence,
For surely *William,* t'is a great offence.

And *william,* I would have you understand,
Weele pay your Maister for the Wine we have,
Vintner O Lord forsooth, as sure as in my hand,
Widdow *William,* we come not to intreat or crave,
We met together *william,* at your doore,
And entred for a Pint, which fals out more.

William, we will not be beholding[75] (see yee)
Unto your Maister more then to another:
T'is for good Wine and welcome, we come to yee,

Or farewell *william,* and you were my Brother:
And therefore *william* this abuse we scorne,
For we are *London-Gentlewomen*[76] borne.

Widdow Why *william* know, heere's neither *Cisse* nor *Kate,*[77]
Vintner No, so God helpe me, I do see you are not,
Widdow Thinkes sawce your fellow, we use Parrets prate,[78]
William our talke is honest, and we care not
If all the parish were in place to heare it,
No by this Cup, (*Vint.*) Ifaith you need not sweare it.

Forsooth, I trust your Wine was very good?
Widdow *William* I graunt the wine was not amisse,
But that base Boy hath vex't me to the blood:
A Man, *william* would nere have offer'd this;
The Proverbe sayes, t'is Manners that doth make,[79]
William, give Guests good words for manners sake.

William when cam'st thou in this house to dwell?
Vintner Forsooth about three yeares agon[80] last May,
Widdow *William,* serve God, and please thy Maister well,
T'will be thine owne *William,* another day:
Your Maister's marri'd *William,* is he not?
Vintner Yes forsooth, yes; a Mistresse I have got.

Widdow *William,* your Maister hath no Children by her?
Vintner No forsooth, but I thinke she be with Child,
To have a Boy she hath a great desire,
Widdow So would not I (*william*) for Boyes be wilde:
Though Girls cry (*william*) till they be bepist,
William, give me a Girle, take Boyes who list.

Wife Coussen you do forget you selfe methinke,
When *Besse* and *I* come home, we shall be chid,
Widdow Pray fill the Cup to *william,* let him drinke,
Vintner *I*n truth forsooth tis the last thing *I* did.

Wife Good *william* drinke, I prethee *william* doo,
Vintner Forsooth *I* pledge you, and *I* thanke ye too.

Widdow William let's know to pay, and there's an end?
Vintner Marry forsooth three shillings and a penny,[81]
Widdow William lay downe their mony, none shall spend,
Coussen, and *Besse,* pray'y do not offer any:
Harke, Bow-bell rings,[82] before the Lord tis late,
William good night, prethy take up thy Plate.

FINIS.

[The following appears in the 1602 edition, but not in the 1609, 1615?, 1619, or 1627 editions. It precedes the conference between a gentleman and a prentice.]

GENTLEMEN.

Chaucer, *our famous rever'nt English* Poet
When Canterbury *tales he doth begin,*
(Such as have red his auncient verses know it)
Found store of Guests in South-warke *at an Inne,*
The Taberd[83] *cal'd, where he himselfe then lay,*
And bare them Pilgrimes company next day.

A Kentish journey they togither tooke,
Towards Canterbury *marching nine and twentie*
Knight, Marchant, Doctor, Miller, Squire, & Cooke,
Scholler, *and* Saylor, *with Good-fellowes plentie,*
But of blithe Wenches scarcitie he hath
Of all that Crue none but the wife of Bathe.

A London *Taverne puts their Inn downe*[84] *then*
Wherein three Citizens; Wife, Widdow, Mayde,
Did kindely meete, and talke, and drinke like men,
And one spent more then sixe of tother payde.

Not penny a quart,[85] *dull Ale, nor drowsie Beere*
But spritely wine, that makes the wit shine cleere.
S.R.

[The following appears in the 1619 and 1627 editions, but not in the 1602, 1609, or 1615? editions. It immediately precedes the wife-widow-maid dialogue.] The copy text is the 1619 text.

By your leave Readers.
Kinde loving Friends, since thus our case doth stand,
That we are fall'n into the Printers *hands;*
And have before this time been often prest,[86]
To make our private meeting, publicke jest;
And that we must endure, and be content
What Men put on us in their merriment:
Pray let us not be too much play'd upon.
Wee met indeed, ti's true, and past and gon:
Merry wee were, yet free from all offence,
And there was no man charg'd with our expence;
Unto a penny wee our reckning payd:
Then who can blame the Widdow, Wife and Mayde,
For meeting, and kind drinking each with other?
Men can their owne carowsings closely smother,
Their Pottles and their Gallons, hand to hand,
Their drinking Healthes untill they cannot stand:
And yet there is no Bookes in Rime to show it:
But well, weele have a Wench shall be our Poet,[87]
And pay them home, because they doe provoke:
So pray reade on, weele stand to all wee spoke.
Wife, Widdow, Mayde

[The following appears in the 1602 edition, but not in the 1609, 1615?, 1619, or 1627 editions. It precedes the wife-widow-maid dialogue.]

A Conference betweene a Gentle-*man and a Prentice.*

Prentice. What lacke you Gentle-man? see a new Booke new come foorth, sir: buy a new Booke sir.

Gentleman. New Booke say'st: Faith I can see no prettie thing come foorth to my humours liking. There are some old Bookes that I have more delight in then your new, if thou couldst helpe me to them.

Prentice. Troth sir, I thinke I can shew you as many of all sorts as any in *London,* sir.

Gentleman. Can'st helpe mee to all *Greenes*[88] Bookes in one Volume? But I will have them every one, not any wanting.

Prentice. Sir; I have the most part of them, but I lacke *Conny-catching,*[89] and some halfe dozen more: but I thinke I could procure them. There be in the Towne I am sure can fit you: have you all the Parts of *Pasquill,*[90] sir?

Gentleman. All the Parts, why I know but two, and those lye there upon thy stalle; them I have: but no other am I yet acquainted with.

Prentice. Oh, sir, then you have but his *Mad-cappe,* and his *Fooles-cappe,* there are others besides those: looke you heere, a prettie Booke Ile assure you sir. T'is his *Melancholy,*[91] sir: and ther's another and you please sir: heer's *Morall Philosophy*[92] of the last edition.

Gentleman. What's that with *Nashes* name to it there?

Prentice. Many sir, t'is *Pierce Penny-lesse,* sir; I am sure you know it: it hath beene a broad a great while[93] sir.

Gentleman. Oh, I thou say'st true, I know't passing well:

is that it. But were's the new Booke thou tel'st me off, which is it?

Prentice Marry, looke you sir, this is a prettie odde conceit, Of a Merrie meeting heere in *London,* betweene a *Wife,* a *Widdow,* and a *Mayde.*

Gentleman. Merrie meeting, why, that Title is stale: Ther's a Booke cal'd, *T'is merry when knaves meete.*[94] And ther's a Ballad, *T'is merry when Malt-men meete:* and besides, there's an olde Proverbe, *The more the merrier:*[95] And therefore I thinke sure I have seene it.

Prentice. You are deceived sir, Ile assure you, for I will bee deposed upon all the Bookes in my Shoppe that you have not seene it; t'is another manner of thing then you take it to bee, sir: For I am sure you are in Love, or at least will bee, with one of these three: or say you deale but with two, The *Widdow* and the *Mayde;* because the *Wife* is another mans commoditie: is it not a prettie thing to carry *Wife, Mayde,* and *Widdow* in your pocket, when you may as it were conferre and heare them talke togither when you will? nay more, drinke togither: yea, and that which is a further matter; utter their mindes, chuse Husbands, and censure Complections;[96] and all this in a quiet and friendly sort, betweene themselves and the pinte-pot, or the quart quantitie, without any swaggering or squabbling, till the Vintners pewter-bearer in a Boyes humour gave out the laugh at them.

Gentleman. Thou say'st well, be-like thy Booke is a conjuring kinde of Booke for the Femenine Spirits, when a man may rayse three at once out of his pocket.

Prentice. Truely sir, Ils assure you, you may make vertious use of this Booke divers wayes, if you have the grace to use it kindly; as for ensample: sit alone privately in your Chamber reading of it, and peradventure the time you bestow in viewing it, will keepe you from Dice, Taverne, Bawdy-house, and so foorth.

Gentleman. Nay, if your Booke be of such excellent qualitie and rare operation, wee must needes have some Traffique together. Heere take your money, i'st sixe-pence?

Prentice. I certaine tis no lesse, sir: I thanke yee sir.

Gentleman. What is this an Epistle to it?

Prentice. Yes for-sooth: yes ti's Dedicated:

To all the plea-saunt conceited[97] London *Gentlewomen that are friendes to mirth,* and enemies to dull Melancholy.

Kinde Gentlewomen of the kinder sort,
Which are no kindred unto dogged natures:
Though some of you keepe prettie Curs for sport,
Yet you your selves become no currish creatures;
But in you mirth have good conceipts and wittie,
True London *bred, in* England's *famous Cittie.*

To you this merry meeting is presented,
As the best worthy for to entertaine it.
It scornes the fingers of the discontented,
And bids a figge for them that do disdaine it:
Ti's not for sullen sad-ones, peevish brave,
That nothing but the Asses vertues[98] have.

The lumpish leaden melancholy thought,
That's next dore-neighbour to a frantique braine,
Whose doltish understanding's good for nought,
And is an out-cast to a pleasaunt vaine:
Smyling as often as Powles-*steeple daunces;*[99]
Let her goe lowre with crabbed Kate *and* Fraunces,

And take her liquor by the Dram and ounce
With Faith I cannot drinke, cry fie, and frowne,
Let her all good Societie renounce,
And turne a scurvey barren witted clowne:
She is too base, in any Common-wealth,
To be at drinking of a Gossips *health.*

Let such go keepe their chamber and their dyet,
And looke as pale as any Parris *plaster,*[100]
And let their husbands never live in quiet
Unlesse the Fanne and Farthing-gale[101] *be master:*
And let them be even at the best they can
Both crosse-consumers,[102] *and crosse lucke to man.*

Their lives are nothing els but fretfull humours;
They know not how to thinke a courteous thought;
Their tongues are swolne with prid's corrupted tumors
Turne Inside out-ward, all's (alike) starke naught.
Then let them be casheer'd[103] *and walke aloofe,*
Such paltry wenches are not Clarret-*proofe.*

But as for you good liquor taking Dames
That prove most friendly in your dayly greeting;
And do deserve right loving Gossips *names,*
The Pynt and quart be'ng witnes to your meeting
Why much good de'e,[104] *pray sit yee merry all,*
For t'other Pynt to make it even, call.

Who hath to do with what you please to take,
It is well knowne to be your owne you spend
To every foole account ye need not make,
You pay for that you have and there an end:
There's many deale upon the score for wine,
When they should pay forget the Vint'ners *Syne.*[105]

You are like Dido[106] *that same famous Queene*
That dranke a health unto the wandring Prince;

Such a Carrowse, the like hath not beene seene
In Carthage, *to that houre nor never since:*
She ply'd him with the Wine in golden Cup,
Turning the liquor in; the bottome up.

So did Semiramis,[107] *King* Ninus *wife,*
When she obtayn'd three dayes to rule the Crowne
She proov'd a good companion all her life,
And hand to hand dranke all her Nobles downe:
And all chiefe Wenches at a Gossips feast,
She made them Ladyes every one at least.

Cato,[108] *for wisedome being surnam'd the* Wise,
The learned and the witty sentence speaker,
Did marrie one just of the Gossips sise:
And in discretion never sought to breake-her:
Though he the art of knowledge did professe,
She would not drinke a droppe of Wine the lesse.

Therefore you shall not greatly need to care,
For every busie tongue that doth abuse-you:
But if that in a private roome[109] *you are,*
And have a Drawer that good Wine will chuse-you,
With frolique myrth this measure still applie,
Tune your Tongues low, take not a Cuppe too hie.[110]

FINIS

[In the 1615?, 1619, and 1627 editions the following stanzas are inserted immediately after the Wife says, "A Gossips round, that's every one a Cup."] The copy text is the 1619 text.

Musitians comes in.

Widdow Coussen, heer's Fidlers, lets us heare a Song:
But looke my friendes, it be a pleasing thing.

Mayde I am afraid then we shall stay too long.
Widdow No, no, I warrant: come on, quickly sing.
Wife Let it touch men I pray in any case:
This Youth (mee thinkes) will doe it with a grace.

The Songe.

What's a womans chiefe delight?
To give man his hearts content:
How doth hee the same requite?
Love her till the sport be spent.
You that doubt it, doe but try,
Men will flatter, cogge,[111] and lye.

With bewitching words they sue,
Vowing constant faith and love;
Women thinke their oathes be true,
Till (poore soules) they trie and proove,
Then they finde, when helpe is past,
For a night their love doth last.

Their owne Stories tell their lives,
How unconstant they have dealt;
Honest *Widdowes, Maides,* and *Wives,*
Have their double dealing felt:
All will say that are not blinde,
Men are false, and Women kinde.

When they vow, trust not their swearing,
When they smile, thinke they will frowe,
Give their flattering but the hearing,
If they can, thei'le put you downe:
Since they seeke your overthrow,
Keepe them from the thing[112] you know.

For to be in great request,
Make your love exceeding strange,
Trie good earnest, out in jest,
Deale with flatterers by change:
  As they come, so let them passe;
  Turne dissemblers out to grasse.[113]

FINIS.

Widdow Now God-amercy Boy, this Song is true,
I prethee drinke, tis good to mend thy voice.
Wife Hast thou not such another that is new?
Boye Yes, I have one is call'd, *The Maydes bad choyce:*[114]
  Pen'd by a Mayde her selfe, whose constant truth
  Was lately wronged by a Merchants Youth.

Widdow. Sing it prethee.

The Song.

You *London* Maides, give eare to me,
  That am in Love your owne,
And borne within the Citie walles,
  well friended, and well knowne.

My selfe I will not seeme to praise,
  It were a note of pride:
What beautie there is in my face,
  Or comely limbes beside.

My ready witte, and quicke conceit,
  To breake a nimble jest;
And all good parts, and qualities,
  I meane to let them rest.

The Art I have in Needle-worke,
Imbrod'ry rich in Gold:
With Lace and Stich, and every thing.
That may or can be told.

For Dauncing, and my skill in Song,
I must, and will be mute:
My playing on the Virginals,
And tickling of the Lute.

Ile burie all mine owne good parts,
And of a Youth will speake
Whose most unkinde bad qualitie
Doth make my heart to breake.

How hee is calde, I will conceale,
And not reveale the same;
Because Ile leave him like a *Jew,*[115]
Without a Christian name.

Hee plide mee long, as Suters doe,
(I meane these subtill men)
And wee had often meeting too,
It skils not where, and when.

Hee vow'd hee lov'd mee constantly,
Farre dearer then his life:
And would himself, destroy himselfe,
Except I were his wife.

I being (as poore wenches bee)
Most kinde, where love doth sting:
Consented too, (I shame to tell:)
And let him doe the thing.

This done, which cannot be undone,
(Tis now sixe months too late:)

I am turn'd off, my Youth hath got
  Another loving mate.

One that hath neither witte nor wealth,
  Beautie, nor comely grace:
One that is Kitchin-stuffe to mee,
  Her stocke is knowen so base.

Fie, who would trust this wicked world?
  Maidens take heed, be wise:
I am not *Widdow, Wife,* nor *Mayde,*
  But of another size.[116]

FINIS

Mayd. I like this Song exceeding wel indeed:
Heer's sixe pence toward the Musick with my heart.
Wife. *Besse,* tis good warning wench for you; take heed,
Mayde. Ile see him hang'd would play me such a part:
  Hee that should come and offer but to feele,
  I would en'e scorne that fellow with my heele.

[The following are additional stanzas in the 1619 and 1927 editions that follow the penultimate stanza in the 1609 edition. The copy for the following is the 1619 text.]

Vinter. Now Gentlewomen, I entreate you speake,
And name the wine, a pinte I will goe fill.
Wife. No *William,* no; there's many Vintners breake,[117]
Let it alone, prethee, kinde hearted *Will,*
  It is enough, if you one rule doe keepe,
  And that is this; Nicke not your Pots too deepe.[118]

There is much knavery in your trade for that,
Which will not thrive, who ever use the same:
Draw briske to *Londoners,* let Clownes[119] drinke flat,

That take in wine but onely for the name;
    Out-face the Fooles, but with a cogging[120] tale,
    For all their judgement's in a pot of Ale.

You can perswade them that their taste is bad,
And boast your wine, that there's no better drawne,
The like in *London* is not to be had;
When all is false, and but an outward fawne.
Widdow. Coussen, wee know Vintners can doe amisse,
    But we might have drunke *Williams* pinte by this.

Vintner. Troth you shall have it instantly, I runne.
Wife. Why this is your fault Coussen, you'le not leave.
Widdow. Tut, hang him knave: this pinte, and we have done,
So much in measure, hee did us deceive:
    Did you not make how e'ry Pot lackt filling,
    Wee'le take it kindly, cause hee gives it willing.

Vintner. Heere Gentlewomen, and I thanke you all.
Wife. This is a cuppe of Clarret doth excell.
Vintner. At any time, when you doe please to call,
Upon my honestie Ile use you well,
    While with my Master I remaine a dweller,
    You shall command the best that's to the Seller.

NOTES

1. John Deane was a bookseller in London from 1601 to 1619. His shop was just under Temple Bar near Fleet Street. Deane published several other pamphlets by Rowlands and three pamphlets by Nicholas Breton. Two pamphlets by Breton are mentioned in *Tis Merry* in "A Conference betweene a Gentleman and a Prentice."

2. This is omitted in editions published after 1609.

3. That is, *Tis Merry*. I.S. personifies the book as master of his household and as one who "medlest" not with virtuous women.

4. Filled to overflowing.

5. Sneer.

6. Meteor.

7. The 1602 edition names Ioh. (i.e., John) Strange, but I can locate no such individual in the historical record.

8. This is probably a reference to a pie from the Dagger, a well-known pub in Holborn. "Dagger" is also appropriate in describing the Widow, who is throwing verbal daggers at husbands.

9. Taverns sold wine to the more prosperous and alehouses sold beer and ale, usually to the less prosperous. There were far fewer taverns than alehouses in the early modern period.

10. Pawnshops were an integral part of the early modern economy. In 1603 legislation was passed against pawnbrokers selling stolen goods. See John Webster and Thomas Dekker, *Westward Hoe* (London, 1607), 2.1: "You must to the *Pawn* to buy lawn."

11. Fine linen.

12. Something unforeseen must have happened.

13. The name of the maid.

14. In faith.

15. Evasions.

16. Suggest.

17. That is, red wine. This word originally referred to wines of yellowish or light red color.

18. Drinking reluctantly.

19. Be without.

20. Ruffs, often made of lawn, came into fashion in the sixteenth century. John Stow says that ruffs became essential wear for men as well as women who wanted to keep up with fashion (*The Annals; or, A General Chronicle of England* . . . [London, 1615]), 867–69. According to Phillip Stubbes, some men wore "great and monsterous ruffes . . . whereof some be a quarter of a yard deep, yea some more, very few less." If caught in a wind, the ruffs "goe flip flop in the winds like rags flying abroad, and lye upon their shoulders like the dishcloute of a slutte" (*Anatomie of Abuses* . . . [London, 1583], D7v). The maid in the woodcut from the 1627 edition is not wearing a ruff, as they were going out of fashion.

21. Tapster. Shakespeare, *I Henry IV* (1596–97) 2.4.22–24: "Ned, I give thee this pennyworth of sugar, clapp'd even now into my hand by an under-skinker."

22. A street within the city of London that runs from Watling Street to Bucklersbury, named for Alen le Sopar. See John Stow, *A Survey of London* (1603; Oxford: Clarendon Press, 1971), 2:251.

23. London Wall, built in C.E. 434, ran from Broad Street to Cripplegate inside the wall of the city of London.

24. This was a street off Cheapside within the city of London. According to Stow, grocers, pepperers, and apothecaries were located on Bucklers-berry (*Survey of London,* 1:260–61). In Shakespeare's *Merry Wives of Windsor* (1597), Falstaff says Mrs. Ford is not like those who "come like women in men's apparel, and smell like Bucklersbury in simple time" (3.3.71–73).

25. One who deals in cloth.

26. The Widow was probably in service.

27. A pottle is equal to two quarts. Sack is a class of white wines imported from Spain

and the Canary Islands. Burned sack is heated or mulled wine, but it may also refer to wine to which burnt sugar has been added. See Shakespeare's *Merry Wives of Windsor* (2.1.214–15): "I'll give you a pottle of burnt sack." In a dialogue entitled *Wine, Beere, Ale, and Tobacco* (London, 1630), the three drinks contend with each other to decide which is superior. Water ultimately determines that each has its place: wine shall be in demand among courtiers, gentlemen, and practical wits; beer shall be the drink of citizens; and ale shall be the drink of those who live in the country. The Widow may have ordered wine because of her class pretensions.

28. A quick and lively dance, introduced ca. 1541.

29. This was a popular song of the time. Perhaps the Widow is implying how up-to-date she is in matters of music.

30. Shakespeare, *Measure for Measure* (1604): "Why, you are nothing then: neither maid, widow, nor wife?" (5.1.177–78)

31. Close.

32. The average age at first marriage for women during this period in England was twenty-five, although members of the aristocracy and upper gentry married younger. Alexander Niccholes states that fourteen was the best age for marriage (*A Discourse, of Marriage and Wiving . . .* [London, 1615], 11). Perhaps the Wife is implying that she wishes she had married before age fifteen because she was already "mar'd."

33. See Morris Palmer Tilley, *Dictionary of Proverbs in England in the Sixteenth and Seventeenth Centuries* (Ann Arbor: University of Michigan Press, 1950), F363.

34. "Head" refers to a husband and "body" to a wife.

35. A pun on "maidenhead" or "hymen."

36. Belts worn around the waist.

37. This is an old proverb about a woman who dies a virgin and leads apes in hell because she has no children. See Shakespeare's *Taming of the Shrew* (1593–94): "I must dance barefoot on her wedding-day / And for your love to her lead apes in hell" (2.1.33–34).

38. Taurus, the bull, has horns like those of a cuckolded husband; therefore, cuckolds are under the influence of Taurus. (A cuckold is a husband whose wife has a sexual affair.)

39. Another reference to horns and cuckoldry.

40. Disturbance.

41. Rabbit; a term of endearment for a woman.

42. Refers to pregnancy.

43. The Widow's husband probably had red hair. The following ballad is reprinted from *The Bagford Ballads,* vol. 3, ed. Joseph Woodfall Ebsworth (Hertford: Ballad Society, 1878), 495.

The West-Country Counsellor

Nay I further declare, you may know by their Hair,
If it be Red or Yellow, then then you may swear
They will never prove true, but will love more than you;
And the sandy Complexions are Flatterers too:

Have a care of such men, for theres's scarce One in Ten
But are False and Deceitful; be careful, O then.

But the Black and the Brown, both in City and Town,
Are delightful and pleasant, they seldom can frown;
By the Powers above, they are all over love,
And as Loyal they are as the dear tender Dove:
Lasses, these are the Men that will honour you then,
There's not one of them false in Fourscore and Ten.
c. 1684–85

44. The Widow is comparing the inconstant love of red- and yellow-haired men to the sexual exploits of Greek youth who tried to obtain the "golden fleece" of Greek maidens. In so doing, she alludes to the mythical Jason's search for the Golden Fleece.

45. That is, his face looks like his backside because he lacks facial hair.

46. Tilley, *Dictionary of Proverbs,* M79. See also Shakespeare's *Two Gentlemen of Verona* (1594): "the old saying is, / Black men are pearls in beauteous ladies' eyes" (5.2.11–12).

47. A black-haired man.

48. This is an expression used to gain attention. "Anan" is an old form of "anon."

49. See John Heywood, *A Dialogue of the Effectual Proverbs in the English Tongue Concerning Marriage,* ed. John S. Farmer (London, 1906): "enough is as good as a feast" (137).

50. That is, a day kept in celebration of an event in the life of the Virgin Mary: March 25 (Feast of the Annunciation); Dec. 8 (Conception of the Virgin); Sept. 8 (Feast of the Birth of Mary); Aug. 15 (Feast of the Assumption).

51. See Fynes Moryson, *An Itinerary* (London, 1617), bk. 3, pt. 3, ch. 3, p. 152: "because the taste of the English is thus delighted with sweetenesse, the Wines in Tavernes . . . are commonly mixed at the filling thereof, to make them pleasant." Adding sugar to beer would also decrease the head (i.e., the foam).

52. Know.

53. That is, the youth who bent a coin and sent it as a love token. An "angel" was a gold coin issued from 1470 to 1634, worth between six shillings, eight pence and ten shillings. It was believed that a bent coin brought good luck, as glossed in *The Complete Works of Samuel Rowlands, 1598–1628,* vol. 3 (Glasgow: Printed for the Hunterian Club, 1880).

54. Niccholes advises men not to choose a wife who is "of too dwarfish a size, and kindred, to store thee with a generation of Pigmies, dwarfes, halfe men, that want the Majesty and power of heigth and strength" (*Discourse,* 10). In *Tis Merry,* the Maid rejects a short suitor.

55. If.

56. Smoking began in England in 1587, with the return of Sir Francis Drake. He brought with him a load of tobacco leaf pirated from the Spanish, along with some Roanoke colonists who had learned the smoking habit from American Indians. Although some people believed that tobacco could cure any malady, including the pox, James I argued that it jeopardized the state because it led to lust and drunkenness,

caused soldiers to lag behind to smoke, and cost too much (at least three shillings an ounce). In addition, smoke "makes a kitchin also oftentimes in the inward parts of man, soiling and infecting them, with an unctuous and oily kind of Soote, as hath bene fond in some great *Tobacco* takers, that after their death were opened" (*A Counterblaste to Tobacco* [London, 1604], D1r). Smoking occurred frequently in taverns and alehouses.

57. A shrub burned to sweeten the odor in a room.

58. Poor cuts of meat.

59. When I was in bed giving birth.

60. Perhaps the Wife dreams of sexual fantasies with a yellow-bearded man and a neutered cock rooster, while the Widow dreams of cats (who were considered deceitful and sexually promiscuous and were identified with women). See Sara Mendelson and Patricia Crawford, *Women in Early Modern England, 1550–1720* (Oxford: Clarendon Press, 1998), 61.

61. That is, the Wife's fastidious neighbor, about whom they are gossiping. The phrase has sexual overtones.

62. This refers to the oath "By St. Mary of Egypt." See Ben Jonson's *Bartholomew Fair* (1614): "Marry gip, goody she-Justice, Mistress French-hood!" (1.5.15). In her youth, St. Mary of Egypt (fifth century?) was a prostitute, not to earn money, but to gratify her lust. After she joined a pilgrimage to Jerusalem and corrupted some of the pilgrims, she was kept from entering a church by an invisible force. While praying to the statue of the Virgin, she realized her sin, whereupon the statue spoke to her and told her to go over the Jordan River, where she would find rest. She did so and lived about forty-seven years in the wilderness. See Alban Butler, *Butler's Lives of the Saints,* vol. 2, ed. Herbert Therston and Donald Attwater (London: Burns and Oates, 1956), 14.

63. In the know.

64. A kind of sausage.

65. Perjure yourself.

66. French kiss.

67. That is, drink more, as glossed in *The Complete Works of Samuel Rowlands, 1598–1628,* vol. 3.

68. Memorandum books used for keeping notes, with pages of wood, slate, or vellum.

69. A liqueur made from or flavored with the juice of the sundew plant, which was thought to restore health. See Nicholas Breton's *Longing of a Blessed Heart* (1601), reprinted in *The Works in Verse and Prose of Nicholas Breton,* vol. 1, ed. Alexander B. Grosart (Glasgow: Printed for the Hunterian Club, 1980): "The *Rosa solis* the sicke soule reviveth" (p. 13, col. 2).

70. Perhaps the Widow is telling the Vintner's Boy that she is as good as his mistress and hence a person to be respected.

71. Your Maisters live, you slave, by such as we.

72. Hurt, injure.

73. The main thoroughfare to London Bridge and one of the authorized places in the city for the sale of fish.

74. The Widow repeats "William" twenty-eight times, probably to taunt him and assert her superiority.

75. Beholden.

76. Gentlemen and their immediate families made up about 2 percent of the population of England during this period. See Keith Wrightson, *English Society, 1580–1680* (New Brunswick, N.J.: Rutgers University Press, 1982), 24. Landed wealth was most important in determining gentleman status, but the category "gentleman" (and "gentlewoman") was not legally defined. The Wife, the Maid, and the Widow would probably not have been considered gentlewomen.

77. We are not to be addressed as common women, as glossed in vol. 3, *The Complete Works of Samuel Rowlands, 1598–1628,* 24.

78. Do you think, saucy fellow, that we prate like parrots?

79. That is, manners make the man. Tilley quotes from *Tis Merry* in giving an example of the proverb (*Dictionary of Proverbs,* M629).

80. Ago.

81. A shilling was the daily wage of a building craftsman in 1600. If a gallon of sack cost between three shillings, ten pence and four shillings, eight pence in 1598–99, and a gallon of claret cost between one shilling, eight pence and two shillings in 1600, then the Wife, the Maid, and the Widow clearly drank a great deal of alcohol. See André L. Simon, *The History of the Wine Trade in England* (London: Wyman and Sons, 1906–9), 3:291.

82. According to Stow the five bells of St. Mary-le-Bow in Cheapside, London, were to "bee nightly rung at nine of the clocke" (*Survey of London,* 1:255). Built during the reign of William the Conqueror, the church was named le-Bow because it was the first church in London to be built on arches of stone (227).

83. This was the tavern in Southwark where the pilgrims in Chaucer's *Canterbury Tales* gathered. In Rowlands's pamphlet, there are more women in the tavern.

84. That is, the London tavern is better than the Taberd [Tabard] Inn because more of its patrons are "blithe wenches."

85. That is, the cheapest. Penny ale, or common thin ale, is mentioned in *The Vision of William Concerning Piers the Plowman in Three Parallel Texts* (B Text; ed. Walter W. Skeat [Oxford: Clarendon Press, 1886], pt. 15, l. 310) as fit only for strict-living friars.

86. Probably a sexual pun on "pressed in print."

87. The Wife, the Widow, and the Maid call for a woman to be their poet.

88. Robert Greene was a playwright and pamphleteer who lived from ca. 1560 to 1592. Among his works are *Pandosto,* the source for Shakespeare's *Winter's Tale,* and the play *The Honorable History of Friar Bacon and Friar Bungay.* Greene was much too prolific a writer to have all his publications gathered in one volume.

89. *Conny-catching* was published in three parts in 1591–92. Greene also wrote *A Disputation betweene a Hee Conycatcher and a Shee Connycatcher, whether a Theafe or a Whore is most hurtfull in Cousenage to the Common-wealth* (1592).

90. This probably refers to Nicholas Breton's *Pasquils mad-cap,* which was published anonymously in 1600, and *The second part of Pasquils mad-cap intituled: the fooles-cap* (1600), rather than to *The First parte of Pasquil's Apologie* (1590), doubtfully attributed

to Thomas Nashe. Pasquil was originally the name of a Roman pillar on which libels and defamatory verses were posted.

91. This probably refers to Breton's *Melancholike humours* (1600).

92. This work is not known to have been written by Breton, Nash, Greene, or Rowlands. The reference may be to *The Moral Philosophie of the Stoicks,* written in French by Guillaume Du Vair in 1585 and translated into English by Thomas James in 1598.

93. Nash's popular pamphlet *Pierce Pennilesse his Supplication to the Divell* was published in 1595, seven years before *Tis Merry.*

94. Rowlands is provocatively drawing attention to *Merry Meeting; or, 'Tis Merry when Knaves mete,* one of two pamphlets by him that were deemed so offensive they were publicly burned in the kitchen of the Stationers Company on 26 October 1600. Apparently the Gentleman was unaware of this pamphlet.

95. Tilley quotes from *Tis Merry* in giving an example of this proverb (*Dictionary of Proverbs,* M60).

96. This may refer to hair color, as the Widow censures red- and yellow-haired men.

97. Intelligent, clever.

98. Stupidity.

99. Perhaps this is a reference to rope dancing from the steeple of Saint Paul's Cathedral. According to Raphael Holinshed, at the coronation of Edward VI a man "came from the battlements of the steeple of Paules church upon a cable, being made fast to an anchor by the deanes gate, lieng on his breast, aiding himselfe neither with hand nor foot, and after ascended to the middest of the cable where he tumbled and plaied manie pretie toies, whereat the king and the nobles had good pastime" (*Chronicles,* vol. 3 [London, 1587], 866). Presumably, the rope dancer wasn't smiling.

100. A fine white plaster made of gypsum from Montmartre, Paris.

101. A framework of hoops, usually of whalebone, worked into cloth and used to extend the skirts of women's dresses.

102. That is, consumers of coin. The figure of a cross was often stamped into one side of a coin.

103. Dismissed.

104. Much good may it do you, as glossed in Rowlands, vol. 3.

105. The narrator emphasizes that the three women pay their tavern bills, unlike many people who ran up sizable debts.

106. Dido is the legendary founder and queen of the city of Carthage. In Virgil's *Aeneid,* the shipwrecked Aeneas is brought by Venus to Carthage, where Dido falls in love with him and plies him with drink (bks. 1 and 4). Christine de Pizan comments that "Dido's love for Aeneas was far greater than his love for her. . . . He departed at night . . . without her knowledge. This was how he repaid his hostess" (*The Book of the City of Ladies* [New York: Persea Books, 1982], bk. 2.55.1, p. 189).

107. According to legend, Semiramis ruled for forty-two years after the death of her second husband, Ninus, king of Assyria. She was famous as a warrior and as the builder of Babylon. In another account, Ninus gives Semiramus the throne for five days. On

the first day she holds a magnificent banquet; on the second, she imprisons her husband. See Siculus Diodorus, *Bibliotheca historica* (Library of history) (Loeb Classical Library, 1946), bk. 2.

108. Marcus Porcius Cato (234–149 B.C.E.), who wrote maxims and rules for everyday life, "used to say that the man who struck his wife or child, laid violent hands on the holiest of holy things" ("Marcus Cato," in *Plutarch's Lives* [Loeb Classical Library, 1914], bk. 20, p. 2). After his first wife died, he married a young girl "when he was long past the marrying age" (24.1) and "fell under no slight or insignificant censure" ("Comparison of Aristides and Cato," in *Plutarch's Lives,* bk. 6, p. 1).

109. The Wife, the Maid, and the Widow are drinking in a private room where they need not be concerned with people watching how much they drink.

110. Too much.

111. That is, cheat. See Shakespeare's *Much Ado About Nothing* (1598–99): "boys, / That lie and cog and flout, deprave and slander" (5.1.94–95).

112. Sexual intercourse.

113. The fourth husband in *A whole crew of Kind Gossips* says, "I will not be a Wittoll and an asse, / But even next Summer turne my wife to grasse."

114. Hyder E. Rollins suggests that "A pleaseant newe ballad Called the maydens choyce," entered in the Stationers Register by John Danter on 26 August 1591, may have been preserved in the 1619 edition of Samuel Rowlands's *Wel met, Gossip or Tis merry* (*An Analytical Index to the Ballad Entries [1557–1709] in the Registers of the Company of Stationers of London* [Chapel Hill: University of North Carolina Press, 1924], 143.)

115. Just as Jews do not have Christian names, given only at baptism, the Widow will not name the unkind youth.

116. In other words, her size is that of a six months' pregnant woman.

117. Mistake.

118. A deceptive bottom in a can of beer, by which customers were cheated.

119. Country people as opposed to sophisticated Londoners.

120. Deceitful.

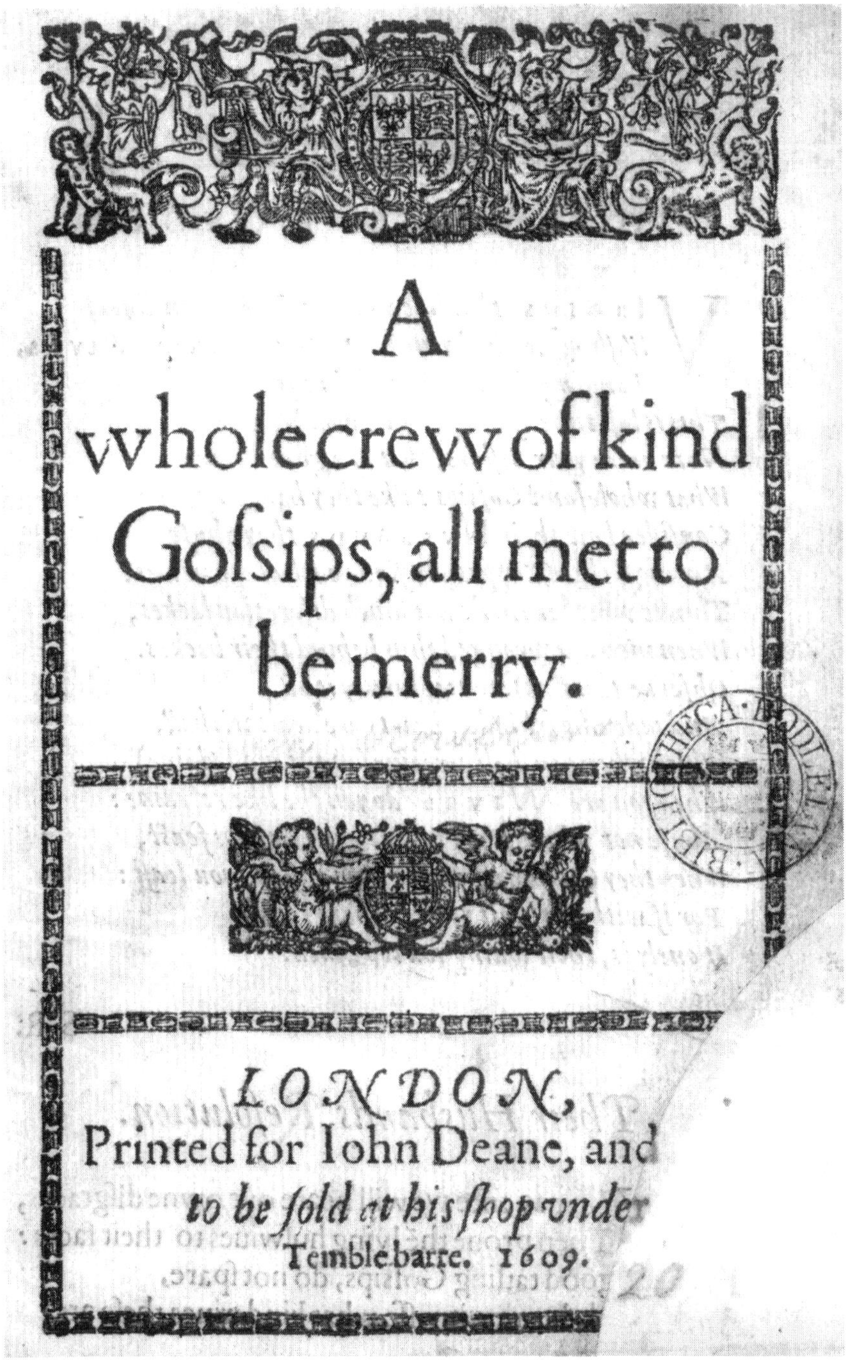

A

whole crew of kind Gossips, all met to be merry.

LONDON,
Printed for Iohn Deane, and
to be sold at his shop under
Temblebarre. 1609.

A whole crew of kind Gossips, all met to be merry. London, Printed for John Deane, and to be sold at his shop under Temblebarre, 1609.

To the Maids of LONDON.

VIRGINS, *that live your weary Maiden-lives,*
Wishing with al your harts that you were WIVES;
Longing continually to heare it saide,
This is last time of asking, farewell MAIDE.
Note heere your Sisters, that are gone before,
What wholesome Gossips[1] *talke they have in store:*
Consider how their HUSBANDS *they abuse*
Amongst their Cuppes, to finde each other newes:
Thinke whether ther's not much discretion lackes,
When men are wronged thus behind their backes.
Observe this Conference, survey it all,
And judge how kindest hearts are dealt withall,
Which when you shall perceive (as t'is most plaine)
When you are WIVES *do you the like refraine:*
Abuse not HUSBANDS *at each Gossips feast,*
When they (good harmelesse men) offend you least:
For if with any fault you can them touch,
It onely is, their loving you too much.

S.R.

Their Husbands Resolution.[2]

With patience we will heare our owne disgraces,
Then prove them lying huswives[3] to their faces:
Proceed good tatling Gossips, do not spare,
And Maids beare witnesse what kind wives these are.

A whole Crew of kind Gossips, all *met to be merry.*

My Maisters that are married looke about,
For matter of complaint is comming out
Against your persons, stand upon your gard,
Either your wives be bad, or you deale hard:

Your credits are in question very farre,
And now or never, either make or marre.
You are accus'd of many haynous things,
And swift report hath very nimble wings.
It flyes about the Towne from eare to eare,
And most will credit even all they heare.
What will the world suppose, to have your wives
Give out, their husbands live such odious lives?
What will our Batchelers and Maidens say,
That are preparing for their wedding day?
Why, they will censure of the married life,
To be a state full of Domesticke strife.
Stand to it stoutly, now as you are men,
First heare them speake, and shape an answere then,
They are no lesse then halfe a dozen strong,
Arm'd with such tongues as will endure no wrong
Six Gossips that of late together met,
Besprinckled finely, well with Clarret wet:
Apt to discourse of all that ere they knew,
As tis the humor of the Gossip-crew,
Did find themselves greatly agrieved all,
And each her husband into question call.
The first of them, a gallant propper Dame,
With tongue inough, and courage to the same,
That dranke carouses to the other five,
And had a care to see the Vintner thrive:
That had her pint for pint, her quart for quart,
Loving a cup of Clarret with her hart:
That scorn'd to be intreated for her drinke,[4]
But would hold out, when twenty Wenches shrink;
And take her cups, even with a courage downe,
Play the good fellow kindly, spend her Crowne[5]
With any he that durst, a merry wife,
That never plaide the Mizer in her life:
Onely her husband did a humour[6] see,
Which did not like him, she was too too free;[7]
And that (indeed) will not do very well,

For divers reasons which a man might tell:
But we will leave them to be thought upon,
And turne her to her tale, which thus goes on.[8]
Kind Gentlewomen, though I sport and jest,
I have small cause to do it, I protest,
If you knew all the crosses Fortune brings,
Ah little do you know where my shoo wrings.[9]
I am oft merry, and I cannot chuse,
If one should hang me, pleasure I must use:
Unto the Proverbe I do still agree,
Care kil'd a Cat,[10] so shall it not do me.
Yet I am husbanded with such a Clowne,
'Twould pul a merrier heart then mine is downe:
Theres nothing in him, tis a very Gull,[11]
His mind's of Money bags, to fill them full:
Ther's nothing that comes from him with good will,
But he is ever grudging, grumbling still:
Let me but aske him somewhat for to spend
At such a time as this, with friend and friend;
His purse will be a comming out so slow,
And such a dogged looke he will bestow,
With minde unwilling going thereabout,
I could spend thrice as much ere it comes out.
Is this the way to please a womans minde,
That is unto good fellow-ship inclin'de?
And never to this day regardeth drosse,[12]
Sometime a Crowne, and sometime ne're a crosse:[13]
To take allowance at a wretches hand,
Not having Gold and Silver at command.
Whom doth he spare for, we no children have?[14]
Indeed he doth allow me to go brave,[15]
But that's his credit, full as much as mine,
And now and then at meales a pint of wine:
Marry sir Muffe,[16] yea, and Gra-mercy[17] horse,
I will have more, by faire meanes, or by force:
I scorne to take allowance like a child,
There's nothing got, when women be too mild.

This by my Sister *Sara* prove I can,
All London doth not yeeld a kinder man
Then *Thomas* is, yet at the first I know,
He did but use her (as they say) so so.
But what did she? Marry, grew somewhat stout,[18]
And when he look't for kindnesse,[19] loure and pout,
With pish and phew, no joy (poore soule) I have,
I could now wish, that I were in my grave;
And sigh, and weepe, and often eate no meat,
And then the Asse (her Husband) would intreat,
I prethe (sweet-Hart) what dost ayle my deare?
Why should this sorrow in thy lookes appeare:
Dost thou want any thing, I prethe speake,
Then would she sigh, as if her hart would breake,
And make as though she wept, and rub her eies,
Till her kinde foole in earnest fits and cries,
Protesting to doe ought that might her please,
Then laying open to him hir disease,
She told him that her onely griefe of mind
Proceeded from hard usage she did find:
For other women (to her extreame care)
Were full of Money, when her purse was bare.
He hearing this, accounted it good hap,[20]
And threw a bag of Angels[21] in her lap:
Then tooke her by the hand, and (kissing) swore,
While he had coyne, she should complaine no more:
So to this day his honest word doth keepe,
Onely because his wife did sit and weepe.
Now which of us will not almost do so,
Our teares are cheape and plenty, you do know,
For be it spoke in secret twixt us heere,
A penny for a pottle[22] is too deere.
Well, I intend to try my Sisters tricke;
Ile first be sullen, after Ile be sicke:
And if one after t'other will not doo,
I will be sullen, sicke, and dogged too,
And chafe, and pout, and loure, and fret, and sweat,

And in a Weeke not touch a bit of meat;[23]
And when my Husbands tongue he stil doth hold,
Then I will be most apt to braule and scold;
But when he speakes, and would have me reply,
I'll hold my peace, and (frowning) looke awry.[24]
These are the rules that I intend to keepe,
A Shroe is ten times better then a sheepe.[25]

The second Gossip.

Next unto her a pretty neate[26] one sat,
Which tooke a cup of wine, and dranke up that:
Then filling it unto another, said,
Ah, wish I could, that I were yet a Maid.
We are so forward in our youth you know,
When past a dozen yeares we once do grow,
We long, and wish, and looke, and daily thinke
For you know what, *Cupid* is meat and drinke
Unto our hungry thoughts, his praise we sing;
Forsooth a Husband is your onely thing.
Poore foolish Girles, we know not what we doe,
But take a pride when fellowes come to woe,[27]
Ile tell you one thing, but no words Ile have,
I know I speake it to the wise and grave:
When I was Maid, with Chalke behind our doore,[28]
Some five and forty Suitors I did score:
And I would use the fooles alike (all kinde)
For which, continuall favours I did finde:
Ile tell you truth, the Gloves[29] which some did give,
Are more then I can weare out while I live.
Each was resolv'd, he did my love possesse;
For like a crafty queane[30] (I must confesse)
I gave kinde words, and smiles, and kisses too,
And things that shall be namelesse I did doo:
Which shall be left to youth, 'tis gone and past,
I have not bin the first, nor shall be last

Of waggish[31] Wenches: for when we are gone,
Ther's little ones new bred are growing on.
But (in good sadnesse) I am plagued now
For all my knavery, and Ile tell you how.
Of all my choise (for forty five was plenty)
I tooke a Clowne the very worst of twenty,
Indeed he doth allow me Coyne at will,
For to be-lye[32] the Divell it is ill:
But heere's his fault, hee'le crosse me many a way,
When I would have my humour, he sayes nay.
Let me bid one do this, he sayes do that,
My wife talkes oftentimes she knowes not what;
Yea, when that many strangers are in place,
Hee's not asham'd to offer this disgrace,
For which we two have often fallings out,
And sometimes at the fist we have a bout.
I care not greatly whosoere it know,
If he strike me, Ile match him blow for blow;
For though he be my head (as people talke)[33]
about his pate my fists sometimes doth walke;
He shall have even as good as he doth bring,
I will not dye in's debt for any thing.
Unto my Parents I do seeme the liker,[34]
For well I wot, my Mother was a striker:
And I have seene her take my Father downe,
That he was even affraid to see her frowne.
He would sometime come wrangling in a dore,
But when my Mother with a cudgell swore,
and said but to him, *Richard shall I come?*
Why present he had not a word but *Mum.*
I noting this, unto my selfe would say,
That same tricke wil I have another day:
For if I meet with one that's like my Father,
Ile take no blowes, Ile see him hanged rather.
Indeed I finde my Husband but a bragger,
His humour is, he will a little swagger,
And seemes as if he were Knight of the Sunne.[35]

But let me stand to him, and he hath done.
At first (indeed) he put me in a feare,
When as I heard him but begin to sweare:
Then spake I faire, and to him was right kinde,
Thinking to put him in a better minde.
I tride him thus a while, but t'was a wonder
How he would dominiere, and keepe me under.
Nay then (quoth I) Ile try my Mothers tricke,
And valiantly tooke up a Faggot-sticke.[36]
(For he had given me a blow or twaine)
But as he likes it, let him strike againe,
The blood ran downe about his eares apace,
I brake his head, and all bescratch't his face:
Then got him downe, and with my very fist
I did bepommell[37] him untill he pist.
So from that houre unto this present day,
He never durst begin another fray:
But is content to let all fighting cease,
A Faggot-sticke hath bound him to the peace.

The third Gossip.

Well done in truth, yea, and Gra-mercy *Besse,*
Would I had part of thy brave valiantnesse,
I lacke it wench (in sadnesse) very much:
For I have one all Hell affoords none such,
He useth me in all things as he list,[38]
Oh that I could but rule him with my fist,
As thou doest thine, how happy should I be,
If I had but a courage like to thee;
It grieves me to the hart I cannot doe it,
Nature hath not enabled me unto it:
I have as tall a tongue as others have,
And can affoord him Rascall, drunkard, knave,
Gull, coxcombe, noddy, ideot, and asse,
The veryest Calfe that ever went to grasse,

Block-headed buzzard, and a hundred like,[39]
But I could never have the heart to strike:
If that I durst once venter[40] for to beat him,
As in mine anger I could even eat him,
In conscience I might be his Maister sure,
If I the tryall of it durst endure.
Sometimes methinkes I could a cudgell take,
But then my very heart begins to quake,
For to my selfe my inward thoughts do speake,
My husband is too strong, and I too weake:
Which makes me often wish I had the power
To make my selfe a man but halfe an houre,
That so I might revenge my selfe a while,
I would be talkt of many a hundred Mile
For valour, I should make him tremble then;
And be example unto other men.
Oh I would teach my dominiering youth,
To strike a woman while he liv'd in truth.
One time he came home drunke, and then thought I,
Now for to cudgell him I will go try.
His case was then so weake he could not stand,
And I might easie get the uper hand:
But I conceiv'd twill turne unto my sorrow,
The drunken foole would thinke upon't to morrow:
And then I shall be sure to pay for all,
I know the weakest must unto the wall.[41]
This made me very fearefull to proceed,
And for my life I durst not do the deed:
But in his way I set a little stoole,
And over that, downe comes my reeling foole:
That was to plague him somewhat for his sins,
For I am sure it mortified his shins,
And then I seem'd to be exceeding sad,
Saying deare husband what a fall you had?
Give me your hand that I may helpe you rise;
And tooke a handkerchief, and wip't mine eyes,
As if that I had wept for very griefe,

Being my selfe the causer of it chiefe:
But of a troth[42] (as you may well beleeve)
I laugh't most bravely at it in my sleeve.
And then into a chaire I did him set,
Asking him if a Chirurgion[43] should be set,
And tying of a Kirchiefe 'bout his hed,
I left him fast asleepe and went to bed:
All this I did to please in outward showes,
Being my pollicy to scape from blowes.
But the next morning in his sobernesse,
I rang his eares a peale, you'le hardly gesse.
Thou filthy beast (quoth I) hast thou no shame,
To make thy selfe a common laughing game,
art thou a man thus to abuse thy wife?
Assuredly, 'tis pitty of thy life.
I sit all day even like a prisoner heere,
and thou com'st home laden with Wine and Beere,[44]
and if I tell thee for thy good thereof,
(Like all lewd Knaves) good counsell thou do'st scoffe.
My tongue thou tearmest but a Serpents sting,
Thus doth the divell lead thee in a string,[45]
Thou hast no power good Motions to imbrace:
Cam'st thou not home last night in scurvy case,
Bleeding, and hurt, my sorrow to provoke?
It were no matter if thy necke were broke.
Thus did I rattle him, till choller grew,
And then he at my head a Cushion threw;
Saying, there skold, take somewhat for thy paines.
Go to (quoth I) y'are best beat out my braines
With Cushions[46] now, to make the proverbe true,
Then out goes he to meete the cursed crue,
And to inquire who t'was did hurt him so,
But Ile keepe that (my wenches) close, I trow.

The fourth Gossip.

Well Gentlewomen (said the fourth) I see
You have great reason to complain all three,
Upon your husbands, they are bad indeed,
But I have one (in conscience) doth exceed:
The chiefest thing wherein he takes delight,
Is to be up at Dice and Cards all night.
He is a Gamester, though no Cocke of game,
For I do find he doth his busines lame,[47]
In things (you know my meaning) scant worth praise,
But fast and welcome as a number sayes,
Al's one for that, my care hath ever bin,
Because he will not stay a nights within,
But runneth still abroad from place to place,
Wasting away his Money lewd and base:
His Gamesters companies heele not refuse,
For all the milde behaviour I can use;
Intreat him, kind deare husband play no more,
And speake him faire untill my tongue be sote [sore],[48]
Request him if in love with Cards he be,
That he would play at *Noddy* but with me,
Or if he love the Tables so a life,
Why then to play at *Dublets*[49] with his wife.
No, no, t'is death unto him, out he must.
To keepe the Money in his purse from rust:
Novum and *Passage,* scoure his Mettall bright,
New-cut[50] even makes a Begger of him right.
Looke heere's the best apparrell that I have,
The very wedding Gowne my Father gave:
He never gave me yet a paire of Gloves,
I am beholding[51] more to others loves
Then unto him, in honest manner tho,
And (Gossips) I beseech you take it so.[52]
There are kinde Gentlemen, some two or three,
And they indeed my loving Kinsmen be,
Which will not see me want, I know it I,

Two of them at my house in Terme time[53] lye,
And comfort me with jests and odde device,
When as my Husbands out a nights at Dice.
For if I were without a merry friend,
I could not live a twelve-month to an end:
One of them gave me this same Ruffe of Lawne,
It cost three pound, but last weeke in the Pawne.[54]
Do y'thinke my husband would have bin so free?
Alas he never made so much of mee.
Nay t'other day at Church I spide a Hat,[55]
My minde and eye was never off from that,
The onely fashion to content alone,
Yet thinke you he would buy me such a one.
No, I protest, but when I made the motion;
Oh wife (said he) pray where was your devotion?
Go you to Church to find new fashions out?
Is this the exercise you are about?
In that same sacred place (ordaind for Prayer)
Are you so void of feare and devout care?
How now (quoth I) heere's Vice will folly teach,
Take in your Geese, the Fox begins to preach,[56]
What have we heere: a mortified man?
Is Dice and Cards become a Puritan?[57]
Oh admirable change, I pray *New-cut,*
Into what devout humour are you put?
And thus I fitted good-man counterfeit,
For he had put me in a chasing heat,
And surely being mov'd, I home can speake;
Some wit I have, a Knavish jest to breake.
My husband he was husht, and went his way,
The Cox-combe Asse had not a word to say:
But in a doores he got exceeding grim,
'Twas next day noone ere I set eyes on him.
This man wil talke full well, and speake of heaven,
Yet leaves his loving wife at sixe and seaven:[58]
Goes forth one day, and commeth home the next,
To prove this lawfull, sure he hath no text.

Wel, ere the weeke do end, I make no doubt,
But we shal have another falling out,
Ile crosse him he was never better crost,
And put him in a heat against the frost
For that same Hat, wherein he did me wrong,
(As you know what it is when women long)
He shall repent it (marke what I do say)
Ten times within a Twelvemonth and a day,
Ile keepe the rest of that I have intended,
A little saide (they say) is soone amended.
But even as true as I was borne a Maid,
I owe him that good turne which shall be paid.

The fift Gossip.

Sure (quoth the fift) I do not meane to flatter,
Were all such husbands hang'd, it made no matter.
I have a sound card[59] for a womans stay,
Hee's drunke but once a week, that's e'ry day.
Oh 'tis the filthiest man I do protest,
That ever was of giddy pate[60] possest:
Himselfe all day in Tavernes he bestowes,
and comes to bed at night in shooes and hose;
And there he lyes as cleanly as a Hog,
Perfum'd as sweet as any stinking Dog,
With filthy leaves he smoakes his head with all,
Such Weeds, as *Indians* do *Tobacco*[61] call:
But sure as *Black-amores*[62] looke outward skin,
So Collier-like[63] are English-men within,
That take such trash: for there be Doctors say,
The memory of Man it doth decay,
and poysoning the braine, it makes it dul,
When loathsome vapours fil each passage ful.
I am a woman, yet ile undertake,
The credit of this fire-worke quite to shake,
Gainst any Maister-gunner of the trade.

No reason in the world that can perswade
Vertue remaineth in a little smoake,
That to our sences doth offence provoke:
Hold but your face where wood a kindling lyes,
Apply the Medicine to your nose and eyes,
Into your mouth let it have passage free,
And note how welcome this same stuffe will be,
Fye out upon't, it makes a filthy smell,
My nose likes a *Sir-reverence*[64] as well.
I thinke a thousand times I do complaine,
And tell my husband that he should refraine
This making of a Chimney of his nose:
He had a breath as sweet as any Rose[65]
Before he used this same scurvy tricke,
But now, if I do kisse him I am sicke,
With this same fough;[66] beshrow your heart say I,
Tobacco stinkes, you poyson me, I dye.
Then what does he, but sayes, Go hang thee Queane,
This wholesome Phisicke[67] keepes my body cleane,
Ile take it for to anger thee withall:
Then for a Candle and a Pipe hee'le call,
A Trencher[,][68] Whore, let there a Rush be got,
Some Paper, make the Fire-shovell hot,
A Knife, some Match, and reach a little Wyre,
A Tinder-box, fetch me a coale of Fyre.
Why heeres a stirre, what woman can endure it?
And yet this life I have (Gossips) assure it.
But now and then I fit him in his kinde,
When any smoaky stuffe of his I finde:
For when I meet with his *Tobacco* Box,
I send it to the privy with a pox.[69]
Then hee'le go raging up and downe, and sweare,
He misseth such most rare and wholesome geare,[70]
The like did never grow on *India*[71] ground,
and every ounce for goodnesse worth a pound.
Thus doth he live, and make a daily course
To smoake himselfe, keeping an empty purse,[72]

With Beere, Wine, and *Tobacco,* what cares he,
Sinke I, or swim, it matters not for me.
Is this a life, judge Gossips, judge I pray?
My discontent succeedeth day by day.
When first I married with this drunken drone,
I was a propper wench it is well knowne:
And though I say't that should not, one or other,
In all our parish was not such another.
I did refuse as handsome men and wise,
As ever girdle[73] girt, let that suffice.
And if good Fortune I had not withstood,
I might in Conscience sure have worne a Hood.[74]
My husband had as much with me (that Curre)
as Mistres *Susans* husband had with her:
Besides I know all you that are in place,
Will judge that I have farre a better face,
More propper body, and for hand and foot
Ile put her downe, and give her legges to boot:
Yet notwithstanding my good parts, you see
How Lady-like she is maintain'd to me.
But well, if I proove widdow ere I dye,
It shall go hard but I will looke as hye.[75]

The sixt Gossip.

Friends (quoth the sixt) each hath reveal'd hir griefe,
Yet give me leave to thinke that mine is chiefe:
Would with your worst I might a husband change
Sure I would thinke my hap lesse hard and strange,
Your five indeed are bad, I must confesse,
But mine is even the worst of all the Messe.[76]
All yours may be indur'd, but tis a hell
When men do love their neighbours wives too wel.
Thinke that I doe not speake it of ill will,
(As true as this is wine I meane to fill)
Nor out of jealousie, take it not so,

Into that humour I did never grow:
I speake it Gossips (first Ile drinke) do y'heare?
Ev'n from the wrongs that I do know I beare.
My Husband's lewd, given to go astray,
His love to me now daily doth decay,
Quite altred from the man that he hath bin,
Even given over to the fleshly sin.
Ther's not a Whore in *London* nor about,
But he hath all the haunts to find her out.
He knowes the Pandars that can fit his turne,
And Bauds[77] that helpe good fellowes to the burne:[78]
Taffity Queanes,[79] and fine light silken Whores,
That have the gift of pox[80] in their owne pores,
and can teach French[81] in halfe a day by noone,
as leacherous as a Monkey[82] or Baboone,
That daily go like Ladies in attire,
And live by hackning out themselves to hire,[83]
More common rid, re-rid, and ridden over,
Then any Jade betwixt Gravesend and Dover:[84]
And let me aske, what's such a one, or she
With Fan and Maske? His Cozens[85] all they be.
What's she that hath the jewell in her haire,
and on her backe the Cobweb-Lawne[86] most rare,
Having a Vintners bush upon her head,[87]
All trim'd with shoo-strings,[88] tawny, greene and red;
Whose Fan weighs more, tride onely by the Feather,
Then all her honest trickes,[89] being joyn'd together:
Forsooth his Cozen, shee's most neere of kin,
This lying humour he is ever in.
He hath all that to villany belongs,
The hugest number of such baudy songs,
You even would wonder (Gossips, this is plaine)
That any man could beare them in his braine.
He hath a song cald, *Mistris will you do?*
And *My man Thomas did me promise*[90] to,
He hath the *Pinnace*[91] *rigd with silken saile,*
And pretty Birds, with *Garden Nightingale,*

Ile tye my Mare in thy ground a new way,
Worse then the Players sing it in the Play,
Besse for abuses, and a number more,
That you and I have never heard before.
And these among those wenches he doth learne,
Which by activity[92] their livings earne.
His Crownes upon them frankly he bestowes,
Not caring for his wife, or how she goes:
Let me complaine for any kind of stuffe,
What answeres he? Thy clothes are good enough,
I like thee well, and should if thou went'st worse.
These are his cogging[93] trickes to save his purse,
So he may spare to spend it upon me,
He never doth regard on whom it be.
Let me but walke with him along the street,
'Tis wonderfull how many he doth meet,
That do salute him, looking all like queanes;
But then heele scarcely speake by any meanes,
Onely he winkes on them, and passes by,
Making account, *The blind eates many a Fly.*[94]
But I can smell the Knavery of him out,
And very shortly (I do make no doubt)
To take him napping, I have laid a plot
Shall coole the Gentleman is growne so hot.
I say no more, there's somewhat in the winde,
The Cat oft winkes, and yet she is not blinde.[95]
All friends, no words, be merry, come who drinks?
Little our goodmen knowes what their wives thinkes.
Let's point a time when we shall meet againe,
and she that failes; we will injoyne this paine,
Five shillings to be spent in Wine, pawne downe,[96]
Gossips, for good example there's my Crowne.

The end of the Sixe Gossips.

Sixe HUSBANDS.

Pray Maisters give us leave a while,
Now you have heard our wives:
Weele overthrow them horse and foote,
Or else weele loose our lives.

Six honest HUSBANDS give their Wives the lye.

The first accused by his Wife to bee Miserable.

There is ancient Proverbe us'd of old,
The first tale's good, untill the next be told.[97]
a lyers tongue, is tearmed falshoods mint,
We have beene slandered by our wives in print,[98]
Yet have bin silent it appeares too long,
The world may censure we have done them wrong,
Because with silence it hath past away.
But Gentlemen, now give us leave I pray
To use apologie, and by no meanes
Give credit to such cunning crafty queanes:
For they have slandred us, upon our lives;
The case may be your owne if you have wives:
and therefore be not partially inclin'd,
But heare the matter with indifferent mind.
A Taverne for their parly[99] they did chuse,
and there (forsooth) as pratling Gossips use,
Like *Catoes* wife,[100] they presently be led,
To utter all that comes into their head.
And first my *Jone,* (a very prating Dame)
Of sparing, and of hardnesse doth me blame:
She wanteth money (as she sayes) to spend,
Sirs, can a man get Coyne unto that end?
My purse she sayes is slowly comming out,
But her hand is too nimble thereabout;

Sheele set it going, she can make it flye,
And if I speake, she answeres, *What care I?*
Ile be maintained Gentle-woman like,
Then bends her fist as if she meant to strike,
That sometime I am glad to speake her faire
For quietnesse: and tis an honest care,
To have commaund, onely by manly carriage,
For I do know the civill warres of marriage
Too well, by divers of mine neighbors lives,
That are ore-macht in combat with their wives;
Blowes therefore we do never put in ure,[101]
But a Shrowes[102] tongue I daily do indure.
Give me some Money, Money is her song,
She loves to be a spending all day long.
Housholders judge, if al things be not deere,
She gets me not a penny in a yeere,[103]
And spends me pounds a weeke, yet stil complaines,
That never taketh any other paines,
But starch a Ruffe,[104] and sit and pricke a clout,[105]
Then walke abroad, this worke she goes about.
Shal I maintaine an ydle huswife so?
There's not an honest man but will say no.
He that doth let his wife have what she wil,
Being a Foole, sheele keepe him Woodcocke[106] stil.
No, Ile be head, my title Ile not lose,
Shee's wel maintaind, as all my neighbors knowes:
Nay Ile be sworne it makes my purse-strings cracke,
To ruffle her in her pride, and gowne[107] her backe:
She hath six Gownes for wearing ne're the worse,
I would I had five of them in my purse:
But tis her humour, and it must be thus,
Pride pleaseth them, how ere it pincheth us,
There's not a new-found toy,[108] if once they crave it,
Poore husbands shall not rest untill they have it.

The Second, charged by his Wife to crosse her in her humour.

Next I am blam'd, my huswife wants her will,
She tels her Gossips I do use her ill:
And yet she doth confesse that I am kinde,
In letting her have Money to her minde.
Yet that's not all the Gentlewomans longing,
Theres other matters to her humours wronging.
She would be Maister to command in all,
Do what she list: check me, marry[109] and shall.
She sayes I crosse her, but she crosses me
In my affaires, stil busie[110] she will be:
I must yeeld her account whether I go,
In every thing, Good-man why do you so?
This likes not me, prethe[111] let's have it thus,
I scorne to see my neighbour put downe us;
We wil have Plate[112] as rich as they have any,
And yet not be beholding for a penny.
How like an Asse my foolish husband goes?
Buy me a Sattin doublet[113] to them hose.
I can be wel content with going plaine,
But that my wife is of another vaine:
She sweares she will go brave, I shal maintaine her,
Or 'tis an argument[114] I do disdaine her;
And that her onely care to go so fine,
Is but for credit both of hers and mine.
Indeed by this my credit sure is tride,[115]
For I owe much to maintaine her in pride.
With Mercers Bookes[116] I am acquainted still,
And large I furnish out the Taylors Bill.
This is the onely credit that I get,
For bravery to run my selfe in debt.
And when I tell her private twixt us two,
Wife let's be wise, these courses will not do,
You do not go according to my purse,
In parish charges I shall speed the worse,[117]

We must be wise, if you farre meaner went,
It would best please, pray, who should you content
But me? Therefore go to your husbands minde,
And I shal take it (Love) most wondrous kinde.
Oh on the sodaine how sheele rage and sweare,
That none in London baser minde doth beare.
Sheele call me Gull, and sit her downe and cry,
Then out in tearmes,[118] What cursed hap had I?
Weary I am of this same wretched life,
Wouldst thou have me go like an Oyster wife?[119]
Oh scurvy minded man, I even scorne thee,
And could finde in my heart base slave to (____)[120] thee.
Goest thou about to offer this disgrace?
I would that I had never knowne thy face:
When first I saw thee, surely I was mad,
For choyce of fourteene propper men I had;
Yea, even as handsome creatures to mine eye,
As ere were girt in Girdles[121] (t'is no lye)
And yet I left them all to marry thee.
What greater crosse then this could light on me,
To have a fellow grumbling at me still,
And all I have comes from him 'gainst his will:[122]
O wretch, O Lob, who would be thus beclown'd?[123]
I deserve better for two hundred pound.
Two hundred pound in Gold my Father gave,
To match me with this miserable Knave,
Whom with my very heart I do disdaine,
Oh would my bargaine were to make againe,
Then I would flaunt it, I would cut it out,
And wiser, ere I leapt would looke about:
I would have none, but I would make him sweare,
That when I list I might the breeches weare,[124]
My sisters life is happy I may say,
Her husband dares not crosse her any way,
She sayes in's life he never gave her checke,
But can have any thing even with a becke:[125]
And why not I attaine the like degree,

That am as proper (I am sure) as she?
Nay, and a little fairer too, I know,
Who sees both faces, he will sweare 'tis so,
But well within my head I have a tricke,
Some have their foreheads swell that be not sicke:[126]
Ile have my will to be maintain'd in all,
And if one will not then another shall.
Maisters how like you this? judge I beseech,
(On Monday last this was her very speech)
Nay, and she stands unto it wondrous bold.
The first tale's good, untill the next be told,
Upon my life this is a womans vaine,
To wrong her husband first, and then complaine.

The third charged by his wife to bee hard and cruell.

Marry a Widdow? Oh that I were free,
Such mischiefe never more should light on me:
Ile pawne my heart, my dearest blood,
Not one amongst five hundred that prooves good
They are not kind, they cannot right be said,
To have such pure affection as a maid:
Ile stand to it, and bring my wife to sweare it,
And Batchelers beleeve it, you that heare it,
Though I (till death do baile[127] me) am fast bound,
(*Would t'were to morrow for five hundred pound*)[128]
Yet by my harmes, I would have you escape,
That have a Divell in a womans shape:
A woman Divel, and a Divell wife,
That makes me weary of a husbands life.
I cannot speake with tongue, nor write with pen
The wofull state of such distressed men
As I my selfe, yet somewhat may suffice,
To paint her in this paper to your eyes:
That those which with such creatures would be doing,

May by my patterne go to hell a woing,
She is most impudent, and shamelesse bold,
Since I was borne I neare heard such a scold.
When she is up, she railes me out of dore,
When I come in, she raileth ten times more:
If I intreat her, she will sweare and curse,
If I say nothing, she growes worse and worse:
I am as patient as a man can be,
When this vile woman thus tormenteth me.
If I be hungry and demaund some meate,
Shee'le wish me choak't with the next bit I eate,
Then with a dogged countenance will say,
Spight of my heart I shall her leysure stay.[129]
If I do reason mildly with her then,
For every word I speake, she gives me ten,
And tels me of her t'other husbands praise,
With whom she lived all her happy dayes,
That he would weepe, even at her finger ake,
And to content her any paines would take.
He was the kindest loving man alive,
And day and night to please his wife would strive:
Then wishes in his grave with him she lay,
Amen, thinke I, that were my happy day.
For sure a man that's mach't with such a wife,
Hath but two happy dayes in all his life.
The first of them's the day whereon they marry,
For then the thing for which they long did tarry,
With wishing and much expectation still,
Is with great joy effected to their will.
The second merry day we married have,
Is when our wives are carried to their grave:
For we are freed from former thraldome then,
And shaking off the yoke, become free men.
Then we may joy that we have got release,
Attaining to a Batchelers sweet peace,
When Serpent dies, adue poyson and sting:
When my wife's gone, farewell venomous thing.

But that's not like to be a long time yet,
Death is too slow in challenging his debt,
Such happinesse to me it will not bring,
She will live longer then a better thing.
The other day a cunning prancke she plaide,
One of her Gossips she brought to perswade,
That I should furnish her in hast to ride
Unto a Gentlewoman, neare allyed
Unto my wife; to see her being sicke:
I did it, but was couzen'd[130] by the tricke,
It was her Cozen as they both gave out,
But sure they kindred made of me, I doubt.
I sent one after them to be my spye,
An honest friend I know, that will not lye:
He sayes both Gentleman and Boore,[131]
Do all report my Cozen is a Whore,
And she hath gallants haunt her far and neare,
What should my wife and her consort do there?
No goodnesse sure, a mischiefe take them both;
To weare a paire of hornes[132] I would be loth:
But who can helpe, the deed once being done,
It is a thred so close with cunning spun.
But Maisters keepe it secret I do pray,
Do not acquaint my wife with what I say:
Harke in your eare, *If I can prove her so,*
Ile be divorcst,[133] and farewell all my wo,
I do intend to let her have full scope,
And then a whore will prove a whore I hope:
Let her keepe company with whom she list,
Let her suppose mine eyes be dimn'd with mist,
Let her not care into what sinne she sinkes,
Ile come upon her when she little thinkes:
And where she takes me for a silly mome,[134]
For all her knav'ry then Ile pay her home.

The fourth complained by his wife to be a common Gamester.

Neighbours, now you have done, my turn is next,
That beyond reason with a wife am vext,
At first a Begger, once scarce worth a lowse,
Whom I have made the Mistris of my house:
Even my Maid, a very Kitchin drudge,
Of whose conditions I intreat you judge.
Daily till ten a clocke a bed she lyes,
And then againe her Lady-ship doth rise,
Her Maid must make a fire, and attend
To make her ready, then for wine sheele send,
(A morning pinte) she sayes her stomack's weake,
And counterfeits as if shee could not speake,
Untill eleven, or a little past,
About which time, ever she breakes her fast,
Then (very sullen) she wil pout and loure,
And sit downe by the fire some halfe an houre.
At twelve a clocke her dinner time she keepes,
Then gets into her chaire, and there she sleepes
Perhaps till foure, or somewhat thereabout,
And when that lazie humour ir [is][135] worne out,
She cals her dog, and takes him in her lap,[136]
Or fals a beating of her maid (perhap)
Or hath a Gossip come to tell a Tale,
Or else at me sheele curse, and sweare, and rale,
Or walke a turne or two about the Hall,
And so to supper and to bed, heeres all
This paines she takes, and yet I do abuse her,
But no wise man I thinke so kind would use her:[137]
I am a Foole to suffer that I do,
Yet love and kindnesse leads me so thereto,
I cannot chuse but yeeld unto her still,
This makes bad wives to let them have theyr will:
And thus they grow from evill unto worse,
Yet when I do intend another course,

It will not be, she shewes her cunning art,
It over-comes my honest, true, kinde heart:
Sometimes her lookes will carry such a sway,
That for my life I cannot say her nay:
Sometimes her teares do charme me in such wise,
That I give credit to deceiving eyes.
Sometimes her words in such great force do stand,
I yeeld to every thing she doth demaund:[138]
And sometimes her out-ragious madding fits,
Makes me as mad as she, beside my wits.
And where she sayes I am a gamester, sirs,
'Tis but a villanous device of hers,
That men should of this hard opinion be,
If that we do not thrive, 'tis long of me.[139]
Beleeve it not, alas it doth appeare,
That I play scarce at Tables in a yeare:
Dice I detest, and Cards as much I hate,
Neither am I as she sayes out so late;
As was reported when your wives and shee
At Vinters Hall,[140] were making their tongues free.
What is it that such tatling Gossips dare not?
To wrong their husbands, nay (themselves) they care not;
For rather then with silence they will sit,
Against themselves they'le uttter [utter] out their wit,
As my wife did in one complaint she made,
about a Hat, that I to her denaide,
'Twas her devotion at the Church to spy it,
And there continually (she sayes) she ey'd it,
With great affection, yet by me denide.
Where were your thoughts, on Prayer, or else on Pride?
This shewes what follies they do entertaine,
and that their speeches (like themselves) be vaine.
All men that know what creatures women are,
For tatling of their wives do little care.
'Tis but a breath, even like *Tobacco* smoake,
Which if they should not utter, they would choake.
If they conceive a thing within their minde,

(Althaugh the substance of it be but winde)
*I*t must be utt'red forth, and have quicke vent,
Or with themselves they grow most discontent.
Well, *I* am further charged with untruth,
By this my male-contented[141] female youth.
She sayes *I* never gave her gowne? Oh lye,
Who paide for that last weeke, belike not *I:*
I give her Money still, and she buyes stuffe,[142]
But now *I* smell a Rat, *I* have enough
Belike some Gallants do their bounty show,
And for her kindnesse, kindnesse they bestow;
She Traffickes[143] with them, changing ware for ware,
and so my money in her purse doth spare:
*I*t may be thus, and now *I* much suspect,
Unto my browes ile have a more respect,
I have beene troubled much with head-ache[144] late,
Something *I* feare doth swell about my pate:
Most curiously *I* will observe the thing,
*I*f it do bud as now tis toward the Spring,
I will not be a Wittoll[145] and an asse,
But even next Summer turne my wife to grasse.[146]

The fift, complained on by his wife to be a common Drunkard.

My Maisters heer's good stuffe, if this geare[147] hold,
When honest men by sluts ate [are] thus contrould:
*I*n absence, to have credit overthrowne,
And we made Guls for them to play upon,
Shall we endure it, and be made fooles still:
No, Ile curbe mine, upon my life I will,
And keepe her somewhat shorter in a doore,[148]
A Taverne tell-tale she shall be no more.
Neighbours, I thinke you know me, all are heere,
Although I love a Cup of Wine or Beere:
And as good-fellow, sometime trade therewith,

Yet did you never see me *Smug the Smith*?[149]
Did any of you ever know me reele?
Or in a storme of Ale turne up the Keele?[150]
In all your lives did any see me so,
That with these paire of legs I could not go?
pray speake my Maisters, for I may mistake,
A man will venter much for good wines sake.
But if I have bin sometimes over-shot,[151]
In calling for too much by t'other pot;
Shall my wife chatter till her tongue be weary,
And terme me Drunkard, when I am but merry;
Wil any loving wife be so unkinde?
Or doth not duty and good manners binde
A woman to forbeare, to winke, and hide,
And not to raile, to slaunder, and to chide,
She might have saide in private certainly,
Husband, last night you sung a pot to hye,[152]
Or my deere love, pray thee where hast thou bin?
In truth (Sweet-hart) you are a little in.
All this were well indifferent to be borne:
But shall she lay me open (as in scorne)
To her companions scoffing at me so,
As if I daily could not stand nor go.
She tearmes me *Sound card*[153] *for a womans stay,*
Drunke once a weeke, and that is every day,
The filthiest Drunkard (thus she doth protest)
That ever was of giddy braine possest.
And further, to the world she doth disclose,
That I come into bed in shooes and hose:
And horrible Tobacco do so drinke,[154]
That she is almost poyson'd with the stinke.
Well, this is good, but marke the end at last,
In a new mould this woman I will cast,
Her tongue in other order I will keepe,
Better she had bin in her bed asleepe,
Then in a Taverne, when those words she spake;
A little paines with her I meane to take:

For she shall find me in another tune,
Betweene this February and next June:
In sober sadnesse I do speake it now,
And to you all I make a solemne vow,
The chiefest Art I have I will bestow,
About a worke cald taming of the Shrow.[155]
It makes my heart to fret, my lookes to frowne,
That we should let our wives thus put us downe.
But for mine owne part I have now decreed,
To do a good and charitable deed.
If she begin her former course a fresh,
I have a tricke to mortifie her flesh:
Unto you all example I will give,
Perhaps youle thanke me for it while you live.
But for your selves, to nothing Ile perswade,
Because the blame on me shall not be laid:
Other mens wives I meane to let alone,
I shall have worke enough to tame mine owne.

The sixt complained on by his wife to be unconstant to her, and haunt Whores.

Sweare not, for I beleeve your word in this,
No kind of crosse like a bad woman is:
I know your hands are full, neighbour 'tis true,
And so is each mans heere, no lesse then you.
I share in Shrow indifferent well,
One that doth make my house resemble hell:
Because her divellish nature is so bad,
No quietnesse can at her hands bee had.
Will you beleeve me? Sirs I will not lye,
She hath the most accursed jealons [jealous][156] eye
That ever I have knowne, or ever shall:
And I perceive, that heere's none of you all
Equall with me, for wicked womans flesh;
Shee'le raile all day, at night begin a fresh,

And with that tune into her bed she lyes,
Scolds in her sleepe, and scolds when she doth rise.
And why is this thinke you? Marry Ile tell,
She sayes, *I love my neighbours wives too well,*
But if I were this instant houre to dye,
Ile take it on my death that she doth lye.
Sometimes I aske my neighbours how they do,
Give them a pinte (perhaps) and kisse them to:
Why what of this? and if a man do so,
May't not be done, and yet no evill grow;
Kindnesse may lead a man unto kind carriage,[157]
And yet he may be constant in his marriage,
But for my wife I do not care a pin,
What scurvy mind soever she be in,
To slander me with whores, my credit's knowne,
She hath a lying tongue (friends) of her owne,
To say that *I* bad houses do frequent,
And there on common whores my love is spent.
I never was in baudy house but twice,
And there indeed a friend did me intice
To see some fashions, onely there we dranke,
And saw a gallant Quene, her name was *Franke,*[158]
In a silke gowne, loose bodyed,[159] so was she,
Not that *I* tride, but as they told me:
She gave us good *Tobacco,* sweet, and strong,
And of meere kindnesse sung a Bawdy song.
This *I* protest was even all we did,
Yet oh when I came home, how I was chid:
Some Rascall told my wife, that ought me spight.
And I was villaind[160] for it sound at night.
And ever since if any strife arise,
She asketh me where Mistris *Francis* lies:
Cals her my whore, and sayes that I and she,
Both of a haire and of a humour be.
But well, It skils not, let her talke and spare not,
I have set downe my rest, in troth I care not:
I see it is no wisedome any way,

To storme in mind at that which women say.
Their mouths cannot containe their tongues within,
For when they're maids, ere wedlocke they begin,
At every meeting, then they do discover
The disposition of each kind of lover.
Jone hath a propper handsome man in truth,
But *Judiths* is not halfe so kinde a youth:
Nan knowes not what a Jewell she hath got,
But *Dorothies* sweet-hart, I like him not.
Thus being Maides, they do their Lovers use,
And being Wives their Husbands they abuse.
Therefore in this case let us be content,
Tis now too late our bargaines to repent:
But let us hope they'le shortly to their grave,
And then we quyet lives a peece shall have:
And he to whom kind *Death* this freedome gives,
Let him take heed of wiving while he lives.

FINIS.

[The 1613 edition concludes with the following:]

The Censure of the Batcheler and the Mayde, upon the former Complaints.

Batcheler.

Good sister Mayde, I am amaz'd in minde,
To heare that married Wives deale thus unkinde
Against their Husbands, when the Gossips meet:
Mee thinkes to live still Batcheler is sweet,
For what I read heere of their jarring strife,
Makes mee afraide to enter married life.

Mayde.

Friend Batcheler, I doe not blame your care,
But doe confesse ti's fit you should beware
How you doe match your selfe unto a Shrow;
For there's too many of that kind, I know:
But seeing Men in witte put Women downe,
And there be civill Wenches in the towne;
Mee thinkes a wise-man may imbrace the one,
And let the Gossips with long tongues alone.

Batcheler.

Wench, thou sayst true; but how can we doe this,
When such false shewes with woman-kind there is?
Still humour them, and have most sweete behaviour:
But crosse their follies, worse then Gall they favour.
Why thou thy selfe (I speake it to thy prayse)
Art a kind creature, all that know thee sayes;
Yet it is doubtfull, when th'art once a Wife,
How with a Husband thou wilt lead thy life.

Mayde.

Brother, tis true; but ist not so with you,
That are of this same smoth-face civill crew?
Love's in your lips, your eyes, your smiles, your tongue;
And yet all this, from cunning may be sprung:
As you of us, so we of you, make doubt;
But both must venter, eare we find it out,
And marry for it: But chuse Mayden love,
For Widdowes alwayes prating Gossips prove,
Upon their former Marriage, bold they beare them.
In trueth we Maydes are oft asham'd to heare them:
But I will cease and end with blushing feares,
Least I doe bring them all about mine eares;

For some of them will swagger worse then Men:
So farewell Brother, till we meete agen.

Batcheler.

Thankes gentle Sister, thou hast taught me wit,
I'le neare have Widdow, heere's my hand on it:
Lets get good-will of Father and of Mother,
And then weele marry, and goe try each other.

NOTES

1. From "God" (God) + "sib" (related, akin). The term was originally used to describe godparents of either sex. It also applied to a woman's female friends invited to be present at a birth. Here it is used to describe women who, in Samuel Rowlands's opinion, delight in idle talk.

2. Missing in the 1613 edition.

3. Housewives or worthless women.

4. She didn't need to be pressed to drink.

5. Money (i.e., five shillings). A shilling equals twelve pence or one-twentieth of a pound sterling.

6. A bad mood or temper.

7. This probably refers to being too free with one's money, but it also has sexual overtones. In early modern popular literature, women were often represented as spending all the money men had.

8. *The First Gossips Complaint* is inserted at this point in the 1613 edition. The wives and husbands alternate speeches rather than all of the wives speaking first followed by all of the husbands.

9. Presses painfully upon my foot; or, figuratively, how much I suffer. See Thomas Lodge's *Rosalynde* (1590): "'I am glad (quoth Ganymede) you looke into your owne faults, and see where your shooe wrings you,'" quoted in Morris Palmer Tilley, *Dictionary of Proverbs in England in the Sixteenth and Seventeenth Centuries* (Ann Arbor: University of Michigan Press, 1950), M129. See also the *Oxford English Dictionary* (hereafter cited as *OED*), which quotes from *A whole crew.*

10. See Shakespeare's *Much Ado About Nothing* (1598–99): "What though care kill'd a cat, thou hast mettle enough in thee to kill care" (5.1.132–34).

11. The first wife describes her husband as an ignorant peasant who lacks manners and a fool who is easily imposed upon.

12. Worthless matter.

13. A coin with the figure of a cross stamped on one side; also a vexation.

14. When a couple did not have children, it was usually considered the fault of the woman. Often, childless women were not accorded respect, and some people even believed that childlessness was a punishment for sin.

15. Dressed in the latest fashion.

16. A derogatory term for a German or Swiss person.

17. Thanks to.

18. Proud, arrogant.

19. Affection.

20. Fortune.

21. See *Tis Merry,* n. 53.

22. See *Tis Merry,* n. 27. If a gallon of claret cost between one shilling, eight pence and two shillings in 1600, then a penny per pottle was a very good price.

23. Solid food.

24. Look with distrust or disdain. See the *OED,* which quotes from *A whole crew.*

25. "It is better to be a shrew than a sheep" (Tilley, *Dictionary of Proverbs,* S412). Tilley also cites John Lyly, *Euphues and his England* (London, 1580), in *The Complete Works of John Lyly,* ed. R. W. Bond (Oxford: Clarendon Press, 1902), 2:223: "Wher-by they noted, that although the virgin were somewhat shrewishe at the first, yet in time shee myght become a sheepe."

26. Elegantly dressed.

27. Woo and woe.

28. She counted her suitors by making chalk marks on her door. This may refer to the custom of keeping account of credit in an alehouse by making chalk marks on the door.

29. Gloves, which usually cost between two pence and one shilling, were often given by a man to his beloved as a promise of marriage. Gloves were manufactured in England beginning in the late sixteenth century.

30. Conniving woman. This term has sexual overtones. See *Tis Merry,* n. 61.

31. Playfully mischievous; also wanton, loose.

32. Tell lies about.

33. The second gossip expresses skepticism about the belief that a wife's husband is her head. See *Tis Merry,* n. 34.

34. More like.

35. Filled with self-importance.

36. A stick for kindling.

37. Beat him with a stick.

38. Pleases.

39. Laura Gowing discusses the language of insult in *Domestic Dangers: Women, Words, and Sex in Early Modern England* (Oxford: Oxford University Press, 1996). A "noddy" is a simpleton or a fool; the implication is that the person has been cuckolded. See James T. Henke, *Courtesans and Cuckolds: A Glossary of Renaissance Dramatic Bawdy (Exclusive of Shakespeare)* (New York: Garland, 1979), 178. A "buzzard" is a stupid person.

40. Venture.

41. That is, the weakest must give way. See Shakespeare's *Romeo and Juliet* (1595–96): "Women, being the weaker vessels, are ever thrust to the wall" (1.1.15–16).

42. Truly.

43. Surgeon.

44. The third gossip complains of being restricted to her home and of her husband's drinking. Ironically, she delivers her complaint while drinking in the tavern.

45. Have you under control.

46. Tilley quotes *A whole crew* to illustrate the proverb "To kill a Man with a cushion" (*Dictionary of Proverbs,* M398). See also the anonymous play *The Taming of A Shrew* (1607): "Why Tapster I say, / Fill's a fresh cushen [cushion] heere" (A2r, ll. 6–7). In this context, a cushion is a drinking vessel.

47. A cock bred and trained for cockfighting. In other words, her husband is not a good lover.

48. A misprint for "sore," to rhyme with "more." The 1663 edition uses "sore."

49. Noddy is a card game that resembles cribbage. Tables is the game of backgammon, while dublets is a game similar to backgammon. The fourth wife is being sexually suggestive in asking her husband to play these games with her.

50. Novum is a game of dice played by five or six people. See Shakespeare's *Love's Labour's Lost* (1594–95): "Abate throw at novum, and the world again / Cannot pick out five such" (5.2.544–45). Passage is a dice game. New-cut is a card game. See John Lane, *Tom Tel-Troth's Message* (London, 1600): "New cut at Cardes brings some to beggarie" (21).

51. Beholden or indebted. This form of the past participle appears frequently in Rowlands's pamphlets.

52. The fourth gossip says that she is indebted to other men, who give her clothes, but she wants the assembled women to know that her relationships with these men are chaste.

53. The period when law courts are in session.

54. See *Tis Merry,* nn. 10 and 20. A shilling was the daily wage of a building craftsman in 1600, so three pounds for a ruff was very expensive (there are 20 shillings in a pound). In 1591, Queen Elizabeth paid ten pounds, ten shillings for three ruffs and three pairs of cuffs of lawn edged with bone lace. See Herbert Norris, *Costume and Fashion,* vol. 3: *The Tudors* (London: Dent and Sons, 1938), bks. 1 and 2.

55. See Anonymous, *The proude wyves Pater noster* (London, 1560): "To chyrche they be come this is no lye / Unto theyr pewe there for to knele / . . . / . . . / . . . / Beholdynge theyr aparell of eyther syde" (17–22).

56. In other words, her husband is a hypocrite. See Tilley's *Dictionary of Proverbs,* in which he quotes from John Heywood's *Proverbs and Epigrams* ([London, 1562], 153): "'When the foxe preacheth, then beware our geese" (F656) and from *A whole crew.*

57. Her husband, who spends his time gambling, is now acting like a Puritan, chastising her for noticing fashionable clothes in church.

58. Uncertain of what to do next. In dicing, this means risking all of one's property on the roll of the dice.

59. Successful playing card to fit into the gossips' previous talk of card games.

60. Dizzy or intoxicated from smoking tobacco.

61. That is, American Indians. For information about tobacco, see *Tis Merry,* n. 56.

62. "Black-amores" refers to black-skinned Africans (e.g., Ethiopians) or black Moors, as opposed to natives of Mauretania, a region of North Africa corresponding to parts of Morocco and Algeria. Later, the term *Moor* was used for members of the Berber and Arab races, most of whom were Muslims. The Moors conquered Spain in the eighth century. See Walter Raleigh's *Historie of the World,* vol. 1 (London, 1614): "The Negro's, which we call the BlackeMores" (95).

63. This is an allusion to the dirtiness of the coal trade and the idea that people who smoke become black inside. See *Tis Merry,* n. 56. The color black was associated with dirt and evil in the early modern period.

64. Human excrement; or a corruption of *save reverence,* which was said as an apology before comments that might be thought objectionable.

65. In *A Counterblaste to Tobacco,* James I says that "herein is not onely a great vanitie, but a great contempt of Gods good giftes, that the sweetenesse of mans breath, being a good gift of God, should be wilfully corrupted by this stinking smoke" (London, 1604), D1v.

66. Smell.

67. This refers to the belief that tobacco prevented or cured venereal disease as well as most other diseases. Rowlands wrote about forty poems that focus on or include references to smoking. In an epigram from *Humors Antique Faces: Uncollected Poems, 1604?–1617* (Gainesville, Fla.: Scholars' Facsimiles and Reprints, 1970), Rowlands states:

A Poore Slave once with penurie afflicted,
Yet to Tobacco mightily adicted
Sayes, they that take Tobacco keepes their health,
Are worthie fellowes in a common wealth.
For if (sayth he) Tobacco were our cheare,
Then other victuals never would be deere.
Fye on excesse it makes men faint and meeke,
A pennie loafe might serve a man a weeke. (136)

68. A trencher is a wooden platter. Perhaps the fifth husband is calling for a platter on which to roll his cigarettes.

69. An exclamation of irritation,

70. The tobacco sent to the privy or toilet.

71. America. See Samuel Purchas, *Purchas his Pilgrimage . . .* (London, 1614): "The name of India, is now applied to all farre-distant Countries, not in the extreme limits of Asia alone; but even to whole America, through the errour of Columbus" (451).

72. Tobacco cost at least three shillings an ounce or three pennies a pipeful when it was first introduced into England. During James I's reign, a pound of tobacco cost between ten and eighteen shillings. In an attempt to discourage tobacco smoking,

James I raised the import duty on tobacco from the colony of Virginia to six shillings, ten pence per pound; under Elizabeth it had been just two pence per pound.

73. A belt customarily worn by a man around his waist to carry a purse or weapon.

74. This probably refers to a French hood, not to a religious hood. The fifth gossip asserts that she remained true to her husband despite her handsome suitors. If she had not withstood them, perhaps they would have given her lavish headwear. According to Raphael Holinshed, the day after her marriage to Henry VIII, Anne of Cleves was "apparelled after the English manner, with a French hood, which became hir exceeding well" (*The Third Volume of Chronicles, beginning at duke William the Norman* [London, 1586], 950). In *Pedigree of the English Gallants* (N.p., 1653), John Bulwer writes, "Our enormous French hoods that vaine modell of an unruly member, the tongue, an abusive invention might be derived from some unicorn-like dress of haire among the barbarous Indians" (quoted in James Robinson Planché, *A Cyclopaedia of Costume*, vol. 1 [London: Chatto and Windus, 1876], 296–97).

75. Proudly. In other words, she will dress well even if she is widowed.

76. Party or group.

77. Pandars and bauds are pimps.

78. According to Robert Nares, "burning" is "one of the names for a disorder which has no decent appellation"—in other words, venereal disease (*A Glossary; or, Collection of words, phrases, names, and allusions* . . . [London: R. Triphook, 1822], 65).

79. Overdressed whores.

80. Venereal disease.

81. The language of sex and thieving.

82. Monkeys were thought to be addicted to lechery. See Shakespeare's *Othello* (1603–4): "hot as monkeys" (3.3.403).

83. Letting themselves out for hire as hackney horses.

84. From west Kent to east Kent.

85. According to the *OED*, "Cozen" was first used for "strumpet" in 1700. In this context, "Cozens" refers to women with whom the sixth wife says her husband is sexually involved.

86. A very fine transparent fabric.

87. The sign for a tavern was often an ivy bush. See Shakespeare's *As You Like It* (1599): "Good wine needs no bush" (epilogue). Elaborate high headdresses were more typical of the late rather than the early seventeenth century.

88. The first usage in the *OED* is dated 1616. Shoe ties of colored ribbon were used in the early seventeenth century. The sixth wife says that her husband's whore trims her elaborate headdress with colored shoe ties.

89. Feathers were often worn by women in their fans. The sixth wife is punning on the lightness of the woman's sexual behavior.

90. In volume 3 of *The Complete Works of Samuel Rowlands, 1598–1628* (Glasgow: Printed for the Hunterian Club, 1880), 44–46, Rowlands identifies this as coming from John Fletcher's *Monsieur Thomas* (1614–17), act 3, sc. 3:

My man Thomas
Bid me promise
He would visit me this night.
Thomas.] "I am here, love;
Tell me, dear love;
How I may obtain thy sight."
Maid.] Come up to my window, love;
Come, come, come!
Come to my window, my dear;
The wind nor the rain
Shall trouble thee again,
But thou shalt be lodged here.

91. A prostitute. The song is quoted in volume 3 of *The Complete Works of Samuel Rowlands, 1598–1628,* from a manuscript dated prior to 1609:

"A pinnace rigg'd with silken saile,
What is more lovely then to see?
But still to see is small availe:
I must aboord, as thinketh mee.
To see is well,
But more to tell
Lackes more then sight, you will agree." (45)

92. Prostitution.

93. Cheating.

94. See Tilley, *Dictionary of Proverbs,* B451; *Fergusson's Scottish Proverbs* (ms., 1598), in *Fergusson's Scottish Proverbs from the Original Print of 1641 together with a Larger Manuscript Collection,* ed. E. Beveridge (N.p., 1924): "Blind folkis eate many flies" (no. 301).

95. See Tilley, *Dictionary of Proverbs,* C169, which cites *A whole crew.* See also Mother Watkins Ale (ca. 1590), quoted in John Payne Collier, *Broadside Black-Letter Ballads, printed in the sixteenth and seventeenth centuries chiefly in the possession of J. Payne Collier* (London: Printed for private circulation by Thomas Richards, 1868): "'Cat will after kind, All winkers are not blind'" (254). The sixth wife says that she is not blind to what her husband is doing.

96. A security deposit.

97. See Tilley, *Dictionary of Proverbs,* T42, who cites Robert Greene, *Mamillia: The Second Part of the Triumph of Pallas* (London, 1593). The "honest" husbands dismiss their wives' complaints with this proverb, which the second husband later repeats.

98. In an interesting reversal, the men complain that they have been silent while their wives have slandered them in print.

99. A conversation or conference.

100. According to Plutarch, "what was most disgraceful of all, even Cato's [the Younger's] wife Atilia was not free from such transgressions [unchastity], but although

he had two children by her, he was forced to put her away because of her unseemly behaviour" (*Plutarch's Lives* [Loeb Classical Library, 1919], bk. 8, ch. 24, p. 293).

101. Into use.

102. Scolds; angry, contentious women who are said to talk too much. Occasionally, men are referred to as shrews. See Shakespeare's *Taming of the Shrew* (1593–94): "By this reck'ning he is more shrew than she" (4.1.84–85).

103. Woman's work was primarily in domestic production or helping in her husband's trade. At most, a woman's wages amounted to a shilling per week, or a little over two pounds per year if the work was steady (Amy Louise Erickson, *Women and Property in Early Modern England* [New York: Routledge, 1993], 15). See also Alice Clark, *Working Life of Women in the Seventeenth Century* (1919; London: Cass, 1968); Sara Mendelson and Patricia Crawford, *Women in Early Modern England, 1550–1720* (Oxford: Clarendon Press, 1998).

104. See *Tis Merry*, n. 20.

105. To sew or do needlework. "Clout" may be applied contemptuously to any article of clothing. See Helkian Crooke, *Mikrokosmographia. A Description of the Body of Man* (London, 1616): "Women . . . live an idle and sedentarie life, pricking for the most part upon a clout" (274).

106. Proverbial: an easily ensnared bird; therefore, a fool.

107. The *OED* cites *A whole crew* as a text that uses *gown* as a verb.

108. A whim; a trinket. The term is applied contemptuously to anything small, flimsy, or inferior of its kind. See Shakespeare's *Taming of the Shrew* (1593–94): "Here is the cap. / . . . / . . . / Why, 'tis . . . / A knack, a toy, a trick, a baby's cap" (4.3.63–67).

109. An expression of indignation.

110. Prying, meddlesome.

111. Pray thee.

112. Utensils for the table, originally of silver or gold.

113. A close-fitting body garment, with or without sleeves, worn by men from the fourteenth to the eighteenth centuries. Phillip Stubbes states in *Anatomie of Abuses* (1583) that "'the women also have doublets and jerkins as the men have, buttoned up to the breast, and made with wings, weets, and pinions on the shoulder-points, as man's apparel in all respects; and though this be a kind of attire proper only to a man, yet they blush not to weare it.'" He describes male doublets as having "'great bellies . . . hanging down beneath the groin . . . stuffed with four or five, or six pounde of bombast at the least'" (quoted in Planché, *Cyclopaedia of Costume*, 179). These garments greatly disproportion the male body, according to Stubbes.

114. It is clear proof.

115. Tried.

116. The accounts of dealers in fabrics.

117. Perhaps the second husband worries that the elegance of his wife's clothes will cause the parish to assess him at a higher tax rate.

118. In so many words.

119. According to the second husband, his wife accuses him of making her dress like

a woman who sells oysters—in other words, like a lower-class woman. In Richard Brathwait's "A Shrow" (in *Essaies Upon the Five Senses* [London, 1620]), the mother of the shrew was an oyster wife whose "sole note (being the voice of her vocation) eccoed, *New wainflete Oysters*" (134).

120. The word—perhaps "kill" or "cuckold"—is so offensive that the second husband cannot utter it.

121. The fifth wife, not the second wife, says this ("As ere were girt in Girdles").

122. Inclination or sexual desire. This pun is repeated when the second wife states that she'll have her "will to be maintain'd in all."

123. A Lob is a clown. To be beclown'd is to be made ridiculously into a clown.

124. To rule or assume the authority of the husband. This term was first used in the sixteenth century.

125. The slightest command.

126. That is, they are not cuckolded.

127. Release.

128. Perhaps the third husband is saying that he would give five hundred pounds if his wife should die the next day.

129. Despite my heart (with a pun on "spite"), I keep her from her leisure.

130. Defrauded, here by a reputed cousin who was, according to the third Husband, a whore.

131. Peasant.

132. The third husband fears that his wife has committed adultery and thus has caused him to be cuckolded or to wear horns.

133. See Heale's *Apologie For Women,* n. 171.

134. Fool (Latin *momus*).

135. *Ir* also appears in *The Complete Works of Samuel Rowlands, 1598–1628;* in the 1663 edition, *ir* has been changed to *it.*

136. Johannes Caius writes of the spaniel: "These dogges are litle, pretty, proper, and fyne, and sought for to satisfie the delicatenesse of daintie dames, and wanton womens wills, instrumentes of folly for them to play and dally withall, to tryfle away the treasure of time. . . . These puppies the smaller they be, the more pleasure they provoke, as more meete play fellowes for minsing mistrisses to beare in their bosoms, to keepe company withal in their chambers, to succour with sleepe in bed . . . to lay in their lappes." (*Of Englishe Dogges, the diversities, the names, the natures, and the properties,* trans. Abraham Fleming [London, 1576], 20–21).

137. To be sexually intimate with her.

138. This is exactly what the wives say happens when a woman cries or turns on her charms. See the comments of the first gossip on pp. 71–72.

139. If we are not prosperous, the husband is to blame.

140. The tavern that is the setting for the first part of the pamphlet.

141. That is, malcontent (with a pun on "male"). See Shakespeare's *III Henry VI* (1590–91): "how like you our choice, / That you stand pensive as half malcontent?" (4.1.9–10).

142. Fabric.

143. Has illicit dealings (i.e., sexual relations).

144. Perhaps his horns are growing because of his wife's trafficking with gallants.

145. Contented cuckold.

146. The fourth husband plans to turn his wife out to pasture; that is, he plans to force her to leave his house.

147. Nonsense.

148. Indoors or at home.

149. Proverbial: intoxicated.

150. Ale was the drink of the lower classes. To turn up the keel was to fall down drunk like a boat capsizing.

151. Intoxicated.

152. Got drunk.

153. See n. 59.

154. To inhale tobacco smoke. See Ben Jonson's *Every Man in His Humour* (1598): "The most divine tobacco that ever I drunke" (3.2.327–28).

155. Perhaps the fifth husband is referring to Shakepeare's *Taming of the Shrew,* written in 1593–94, or to the anonymous play *The Taming of A Shrew,* written in 1607.

156. The word "jealons" also appears in *The Complete Works of Samuel Rowlands, 1598–1628.*

157. Behavior; treatment of others.

158. Short for Francis; also refers to a pigsty. Francis is also the name of the prostitute in Thomas Nash's erotic poem "The Choise of Valentines" (1593?).

159. Loose-fitting, suggesting sexual availability. *Night-Raven* (London, 1620) describes a young woman who is consorting with a lecher as being as "loose of body as she was of gowne" (C1r).

160. Abused like a villain.

2 “Women, their mindes are crystall”: Christopher Newstead’s Arguments for the Superiority of Women

CHRISTOPHER Newstead’s *Apology For Women; or, Women’s Defence,* published in 1620, argues for the superiority of women because they are more virtuous than men. Although Newstead writes that women are “the weaker vessels” and that a woman’s sensual body is “an *Asia,* full of delights,” he asserts that women overcome their frailties and act more virtuously than men despite initial inferiority. Newstead’s pamphlet thus belongs in the category of pamphlets that praise women while undercutting them.

An Apology For Women was entered in the Stationers Register on 27 December 1619 and printed in December 1620 for R. Whittaker by Edward Griffith, who printed many sermons. Although Newstead makes no mention of it, *A Short-Title Catalogue of Books Printed in England, Scotland, and Ireland and of English Books Printed Abroad, 1475–1640* lists *An Apology* as a response to Joseph Swetnam’s 1615 pamphlet *The Araignment of Lewde, idle, froward, and unconstant women.*[1] Because *An Apology* had only one printing, it apparently was not a popular pamphlet.

Probably in the hopes of preferment, Newstead dedicated his pamphlet to Mary Beaumont, the second wife of Sir George Villiers, Knight of Brooksby, and the devoted mother of George Villiers, the first Duke of Buckingham and King James’s favorite. Although some historians have been critical of Mary Beaumont,[2] her son idolized her and she was considered a powerful woman in the king’s court. In 1618, a year before the completion of Newstead’s pamphlet, she had been granted by King James the title of Countess of Buckingham.[3] The previous year she may have been instrumental in securing the extravagant dowry of 10,000 pounds from Lord Chief Justice Sir Edward Coke for the marriage of his daughter Frances to her eldest son, Sir

John Villiers, against the wishes of the bride's mother.[4] According to Roger Lockyer, the countess exerted some influence on appointments, particularly those about which her son had no definite preference, but she did not have as much power as some thought.[5] King James was concerned about her Roman Catholic leanings and in 1622 asked William Laud, later Archbishop of Canterbury, to speak to her about her faith. Nevertheless, by 1622 the countess had openly converted to Roman Catholicism.[6]

Other pamphlets were dedicated to the Countess of Buckingham, although Newstead's *Apology* appears to have been the first. In 1622 John Taylor dedicated *The Life and Death of the Most Blessed Among Women, the Virgin Mary Mother of our Lord Jesus* to "The Right Honourable and truly vertuous Lady, and Noble Patronesse of good endevors, Mary Countesse of Buckingham," indirectly comparing the mother of Christ to the mother of James's favorite. In 1627 *The Life of B. Aloysius Gonzaga of the Society of Jesus,* written in Latin by Virgilio Cepari, was dedicated by the translator, R. S.[tanford?], "To The Most Honourable The Lady Mary Countesse of Buckingham." R.S. desired that his translation would "both encourage and instruct you in that happy course of Vertue, which so prosperously you have begun," a reference to the countess's conversion to Roman Catholicism.[7]

In his dedication to the countess, Newstead affirms that she outshone all women, among whom there were a multitude of stars. Calling her an "exquisite Lady," he asks her to "nourish" his pamphlet, which he terms "this obortive Bacchus." (Bacchus, the god of wine, was born from the thigh of his father, Jove, into which he has been sewn after his mother, Semele, died after being impregnated by Jove.) By alluding to a male who assumed a female role, Newstead may have been describing his own writing of, or giving birth to, *An Apology*. He wrote that he hoped to present the countess "with a more richer Prize" if Minerva granted his Muse "safe returne" after her "traffiking in her Indies." Two years after publishing the pamphlet, Newstead was appointed chaplain, at a salary of fifty pounds a year, to Sir Thomas Roe, ambassador to the Ottoman Porte in Constantinople and a commercial agent for the Levant Company. Newstead's effusive praise of the countess may have influenced his appointment, which he held until 1628, but he never wrote the "more richer Prize" and Constantinople was hardly "an *Asia,* full of delights." Roe wrote approvingly of Newstead but sent many missives to the Duke of Buckingham detailing the chaos in Constantinople and expressing a desire, which Newstead probably shared, to leave the remote appointment.[8]

Newstead was about twenty-three years old when he wrote *An Apology,* his only published work. He had been raised in Somercotes in Lincolnshire, the third son of Thomas Newstead, and matriculated from St. Alban's Hall, Oxford University, in 1619, although there is no record of a degree until he received a Bachelor of Divinity degree in 1631.[9] In 1629, following his return from Constantinople, Newstead was appointed vicar of Abingdon St. Helen, Berkshire. He married Mary Fulhurst in 1631. Roe intervened with Archbishop Laud on Newstead's behalf to have him appointed minister to the parish at Stisted. The Lords finally presented Newstead with the Stisted parish in 1642, but Newstead wrote that he could not enter the church because the parish women threw stones at him. Later he gained possession of the rectory, but in 1643 depositions were filed against him citing many abuses, such as his declaring "malignity against the Parliament," preaching "that Papists are saved as well as Puritans, but that a Papist must go a little farther," burying "corses with crosses on the breast," and "choosing those of most base and lewd life for his churchwardens."[10] In 1645 his position as minister of Stisted was sequestered, or taken away, but his wife was awarded one fifth of the parish proceeds by the committee for plundered ministers. Newstead was then appointed preacher at Maidenhead in Berkshire. At the time of the Restoration, in 1660, he was prebendary of Cadington Minor in St. Paul's Cathedral. Newstead died in 1662.

An Apology For Women belongs in the *querelle des femmes,* the tradition of texts that ostensibly praise women, such as Giovanni Boccaccio's *De Claris Mulieribus* (ca. 1360), Christine de Pizan's *Book of the City of Ladies* (ca. 1405), Geoffrey Chaucer's *Legend of Good Women* (1386), Henricus Cornelius Agrippa's *Declamation on the Nobility and Preeminence of the Female Sex* (delivered in 1509, published in 1529), Sir Thomas Elyot's *Defence of Good Women* (1540), and Edward Gosynhyll's *Prayse of all women, called Mulieru pean* (ca. 1542). Like Boccaccio, Chaucer, Elyot, and Gosynhill, and unlike Pizan[11] and Agrippa, Newstead does not praise all women. Rather, he divides them into three categories: "those who have both a Theoreticall and Practicall knowledge of vertue by themselves, understanding those things that are good, and willingly desiring to effect them"; those who desire to be good because they "know not that which is honest by themselves, yet they obey others rightly admonishing them"; and those who are "the dregges and scumme . . . of woman kinde." He excludes the third category, the women on whom the writers of antiwomen pamphlets focus, from "under the shield of [his] defence."

Newstead contends that women have the same "specificall essence" or souls as men and that women at first were inferior because of Eve's sin but have become superior because of their virtue. In language similar to Hic Mulier's, Newstead states that "each man . . . is metamorphosed into a woman" and that men have "womanized their affections." Women regained superiority through their industry, which, according to Newstead, was much more difficult than retaining their virtue: "*Eve* then tempted *Adam,* but now *Adam* tempts *Eve:* and it is better to bee conquered by Nature, then by Art." In Newstead's view, because they overcame their inferiority by means of their virtue, women are superior to men, who are seduced by society.

Following his initial chapter, "Of Women in generall," Newstead structures his defense with ten chapters, each elaborating a quality that makes women superior, followed by a concluding chapter. The chapters on beauty and constancy, as well as such details as women being less gluttonous than men, echo chapters in Agrippa's *Declamation.* These texts differ from Chaucer's *Legend,* Boccaccio's *Concerning Famous Women,* and Pizan's *Book of the City of Ladies,* all of which are structured around catalogs of allegedly good women. Although Newstead and Agrippa include their own catalogs, they are not major structuring devices.

Newstead focuses on religious piety, continency and chastity, fortitude and magnanimity, constancy and true love, freedom from gluttony, dexterical wits, and wisdom and beauty. He also includes chapters on how women are a comfort to men and how children are most obliged to their mothers. Similar to his argument about female superiority, Newstead argues in the chapter entitled "Of their Continency and Chastity" that women are more chaste than men because their desires are more immoderate. He commends women because they live "chaste in the *Asia* of their bodies." Using the work of the poet Michael Drayton to support his argument, Newstead creates a new double standard: if women are unchaste, they are only half evil because it is difficult for them to remain chaste; however, if men are unchaste, they are wholly evil.

It is difficult to assess the tone Newstead uses in *An Apology,* much as it is difficult to assess the tone in Boccaccio's *Concerning Famous Women,* Chaucer's *Legend,* and Agrippa's *Declamation.* Believing women to be inferior to men in body and mind, Boccaccio praises women who are manly, particularly if their alleged manly virtues are on behalf of men. He also praises women who are chaste, silent, and obedient. As Albert Rabil Jr. summarizes in his introduction to Agrippa's *Declamation,* "Women were his subject, but Boccaccio's standard remained male."[12] The attitude of Chaucer's narrator in *The Legend of Good Women* is also contradictory. Women are praised only if they sacrifice themselves for the ideal of chaste love—a male definition of female virtue.[13] Both Boccaccio and Chaucer, while overtly praising women, thus undercut their defense of women.

Agrippa is more praiseworthy than the other authors mentioned above because he believed in the superiority of all women over men, though his tone is difficult to determine; for example, he argues that women are superior in virtue because they are not "disfigured by baldness" or "covered with ugly hair" and that they are more modest when they drown because they float face down, unlike men, who immodestly drown facing up.[14] Are these comments made to praise women or to amuse Agrippa's mostly male audience? Either way, Agrippa set out to marshal every possible argument in praise of women. The tract operates as a rhetorical exercise to prove the given assumption of women's superiority in the most persuasive and dazzling way possible. Although Newstead eliminates "the dregges and scumme" of women from his apology, like Agrippa he develops his defense to most convincingly and, often, playfully prove his premise of women's superiority.[15]

Both Agrippa's and Newstead's tones, though frequently humorous, become serious when the authors argue that women lacked the opportunity for education. After describing women who excelled in the past, Agrippa states that the "freedom that was once accorded to women is in our day obstructed by unjust laws, suppressed by custom and usage, reduced to nothing by education." Women have "no other prospect than needle and thread."[16] Newstead states that women's lack of freedom and education, or "want of imployment, corrupts the bravest spirits; the fountain of their vertue, corrupts by standing. Want of use, causeth disabilitie; but custome, perfection."

In the chapter entitled "Of their Fortitude and Magnanimity," Newstead argues that women have "the same vigour, and can, as well tolerate labours, as men, if they be accustomed to them." He includes a catalog of women who fit this description, among them the Amazons, Artemisia, Semiramis, Vaodica or Boudicca, and Joan of Arc. The list concludes with Queen Elizabeth, who died sixteen years before Newstead wrote his pamphlet, and Blanche, Dutchess of Orleans, whom Newstead playfully quotes telling King Philip that she would not have been reviled by him if "she had a paire of ____." Answering an imagined argument that men are physically stronger than women, Newstead counters with "many beasts [are] stronger then men" and "Valour consists in the minde, not in the body." He then provides a list of women who love valor; it facetiously includes Damatria, who told her son to stand closer to his enemy if his sword is too short.

In the fifth chapter of *An Apology,* Newstead contends that friendship between a woman and a man has "a greater Sympathy of affections" than friendship between men. Friendship among women is not mentioned. The superiority of a man's friendship with his wife over friendships with other males runs counter to prevailing seventeenth-century opinion. In "Of Friendship," Michel de Montaigne states that neither "the ordinary sufficiency of women" nor "their mindes [are] strong enough to endure the pulling of a knot so hard, so fast, and durable."[17] To counter such arguments, Newstead includes a catalog of women who proved themselves loyal to their husbands, several of whom did so by dying with their husbands and the rest of whom refused to remarry after their husbands died. Newstead next argues that woman are superior to men because they have more dexterous wits. As proof he cites the Muses, "the fountaine of all wit," and the Greek poet Sappho, the "quintessence . . . of wit." The seriousness of Newstead's pamphlet may be undercut, however, as he also contends that women are superior to men because they are less gluttonous.

Among contemporary texts, Newstead cites Michael Drayton's *English Heroical Epistles* (1599), Philip Sidney's *Countess of Pembroke's Arcadia* (1655), and John Barclay's *Euphormio's Satyricon* (1605), and he probably refers to *Love's Labour's Lost* by Shakespeare, whom he calls "a modern Poet."[18] He also cites contemporary or near-contemporary historical texts, including John Speed's *History of Great Britain* (1611), Edward Hall's *Chronicle* (1548), Edward Grimston's translation of John de Serres *Generall Historie of France* (1611), and William Camden's *Britannia* (1607). In addition, Newstead refers to John Foxe's *Book of Martyrs* (1589), Petrarch's Latin works, Erasmus, Osorius, Galateo, and Lipsius, all nonclassical authors. Most of Newstead's citations are from classical Greek and Roman authors, his favorites being Seneca's *Epistles* (1614) and plays, Aristotles's *Ethics* (1581) and *Magna Moralia* (1596), Livy's *Historiae Romanae Decades* (1589), Diodorus of Sicily's *Library of History* (1569), and Cicero's *Orations* (3 vols., 1616). (The dates for the classical Greek and Roman authors indicate editions available in England during Newstead's life.) In both the text and margins Newstead refers to Aesop, Ovid, Euripides, Plato, Homer, Sappho, Achilles Tacitus, Aelian, Aeneas Silvius, Plutarch,

Lucan, Juvenal, Suetonius, Justin, Velleius Paterculus, Diogenes Laertius, Horace, Tacitus, Rufius Festus, and Herodotus. His many references provide a list of texts with which a well-read Oxford undergraduate would have been familiar in 1619.

In fact, that undergraduate might have been able to improve on Newstead's references. Newstead often incorrectly quoted from memory, as I note on numerous occasions in my annotations. Sometimes references to epistles or chapters are inaccurate, and sometimes the actual words are changed (this happens often in his quotes from Seneca). In some cases Newstead may have misremembered; in others he may have changed the words to better fit his argument. For example, in his chapter on women's beauty, he no doubt changes Tacitus's text to make his argument stronger. According to Tacitus, Germanicus's speech calms his legionaries, while in Newstead's version Agrippina (Germanicus's wife) calms the revolt. Newstead also changes "your" and "you" to "their" and "they" in Drayton's poem to make the pronouns fit his argument. These liberties and inaccuracies are difficult for today's readers to accept, but it must be remembered that Newstead's objective was to prove women's superiority by marshaling the work of the authors he had read, even if he had to misquote to prove his point and demonstrate his cleverness. Accuracy in quoting and citation was not taken as seiously in the early modern period as it is today.

In chapter eight of *An Apology,* entitled "Of their Wisedome," Newstead extends the analogy of the head of the family—which in his understanding gives precedence to women—to the head of the state. "A house is, as it were a little Citie, and a Citie, as it were, a great house," he argues; therefore, "Let it appertaine to the Sexe feminine to govern the house . . . who knows how to guide a little, will quickly learne how to governe much." In other words, women would be fit rulers if only they were permitted to rule. He follows this argument with his complaint that women's "want of imployment, corrupts the bravest spirits." Here Newstead incorrectly cites Aristotle's *Politics* (1598) in support of his argument, although Aristotle actually states that those who believe there is no difference between a large household and a small city are wrong. Once again, Newstead has altered his source to support his argument.

In the ninth chapter, entitled "Of their Beauty," Newstead argues that women's superior beauty is easy to prove: "Let each ones sences bee the glasse, in which they view beauty; and then, I thinke, there will be none so hypocriticall, or false, that will not reflexe some shaddow of their pulchritude, by which they may see them to surpasse men." The tenth chapter is concerned with how women are a comfort to men and how "a man is never perfect, untill he be married, till then he is defective, he wants a Ribbe." Women are the sun and men are the moon; her beams cause him to shine.

Newstead's pamphlet ends with a chapter on how children are most obliged to their mothers and then a conclusion, or "Castrophe." He states that mothers are landlords while children are "unruly Tenant[s]" and that mother love usually remains constant because mothers, unlike fathers, are "certain they [the children] are theirs." Also, mothers "love that most dearely, that costs [them] dearest." After naming more virtuous women, Newstead concludes by facetiously stating that he has "touched, not handled [women's] vertues."

Textual Introduction

An Apology For women; or, Womens defence (*STC* 18508) by Christopher Newstead was entered in the Stationers Register on 27 December 1619 and printed by Edward Griffith for R. Whittaker in 1620. It is curious that Newstead, an Oxford undergraduate who had never published anything previously, secured a London publisher. His pamphlet was printed in octavo, small enough to be carried in one's pocket.

A Short-Title Catalogue of Books Printed in England, Scotland, and Ireland and of English Books Printed Abroad, 1475–1640 (vol. 2) lists four copies of the 1620 edition: one each at the Huntington, Folger, and Bodleian libraries and another at the Christ Church Collection at Oxford. For *"Custome Is an Idiot,"* I used the Huntington Library as copy text, of which the Folger Library copy is a duplicate. (I say this based on the fact that the same mistakes appear in both copies: for example, on page 14 of the Huntington copy and the Folger copy the catchword is "[uni]versall," and the word on the top of page 15 is "[uni]versal" [near note 104]; also, on page 15 "vitiate, or in or in vanquishing" appears in both copies [near note 105].)

The marginalia has been moved to the endnotes and enclosed in angle brackets. Much of the Latin in the text was translated into English by Newstead and therefore is not commented on in the endnotes unless it was translated incorrectly or includes a marginal note. The biblical quotes are from the Geneva Bible. The beginning of each chapter has been silently regularized (e.g.,

"REligion" becomes "Religion"), as have words with tildes (e.g., "burthe~" becomes "burthen" and "woma~" becomes "woman") and sharp *s*'s (e.g., "amißa" becomes "amissa"). In the Greek a dot indicates a letter is illegible.

NOTES

1. A. W. Pollard and G. R. Redgrave, eds., *A Short-Title Catalogue of Books Printed in England, Scotland, and Ireland and of English Books Printed Abroad, 1475–1640,* 2d ed. revised and enlarged by W. A. Jackson and F. S. Ferguson, completed by Katherine F. Pantzer (London: Bibliographical Society, 1986), 2:185.

2. Phillipe Erlanger describes her as an "arrogant tiresome intriguer of a woman" in *George Villiers Duke of Buckingham,* trans. Lionel Smith-Gordon (London: Hadder and Stoughton, 1953), 57. Charles Richard Cammell says she was "from first to last ambitious and unscrupulous" (*The Great Duke of Buckingham* [London: Collins, 1939], 55).

3. Roger Lockyer, *Buckingham: The Life and Political Career of George Villiers, First Duke of Buckingham, 1592–1628* (London: Longman, 1981), 34.

4. The marriage did not last. Frances Coke, later Lady Purbeck, began to live apart from her husband in 1622, as he was subject to fits of madness. See Lockyer, *Buckingham,* 117.

5. Ibid., 68, 115.

6. Cammell, *Great Duke of Buckingham,* 150.

7. John Taylor, *The Life and Death of the Most Blessed Among Women, the Virgin Mary Mother of our Lord Jesus* (London, 1622); Virgilio Cepari, *The Life of B. Abysius, Gonzaga of the Society of Jesus* (Paris, 1627).

8. *Dictionary of National Biography* (1959–60), 14:362; Michael Strachan, *Sir Thomas Roe, 1581–1644* (Wiltshire, England: Michael Russell, 1989), 156, 180. In "History of Troubles and Trial," in *The Works of the Most Reverend Father in God, William Laud, Sometime Lord Archbishop of Canterbury,* vol. 4 (Oxford: John Henry Parker, 1854), 6, William Laud states that Newstead served seven years as chaplain. John B. Pearson, in *A Biographical Sketch of the Chaplains to the Levant Company, Maintained at Constantinople, Aleppo and Smyrna, 1611–1706* (Cambridge: Deighton, Bell, 1883), n.p., gives 11 August 1626 as the date Newstead resigned. Pearson has a Mr. Hunt taking Newstead's place as chaplain on 15 June 1627.

9. Pearson, *Biographical Sketch,* 14. Pearson's list of chaplains for Constantinople shows Newstead receiving a Bachelor of Divinity degree in 1621. In *Athenae Oxonienses* (London: Printed for P. C. and J. Rivington et al., 1815), pt. 1, 461, Anthony à Wood lists 21 April 1631 as the date of Newstead's divinity degree, as does Joseph Foster in *Alumni Oxonienses,* vol. 3 (Nendeln, Lichtenstein: Fraus Reprint, 1968), 1064.

10. T. W. Davids, *Annals of Evangelical Nonconformity in the County of Essex* (London: Jackson, Walford, and Hodder, 1863), 483.

11. Although Pizan cites examples of "unchaste" women, she compassionately views them not as inherently bad but as having made unwise decisions. For a discus-

sion of Pizan's examples, see Ann McMillan's introduction to Geoffrey Chaucer's *Legend of Good Women* (Houston: Rice University Press, 1987), 25.

12. Albert Rabil Jr., introduction to Henricus Cornelius Agrippa's *Declamation on the Nobility and Preeminence of the Female Sex,* trans. Albert Rabil Jr. (Chicago: University of Chicago Press, 1996), xix. See also Giovanni Boccaccio's *Concerning Famous Women* (New Brunswick, N.J.: Rutgers University Press, 1963), particularly the introduction by the translator, Guido A. Guarino; the foreword by Marina Warner to Christine de Pizan's *Book of the City of Ladies* (New York: Persea Books, 1982), xxxiv–xxxviii; and McMillan's introduction to Chaucer's *Legend,* 22–25.

13. See McMillan, introduction to Chaucer's *Legend,* 26–27.

14. Agrippa, *Declamation,* 55.

15. See the following discussions of Agrippa's work: Linda Woodbridge, *Women and the English Renaissance: Literature and the Nature of Women, 1549–1620* (Urbana: University of Illinois Press, 1984), 38–44; Constance Jordan, *Renaissance Feminism: Literary Texts and Political Models* (Ithaca, N.Y.: Cornell University Press, 1990), 122–26. See also Woodbridge's discussion of Newstead's work in *Women and the English Renaissance,* 79–81.

16. Agrippa, *Declamation,* 94–95, 95. In *The Renaissance Notion of Women: A Study in the Fortunes of Scholasticism and Medical Science in European Intellectualism* (Cambridge: Cambridge University Press, 1980), 80, Ian Maclean argues that "it would be safer to regard it [the passage decrying women's lack of education] as part of a rhetorical exercise in declamation."

17. Michel de Montaigne, "Of Friendship," *Essayes,* trans. John Florio (London, 1613), bk. 1, p. 91.

18. Newstead quotes "Fat panches make leane pates, / and groser bits / Enrich the ribs, / but bankrout quite the wits," which varies slightly from the text of Shakespeare's *Love's Labour's Lost* but is close enough to suggest that he knew the play, the first quarto of which was printed in 1598.

AN APOLOGY FOR VVOMEN: OR, *Womens Defence.*

Pend by C.N. late of Albane Hall in *Oxon.*

SOCRAT.

Melius eſt mulieri non omnino naſci, quàm conuitijs lacerari.

LONDON,
Printed by E.G. for *Ri. Whittakers*:
and are to be ſold at his ſhop at the
Kings head in Pauls Church-
yard. 1620.

An Apology[1] *For Women: Or, Womens Defence.* Pend. by C.N. late of Albane Hall in Oxon.[2] Socrat. Melius est mulieri non omnino nasci, quam conuitiis lacerari.[3] London, Printed by E.G. for Ri. Whittakers:[4] and are to be sold at his shop at the Kings head in Pauls Church-yard, 1620.

TO THE RIGHT EXCELLENTLY VERtuous Lady, MARY, Countesse of Buckingham,[5] *C.N. wisheth event of all felicitie.*

Madam, *I neede not have a Lanterne & a Candle to investigate a vertuous woman, as* Diogenes *had to finde an honest man:*[6] *they appeare like so many Starres, fixed in this terrestriall Globe. Yet no sooner did the Sunne of your presence enter into the Horizon of my thoughts, but it overshaddowed all the fore-appearers Honour seated in your brest, findes it selfe adorned as in a rich Palace, making that excellent, which makes it admirable, which caused me to present unto your Ladiships protection, this my ill-looking Infant, the madenhead*[7] *(as I may so tearme it) of my invention, conceived in my brains, by the frothy word of many Hyperbolizing selfe-conceitists,*[8] *who deeme it their greatest grace, to be able to disgrace women. If then (exquisite Lady) an over-speedy or weaning desire of repulsing your sexes wrongs, hath caused my braines with* Semele, *to bring forth this obortive Bacchus, or brood. Be you the* Jove *to nourish it in the lap of your good liking, that being wrapt in the swaddling bands of your favour, the cold of contempt may not so easily freeze it.*[9] *And if* Minerva[10] *grant a safe returne to my Muse*[11] *traffiking in her Indies,*[12] *I shall, I hope, presont you with a more richer Prize.*

Your Ladiships unfainedly
devoted in all
observant service,
CH. NEWSTEAD.

TO THE READER.

Courteous Reader, if thy tongue hath not tyed thee to a curst wife, I doubt not, but the generall view of my Subject, wil winne at the least thy ordinarie acceptation. But when by perusing, thou wouldst espy how it is treated of, if thou beest illeterate, and the Curtaine of Ignorance be drawne before the eyes of thy Judgement, I doe not much wey how thou art opinionated of me: if thou commend me, I shal esteeme (as Antisthenes[13] *did, when he was praised of an evill one) rather worse then better of my selfe: for* quicquid pene vulgus laudat, vituperio dignum est: *Whatsoever ignorance commendeth, most usually deserves to be discommended. I had rather with* Lysimachus *the Poet have the approbation of one judicious* Cato,[14] *then the applause of a multitude: the judgements of the judicious, and the vulgar, doe seldome jumpe.*[15] *But if thou beest such an one as* Lucilius *would have his Auditour, neither ignorant, nor learned;*[16] *Because (saith hee) the one doth understand nothing, and the other more then I doe of my selfe. If thou beest, I say, lukewarme in knowledge, and that the* Aurora *of* Minerva,[17] *the dawning of the day of literature, begins to twy-light thy capacitie; Judge favourably of the faults, that thy Eagle-eyed scrupulositie perceives, they may bee errours of ignorance seene to thee: but they are an ignorance of the errours, unseene to me. But if by the Ladder of industry (if any for the subjects sake dare to credit) thou hast ascended the top of* Pernassus,[18] *I neede not tell thee, as the Poet saith of one,* Nemo repentè fuit doctissimus, *that perfection comes by degrees.*[19] Zeuxis *his* Helena *was not suddenly lim'd forth with one Pensil:*[20] *Braines to day are as empty, as* Tellus *his purse of money, may to morrow, with* Midas, *be stuft with the gold of invention.*[21]

Qui non est hodie, cras magis aptus erit.[22] *Whatsoever thou art, unlesse thou be a Brownist,*[23] *I meane obstinate, I doubt not, but it will perfume thy breath, for ever tainting women with reproches. But thou wilt say, thy evill speeches of them proceeds from mirth: thou mayst as well say thou dost lye with them,*[24] *as belye them in jest. No intentions can make absolute evills good. Againe, jests should be* fecetosi, *not* acetosi; *pleasing, not piercing, neither continuall: therefore they are called* sales *of the Latines,* quasi condimenta;[25] *we should use them as Spices, to season our talke, not as the subject of it. But many may say with* Philippus *the Iester,*[26] *that they have got such an habit in speaking ill of them in jest, that they know not how to speake well of them in earnest. And it is a shrewd signe he never meanes well, that speakes alwayes ill. But lest thou turne from them, to jest on mee, for my prolixitie, in bidding mee (as* Diogenes *did the Citizens, that had exceeding ample gates,*[27] *to a little Citie) shut the gates of my Preface, lest the City of my Book*[28] *runne forth, I will leave thee.*

Thine, as thou usest me,

C.N.

AN APOLOGY For Women: OR, *Womens Defence.*

Of Women in generall.

Qui alium sequitur, nihil sequitur,[29] who makes alwayes examples his Copie, shall many times erre from the rules of discretion. Should I tread in the steps of our precisest Methodists,[30] in defining my Subject, I might seeme with *Didymus,* to write that which each one knew, and give a new testimonie of that old and highway *Adage,* λὐχνον ἐν μ́εσιμβρία ἁπτ.ις, to burne Candle at noone day.[31] For what so ignorant a *Licinius,* whose darke capacitie is not enlightened with this little candle of knowledge to know what man is[32] (for every one knowes man in generall, though few in particular themselves) from whom woman differs, onely in a materiall designation, having one and the same specificall essence.[33] Now the golden Ball,[34] which their deserts do challenge, is not honour, nor riches, nor beauty; but vertue. I strive not to make them excell men, as *Caesar* did *Pompey* in dignitie,[35] or as the *Lydeans* Dames did their Husbands,[36] in masterie; but as *Seneca* did his Father,[37] in verture: *Haec ista honesta contentio;* this is an honest contention, or contentious honestie.

It is true, at first, when there was but two actors,[38] upon this Theater of the world, woman was the Syren, that allured man unto evill:[39] but now each man with *Tiresias,*[40] is metamorphosed into a woman: pleasures and delights, are the ingendring Serpents, that have womanized their affections: Men were the more perfect by nature: but women now then they, by industrie, (and it is more difficult to re-obtain vertue, then to keepe it). *Eve* then tempted *Adam,* but now *Adam* tempts *Eve:* and it is better to bee conquered by Nature, then by Art. It is *Catulus* his saying, that he could in those things, which nature gave to man, suffer patiently himselfe to be subdued, but not in those that might be assequuated,[41] and got by our endevours.[42] For to be delinquent or faulty by nature, that is not ours, but natures fault; but to be ill by corruption, that is not natures, but our fault.[43] What if she were an instrumentall cause of our fall, was she not as much the cause of our rising? But wee all sooner forget benefits, then injuries: we are Eagle-eyed in espying their faults, but dark sighted Owles, in perceiving their vertues. But not to make them all alike vertuous, as *Mantuan* would have them vicious,[44] there are of women three sorts: The first are those who have both a Theoreticall and Practicall knowledge of vertue by themselves, understanding those things that are good, and willingly desiring to effect them: and these may I condingly[45] entitle, as the *Romans* did *Titus,*[46] *deliciae humani generis,*[47] the delight of mankinde: each one of these is a *Scipio, qui nihil in vita nisi laudandum, aut fecit, aut dixit,*[48] who neither speake, nor doe any thing, but which is commendable; so apt to all goodnes, that they seeme with *Cato*[49] to be borne to all actions they undertake. The second, are those who though not so excellent, yet laudable: for although we marvell at the greatest, yet wee praise those that are lesse: *non statim statim pusillus est, si quis maximo minus est:*[50] hee is not presently a Pigmy,[51] that is lesse then a gyant. In transcendent things those are great, which are next to the best: those, I say, who with *Licinus*[52] have neede of one to direct them to goodnes; although they know not that which is honest by themselves, yet they obey others rightly admonishing them, and *admoneri velle secunda virtus,*[53] it is a second vertue, to indure reproving: for it argues a willingnesse to bee good: and *pars magna bonitatis est, velle fieri bonum:*[54] the next degree of goodnes, is the desire of goodnes: these may I tearme, as *Plutarch*[55] doth *Alcibiades,* Camelions,[56] from their facilitie of manners, whose mindes bend like the bones of the *Iambulans,*[57] whither you will force them. *Cereus in vitium flecti,*[58] as the Poet saith of yong men, easie to bee drawne either to vertue, or vice. But *natura suis nervis pulcherrimum corpus,*[59] as perfect there is no so heavenly a body, in which doth not hang some clouds of corruption. *Non datur sincerum aliquod sine mali admixtione:*[60] there is nothing so sincere that hath not some admixtion of evill. In this *Attica*[61] and pleasing field of woman, there growe some Thistles among the Violets, and these are the third sort, the dregges and scumme (as the Latines said of the Romanes) of woman kinde: obstinate *Heraclites,*[62] who neither know good themselves, nor condiscend to others admonitions: These I exclude (as *Aristotle* doth them from his Ethicks)[63] from under the shield of my defence, although your foule-mouthed *Mantuans*[64] take occasion to make these the Axeltree,[65] on which the wheele of their tongues do continually run: who, because their deserts could never seate them in the favour of any vertuous women, therefore they empty the dregs of their stomacks upon all, with the Romans, for one Tyrannicall *Tarquinius,*[66] to hate all Kings, like expert Logicians, out of particulars, concluding an universall. Aske them what woman is: and you shall have them speake contradiction *ex tempore:*[67] they are *mala necessaria,* necessary evils: as though evill could be necessary: Since whatsoever is needful, appertaines either to the *esse,* or *bene:*[68] *Esse* of man, and there is nothing necessary either to his essence or perfection that is ill. But lest if I should suffer the Planet of my wit to wander in the whole heaven of woman,[69] and runne at randome in the ample field of their vertues, it might stray perhaps from the path way of Judgement; I will now teather[70] and confine it within the ground-plot of each of their particular qualities.

Of their religious Piety.

Religion meritoriously challengeth to act the first part of their praise: and *Osorius*[71] tels me, that whom we would make immortall, we must prove religious. Our *Matilda Sancti Brigit Hildegard,*[72] the first accusers of the Romish Religion; the learned sister of *Nazianzen, Paula Salvina Celantia,*[73] Pillers of the Church: Holy *Apollonia,* whose celestiall fire of zeale extinguished the smart of this earthly and culunary fire:[74] *Ursula,* who with eleven thousand Virgins suffered Martyrdome,[75] seeme to object envy unto me, in concealing theirs and innumerable other pieties: but, alas, I want not the will, but the power. The Poet bids me looke: *Quid valeant humeri?*[76] And I finde the shoulders of my invention too narrow to beare the burthen of their due praises for Οὐδ΄ οἴμοι δέκα μ[οι] γλῶσσαι δέκα [δὲ] σὸματ́ εις'ν.[77] If I had as many tongues as *Briarius* had hands,[78] I could not enumerate the praises due to their devotions: and it is better your pieties be conceal'd, then insufficiently reveal'd; whiles we praise by halves, we disgrace: an ill Instrument may shame a good worke: the unworthinesse of the agent many times curses a good enterprise. *Caesar* his warres had better beene inveloped in obscurity then divulged by botching *Labio;*[79] Truth is better hid, then wronged by telling.

Of their Continency and Chastity.

Continency is defined by the Prince of Philosophers,[80] when we immoderately desire pleasures, and yet abstaine from them. This definition lookes like *Otho* his life, onely good in the end:[81] the sweet of it, which makes continency a vertue consists as the honey of the Bee, in the Taile (for *Ubicunq desines, si bene desines tota est*)[82] too immoderately to desire pleasures, that argues weaknes: but to be able to cast the cold ashes of restraint, on the burning coles of desires, that the strongest vertue: the object then of continency is pleasures in generall; give mee leave to restraine them onely to Veneriall.[83] The first part of this vertue, *viz.* to immoderately desire, I doubt not but the greatest Mysogunians[84] will grant unto them: for the oracle of our beliefe doth testifie it, tearming them the weaker vessels: and weaknesse alwayes is the most subject to gape after pleasures, and in their bodies (if it may not seeme superfluous) to adde the Sunne of verity the candle light of humane reason. Aire (saith the Philosopher)[85] doth predominate, and where most aire is, there is most *Humidum radicale:*[86] being both of one nature, indifferently hot and moist,[87] where there is most *Humidudum radicale,* there is most ability of body, and where the body is most able, there naturally should be most desire.

Now if any object as a fault, the natural pronenesse of their bodies, *Ciceroes* answere to the Romans refusing *Murena* to be consul, because he had lived in *Asia,* shall be mine, telling them, that was not commendable in *Murena,* that he had never seene, but that he had lived continently in *Asia.*[88] What if their bodies be an *Asia,* full of delights? that is not discommendable: but that their soules, a *Murena,* should live chaste in the *Asia*[89] of their bodies, thats laudable (as *Seneca* saith of *Levanus*) *Hoc multo fortius ebrio ac vomitante populo sobrium esse;*[90] by this they are most vertuous, that their mindes should be sober, amongst the riotous pleasures of their bodies. It is the chiefest part of Continency, that it can, but will not doe ill. Now to prove their voluntary abstinence from those their desires, examples must be my only *Medium,*[91] which although they bee not demonstrable arguments to prove a truth, yet they are probable, for (saith *Cicero*) *ut habet in aetatibus authoritatem senectus, sic in exemplis antiquitas:* ancient examples to present times should be as venerable, as old age to youth.[92] *Optimum ex praeterito consilium praesentis venit,* wee may best judge of the present by things past.[93] *Lucretia,* being asked of her husband, when *Tarquinius* had offered her violence,[94] how shee did? answered, *Quid salum est mulieri amissa pudicitia?*[95] What can be safe to a woman, when shee is bereaved of her chastity? The Romane Lady that never kist man, but her husband, did therefore deemed all men like unto him, to have obnoxious & noysom breaths.[96] The Thebane maide, before *Nicanor* should be the carver up of her virginity, chose to be her owne boistrous Butcher.[97] Our *Matilda,* ere she would assent to the unlawfull sute of King *John,* fled to a Monastery, and there suffered death.[98] And what was the reason that the ancients constituted them the mouthes of their Oracles, and governors of their Temples, but for their chastity and sanctity? and whosoever shall read histories, or looke into these present times, shall find many chaste *Orythyas,* for one *Carneades,*[99] many continent *Clea's* for one *Socrates,*[100] and on the contrary many a lascivious *Caligula,* for one *Messalina,*[101] many an incontinent *Tiberius,* for one *Livia:*[102] but that which gives the most luster of their continency, is, that men who as I have proved should be naturally most chaste, are assailants, whereas they should bee defendants: but now custome hath made it no fault in them; for *Multitudo peccantium tollit peccatum,* the multitude of offenders takes away the offence,[103] and faults are no longer feared, then that they are rare, but our English so *Seneca* tels them,[104] that offences are much greater, as they are more universal. Do they not observe houres, dayes, and all occasions, to batter the walles of their chastity? And what will not importunity and opportunity effect? which as they aggravate the fault in the agent, so they extenuate, though not excuse it in the patient. Certainely, if they should use the like meanes, to obtaine men, a Nay would bee as seldome as treason in the mouthes of most men. Yet so injurious are the censures of these our times, that if a *Jove* vanquish but, or vitiate, or in or in vanquishing, viciate a silly *Jo,* a grave *Cato,* a light or tender Virgin, black infamy shall overcloud, and brand her reputation, not once touching his.[105]

Ille pretium sceleris,
tulit hic Diadewa [Diadema].[106]
Of 'he fault poore she
shall beare the blame,
When he's crown'd with
a Diadem.

As sweetely sings a Lady in our English *Ovid.*

To men is granted
priviledge to tempt:
But in that Charter,
women be exempt:
Their fault it selfe
serves for the faults excuse,
And makes it ours,
though yours be the abuse:

And howsoever,
although by force they win,
Yet on our weakenesse,
still returnes the sinne.[107]

If women bee unchaste, they are but incontinent, and therfore but *semimale,* but halfe evill: If man be unchaste, he is untemperate, & therefore *totaliter malus,* wholy evil,[108] if they be both chaste, shee is continent, and he but temperant, and therefore more to be praised: for *Quamuis aeundem finem uterque pervenerit tamen maior est laus, idem efficere difficiliore materia:*[109] although they both attaine the same end, yet it is the more laudable to effect the same in a more difficult matter.

Of their Fortitude and Magnanimity.

Although continency bee the best fortitude, and it is the greatest conquest, when the body is the Chariot, that carries the minde triumphing over its affections: therefore *Laelius* told his friend, being insnared with the beauty of *Syphax* his wife, that it would be a more noble victory, to conquer his affections to her, then in subduing the husband:[110] *Maximum est imperium imperare sibi,*[111] and he is most valiant that conquers himselfe: yet because you shall not deeme them inferiour to you in warrelike fortitude, take *Seneca's* judgement of them. *Quis dixerit naturam maligne cum mulieribus egisse, par illis mihi crede vigor, &c.* who saith, that nature hath given her favours sparingly to woman, they have the same vigour, and can, as well tolerate labours, as men, if they be accustomed to them.[112] To omit the men-conquering *Amazons,*[113] there is none I know so obscure, to whom the trumpet of fame hath not blowne their valors. *Xerxes* (he that was alwayes last in the field, and first out) seeing *Artemisia* bravely fighting amongst his Captaines, sayd (for even the vicious thinke well of vertue) Οι μ[ὲν] ἄνδρες γεγό νασί υοι γυναῖκες αἱ δ' γυναῖκες ἄνδρες: as there is in man womanish feare, so there is in woman virill audacity.[114]

The Romanes had no lesse fight with the women, then with their husbands, in conquering the *Cimbrians.*[115] *Semiramis* receiving ignominious speeches from the King of the *Indians,* renunciated and sent him word, she intended not to fight with words, but with swords.[116] The ancient inhabitants of this Ile, the Britaines, *Vaodicia* being their General, shaked off the Romane yoke,[117] and most of their prosperous battels were when women did leade them. And was not *France* wholy overrunne by our English, untill (as the French brag) that valorous *Joane* gave life to the French, confronted our brave *Bedford* in the field?[118] And what was the Phoenix of her time, our ever to bee renowned Queene, *Elizabeth,*[119] at whose frowne Kings trembled? And that fiery-spirited *Blanch,* Dutches of *Orleance,* when King *Philip* had given her disgracefull words, replyed, that if (to use my authors words) she had a paire of ____, hee durst not so have reviled her.[120] But thou wilt say, they may have couragious minds, but they want force. Oh! men are stronger then they. So are many beasts stronger then men, *Corpus si magnas habet vires, non aliter quam furiosi validum est:*[121] Valour consists in the minde, not in the body; not Megasomity,[122] but Magnanimity, is the vertue: it is the minde that extols dejected things, illustrates base things, dehonestates[123] great things. They yeeld to men to have windes like *Dionysius* that strong-sided Trumpeter, who with his breath could puffe about Wind-Mils.[124]

So that they have minds able to blow away all base feares: And what more evident signe of their valor, then their love of it? *Homer* induceth *Helena* complaining of *Hymen,* that hee had espoused her to one, who durst not defend her against the enemy.[125] The *Laconians* seeing their husbands feare, lending them wings to flye from the field, asked them if they intended to obscond themselves in their mothers bellies?[126] *Tiphane* perceiving her beloved *Bertrand,* for the sweet of her companie, to let his desire of Martiall affaires quaile within him; told him she should the entirelier love him, if he did stil prosecute the honour and reputation of Chivalry.[127] *Damatria* her sonne complaining of the shortnesse of his sword, bid him stand neerer his enemy.[128] *Venus* did more affect bloudy *Mars,* then timorous & fairefac't *Apollo.*[129] And how many *Katherines*[130] chose rather to bee courted with conquering Launces, then Court-like Rapiers? I might heere *a posteriore* (as the Logicians tearme it)[131] from the effects inferre their fortitudes, women beeing the cause of that *calor coelestis,* the heavenly fire of love, which burnes, as it did in *Lepidus,*[132] all ignoble, and servile feares from mens hearts, the whetstone (as one saith of Anger) that exacuates[133] and sets an edge on mens obtuse and blunt affections: the *Lapis Alchimicus,* the Philosophers Stone,[134] that converts Leaden passions, into any golden sweet content: but that many pens have testified the same, and I am loth to bee a Broker of other mens wits.

Of their constancie and true love.

There is a greater Sympathy of affections in friendships,[135] ὁμοειδης then αὐ. . .οιδεις,[136] betwixt man & woman, then man and man. For you shall not reade of above foure or five couples of men that were linkt together in the bands of faithfull friendship, when Authors swarme with examples betwixt the other. *Similitudo morum,* the similitude of affections, as *Otho* obtained *Neros,* is the cause of virall friendship:[137] but ἡ φυαίς, nature it selfe, is the foundation of conjugall friendship. It is *Jucunda amicitia,* that is the cause of this *vera amicitia.*[138] It is pleasure, that tyes the indissoluble knot of true friendship; delight begins it, honestie confirmes it: for where pleasure is, there is desire of societie, and thats the key, that locks their thoughts together. Shee then that is espoused to one whom shee doth not affect, if shee love another, can not be said to be inconstant, but incontinent. For inconstancie is a negation of constancie: they must then first love, ere they bee inconstant. If then (courteous Reader) thou doest but ballance the scales of thy judgement with impartialitie, duely waying the nature of inconstancie, thou wilt not hereafter so rashly accuse them of instablenes. What if there be one *Helena* amongst all the Graecians; one *Livia* amongst all the Romans; one *Cleopatra* amongst all the Egyptians:[139] wilt thou therefore shoot the arrow of thy same-wounding judgement against all, the Graecians, Romanes and Egyptians? There is no motion, but circular, that is alwayes perfect. All are not Starres, fixed in the Orbe of constancie, there must bee some straying Planets.[140] *Elisa* Queene of Carthage, her Husband being murdered, and afterward beeing sollicited of many for her love, praecipitated her selfe from a Sky-kissing Turret, saying, I come, my *Sychaeus,* I come.[141] *Theogena,* wife to *Agathocles,* refused to depart from him, when all his subjects had relinquisht and forsaken him, saying, *Se non prosperae tantum, sed omnis fortunae inisse societatem,* she was as wel married to him in adversitie, as in prosperitie.[142] And not to stand particularizing, the Getoi women would not be sent from their husbands besieged: but would participate of the same fortune they did.[143] It beeing a custome amongst the Indians, that the women should be buried quick with their husbands, if the thred of their lives were first cut, they so willingly condiscended unto it, that many times one man having two wives, they would be at mortall strife, who should be interred with him.[144] *Martia,* the Daughter of *Cato,* being demanded when she would surcease from mourning for her deceased husband, *Cum & vitae inquit:* When I cease to live.[145] The wife of *Philo,* when shee was asked why shee did not adorne her selfe with Jewels at publike solemnizations, answered, It sufficeth me, that I have for my ornament the vertue of my husband.[146] The Wife of *Pompey* slew her selfe upon his dead corps, from whom, I thinke, the Tragedian took his sentence, *Mors misera non est, commori cum quo velis.*

Pale death to life
is oft of those preferd,
Who are with those,
whom they doe love, interr'd.[147]

Should I stand to enumerate all the regular Matrons that moove within the speare[148] of fidelitie; I might seeme by a Logicall Induction, in reckoning up all particulars, to inferre a generall. Women, their mindes are crystall, which writ on by the Diamond of love, the slubbering[149] fingers of Time can never obliterate or blot forth: Like the state of the world above the Moon, where there is no change.[150] Their minds perhaps, as (*Seneca* saith) a wise mans, may waver, but never alter.[151]

Of their contempt, and freenesse from Gluttonie.

There is none, I thinke, so scrupulously malicious, unlesse hee resemble the Philospher, who doubted whether he were a man or a woman, and therefore would have it decided by disputation,[152] that will suffer any thought to moove within the Zodiake of there imaginations,[153] which doth not in this give Woman the preeminence. Peruse thou all Authors, that have in there writings disgorged and spet forth their venemous rancour against them: and if thou canst finde two of them that were addicted to Gastrimorgisme,[154] I will grant thee to inferre that they are all dishmongers,[155] when the streame of Autors beares floting on their Pageants, innumerable mens names, who by πολυπασία and πολυφαλία[156] have brought both bodies and purses into consumptions. *Philoxenus* wished his necke were as long as a Cranes, that hee might the longer feele the sweetnes of his meat:[157] and he (*qualis vita, finis ita*)[158] having taken a mortall surfet, by devouring almost a *Polypus* of the quantitie of two Ells,[159] desired to comfort his empty stomack, that death should separate his leane soule, from his fat body, that he might eat the remainder. *Sminderides,* whose eyes were sixe times as long shut with Gluttonie, as *Endymions* was with sleepe, from beholding the Sunne, and then forsooth by Love, being awaked from his sluggishnes, he rode a wooing, bravely attended with a thousand Cookes, as many Fowlers, and so many Fishers.[160] How many *Nero's* shall you finde banquetting, and swilling, from midday, to midnight, with *Vitellius,* making (as one saith) their τρυφὴ and ζοφὴ, their π..ιματα: and *honestum et parum est, cui corpus multum,* whose belly is his god, honestie most commonly is his slave.[161]

Of their dextericall[162] Wits.

If the acutenesse of wit doe follow, and be seene by the purenes of the temperature of the body,[163] as without doubt it is: for it heere is usually ἀφὴ ἀκριβεςάτ, the most exact sense of feeling and μαλακότερος σαρκ, a soft temperate flesh, where there is a smirke[164] and quicke wit: women (being they are most commonly imbued with those corporall favours) should by a consequent bee the best ..φυὲς,[165] have the most active, and excelling wits: and when *Aristotle* prefer's the more obtuse and melancholy wit, before the dextericall; it is in affaires where there is time for deliberation: otherwaies the prae-wit excels the post wit,[166] as actions performed in season, doe those which are out of season. For many times, when occasion is offered the prae-wit takes it by the forehead, when the other whiles the time away it: doth search the corners of the braines, for the oyle of inventions, stayes till the doore of answering be shut against it: Like the messenger that came to tell *Cassius* of the victory, when hee had already slaine himselfe in despaire of it:[167] and *elleborum frustrarum iam cutis aegra tumebat.*

In vaine we to invention flye,
When occasion's past, for to reply.[168]

Socrates tearmeth perspicuitie of wit, *aurum divinum,* divine and refined gold, whose Mine is the minde of a woman: And therefore the Muses, the fountaine of all wit, were women:[169] The Sybils, *quarum quot verba, tot Oracula,* whose words as an Oracle to the Romanes, were women.[170] The quintessence, the A *per se*[171] (as one saith of Poets) of wit: the even flowing *Euripus* of faculty, learned *Sapho,* a woman.[172] The daughter of *Tully* being asked in scurrility, by *Metellus* who was her Father? replyed, It would be hard for thee to answere it, by reason of thy Mother, (for shee was esteem'd none of the honestest.)[173] It was a pretty extemporarie sleight of *Semarimus:* who, when the Indian King caused her to ascend his Throne, and gave her authority to command the Souldiours, to doe what she would; she presently bid them kill the King himselfe: and so she obtained his Kingdome.[174] And whose eye is not blinded with malignitie, may see the floud of their wits still to flow in these our times.

It is a more then probable signe, that they excell men in the activenesse of wit, in that (as I have prooved) they are lesse incident to Gurmandizing:[175] for παχεῖα γαστηρ λεπτότατον [οὐ] ...τεινοον:[176] and as a modern Poet pithyly Englisheth:

Fat panches make leane pates,
and groser bits
Enrich the ribs,
but bankrout quite the wits.[177]

Of their Wisedome.

Perspicuitie of wit is of the Moralists[178] made the chiefest part of wisedome, differing solely from it: as *pars* doth a *toto:* as the part from the whole. Indeed, wisedome is nothing but a perfected wit, it being onely necessary by nature: the other parts got by experience. If then women have activenesse of wit, reason will tell you, they most easily attaine to prudence, which is (because the knife of occasion, will not suffer me to shred it into all his[179] parts) either Oeconomicall,[180] or Politicall. Concerning the first, the whole multitude cryes, as they doe to Kings, *Regnant, regnant:*[181] Let it appertaine to the Sexe feminine to govern the house, and so their politikes prudence,[182] who knowes how to guide a little, will quickly learn how to governe much. Our politike Prudence sprung first, from Oeconomicall. And *domus* (saith *Aristotle*) *est quasi parva quae dam civitas, & civitas quasi magna domus:* a house is, as it were a little Citie, and a Citie, as it were, a great house.[183] But let one, who with *Diogenes* could never afford woman a good word,[184] speake for them, saying, that nature had denied unto them strength: for otherwise, their courage beeing corroborated by policy, would bee unconquerable. *Antipater* was accustomed with his Daughter *Phila,* to consult of his most serious and warlike affaires. *Tannaquill,* that politick Romane Dame, obtained by the sleyts of her wits, two Empiredomes.[185] *Agrippina,* when al the Captaines could not asswage the raging of the people, with her sweet and Nectar-flowing words of wit, calmed and pacified them. *Heluna,* the Mother of *Seneca,* was expert in all Science:[186] The Armenians expulsed their King, to have a Woman sway the Scepter of their Monarchy:[187] shewing, that there are women both more wise to judge what is to bee expected, and more constant to beare it when it is hapned. But I may say of their vertues, as one saith of vices; *Multarum latent virtutes, quia imbecilles sunt,* the clouds of obscuritie, many times overshaddow the Sunne of their Vertues from shining:[188] and *haud distat inertia caelcita virtus.*[189] Vertue concealed, is esteemed little better then sluggishnes. They may have nature which begins; Art which directs; but they want use, which perfecteth. *Generosos animos Otium corrumpit:* want of imployment, corrupts the bravest spirits;[190] the fountain of their vertue, corrupts by standing. Want of use, causeth disabilitie; but custome, perfection.

Of their Beauty.

Although it bee a Tenent[191] amongst the Stoicks (who would have men impassionate, & without affections,[192] as *Diodorus* writes of some Arabians)[193] that there is no externall good, addes perfection to a man: Yet the *Peripateticks*[194] hold them, although not necessarie, yet requisite, as one distinguisheth, not absolute: *sed respective,*[195] they doe not concurre to perfection, as it is perfection, but as it is mans perfection: and of all adventitiall, and extrafical goods,[196] *Aristotle* gives the prinicipalitie to pulchritude, which doth not cause vertue, but graceth it.[197] *Plutarch* accuseth *Seneca* of inconsiderate Judgement, in that he accuseth *Virgil* of errour, in saying that *Gratior est pulchro veniens e corpore virtus.*[198]

Plac't with beauty, vertue's like
Rich Pearle set in a Margarite.[199]

Non satis est (saith *Galateus*) *bene quid facere, nisi etiam fiat venuste.*[200] It is not sufficient to performe actions so wel, unlesse also decently. *Sumus omnes* (saith *Osorius*) *natura concinnitatis, appetentes:* wee all naturally desire neatnes, & concinnity.[201] Beautie is call'd of *Plato,* a prerogative of nature, accidentall to few:[202] Of *Theophrastus, silentem fraudem, quod absque verbis persuadebat:* a silent fraud, that perswades without words.[203] Of *Carneades,* ἀδορο.ορητον Βασιλέ..: a Kingdome without a guard; because it commands without compulsion.[204] And therefore saith the Philosopher, If there were any amongst the gods, that did excell in externall lineaments, the rest would deeme it meet that they should governe.[205] The *Catharri* chose them to be libertie free, who were of a comely proportion, the rest they made servile.[206] And if I may not come within the reach of *Juvenals* lash, the *primus Motor,* the abstract of fairenesse, entitled (with reverence be it spoken) his Spouse in the *Canticles,* by the name of faire:[207] Intimating the Adamantine[208] and winning power it hath, with mortals. For beeing the *species* of each object,[209] & impressed in the sence, before it bee in the understanding, it is a good consequent, that whatsoever is most delightfull to the Organical sences, the Intellectuall parts are most willing to receive. I neede not set invention on the racke,[210] to prove their Prerogative in corporall feature, as I have in their internall and mentall forme, since our sensible eyes doe more easily see, then our intelligible understand. I have need of a *Sapho's* wit,[211] to describe the Rose of their beauty; not an *Aristotles* Judgement, to prove it. Let each ones sences bee the glasse,[212] in which they view beauty; and then, I thinke, there will be none so hypocriticall, or false, that will not reflexe[213] some shaddow of their pulchritude, by which they may see them to surpasse men. *Quantum lenta solent inter viburna Cupressi,* as much as the lofty Cypresse doth overpeere the limber shrubbe:[214] or, as one saith of *Ephesius,* καλῶς ἐν μειρακί οις ὅσον Ροδοπη ἐν παρθένοις, as faire not amongst, but above men; as *Rodope,* above the Virgins.[215] The Crasis of their bodies, comes neerest to the Physicians *temperamentum ad pondus.*[216] Although selfe-tormenting envie, which alwaies, *tanquam ignis summa petit,*[217] a perpetuall companion of vertue, seek to congeale vapours in the sky of beauty, with the noisomnesse of its breath, by objecting incontinence unto it, as a Poet sings:

There is no name
(if she be false or not,)
But being faire,
some envious tongue will blot:[218]

As if nature were an Hypocrite, to candie over the bitter Pils of the minde, with sugred outsides. No, no, their externall feature doth strive (as *Paterculus* saith of *Victinius*)[219] with the excellencie of their mindes; whose vertues being a Jewell, inveloped in the silver Ore of their bodies, like *Achilles,* of whom *Maximus Tirrhus* saith, Not onely to bee extold for her golden looks, but because he was adorned with all vertuous qualities.[220] The cord of society (as *Chrysippus* nominates it) or pulchritude, is described to bee a proportionable commixtion of the foure elements in mans body,[221] & where no one element doth predominate in the body, there no one passion doth captivate the soule: for, *Cuius in ullo elementi portio praevalebit, inde moris erunt,*[222] the minde derives his[223] passions from the prevailing element in the body: where *Frigidity*[224] doth predominate, their timorousnes; where *Calidity,*[225] there choler: wherfore *Plato* would have children prohibited, and yong men in the hot Meridean of their age, to abstaine from Wine, becaeuse by califying the body, it inflameth also the minde.[226]

And whereas we see many with *Lepidus,* to have fairer bodies then minds, leaden Rapiers, in golden Sheathes, like *Diogenes* young man,[227] a *Momus* wit in an *Apollo's* body, like *Nereus* Beard in a painted Box,[228] it is not by the instinct of nature, but by the corruption of it: and on the contrary, when wee see many golden qualities placed, as *AEsops* Jewell, in the dunghill,[229] in Leaden bodies, as in *Galba,* of whome *Cicero* said, his wit had an ill lodging;[230] nature doth not imbue them with them, but industry obtaines them, as *Socrates* and our last Cardinall confessed of themselves,[231] The temperature of the body[232] doth but beginne and inchoate[233] our affections, custome and use are of most validity, wherefore generally wee may judge, as an Epigrammatist doth of a slow paced Lordane:[234]

Tardus es ingenio,
ut pedibus, natura etenim dat
Exterius specimen,
quod latet interius.
Thy leaden heeles
no golden wit doe shew:
For in-bred gifts
by outward limbs we know.

Of their comfort to man.

There is nothing more oppugnant[235] to mans nature, then solitude: and therefore he is described to be *animal sociale,* a sociable creature: it is one of the two by which he hath his prerogative[236] of beasts, *Societas illi dominum animalium dedit:* Company hinders from many offences,[237] when *Omnia nobis mala solitudo persuadit,* Solitarinesse perswades to all evill.[238] *Crates* seeing a young man spaciating by himselfe, demanded what he did there alone? *Mecum* (saith he) *loquor,* I talke with my selfe. Take heed then, replied *Crates,* lest *cum homine malo loqueris,* thou conferrest with an evil one.[239] It is better for a man to be with any one, then with himselfe. Art thou with *Metellus* in prosperity,[240] and doth Fortune, with a prosperous gale of winde, blow the Ship of thy life towards the Port of riches? thou canst never by thy selfe, without the cords of friends, cast Anker in the Haven of contentednes: for *Nullius boni sine societate iucunda possessio est:* There is no pleasing possession of any thing without a companion.[241] Again, art thou with *Rutilius* in adversity:[242] & doth the blustring Boreas[243] of mis-fortune, cast thee on the rock of poverty? yet *solamen miseris,*[244] the comfort of friends is comfort: it is a sweete thing in adversity to have, who laments with us our miseries; *ut serenitas gratior in tempestate advenit, sic lugenti amico amicus,* as serenity to Mariners after tempests; so the Sunne-shine of a friends presence, is most gratefull to his correlative, in the tempest of his adversity:[245] *Lacrimis lacrimis miscere iunat.*[246] *Helena* could tell *Hecuba,* that her sorrow was light in respect of hers, because she had coopartners in it: for *magis exurunt, quos secretae lacerant curae.*[247] Care doth most scorch, when we pen it within the narrow compasse of our owne hearts. Wel then, there is no true joy, without a friend, and no friend, in respect of a wife, a woman to a man, who, if thou beest jocund, ads pleasure to thy mirth, and makes the cup of thy heart overflow with the nectar of delight. Art thou sad, and doth care gnaw thy perplexed minde? why, *Est aliquod fatale malum per verba levari,* by words thou must ease it:[248] and who so convenient as a wife to unclapse the bosome of thy thoughts unto? who either bedewing her cheeks with teares for thee, beares halfe thy burthen, or else absterging[249] or wiping with her soft hand teares from thy eyes, as sorrow from thy soule, as *Jocasta* did to *Oedipus* with a consolatory, *Quid iuvat, coniux, mala gravare quaestu?*

What helpes it, Sweet,
to aggravate
By sorrow thy
disastrous fate?[250]

What a Patheticall Oration makes *Messalinus* for women, to associate their husbands in the wars in forraine regions?[251] *Quod honestius, quam levamentum uxorium revertentibus post laborem, &c?*[252] what more convenient, then to have, when wee returne from our labours, then the comfort of our wives, as that one eye of *Minerva* testifieth of them?

And thou shalt finde
in women vertues lie:
Sweote supple minds,
which soone to vertue bow,
Where they, by wisedomes rule
directed are,
And are not forst
fond thraldome to allow.
As we to get are fram'd,
so they to spare:
We made for paine,
they made, our paines to cherish,
We care abroad,
and they at home have care.[253]

I may say of them, as *Euripides* saith of the just man, They seeme *non sibi, sed aliis natae,* not to be borne to themselves, but to others.[254] *Dulces parentes, dulces filiis, dulces fratres, dulces amici, sed dulcissimae uxores.* It is a sweet thing to have parents, children, brothers and friends, but it is most amoene, it is most sweete, to have the comfort of a loving woman,[255] when parents prove unnaturall, children rebellious, brothers unkind, friends unconstant, wives are onely like the Gemelli of *Hypocrates,* inseparable;[256] the sweete that must relish all those sowre potions: a wife is as a good conscience to a man, where-soever she is, there is true peace and joy: a man is never perfect, untill he be married, till then he is defective, he wants a Ribbe,[257] not *uxor fulgit* (as the Civilian saith) *radiis mariti, sed maritus radiis uxoris:* She is as the Sunne, and hee the Moone, the beames of her presence is the cause of his shining. It may be an Axiome as well as an Adage, *Verberat uxorem qui non habet:* unmarried men only beat their wives, who discommend them out of ignorance for wee cannot judge of sweet, untill we taste them:[258] but most maligne them, as *Appius* did *Virginia,* because they cannot obtaine them:[259] and married men dislaude[260] them, because they have them: for *Quicquid domi est, vile est:* we alwaies esteeme the worst of that wee injoy: *praesentium taedio futuri desiderio laboramus,* wee are sick alwayes of the present, and for future things:[261] *tardius bona quam mala sensimus,* wee are more sensible of ill then good, as *Cicero* saith of his *Terentia,* that till he was exilde from her company,[262] hee never knew what content it brought unto him; wee never know what pleasures are, till we bee bereaved of them: widdowers can onely judge of the comfort of a wife.

That Children are most obliged to their mothers.

Educing,[263] education, and affection, are the threefold cords that should tye each childe to the love of its mother: first, by educing or inducing[264] to this world; wherin every mother is as a good Land-Lord to her childe, giving it both house-roome and nutriment, when it, like an unruly Tenant, doth grieve and vexe her, and, which is against the Lease of equity, many times cuts and crops the flourishing trees of their beauty, and growne too great for their places, as many mens minds are for their estates, they seeke for a more ample habitation, neither can they have the Lawyers *bene decessit,*[265] for many times (*Proh dolor*)[266] they ruinate[267] in their departure, their continents, and yet women shew themselves the truest lovers, they love them that hurt them; & that it is better not to beginne a good action at all, then to desist; having begunne, they persevere in their benefits, giving them that *altera natura,* that other nature, education, nourishing our bodies as the Pellicane, though not with the bloud, yet with the substance of their brests,[268] and when they are able instruments to exercise the faculties of the soule, they (and *id maximum beneficium, quod animum reddit meliorem;* that is the greatest benefit which perfects the soule) suckle our mindes with the milke of good manners, training us up, as *Tanaquill* did her sonne, in religion and learning.[269] The two *Gracchi* reaped all the flowers of their Oratory, from the Garden of their mothers vertues.[270] *Caesar* obtained his eloquence by conversing with his mother.[271] And *Socrates,* that Athenian Eagle, exhausted all his wisedome from the well-spring of *Diolinna's* instructions.[272] Lastly, by their affection. *Rutilia* followed her sonne *Cotta* in his exile; and yet when death bereaved her of him, her eyes never shewed, her heart loved him, in *expulso virtutem ostendit, in amisso, prudentiam:* in his exile she shewed her love, in his death, her wisdome.[273] Two Roman Matrons beholding their sons, whom they deemed to have bin slaine in the great battel at *Thraceninus,* their soules as incapable of so inexpected joy, took leave of their bodies.[274] But I need not induce Instances, since they are oftner with *Niobe* & *Satyrus* for overloving,[275] then for not loving them, reprehended. Two reasons may be given, why they doe most affect their children. First, because they are certain they are theirs. Wherfore *Telemachus* being asked, if it were true that *Ulisses* was his father? answered, *Mater quidem ita hoc dicit,* My mother saith he was.[276] Secondly, for that they have most sorrow by them: for *omnis amat beneficia sua,* wee love that most dearely, that costs us dearest.[277] There is one honour (saith *Aristotle*) due to the father, another to the mother: we owe most honour to our father in a Geometricall proportion, in respect of dignitie, but most to our mother in an Arithmeticall proportion, in respect of desert.[278] For we have of them principally, τὸ εἶναι, our essence: Secondly, τιῶ ζοφίω, our nourishment: thirdly, τιῶ παιδίαν, our education: and *amor, amoris magnes est, & durus est, qui amorem non rependit:* Love is the Loadstone of Love, and hee is the most obdure, that doth not repay it.[279] There is no ingratitude comparable to that which is committed against the mother. Every man may say with *Seneca, Quicquid praestiti, infra aestimaetionem materni muneris est.* When I have performed all that I can, I can never recompence her.[280] For hee is never conquered in benefits, whose benefit it is, that he is conquered. I will winde up the clue[281] of this Tract, with that patheticall[282] saying of *Petrarch:*

Cum nihil sit natis
materno magis amore:
Iam mater studiis
est veneranda piis.
Since Mothers most
their childrens states doe tender:
By obsequious dutie,
we them thankes should render.[283]

The Castrophe.[284]

It is no marvell if the *Catharri* would rechange three or foure men, for one woman captivated or taken prisoner:[285] if the Egyptians, & Lycians, would have them rule both in publike, and private:[286] If the Lacedemonians called their wives κυρίας, Ladies: If the Germans paid so deare for their Spouses:[287] If *Plato* held a woman as necessary in a Family, as a King in a Countrey; since they doe excell in all the principall passions of the minde;[288] having, as *Museus* saith of *Hero,* a hundred graces:[289] In continencie, *Cato's;* in fortitude, *Scipio's;* in constancie, *Achates;*[290] in pulchritude, as the Poet saith of *Amarintha,* all beauty; in wit, the Marmulade and sucket of Muses:[291] Cordial Nepenthes of comfort to their husbands:[292] True Pellicans to their children.[293] If Nature, saith *Plutarch,* would see her selfe, woman must be her perspective, or Looking-glasse? Women? What are they? Natures pride, Vertues ornament, Angels on earth, Saints in Heaven; memorable to be registred, worthy to bee served. In a word, if the world bee a Ring, woman is the Diamond set in this Ring.

And now my Pen will needs take his leave of its faire Love, the Paper, with blubbering, as you see these ruder teares of Inke. I may say, as *Festus* saith of himselfe, *Res gestas signavi, non scripsi,* I have touched, not handled their vertues.[294] Wherein I have observed halfe of *AEsops* counsel to *Solon,* Ηκιϛα ἤ ἥδυσα: that his speech should bee either short, or sweet.[295] What I want in suavitie, I have endevoured to supply by brevitie: of which, if any one accuse me, let *Seneca* give a pricke to their Toade-swolne galls with his *Nunquam parum est, quod satis est.* I know, that more may be said of each qualitie; but I desired not to say all, but enough.[296]

FINIS

NOTES

1. An apology is a justification or defense. The *STC* lists this pamphlet among a group published in response to Joseph Swetnam's pamphlet *The Araignment of Lewd, idle, froward, and unconstant women* (1615).

2. Alban was one of the halls of Oxford University. In the early modern period, the halls were essentially hostels or boardinghouses inhabited by independent scholars who were not affiliated with or supported by a college. Alban's Hall was named not for St. Alban but for one of the early owners of the hall; it no longer exists.

3. It is better for a woman not to be born at all than to be tortured by those she lives with. (The translations are mine unless otherwise noted.)

4. Edward Griffen was a London printer, active from 1613 to 1621. He was one of the partners in Eliot's Court Press, situated in the Little Old Bailey. After his death, his business was taken over by his widow and later by his son, also named Edward. Richard Whitaker was a London bookseller, active from 1619 to 1648. He married the widow of Thomas Norton and took over his shop in Paul's Churchyard. From 1643 to 1645 he was a warden of the Company of Stationers.

5. See pp. 109–10 for biographical information about Mary Beaumont, Countess of Buckingham.

6. Diogenes of Sinope was a Greek Cynic philosopher (ca. 400–ca. 325 B.C.E.) who believed that a simple life was the most virtuous and who exposed the hypocrisy of conventional beliefs. Many legends sprang up around Diogenes, including that he spent his life wandering the world with a lighted lantern, searching in vain for an honest man (as an example of his contempt for his generation).

7. First fruits.

8. People with overblown opinions of themselves who exaggeratedly dispraise women.

9. See p. 110 regarding Newstead's reference to the birth of the "abortive Bacchus" as a metaphor for assuming the "woman's part" in his own argument.

10. The Greco-Roman goddess of wisdom, also known as Athena, is used here figuratively (and significantly) as a feminine embodiment of the intellect.

11. In Greek mythology the Muses were nine sisters, daughters of Zeus (king of the gods) and Mnemosyne (Memory), who inspired and presided over poetry and the arts and sciences. Here the Muse appears as a feminine embodiment of the writer's creative faculties, his inspiration.

12. Used figuratively for a region of great wealth to which profitable voyages can be made.

13. A Greek philosopher (ca. 455–360 B.C.E.) and one of the most devoted followers of Socrates, Antisthenes is considered the first of the Cynics. According to Diogenes Laertius (404–323 B.C.E.) in *Lives of Eminent Philosophers* (Loeb Classical Library, 1950), "once when he [Antisthenes] was applauded by rascals, he remarked, 'I am horribly afraid I have done something wrong'" (6.5). <*Misere metui mali aliquid in me admiserim. Petrar. de virt. opin.*> (Miserably, I feared that I might have allowed something evil to come into me.) In Petrarch's *De Virtutis Opinione* (Reputation) (in *Petrarch's Remedies for Fortune Fair and Foul: A Modern English Translation of "De remediis utriusque fortune," with a Commentary,* by Conrad H. Rawski [Bloomington: Indiana University Press, 1991], bk. 1), Reason asks Joy, "How can a name, or anything else, be good if it is based on falsehood" (31).

14. Marcus Porcius Cato (234–149 B.C.E.) was consul in 195 and censor in 184. He was known for his just policy of reconstruction. Lysimachus may be the flutist who performed at a chaotic victory celebration for Lucius Anicus after he conquered the Illyrians in 167 B.C.E., mentioned by Polybius in *The Histories* (Loeb Classical Library, 1995), 30.22.

15. Agree (i.e., move together).

16. <*Tull. de Orat.l.2.*> Lucilius was the first major Roman satirist (?–103 B.C.E.). His writings survive only in fragments. His opinion that the ideal reader is neither the most ignorant person nor the most learned is quoted by Cicero (Marcus Tullius) in *De Oratore* (Loeb Classical Library, 1988), 2.6.25.

17. Aurora was the Greek goddess of dawn; thus the Aurora of Minerva is the dawn of wisdom, or, as Newstead puts it, "the dawning of the day of literature."

18. A mountain in central Greece said to be sacred to Apollo and the Muses and often used figuratively for the abode of poetry or the heights of wisdom.

19. <*Juvena.*> Nobody becomes learned suddenly. Misquoted from Juvenal's *Satires* in *Juvenal and Persius* (Loeb Classical Library, 1940), 2.83, which has "turpissimus" ("most ugly") instead of "doctissimus." Juvenal (ca. 55–ca. 140 C.E.) was a Roman satirist; much of his most scathing writing is directed against women.

20. Zeuxis was a Greek painter (ca. 400 B.C.E.) whose portrait of the legendary Helen of Troy, one of the most famous paintings of antiquity, was a composite of the most beautiful features of many women, not the image of a single woman.

21. The Athenian lawgiver Solon, when asked by the fabulously wealthy King Croesus of Lydia whether anyone could be happier than the king was in his riches, replied that he knew of an honest man named Tellus, a good citizen of Athens, who, while not especially wealthy, had died valiantly defending his country and left be-

hind two upstanding sons. In Solon's view, Tellus's honorable and simple life was superior to Croesus's luxurious life. Solon's reply is described by Herodotus (in *Herodotus* [Loeb Classical Library, 1921], 1.30) and Plutarch (*Plutarch's Lives* [Loeb Classical Library, 1993], 27.4). Midas is the legendary king who, for returning his lost tutor, Silenus, to Bacchus was granted anything he desired. He asked that everything he touched be turned to gold, a gift that had the unfortunate consequence of turning to gold the food he ate.

22. One who is not prepared today will be more prepared tomorrow. Misquoted from Ovid's *Remedies for Love* (Loeb Classical Library, 1979), 94, which has "minus" ("less") instead of "magis" ("more").

23. An adherent or follower of Robert Browne (1550–1633), an English Puritan and Nonconformist who advocated a system of church government later adopted and modified by the Independents and Congregationalists.

24. Newstead puns on "lie" as meaning both "untruth" and "have sex with."

25. Seasonings, spices (lit., salt). In Latin, *sales* was often used figuratively (as here) to describe witty speech.

26. Probably Philippus of Thessalonia, writer and gatherer of a collection of Greek epigrams entitled *Garland,* published ca. 40 C.E.

27. When Diogenes Laertius came to Myndus and found that although the city itself was small, its gates were large, he supposedly cried, "Men of Myndes, bar your gates, lest the city should run away" (*Lives of the Eminent Philosophers,* bk. 6, p. 57).

28. By figuring his book in defense of women as a city, Newstead may be recalling Christine de Pizan's famous defense of women, *Le livre de la Cite des Dames* (1405), translated into English in 1521 by Brian Anslay as *Boke of the Cyte of Ladyes.*

29. <*Sen. Epi.* 33> One who follows another follows nothing. Misquoted from Seneca's *Epistles* (Loeb Classical Library, 1996): "qui alium sequitur nihil invenit" ("one who follows another discovers nothing") (33.10.5). Newstead contradicts this position later (see n. 91).

30. People who are skilled in or attach importance to logical method; not to be confused with the later Christian sect.

31. Didymus was a scholar of immense learning and industry (ca. 80–10 B.C.E.), said to have written more than thirty-five hundred treatises. He was not an original researcher but rather an editor and transmitter of learning that might have otherwise been lost. A "highway adage" is a common proverb. This proverb is not in the extant Didymus fragments.

32. Probably a reference to the Roman Emperor Licinius (r. 308–324 C.E.), the last of Constantine's rivals for sole rule of the Empire and thus seen as the last obstacle to Constantine's establishment of Christianity as the official imperial religion. Some traditions claim that Licinius, like Constantine, was visited by an angel in a dream the night before he defeated one of his rivals; unlike Constantine, however, Licinius was not converted to Christianity by his success. Thus he serves here as a figure of an ignorant person who cannot be enlightened even by divine relevation.

33. That is, while woman's material body was different from (and believed inferior

to) man's, woman's soul—or essence—was thought by some to be equal to man's in the sight of God. See Nancy Tuana, *The Less Noble Sex: Scientific, Religious, and Philosophical Conceptions of Woman's Nature* (Bloomington: Indiana University Press, 1993), 53–60, for a range of views on women's souls.

34. Probably refers to the apple of discord, a golden fruit inscribed "to the fairest." Paris was chosen to settle a dispute among the goddesses Hera, Athena, and Aphrodite, all of whom claimed ownership of the apple. Hera tried to bribe Paris with riches and fame; Athena offered him success in war; and Aphrodite promised him Helen, the most beautiful of women. Paris chose beauty.

35. Julius Caesar (100–44 B.C.E.) defeated Pompey (106–48 B.C.E.) in 48 B.C.E. at Pharsala in the civil wars of the Roman republic.

36. Lydia was a district in Asia Minor conquered by the Persians in ca. 546 B.C.E. After the conquest, the male inhabitants were forbidden to bear arms and subsequently acquired a reputation for effeminacy. Newstead suggests that the Lydian men were overmastered by their wives.

37. The younger—and better known—Seneca (3 B.C.E.–65 C.E.), the Stoic philosopher, was a political advisor and minister to Nero. For eight years there was good government based on compromise and diplomacy, but Seneca asked to retire in 62 when Nero's murderous acts tarnished his reputation. To early modern writers, Seneca was a supreme moral teacher, and his plays were a model for drama. His father (ca. 55 B.C.E.–39 C.E.) wrote *sententiae,* brief pointed sayings of perverse ingenuity.

38. That is, Adam and Eve.

39. In Greek mythology, the Sirens were sea-songstresses who lived on an island near Scylla and Charybdis. They sang to passing ships, luring sailors to their death. Returning home from Troy, Ulysses lashed himself to the mast of his ship so that he might hear their voices yet resist their call. See Homer's *Odyssey,* book 12. Here, the Siren is used as a figure for Eve.

40. According to legend, Tiresias came upon two snakes coupling in the woods and struck them with his staff, whereupon he was transformed into a woman. After living as a woman for seven years, he came upon the snakes again and, striking them a second time, was turned back into a man. Because he was the only living being to have experienced sex as both a man and a woman, he was called upon to adjudicate a dispute between Jupiter and Juno about whether men or women have more sexual pleasure. He agreed with Jupiter that women take far more pleasure from intercourse than men, for which verdict Juno blinded him. To compensate for Tiresias's loss of sight, Jupiter gave him long life and the ability to see the future. Here, Tiresias serves as a type of effeminate man who has been "womanized" by his passions.

41. Gained or obtained, from the Latin *assequor,* a coinage not in the *Oxford English Dictionary* (1989; hereafter *OED*).

42. <*Tull. orat.l.2.*> Not Catullus the poet but Quintus Catulus, who was made consul in 102 B.C.E. In Cicero's *De Oratore,* Catulus says that "no one can achieve high distinction for wisdom and eloquence without a very great amount of zeal and industry and study" (2.89).

43. <*Liv. Dec.*3> Livy's *Historiae Romanae Decades* (*Ab Urbe Condita*). Perhaps Newstead is referring to Livy's account of Appius Claudius, a decemvir who wrongly claimed in 449 B.C.E. that Verginia, a young girl, was a slave so that he could use her to satisfy his lust. Her father killed her rather than let her be defiled, and the decemvirs were forced to abdicate their power.

44. <*Liv. Dec.*3> Baptista Spagnolo Mantuanus (1448–1516), whose Latin *Eclogues,* in imitation of Virgil's, was commonly used as a school text in the sixteenth century. It was translated into English by George Tuberville in 1567. Mantuanus's fourth eclogue contains a lengthy polemic against women, which includes most of the clichés of medieval and early modern antifeminism: women are said to be lecherous, greedy, ambitious, deceitful, inconstant, rebellious, and lazy. According to Mantuanus, men should avoid women as the lamb avoids the wolf. The eclogue provides a catalog of evil women, from Medea to Eve, some of whom (like Semiramis) are praised by Newstead. In Shakespeare's *Love's Labour's Lost* (1594–95), Holofernes quotes the opening lines of Mantuanus's *Eclogues* (4.2.93–94).

45. Condignly or suitably.

46. Titus (39–81 C.E.) led the Roman legions in the sack of Jerusalem in 70 C.E. His brief reign as emperor (79–81 C.E.) was distinguished by his leniency and generosity and was referred to proverbially as a time of ideal government.

47. <*Suet.* I.12.> The phrase "delicae generis humani" was used by the historian Suetonius to characterize the emperor Titus ("The Deified Titus" in Suetonius's *Lives of the Caesars* [Loeb Classical Library, 1997], bk. 8.1). Here and elsewhere, Newstead applies to women compliments originally given to great male leaders and soldiers.

48. <*Paterc. pag.* 125.> Scipio Aemilianus (ca. 185–129 B.C.E.), the grandson of Publicus Africanus. Scipio was seen by Cicero as a paragon of Roman virtue. The quote is from Velleius Paterculus, *Compendium of Roman History* (Loeb Classical Library, 1924), 1.12.3.6.

49. Probably Cato the Younger (95–46 B.C.E.), a Roman statesman who had a reputation for honesty. Cato the Elder hated the Scipio family because he thought that they lived too luxuriously.

50. <*Sen. ep.* 101> "It is no slight thing to be less than the greatest." From Seneca's *Epistles* (100.9.4.), although Seneca does not repeat "statim" and uses "pusillum" instead of "pusillus" and "quid" instead of "quis."

51. One of a race of physically small (less than five feet tall) people of color mentioned in ancient history and tradition as inhabiting parts of Ethiopia or India.

52. See n. 32.

53. Newstead may be referring to Seneca's *On Benefits* in volume 3 of *Moral Essays* (Loeb Classical Library, 1989): "Moneri velle ac posse secunda virtus est" ("The second best form of virtue is to be willing and able to take advice") (5.25.4) and "proximi sunt, qui admoniti in viam redeunt" ("next best are those who return to the right path when they are admonished") (5.25.5).

54. <*Sen. Epist.* 34.> Seneca, *Epistles,* 34.3.

55. A Greek essayist and biographer (46?–120 C.E.), most famous in the early mod-

ern period for *The Parallel Lives,* a book about eminent Greek and Roman figures that was widely available in England as *Lives of the Noble Grecians and Romans* (1579), translated by Sir Thomas North.

56. An Athenian general and statesman (450–404 B.C.E.) who switched sides several times in the course of the Peloponnesian War, betraying both his native land of Athens and the Spartans, to whom he defected after being dismissed from command of the Athenian forces because of accusations that he took part in mutilating the statues of Hermes. In his chapter on Alcibiades, Plutarch refers to him as a chameleon for his ability to adapt himself flawlessly to different manners and customs (*Plutarch's Lives,* 23.4).

57. <*Diod. de Jamb.*> *Diodorus of Sicily* in *The Library of History* (Loeb Classical Library, 1989), tells of an island in the Indian Ocean, discovered by an explorer named Iambulus, where the inhabitants had flexible bones: "the bones of the body have the ability to bend to a certain extent and then straighten out again, like the sinewy parts" (2.55–56). *The Library of History* in forty books (ca. 60–30 B.C.E.) begins with the earliest times and ends with Julius Caesar's Gallic War of 54 B.C.E. The books are a compilation of various sources, much of it contradictory and unreliable. In book 3.18, Diodorus describes an Arabian (Ethiopian) tribe whose members are "insensible" to pain.

58. <*Horat. de Arte Poet.*> "[The beardless youth is] soft as wax for molding to evil" (Horace, *Horace: Satires, Epistles, and Ars Poetica* [Loeb Classical Library, 1991], l. 163).

59. <*Euph. Sat. Apollo.*> A body, by nature, is most beautiful in its own strength. John Barclay's *Euphormio's Satyricon,* written in Latin between 1603 and 1607, is a satire on the Jesuits.

60. <*Phar. in praeda Mar.*> Perhaps a reference to Lucan's *Civil War,* known as *Pharsalia,* though I could find no such reference in that work or in Horace's *Ars Poetica* or Martial's *Epigrams.*

61. The area of Greece surrounding Athens. Pindar uses the epithet "violet-crowned" to describe Athens, perhaps referring to festal wreaths made of violets.

62. Followers of the Greek pre-Socratic philosopher Heraclitus of Ephesus (ca. 535–475 B.C.E.), who believed the only reality was change. Newstead cites them here for their supposed obstinacy.

63. <*Arist. Eth. l.*I.*c.*3.> In book 7 of *Nicomachean Ethics* (Loeb Classical Library, 1994), Aristotle suggests that Heraclitus did not distinguish between his own opinions and established facts (3.4).

64. See n. 44.

65. Axle.

66. Sextus Tarquinius, legendary last king of the Romans (534–510 B.C.E.), raped Lucretia, the wife of Tarquinius Collatinus. His action sparked an uprising led by Junius Brutus, who overthrew him, resulting in the establishment of the Roman republic. The legend of Tarquinius was often invoked in early modern literature to explain the ancient Romans' fierce rejection of monarchy as a form of government.

67. On the spur of the moment.

68. The existence or the good.

69. A metaphor drawn from early modern cosmology. Newstead compares straying from his topic to a planet straying from its course.

70. To tether or fasten.

71. <*Osorius lib. de Christi Nobilit.*> Jerónimo Osório (1506–80), bishop of Silves, wrote *De Nobilitate Civile et Christiana,* which was translated from the Latin into English by William Blandie in 1576. An exemplary prelate, learned scholar, and critic, Osorio gained a European reputation by writing in Latin. His style was so excellent that he was called "the Portuguese Cicero."

72. <Hall.> <*Fox lib. de Mar.*> St. Matilda (897–968), queen of Germany and wife of King Henry I, built and supported many churches and monasteries and lived a life of holy contemplation. St. Brigid of Sweden (1302?–73) founded a monastery for women and protested against abuses in the church, as did St. Hildegard, a Benedictine nun known as Hildegard de Bingen (1098–1179), who prophesized the corruption of the friars and the destruction of the church of Rome. John Foxe discusses St. Hildegard in volume 3 of *The Acts and Monuments of John Foxe* ([New York: AMS Press, 1965], 87–88); Edward Hall does not mention these women in *Hall's Chronicles* (London: J. Johnson, 1809), reprinted from the 1548 edition, entitled *The Union of the Two Noble and Illustre Famelies of Lancastre and Yorke, etc.*

73. Widowed at age thirty-two, St. Paula (347–404) dedicated her life to Christ. She settled in Bethlehem, where she built three monasteries and, with her daughter, helped St. Jerome translate the Bible from Hebrew into Latin.

74. St. Apollonia, martyred in Alexandria in 248, was a holy virgin persecuted by heathens who, after breaking her teeth, threatened to throw her into the fire if she did not speak unholy words. Instead, she flung herself into the fire. "Culunary" refers to a culinary or kitchen fire.

75. St. Ursula, a legendary saint said to have lived between the third and fifth centuries. Although she had dedicated herself to Christ, the son of the king of England desired to marry her and she agreed on the condition that he give her 11,000 virgins, wait three years, and convert to Christianity. After the virgins sailed on a pilgrimage to Rome, two German army commanders, fearing that the women would return and convert the German people to Christianity, asked the king of the Huns to massacre them, which he instructed his men to do.

76. <*Horatius*> "What are the shoulders able to bear?" (Horace, *Ars Poetica,* 40, which has "umeri" instead of "humeri").

77. <*Hom. ad Ili. lib.*2.> Homer, *Iliad* (Loeb Classical Library, 1999): "Not even if I should have ten tongues in ten bodies" (2).

78. In Greek mythology, Briarus was a Titan with one hundred hands.

79. Labeo was one of the members of the conspiracy that murderered Julius Caesar. He committed suicide after the battle of Philippi (42 B.C.E.). Newstead's implication is that had Caesar not been so renowned, Labeo (and others) would not have assassinated him.

80. Aristotle. This definition of continence is central to book 7 of *Nicomachean Ethics.* <*Aristo. Ethi. lib.*7. *cap.*I.>

81. Marcus Salvius Otho (32–69 C.E.), briefly acclaimed emperor of Rome in 69 after organizing a conspiracy among the Praetorians. He commited suicide after his defeat by Vitellius. It was said that nothing in his life became him so well as his manner of leaving it. <*Ausoni. hoc solum fecit nobile quod periit.*> That which has passed away, he made this alone noble. Decimus Magnus Ausonius, a Roman poet, was consul in 379.

82. "At whatever point you leave off living, provided you leave off nobly, your life is a whole" (Seneca, *Epistles,* 77.4.3, which has "ubicumque" instead of "ubicunq").

83. Sexual desires (derived from "Venus").

84. This seems to be Newstead's coinage for "misogynist" (i.e., misogynian). In the anonymous play *Swetnam, The Woman-hater, Arraigned by Women* (1620), Joseph Swetnam's alias is Misogynos, the woman-hater.

85. See Aristotle's *Parts of Animals* (Loeb Classical Library, 1993).

86. Principle or basic humor.

87. In humoral science, the four elements combine the qualities of temperature and moisture: air is hot and moist, fire is hot and dry, water is cold and moist, and earth is cold and dry. The bodily humor of fluid corresponding to air was thought to be blood, which was of all the humors the most hot and moist. A preponderance of blood in one's humoral makeup would result in a sanguine temperament, which was often said to be the best of the four temperaments as it was associated with physical vitality and a cheerful disposition. Women were believed to be colder and dryer than men in their humoral makeup. See Aristotle's *Parts of Animals,* bk. 2.

88. <*Tulli. de Oratore li.*I.> In 63 B.C.E. the Roman orator Cicero successfully defended Lucius Licinius Murena from charges of electoral malpractice. Cicero praises Murena's military service in Asia in his oration "Pro Murena" (in *The Making of an Orator,* 20): "In this command he led an army . . . crossed the face of that Asia of yours, so crammed with wealth and luxury, and yet left behind in it not a trace of acquisitiveness or of extravagant living" (20). Murena became consul the following year.

89. Specifically Asia Minor (the area where Murena served in the army), but figuratively the East in general. Asia is conceived here, as it often is in Western culture, as a land of effeminate pleasures and moral laxity.

90. All of Seneca's epistles are addressed to Lucilius, a Roman knight. No mention is made of Levanus. The phrase is misquoted from Seneca's *Epistle:* "Hoc multo fortius est, ebrio ac vomitante populo siccum ac obrium esse" (18.4.2).

91. This contradicts Newstead's statement at the beginning of chapter 1: "who alwayes makes examples his Copie, shall many times erre from the rules of discretion." See n. 29.

92. Cicero, in *The Making of an Orator,* says the opposite: "Habet autem ut in aetatibus" ("Antiquity does not carry authority in the precedents it furnishes") (169.4).

93. <*Sen. Epis.*18.> Misquoted from Seneca's *Epistles:* "Atque consilium futuri ex praeterito venit" (83.2.6, not 18).

94. Lucretia, a legendary Roman matron, was renowned for her chastity, which was

said to have inflamed the lust of Sextus Tarquinius (see n. 66), the last of the Roman kings. Coming to her house as a guest, Tarquinius raped Lucretia at swordpoint. After informing her husband and father of the deed, she killed herself with a dagger to regain her lost honor. In the early modern period, Lucretia was considered the epitome of wifely virtue and chastity in marriage, and her suicide was seen as exemplary feminine behavior. The story of Tarquinius and Lucretia is related in Livy, *History of Rome* (Loeb Classical Library, 1998), 1.58. Shakespeare commemorates Lucretia in *The Rape of Lucrece* (1594).

95. <*Livi. Deca.*12.> Misquoted from Livy's *History of Rome:* "Quid enim salvi est mulieri amissa pudicitia" (1.58.7.3–4).

96. The "Romane Lady" is Bilia, wife of Gaius Duilius, a Roman commander who defeated the Carthaginians in 260 B.C.E. When he was rebuked by another man in a quarrel for having bad breath, he blamed his wife for failing to tell him. She replied that she thought all men had bad breath. In *Against Jovinianus,* in *The Principal Works of St. Jerome,* trans. W. H. Freemantle, vol. 6 (Oxford: James Perker and Co., 1893), St. Jerome, author of the Vulgate translation of the Bible into Latin, cites Bilia as a model of chastity (1.46). Juan Luis Vives, in *A Very Fruteful and Pleasant Boke Callyd the Instruction of a Christen Woman,* trans. Richard Hyrd (London, 1540), also praises her (g4v–h1r).

97. St. Jerome's *Against Jovinianus:* "Nicanor having conquerored and overthrown Thebes was himself overcome by a passion for one captive virgin, whose voluntary self-surrender he longed for. A captive maid, he thought, must be only too glad. But he found that virginity is dearer to the pure in heart than a kingdom, when with tears and grief he held her in his arms slain by her own hand" (1.41). Vives also mentions her (*Instruction of a Christian Woman,* M4r–v). Once again the maiden remains nameless.

98. A popular legend maintained that Matilda, daughter of Lord Robert Fitzwalter, was wooed by King John after her father was banished for his involvement in a seditious plot against the king. She is said to have resisted the king's blandishments and entered a convent in her native town of Dunmow, eventually becoming a nun. In 1619 Michael Drayton included an imagined exchange of letters between John and Matilda in his collection of poems *England's Heroical Epistles.* <*Speed Chron.*> Matilda is not mentioned in John Speed's *History of Great Britain* (1611).

99. In Greek mythology, Oreithyia, daughter of Praxithea and Erechtheus, king of Athens, was taken against her will by Thracian Boreas, god of the North Wind, while dancing by Ilissus's stream. Here, she is an emblematic figure for a chaste virgin. Carneades was an Athenian Sceptic philosopher (214–129 B.C.E.) who founded the New or Third Academy and was an outspoken critic of dogmatic schools of thought, especially the Stoics. Newstead is saying that there are many more chaste women than chaste men.

100. Probably a reference to a priestess at Delphi who was a friend of Plutarch, who addressed his treatise *Mulierum Virtutes* (On the bravery of women) to her, as well as his essay on Isis and Osiris. Socrates (ca. 469–399 B.C.E.), the Athenian teacher and

philosopher, was considered a model of sexual continence in the early modern period, largely because of a speech by Plato in which Alcibiades, renowned for his physical beauty and eager to have sexual relations with Socrates, relates how Socrates lay with him wrapped in the same blanket all night. In the morning Alcibiades "arose as from the couch of a father or brother" (*Symposium,* in *Plato* [Loeb Classical Library, 1925], 219b–d).

101. Caligula, Roman emperor from 37 to 41 C.E., was renowned for his depravity. By all accounts a vicious psychotic, he is said to have committed incest with all three of his sisters. Valeria Messalina, the third wife of Roman emperor Claudius, was notorious for her avarice and ambition. She was executed in 48 C.E. for committing adultery. In the early modern period, "Messalina" was a type of sexually insatiable woman. See Juvenal, *Satire,* 10.329. Newstead is saying that there are many more depraved men than depraved women.

102. Tiberius, Roman emperor from 14 to 37 C.E., following Augustus Caesar, began his reign as a moderate, even modest ruler. But according to Suetonius, he spent the last years of his life in seclusion on the island of Capri indulging in all manner of vices. The contrast between his sober youth and his "incontinent" old age was legendary in the early modern period. Livia Drusilla (58 B.C.E.–29 C.E.) was the wife of Tiberius Claudius Nero until Augustus compelled her husband to divorce her and then married her himself. She was suspected of committing various crimes to secure the throne for her son.

103. Newstead could have been thinking of Seneca's *On Mercy,* in *Moral Essays* (Loeb Classical Library, 1998): "Facit enim consuetudinem peccandi multitudo peccantium" ("for sin becomes familiar from the multitude of those who sin") (1.22.2.3); or of Seneca's *On Benefits:* "pudorem enim rei tollet multitudo peccantium" ("for the multitude of the offenders will remove the shame of the thing") (3.16.1.5).

104. <*Hall.*> See nn. 37, 72.

105. In Greek mythology, Jove, who was the king of the gods, was notorious for his habit of raping nymphs and mortal women. Jo, a maiden he raped, was turned into a white cow to hide the crime from his wife, Hera. Cato the Younger (see n. 49) lent his second wife, Marcia, to Hortensius. Newstead is illustrating the double standard by which women are blamed for sexual impropriety.

106. <*Juvena. Sat.*> Misquoted from Juvenal's *Satires:* "Ille crucem sceleris pretium tulit, hic diadema" ("One man gets a gibbet, another a crown, as the reward of crime") (13.105).

107. <Drayton Poet.> Michael Drayton (1563–1631) wrote *Poly-Olbion* (1612 [pt. 1], 1622 [pt. 2]), a poetic survey of England and its history, as well as pastorals, Petrarchan sonnets, and odes modeled on those by Horace. Ovid (?43 B.C.E.–17 C.E.) was a celebrated Roman poet known for *Metamorphoses, De Remedis Amoris,* and *Tristia,* among other works. These three couplets are misquoted from "Alice Countess of Salisbury, to the Black Prince" (ll. 33–34, 41–42, 65–66), in Drayton's *Englands Heroical Epistles* (London, 1599), a collection of imagined correspondence between famous English lovers. "Alice Countess of Salisbury, to the Black Prince" is from the first of three

groups on attempted seduction by royalty. Newstead has changed "your" and "you" to "their" and "they."

108. <*Incontinem semi-malus Arist. Ethi-l.7. Continentia melior Tem. Arist. Ethi. l.7.*> Newstead puns on "male" and the Latin *male* (evil). In book 7 of *Nicomachean Ethics,* Aristotle discusses imperfect and perfect self-control, but he concerns himself only with men.

109. <*Sene Epis.*> Misquoted from Seneca's *Epistles* (52.4.7–9), which has "enim ad eundam" instead of "aeundem" and "effecisse" instead of "efficere."

110. <*Livi. deca.*> Gaius Laelius fought under Scipio Africanus Major in his campaigns against the Numidian king Syphax. After Syphax was defeated by the Romans in 203 B.C.E., the entreaties of Sophoniba, the wife of Syphax, won the heart of General Masinissa, described by Newstead as Laelius's "friend." To save Sophoniba from death by the Romans, Masinissa married her. Laelius disapproved, as did Scipio, who told Masinissa that conquering his affection for Sophoniba would represent a greater victory than his defeat of Syphax. Masinissa thus abandoned his new wife, who willingly drank the poison he gave to her rather than submit to the ignominy of captivity. See Livy, *Historiae Romanae Decades,* 30.12–15.

111. See Livy, *Historiae Romanae Decades,* 30.3–15. Newstead is paraphrasing here.

112. <*Sen.ca.*16.> Misquoted from Seneca's *To Marcia on Consolation,* in volume 2 of *Moral Essays* (Loeb Classical Library, 1996): "Quis autem dixit naturam maligne cum mulierum ingeniis egisse et virtutes illarum in artum retrax isse? Par illis, mihi crede, vigor, par ad honesta, libeat, facultas est; dolorem laboremque ex aequo, si consuevere, patiuntur" ("But who has asserted that Nature has dealt grudgingly with women's natures and has narrowly restricted their virtues? Believe me, they have just as much force, just as much capacity, if they like, for virtuous action; they are just as able to endure suffering and toil when they are accustomed to them") (16).

113. A race of female warriors believed to inhabit the borders of the known world. Amazons were said to amputate their right breasts to improve their fighting abilities. In Amazonian society, all household tasks were done by male slaves, and the Amazons were said to kill, cripple, or abandon their male children, keeping only the girls. According to Herodotus in *Herodutus* (4.117), an Amazon was not allowed to wed until she had killed a male enemy. Diodorus describes the Amazons in *Didorus of Sicily* (3.53–55).

114. Xerxes was king of Persia from 485 to 465 B.C.E. In 480 he invaded Greece to punish the inhabitants for participating in the Ionian revolt. At first he met with success, but his fleet was eventually destroyed by Themistocles at the naval battle of Salamis and he was forced to retreat to Asia. Artemesia was ruler of part of Caria under Xerxes. She accompanied Xerxes' invasion with five ships, but, according to Herodotus, she urged him not to attack at Salamis. Trapped there by Greek ships, she sank one of her allies' vessels to cut her way out. Believing that she had destroyed a Greek ship, Xerxes (who was watching the battle from the safety of the shore) said, "My men have become women, and my women men" (Herodotus, *Herodutus,* 8.88, incorrectly attributed in the margin—<*Diodorus lib.*20.>—by Newstead). Newstead also does not

mention that Artemesia's valor was directed against her allies. Diodorus describes the battle at Salamis in *Didorus of Sicily* (40.16–18) but does not mention Artemesia.

115. The Cambrians were a German tribe from North Jutland who invaded Gaul and Spain in 110–105 B.C.E. They were defeated by the Roman general Marius in 101 at the battle of Raudian Plain near Verona in northern Italy. <*Florus de Bello Cim.*> Lucius Annaeus Florus recounts in *Epitome of Roman History* (Loeb Classical Library, 1947) how the Cimbrian women, standing on top of a barricade formed of their wagons, fought with axes and pikes. Following their defeat, they killed their infants and each other (some of them hanged themselves with ropes of their own hair) (1.38). Boccaccio, in *Concerning Famous Women* (New Brunswick, N.J.: Rutgers University Press, 1963), tells a version of this story.

116. <*Diodorus de antiqui.*> In Greek mythology, Semiramis was the daughter of the Syrian goddess Derceto; her second husband was Ninus, king of Assyria. After Ninus's death, Semiramis ruled for many years and was famous for her valor in battle and for building Babylon. The historical figure behind this legend is probably Sammuramat, wife of the Assyrian king Shamshi-Adad V. The king of the "Indians" (or India) was Stabrobates. When India was invaded by Semiramis, Stabrobates accused her of being the aggressor and called her a strumpet. Semiramis replied, "It will be in deeds that the Indian will make trial of my valour" (Diodorus, *The Library of History,* 2.18–19). De Pizan writes of Semiramis conquering India in *Le livre de la Cite des Dames.* Here, "renunciated" means "renounced."

117. Boadicea (or Boudicca) was the ancient British queen of the Icenci whose kingdom was seized by the Romans after her husband's death in 59 or 60 C.E. Boudicca led a revolt against Roman rule, sacking London, Colchester, and Verulanium. After her initial success, her forces were defeated and she committed suicide in 60 C.E. by taking poison. <*Cam. Brit.*> William Camden, in his discussion of "Boodicia" in *Britainnia* (London, 1610), writes that "it was custome verily of the Britans to make warre under the conduct of women" (51). <*Tacitus Anna.* 4.> Tacitus relates Boudicca's story in his *Annals* (Loeb Classical Library, 1925–37), 14.31, 35, 37.

118. <*Grim. his Fran.*> Joan of Arc (1412?–31) was a peasant girl from Domremy, France, who at the age of thirteen began to hear saints' voices telling her to deliver France from the English invaders and place the Dauphin, later Charles VII, on the throne. Dressed in armor as a man, she led a French force that raised the seige of Orleans in 1429 and defeated the English at Patay; in the same year, she saw Charles crowned at Rheims. After failing in an attempt to recapture Paris in 1430, she was captured by the English in Rouen and burnt at the stake in early 1431 as a heretic and a witch. Jean de Serres relates the history of Joan of Arc in *A General Inventorie of the History of France,* bk. 54 (1598; trans. Edward Grimeston [London, 1607]). "Bedford" refers to John of Lancaster, Duke of Bedford (1389–1435) and the third son of King Henry IV. He was regent of British territory in France following the death of his brother Henry V in 1422. Although Joan of Arc won her remarkable victories against Bedford's troops, they never actually faced each other in battle. A fictional confrontation be-

tween Joan (La Pucelle) and her men and Bedford with Talbot and Burgundy is staged in Shakespeare's *1 Henry VI,* 3.2.

119. Queen Elizabeth I of England (1533–1603), renowned for her country's defeat of the Spanish Armada in 1588.

120. <*Fren. Hist.*> Blanche of France, Duchess of Orleans (1328–93), posthumous daughter of King Charles IV of France, would have been queen at her birth had French Salic law not forbidden female monarchs. Instead, at the death of Charles in 1328, Philippe of Valois (1293–1350), a cousin, became King Philippe VI of France, setting aside both Charles's daughter and King Edward III of England, the son of Charles's sister. Here, Blanche says that if she had "a pair of [testicles]," she would have been treated better by Philip. De Serres relates Blanche's early history in *A General Inventorie of the History of France.*

121. <*Sene.*> Misquoted from Seneca's *Epistles:* "Corpus quoque, etiam si magnas habet vires, non aliter quam furiosi aut phrenetici validum est" ("[Without philosophy] the body, too, though it may be very powerful, is strong only as that of a madman or a lunatic is strong") (15.1.5).

122. "Great-in-body," from the Greek *mega* (great) and *soma* (body), a coinage not found in the *OED.* Newstead contrasts "megasomity" with "magnanimity" (greatness of spirit).

123. Dishonors. The *OED* has 1663 as the first usage of "dehonestates" as a verb.

124. <*Aelianus Hist.*> Dionysius is mentioned in Aelian's *Historical Miscellany* (Loeb Classical Library, 1997), but there is no reference to his lungs.

125. <*Hom. Il.l.*3.> In Homer's *Iliad* (3.427–36), Helen of Troy complains to Paris, who has stolen her from her first husband, Menelaus, that he is not strong enough to defend her in battle. She does not explicitly mention Hymen, the goddess of marriage.

126. "Laconians" are Spartans. Aelian, in *A registre of hystories,* mentions the courage of the Laconian women on several occasions but does not relate this specific story. "Obscond" means "abscond" (although this spelling is not in the *OED*) or "conceal."

127. <*Fren. hist.*> See n. 118.

128. <*Erasm. Rhet. Apo.*> Probably from Erasmus's *Apophthegmes* (1542).

129. In Greek mythology, Venus, the goddess of love, had an affair with Mars, the god of war. The story traditionally includes a rejection of her crippled husband, Vulcan, rather than of Apollo, the handsome, youthful sun god. Here, Newstead uses Mars and Apollo as emblematic figures of a soldier and a delicate, even effeminate, youth.

130. Perhaps a generic name for women.

131. Reasoning or arguing from effects to causes or from experience and not from axioms; also inductive, empirical.

132. Pliny the Elder, *Natural History* (Loeb Classical Library, 1942): "Marcus Lepidus after divorcing his wife Appuleia died for love of her" (bk. 7, 36.122).

133. Sharpens. According to the *OED,* the first such usage occurred in 1632 in Ben Jonson's *Magnetic Lady* (3.3).

134. The Stone of the Alchemists, or the Philosophers' Stone, which was believed to have the power to transmute base metals to gold.

135. Newstead's argument that friendships are stronger and more lasting between men and women than between men and men is contrary to much of the early modern thought on the subject. Michel de Montaigne states in "Of Friendship" that neither "the ordinary sufficiency of women" nor "their mindes [are] strong enough to endure the pulling of a knot so hard, so fast, and durable" (in *Essayes,* trans. John Florio [London, 1613], bk. 1, 91).

136. The Greek translates as "made of a similar substance" and "made of the same substance."

137. Nero (37–68 C.E.), Roman emperor from 54 to 68, and Otho (32–69 C.E.) were friends and, in their youth, probably lovers, but they were estranged after Nero fell in love with Otho's wife, Poppaea, for whom he killed both his mother, Agrippina, and his first wife. <*Suet.* p. 250> In volume 2, book 7 of *Lives of the Caesars,* Suetonius describes Otho as holding the first place among Nero's friends "because of the similarity of their characters" (219). Newstead cites this as an example of man's ("virall") friendship.

138. Pleasant friendship, true friendship.

139. Helen of Troy's abduction by the Trojan Paris from her husband, Menelaus, sparked the Trojan War. In the early modern period, Helen was often portrayed as a whorish temptress whose beauty led to the death of thousands of men. In Shakespeare's *Troilus and Cressida* (1601–2), Helen is a source of debasement for the Trojans. For Livia, see n. 102. Cleopatra (69–30 B.C.E.) was the ruler of Egypt and consort of both Julius Caesar and Marc Anthony. In the early modern period she was often seen as a lustful gypsy (i.e., Egyptian, although she was probably Macedonian) and an emblematic figure of "oriental" feminine misrule; she was also blamed for "effeminating" Marc Anthony, whose forces she was (probably falsely) accused of deserting at the battle of Actium. Boccaccio states in *Concerning Famous Women* that Cleopatra was "known throughout the world for her greed, cruelty and lustfulness" (192).

140. In Ptolemaic cosmology, stars were seen as fixed in the outermost of the visible heavenly spheres; their movements were thus uniform. The planets were observed to wander in their orbits, a result of the discrepancy between the circular orbits of Ptolemaic theory and the elliptical orbits that planets actually follow.

141. Elissa was another name for Dido, queen of Carthage. Sychaeus was her husband. In the older version of the story, after Sychaeus was murdered by Dido's brother, Pygmalion, Dido built a pyre and leapt into the flames to escape marriage with the king of Libya. In book 4 of Virgil's *Aeneid,* Dido escapes to Libya and founds Carthage. When Aeneas comes to Carthage, Dido falls in love with him. When he leaves, Dido stabs herself and throws herself on her funeral pyre instead of jumping to her death. <*Just. l.* 18.> Justine relates the history of Dido in book 18 of *The Historie of Justine* (London, 1606). In his account there is no Aeneas, and Dido kills herself by stabbing herself first and then jumping into the flames.

142. <*Just.l.*18.> Agathocles (361–289 B.C.E.), tyrant and king of Syracuse, was twice exiled in conflicts with the ruling oligarchy. In book 23 of *The Historie of Justine,* the author relates how Theogona laments leaving her husband, who is about to die; he wants her to go to Egypt because he fears the tyranny of her nephew after his death. The Latin quote is also from book 23 (2.11–12). See M. Juniani Justini, *Epitoma Historianum Philippicanum Pompei Trogi* (Lipsiae in Aedibus: B. G. Teubneri, 1935), 189.

143. <*Diod.*> The Getae were an ancient people of Thracian origin. Diodorus mentions the Getae in *The Library of History* but does not discuss Getae women. In book 4 of *Herodotus,* he tells of the Getae being conquered by the Persians but also does not mention Getae women.

144. <*Diod.*> Probably alludes to some version of the Hindu custom of suttee. In *The Library of History,* Diodorus describes how, among certain Indian peoples, wives were cremated with their recently dead husbands unless they were pregnant. Diodorus explains that the custom was said to have been instituted to reduce the high instance of women poisoning their husbands because they married too young. The alternative to being burned alive was loss of caste status, which Diodorus suggests was seen as far worse. He claims that when a man had more than one wife, the wives would vie with each other for the honor of being burned with the dead husband (19.33–34). See also Jerome, *Against Jovinianus,* 1.44.

145. In *Against Jovinianus,* Jerome states that "Marcia, Cato's younger daughter, on being asked after the loss of her husband why she did not marry again, replied that she could not find a man who wanted her more than her money." When asked what day she would stop grieving for her deceased husband, she replied, "The same that terminates my life" (1.46).

146. This could be Philo Judaeus, the Jewish philosopher (b. ?10 B.C.E.) about whom little is known.

147. The fourth wife of Pompey the Great was Cornelia, daughter of Metellus Scipio. According to Plutarch, she was well versed in music, mathematics, and philosophy. Cornelia witnessed her husband's assassination on the docks at Alexandria, shortly after his defeat, from aboard a galley in the harbor. Pompey's remains were eventually returned to her (*Plutarch's Lives,* vol. 5, "Pompey," 55.80). <*Sen. Trag.*> The tragedian is Seneca; the line, spoken by Clytemnestra, is from *Agamemnon,* in *Seneca's Tragedies* (Loeb Classical Library, 1938), 202.

148. That is, sphere.

149. Obscuring.

150. In the Ptolemaic system of astronomy, the regions beyond the sphere of the moon were thought to be fixed and unchanging.

151. <*Sen. ep.*55.> Seneca's epistle 55 deals with the imagination's ability to bridge distance, not with constancy as such.

152. <*Rick. Rhet.*> In the early modern period, "the Philosopher" referred to Aristotle.

153. "Zodiac" is used metaphorically for "compass" or "range."

154. Gluttony.

155. A dishmonger is someone who carries on a disreputable trade.

156. With many children and productiveness.

157. Athenaeus of Naucratis tells the story of Philoxenus, the son of Eryxis, who wished he had the neck of a crane to enjoy eating more (*Deipnosophists* [Loeb Classical Library, 1927], 1.6).

158. As a man's life has been, so will be his end.

159. A polypus is a cuttlefish or octopus. An ell is the equivalent of forty-five inches.

160. <*Aelian l.*12.> In book 12.23 of Aelian's *Historical Miscellany,* translated by Abraham Fleming in 1576, Sminderides is described as a "sybarite" given to "gluttony" and "belly cheare." He journeyed to Sicyon and brought back with him "a thousande Cookes, a thousande Butchers, a thousand Foulers and a thousand Fishers." Endymion, the son of Zeus, fell in love with Selene, the moon, who bore him fifty daughters. At her request, Zeus caused Endymion to sleep forever, thus enabling him to stay young forever. Selene joins him each night in his cave while he sleeps and has sexual relations with her beloved without awakening him.

161. Nero, renowned in the early modern period for his gluttony, is emblematic of those rulers whose only concern was their own pleasure. Vitellius, briefly emperor in the year 69 C.E., was also notorious for his gluttony. In *Dio's Roman History* (Loeb Classical Library, 1955), Cassius Dio Cocceianus describes Nero as "the slave of his desire" (61.5) and Vitellius as having been "insatiate in gorging himself, and . . . constantly vomiting up what he ate, being nourished by the mere passage of the food" (64.2). The Greek words translate as "dark luxury," "calamities," and "drunkenness." The Latin translates as "Virtue is not enough, for one whose body is considerable."

162. Dexterous, skillful, adroit.

163. Temperament, referring here to the tempering or mixture of the four humours.

164. Ready, smart.

165. Talents.

166. "Prae-wit" probably means one's first response; "post-wit," one's response after deliberation.

167. <*Paterc.* pa. 122.> Cassius was one of the Republican conspirators who assassinated Julius Caesar. At the battle of Philippi, just before the messenger arrived to report that Brutus was victorious, Cassius committed suicide under the mistaken impression that his forces had been defeated (Velleius Paterculus, *Compendium of Roman History,* 2.70). See Shakespeare's *Julius Caesar* (5.3).

168. <*Persius.*> Misquoted from Persius's *Satires,* in *Juvenal and Persius* (Loeb Classical Library, 1940): "Elleborum frustra, cum iam cutis aegra tumebit" ("It is too late to call for hellebore [i.e., medicine] when the skin is already swollen and diseased") (3.63). The couplet that follows in the pamphlet could be construed as a loose translation.

169. The ideas of Socrates, who never actually wrote anything, are set forth by Plato and Xenophon.

170. The Sibyls, who lived in temples, were the female prophets of pagan antiquity. They acted as the mouthpieces of various gods, dispensing advice and delivering oracles.

171. By itself.

172. The Euripus is a narrow strait in the Aegean Sea that separates the island of Euboea from the Greek mainland. The tides of Euripus are remarkably strong, and the name came to be used figuratively for any strong current. Here, the strong current of the Euripus is used to describe Sappho (b. ca. 612 B.C.E.), a female Greek lyric poet whose work was collected into nine books and has survived mostly in fragments. De Pizan, quoting Boccaccio, says that "'Sappho . . . frequented the heights of Mount Parnassus. . . . [and] kept company with the Muses'" (*The Book of the City of Ladies,* trans. Earl Jeffrey Richards [New York: Persea Books, 1982], 1.30.1). Plato termed Sappho "the tenth Muse." <*Aeneas Syl.*> Aeneas Silvius, who became Pius II, wrote in *The Commentaries of Pius II* (trans. Florence Alden Gragg [Northampton, Mass.: Smith College Press, 1957]) that Sappho was "an extraordinary woman and most accomplished poet whose equal has never been seen during all the centuries since" (10.634).

173. Marcus Tullius Cicero (106–43 B.C.E.), a Roman statesman and orator, had a daughter named Tullia (ca. 79–45 B.C.E.) of whom he was very fond. Upon her death, he wrote the treatise *De Consolatione,* which has since been lost. Q. Caecilius Metellus Nepos, a member of Pompey's party in Rome, served as tribune in 62 B.C.E. and in that office violently opposed Cicero, whom he prevented from addressing the people on the final day of his consulship, as was traditional. "In scurrility" refers to a coarse jesting manner.

174. <*Aelia.l.7.*> Alienus tells this story in book 7 of *Historical Miscellany.* See also n. 116.

175. Predisposed to gourmandizing or eating excessively.

176. <*Lab. in Juve.*> Juvenal speaks of gourmandizing in satire 11, "Extravagance and Simplicity of Living."

177. Perhaps Newstead is referring to Shakespeare *Love's Labour's Lost* (1594–95): "Fat paunches have lean pates, and dainty bits / Make rich the ribs, but bankrout quite the wits" (1.1.26–27). In a chapter entitled "Whether the internall faculty may bee knowne by the externall phisiognomy and visage" in *The Optick Glasse of Humors* (London, 1607), Thomas Walkington cites Newstead's lines exactly and attributes them to "a moderne english poet of good note" (3.22). *The Optick Glasse* is considered a predecessor to Robert Burton's *Anatomy of Melancholy* (1621).

178. <*Mag. in Aris. l.3.*> Aristotle does not discuss wit and wisdom in volume 18 of *Magna Moralia* (Loeb Classical Library, 1997), but in book 5 of *Nicomachean Ethics* he defines wisdom as scientific knowledge and intuitive intelligence (7.5).

179. Its.

180. Economical (i.e., a reference to the management of a household as opposed to the management of a state).

181. They reign, they reign.

182. That is, prudence in political or public affairs.

183. In book 1 of *Politics* (Loeb Classical Library, 1932), Aristotle says that those who think there is no difference between a large household and a small city are wrong: there is a difference in kind between the master of a family and a statesman (2).

184. See n. 6. In William Goddard's *Satirycall Dialogue; or, A Sharplye-invective con-*

ference, betweene Allexander the great, and that truelye woman-hater Diogynes (Low Countries, 1616), Diogenes says, "Vertue in women is as cold as Ice: / Nothinge is warme in them unlest' be vice" (C1r).

185. <*Diod.l.*18.> Antipater (397–319 B.C.E.) was a Macedonian general under Philip II and governor of Macedon under Alexander the Great. After Alexander's death he defeated the rebellion of the Greek cities. Antipater's daughter Phila was reputed to have been "of exceptional sagacity," and it is said that her father conferred with her "about the most important matters when she was still a child" (Diodorus, *The Library of History*, 19.59). Tanaquil was the wife of the Roman king Tarquinius Priscus, said to have lived from 616 to 579 B.C.E. After the king's murder, Tanaquil secured the succession for her son-in-law Servius Tullius. <*Liv. De.*3.> Livy tells her story in *Historiae Romanae Decades* (1.34).

186. <*Tac. Ann. l.*6> Agrippina, the granddaughter of Caesar, wife of Germanicus, and mother of Caligula, lived from ca. 14 B.C.E. to 33 C.E. Her part in calming a rebellion of her husband's legionaries is related by Tacitus in his *Annals* (1.40–43). Agrippina's tears shamed the soldiers and made them reconsider their actions, but according to Tacitus it was Germanicus, not his wife, whose speech finally ended the revolt. Tacitus quotes Pliny to tell how Agrippina prevented the demolition of the Rhine bridge by her words (*Annals*, 1.49). Seneca's mother was named Helvia.

187. Armenia is a region of Asia between Asia Minor and the Caspian Sea that includes the source of the Tigris and Euphrates rivers. King Artaxias of Armenia was deposed by his subjects in 20 B.C.E., and shortly thereafter the region was assimilated into the Roman Empire. Tacitus relates that in the confusion that resulted in Rome's attempt to control the region, the Armenians chose for their ruler Queen Erato, wife of a previous king, who reigned only briefly (*Annals*, 2.4). <*Diodorus*> Diodorus describes how Semiramis quarried a stone that was 130 feet long and 25 feet thick and wide from the mountains of Armenia and had it hauled to Babylonia to be set up as an obelisk (*The Library of History*, 2.11.4–5).

188. <*Sen. ep.* 42.> Seneca's *Epistle:* "Multorum, quia inbecilla sunt, latent vitia" ("In the case of many men, their vices, being powerless, escape notice") (42.3).

189. Celestial virtue cannot be distinguished from ignorance.

190. Newstead may have been thinking of Seneca's *Epistle:* "quae saepe generosos atque acerrimae indolis viros corripit" ("this often seizes upon the noblest and most spirited men") (24.25.4).

191. Belief, tenet.

192. The Stoics were adherents of a philosophy, first expounded ca. 300 B.C.E. by Zeno of Citium in Athens, that stresses virtue as the highest good and inculcates control of the passions and indifference to pleasure, pain, and death. Adherents were called Stoics because they met in the Stoa Poecile, a colonnade near the Agora, to hear their master lecture. Here, "impassionate" means "without passion."

193. <*Diod.l.de Antiq.*>

194. Aristotelians, from Aristotle's habit of walking about (from the Greek *peripatetikos*) in the Lyceum while teaching.

195. But in each respect.

196. Adventitious or not inherent; superficial goods. "Extraficall" does not appear in the *OED.*

197. <*Arist. Eth.* l.2.> In book 2 of *Nicomachean Ethics,* Aristotle is concerned with moral virtue, not beauty ("pulchritude"). In the *Metaphysics,* he states, "in many cases the Good and the Beautiful are the beginning both of knowledge and of motion" (5.1.3).

198. Seneca quotes Virgil's *Aeneid* (5.344): "gratior et pulchro veniens e corpore virtus" ("Worth shows more pleasing in a form that's fair") (*Epistles,* 66.2.2). He also writes that Virgil is wrong: "For virtue needs nothing to set it off" (ibid.). I can find no reference to Plutarch's accusation. The couplet that follows in the pamphlet is a loose translation.

199. Precious stone.

200. <*Gal. de Mor.*> Antonio de Ferrari Galateo (1444–1517) wrote *De morbo articulorum, podagra et morbo gallico* (1494), from which the quote is probably taken.

201. <*Osor. de Glor.*> The quote is probably from Jerónimo Osório's *De Nobilitate Civili et Christiana* (1576). See n. 71. "Concinnity" refers to harmony between parts. The *OED* (s.v. "concinnity") cites John Donne's *Sermons:* "This world a frame of so much harmony, so much concinnity and conveniency."

202. "Accidentall" means "incidental" or "nonessential."

203. Theophrastus (ca. 370–ca. 285 B.C.E.) collaborated with Aristotle and was head of the Lyceum. He wrote many works in the Aristotelian tradition, some of which still survive. Diogenes Laertius describes his life, lists his works, and relates his will in *Lives of the Eminent Philosophers* (1.5.36).

204. <*Laert. vita Car.*> See n. 99. In "The Life of Carneades," in Diogenes Laertius's *Lives of the Eminent Philosophers,* there is no discussion of a kingdom that does not need a guard because it runs without force. The Greek is translated as, "They asked him" (5.19.5).

205. In *Politics* (Loeb Classical Library, 1932), Aristotle is not in favor of good looks determining who should rule (3.7.2–4).

206. <*Diod.l.de Ant.*> May refer to the Catheri (Greek for "pure ones"), who were a sect of extreme ascetics in the south of France in the late twelfth and early thirteenth centuries. The Albigensian Crusade succeeded in suppressing them. The Catheri ordained women. Donne refers to them as "false" puritans (John Donne, *Sermons,* ed. George R. Potter and Evelyn M. Simpson [Berkeley: University of California Press, 1953–62], 1.186–89).

207. <*Sacra miscere profanis. Persius Sat.*> On Juvenal, see n. 19. Newstead imagines that Juvenal would criticize him for defending women by using the erotic material of the Canticles, the Old Testament book also known as the Song of Solomon or the Song of Songs. It is an erotic marriage poem that, in the early modern period, was often interpreted allegorically as an expression of the love of Christ for his bride, the Church. The passage Newstead refers to is, "My love, beholde, ye art faire" (Song of Sol. 1.14). The primus Motor is the first mover (i.e., God). <"Sacra miscere profanis"> "To mix the sacred with the profane"; attributed to Persius (34–62 C.E.), a Stoic satirist (see *Satires,* 5.122).

208. Impregnable to any application of force. Theophrastus called adamant the hardest crystalline gem known; it later became synonymous with the diamond.

209. Refers to outward appearance, the visible image, the immediate object of vision. "Organical sences" refers to the physical senses (i.e., those embodied in an organ). The organical senses were opposed to the intellect. Newstead says the intellect willingly receives those who are beautiful.

210. An instrument of torture usually consisting of a frame with a roller at each end to which the victim was fastened by the wrists and ankles and then stretched. Newstead is saying that he does not need to strain or stretch his argument that women are physically more beautiful than men because this is something the eyes can see.

211. See n. 172.

212. Mirror.

213. Reflect.

214. Virgil, *Eclogues*, 1.25.

215. <*Achil. Tac. lib.*8.> The Greek is from *The Adventures of Leucippe and Clitophon* (8.12.13) in *Achilles Tatius* ([Loeb Classical Library, 1917]) by Achilles Tatius, a Greek writer of romances who lived in the second century C.E. Rhodope took a vow to remain always with Diana and shun the company of men. In anger Venus punished her by making her fall in love with Euthinicus, a youth from Ephesus, who was "as faire amongst men as Rhodope was accounted amongst women" (Loeb ed., 147). Diana retaliated by changing Rodope into a fountain. Newstead's misquoted Greek translates as, "Beautifully among the boys as much as Rodope among the girls." *The Adventures of Leucippe and Clitophon* was first translated into English in 1597.

216. "Crassis" refers to the combination of humors that constitute a state of health. "Temperamentum ad pondus" translates as "moderation with respect to stability of character." The phrase refers to the ideal (and unattainable) body in which all four humors are perfectly balanced.

217. Seeks as much for the substance of fire.

218. I have not been able to identify the author of this quote.

219. Caius Velleius Paterculus, a Roman historian (ca. 19 B.C.E.–ca. 30 C.E.) who served in the legions under Tiberius and wrote a history of Rome in two books. I cannot find a reference to Victinus in Paterculus's *Compendium of Roman History*.

220. "Achilles" may refer not to the well-known hero of Homer's *Iliad* but to the son of Zeus and Queen Lamia, renowned for his godlike beauty (which may well have been transferred to the Greek hero in the early modern period). "Maximus Tirrhus" refers to Maximus of Tyre (ca. 125–185 C.E.), the author of forty-one extant lectures that are eloquent exhortations to virtue.

221. <*Dioge: Laer. in vita cry.*> The cord of society, defined as "pulchritude" or "beauty," is seen here as the force that binds society together. Chrysippus was a Stoic philosopher who lived from ca. 280 to 207 B.C.E. Diogenes Laertius discusses Chrysippus's life and lists the works ascribed to him, one of which is entitled "Of the Good or Morally Beautiful and Pleasure" (*Lives of the Eminent Philosophers*, 7.179). Only fragments of Chrysippus's writing remain. A commixtion is a mixture. For the four elements, see n. 87.

222. <*Sen de Ira l.2. c.9.*> Misquoted from Seneca's *To Novatus on Anger,* in *Moral Essays* (2.19.2), which has "mores" instead of "moris" and "illo" instead of "ullo."

223. Its.

224. The cold humour.

225. Warmth, heat.

226. Plato maintained that wine heated the soul as well as the body (*Timaeus,* in *Plato* [Loeb Classical Library, 1929], 60a). Because the humoral makeup of children and young people was already warmed by the natural heat of youth, he prohibited the drinking of wine by children and suggested that young men should be more careful than old men to drink in moderation (*Laws,* in *Plato* [Loeb Classical Library, 1926], 666a). "The hot Meridean of their age" refers to the prime of life, an age that is associated with summer in humoral theory as well as with noontime, when the sun is at its height. "Califying" refers to calefying or heating.

227. May refer to Marcus Aemilius Lepidus (d. 13 or 12 B.C.E.), triumvir with Mark Antony and Octavian, who lacked the character and energy to use the advantages he was given by his high birth and Caesar's favors. Marcus Aemilius Lepidus was the grandfather of the Marcus Lepidus mentioned in n. 132. Diogenes Laertius supposedly said to him, "'Are you not ashamed . . . to draw a dagger of lead from an ivory scabbard?'" after "noticing a handsome youth chattering in unseemly fashion" (*Lives of the Eminent Philosophers,* 6.65).

228. Momus was the Greek god of ridicule; *momus* is also Latin for "fool"—thus, a foolish critic or buffoon. Apollo was the Greek sun god, emblematic of youthful masculine health and beauty—another example of a person with a body fairer than the mind. Nereus was an ancient Greek sea-god, the father of the Nereids (water nymphs), who was able to prophesy and to change his shape at will. Perhaps Newstead is commenting on the attractiveness of the exterior of the box and the lack of substance or changeableness of the beard within.

229. The first fable in many collected works of Aesop, the legendary Greek author of animal fables who wrote ca. 600 B.C.E. This fable is the tale of a rooster who finds a jewel in a pile of dung. He realizes the jewel is beautiful and valuable, but because he cannot eat it or use it, he leaves it where it is. The jewel, Aesop implies, is his own book of fables; the rooster, the foolish man who sees no application for them. *Aesop's Fables* was translated from the French into English and published by Caxton in 1484.

230. Physical bodies are described as "leaden" because they are made of gross, heavy matter as opposed to the airy nature of the soul or the intellect. Servius Sulpicius Galba was a Roman orator who served as consul in 144 B.C.E. In *The Making of an Orator* (1.53.227), Cicero characterizes Galba as a harsh speaker (1.53) and accuses him of playing on the emotions of his auditors to gain acquittal for his crimes. While disapproving of some of Galba's tactics, Cicero concedes that he "spoke like a god" (1.10.40).

231. Socrates believed that human beings were born with an innate knowledge that could only be brought to consciousness through a constant process of questioning and self-examination. (See n. 100 for more on Socrates.) The last Catholic cardinal of

England was Cardinal Wolsey (ca. 1475–1530), archbishop of York and Henry VIII's chancellor. Wolsey was the son of a butcher from Ipswich, and thus his rise to the highest offices of the English church and state provides a striking example of the industrious cultivation of "golden qualities."

232. Here as elsewhere (see, e.g., n. 163) Newstead uses "temperature" instead of "temperament" (i.e., a person's psychological makeup). He asserts that while a person's temperament (determined by the proportions in which the humors are mixed in the body) may incline her or him to enjoy some things and avoid others, these predispositions can be modified by the force of custom and habit.

233. Bring about (used here as a verb).

234. An epigrammatist is a maker of epigrams, which are short poems that end in a witty turn of thought. A lurdan is a sluggard or a loafer, from the French *lourd* (heavy). The Latin is roughly translated by the verse that follows in the pamphlet.

235. Repugnant, antagonistic, contrary.

236. Superiority.

237. <*Sen. epis.* 10> Misquoted from Seneca's *On Benefits* (4.18.3.1), which has "dominium" instead of "dominum" and "omnium" instead of "dominium" ("Fellowship has given to him dominion over all creatures").

238. Misquoted from Seneca's *Epistles* (25.6.1), which has "persuadet" instead of "persuadit."

239. <*Seneca.*> Crates of Thebes was a Cynic philosopher (ca. 365–285 B.C.E.) and a pupil of Diogenes of Sinope. Because he consoled people in distress and reconciled enemies, he was greatly beloved. "Spaciating" means "strolling." The Latin is from "On Living to Oneself" (*Epistles,* 10.1.8–10), in which Seneca tells his friend Lucilius that he trusts him to be by himself.

240. Q. Caecilius Metellus Macedonicus, a Roman general and consul who died in 115 B.C.E. He was often cited in antiquity as an example of human felicity, for he had honorably fulfilled all the highest offices of the Roman state, triumphed in war, and died at an old age, leaving four adult sons, three of whom had also been elected consul. Metellus Macedonicus should not to be confused with Metellus Nepos (see n. 173).

241. Misquoted from Seneca's *Epistles,* 6.4.8, which has "socio" instead of "societate" ("No good thing is pleasant to possess without friends to share it").

242. Rutilius Rufus (b. ca. 158 B.C.E.), a Roman statesman, historian, and orator. As a legate to the governor in Asia, he attempted to protect the people from tax extortion, which angered the extortionists, who banished him from Rome in 92 B.C.E. Newstead uses Rufus's career as an example of undeserved adversity.

243. The mythical god of the North Wind.

244. A solace from misery.

245. <*Lip. epis.* 62.> Justus Lipsius (1547–1606), a humanist scholar who wrote a treatise on letter writing. The reference is to his *Epistolae,* but not epistle 62. His correlative refers to his wife.

246. From Seneca's *Agamemnon:* "Lacrimas lacrimis miscere iuvat" ("Tis sweet to mingle tears with tears") (664).

247. Helen, who was carried away from her husband, Menelaus, by Paris (which precipitated the Trojan War) could tell Hecuba, who saw her son Hector and her husband, Priam, brutally murdered in the war, that her own grief was less than Hecuba's because Helen was not alone. (See n. 125.) The Latin is quoted from Seneca's *Agamemnon:* "Griefs bring more smart where they wound in solitude" (665).

248. <*Ovidus de Trist.*> Ovid's *Tristia* (Loeb Classical Library, 1988): "'Tis something to lighten with words a fated evil" (5.1.59). Note that Ovid uses "aliquid" instead of "aliquod."

249. Wiping away.

250. <*Sen. Tra. Oedi.*> In Seneca's dramatization of the myth of Oedipus, when Oedipus, king of Thebes, bemoans the troubles that have beset his kingdom, his wife, Jocasta (who unbeknownst to them both is also his mother), comforts him by giving him the following stoic advice: "What boots it, husband, to make woe heavier by lamentation?" (*Oedipus,* in *Seneca's Tragedies,* 81–82). In other words, Oedipus should face his troubles with equanimity. Note that Seneca uses "conjunx" instead of "coniux" and "quaestu" instead of "questu."

251. <*Tacitus Annal.*3. *& Valeri. pro iii, Livi Deca.*> Marcus Valerius Messalinus, a talented orator and legate of Illyrium in 6 C.E. In his *Annals,* Tacitus describes Marcus Valerius Messalinus's attempts to persuade the Romans of the necessity of having women accompany the soldiers on their expeditions (3).

252. Misquoted from Tacitus's *Annals:* "laborem quod honestius quam uxorium levamentum" (3.34.11).

253. <*Sir Philip Sidney.*> The poetry is from the third eclogue of Sidney's *Countess of Pembroke's Arcadia (The Old Arcadia)* (ed. Jean Robertson [Oxford: Clarendon Press, 1973], 263). In the dialogue between old Geron and young Histor, Geron tries to convince Histor to marry. "One eye of Minerva" refers to Sidney, the Elizabethan poet and courtier, often represented after his death as the epitome of courtly grace and eloquence. Minerva, also known as Athena, was the Greco-Roman goddess of wisdom. Thus, to be an eye of Minerva is to be extraordinarily perceptive and intelligent. "Forst" means "forced."

254. <*Euri. Trag.*> A Greek tragedian from Salamis (?485–406 B.C.E.). Of his ninety-two dramas, nineteen survive. He is not known as a supporter of women.

255. <*Pet. de reemr. fortu.*> Petrarch's *De remediis utriusque fortune* is a series of dialogues between joy and reason (book 1) and sorrow and reason (book 2), but reason has little that is positive to say about wives (see n. 13). The Latin *amoene* means "pleasant" or "agreeable."

256. Gemels are twins. Hippocrates discusses twins and why they are alike in *Regimen,* in *Hippocrates* ([Loeb Classical Libary, 1923], 1.30).

257. "Wants," as in "lacks." Newstead refers to the bibical legend that Eve was created from one of Adam's ribs while he slept (Gen. 2.21–24). This notion provides one of the biblical justifications for marriage: because woman comes from man's rib, the sacrament of marriage can reunite the two, making them "one flesh."

258. "He that has no wife beats her often" (Morris Palmer Tilley, *Dictionary of Prov-*

erbs in England in the Sixteenth and Seventeenth Centuries [Ann Arbor: University of Michigan Press, 1950], W357). "Discommend" means "find fault with."

259. Appius Claudius, one of the decemvirs, became enamoured of Virginia. So as to possess her, he ordered that she be taken as a slave. To keep her from being taken, her father, a centurion, stabbed her to death. The story has been told by Livy (*Historiae Romanae Decades,* 3.44–58) and retold by Petrarch in "Beautiful Children" (dialogue 72 in *De remediis utriusque fortune*) and by Geoffrey Chaucer (*The Doctor's Tale* [1477].

260. Dispraise.

261. We too suffer the tedium of the present the desire for the future.

262. <*Tull. orat.*> Terentia was Cicero's first wife, a woman who supposedly had great influence over him. He divorced her in 48 B.C.E., after thirty years of marriage, in order to marry the young Publilia, from whom he was almost immediately divorced. In *Letter to Atticus* (Loeb Classical Library, 1999), Cicero says that Atticus has exhorted him to hide the depth of his grief for Terentia (15 Mar. 45 B.C.E., letter 258 [12.20]).

263. Eliciting from a condition of potentiality.

264. Leading a person by persuasion.

265. He withdrew well. "Decessus" means "death."

266. Oh, sadness.

267. Bring ruin upon, destroy.

268. The pelican was popularly believed to peck its own breast to draw forth blood to feed its young and was thus commonly used to suggest parental self-sacrifice.

269. <*Livi.*> Probably refers to Servius Tullius, a child whom Tanaquil and her husband, the fifth king of Rome, raised as their own after flames were seen bursting from his head as he slept. He later married their daughter. Tanaquil's actions upon her husband's death secured the throne for Servius (Livy, *Historiae Romanae Decades,* 1.39). See also n. 185.

270. The Gracchi—Tiberius Gracchus (163–133 B.C.E.) and his brother, Gaius Gracchus (153–121 B.C.E.)—were orators who both held the office of tribune in Republican Rome. They were assassinated in response to their sustained agitation for land reform to benefit small farmers. Their mother, Cornelia (Scipio's daughter), is praised by Plutarch for her wisdom. He attributes both sons' education and love of virtue to her careful upbringing. See "Tiberius and Caius Gracchus," in *Plutarch's Lives* (Loeb Classical Library, 1921), 10:1.

271. <*Sueto.*> This tradition is not mentioned by Plutarch or by Suetonius in *Lives of the Caesars.* In *A Dialogue on Oratory* (Loeb Classical Library, 1963), Tacitus speaks of "the good old days" when "every man's son . . . was brought up not in the chamber of some hireling nurse, but in his mother's lap, and at her knee" (28). He cites Cornelia (mother of the Gracchi), Aurelia (mother of Caesar), and Atia (mother of Augustus) and concludes, "thus it was that these mothers trained their princely children" (28).

272. Socrates is not traditionally identified with an eagle, but eagles were renowned for their natural nobility, courage, and keen perception—all qualities for which Soc-

rates is famous. In Plato's *Symposium,* Socrates relates how Diotima, "a woman who was deeply versed . . . in many fields of knowledge," taught him the true philosophy of love (201d).

273. <*Sen. ad Hel.*> When C. Aurellus Cotta was exiled, his mother, Rutilia, followed him because she preferred her own exile to losing him. When he died, she let him go bravely, and no one saw her cry. The quote is from Seneca's *To Helvia His Mother on Consolation,* in volume 2 of *Moral Essays* (16.7).

274. <*Petrar. de Mater*> Newstead is probably referring to Petrarch's *De Viris Illustribus* (1338–39), which included twenty-three illustrious men of Rome in its first version, or to *Rerum Memorandum Libri* (1343–45), an unfinished work that illustrates the seven cardinal virtues through stories of Greek, Roman, and contemporary subjects.

275. In Greek mythology, Niobe, daughter of Tantalus and wife of Amphion, king of Thebes, was inordinately proud of her twelve children (six sons and six daughters). Carried away by pride, she chided Leto, the mother of Apollo and Diana, for having only two children. To avenge Niobe's insult, Apollo and Diana killed all of Niobe's children. Niobe's lamentation became legendary: she was inconsolable and could not stop weeping, even after she was transformed into a stone by grief. Satyrus was an Athenian actor who supposedly taught Demosthenes, the renowned orator (384–322 B.C.E.), how to give his words greater effect by accompanying them with appopriate sentiment and actions (see "Demosthenes," in volume 7 of *Plutarch's Lives* [Loeb Classical Library, 1928]). Here, these two very different figures are used by Newstead as examples of the passionate expression of emotion.

276. When Pallas Athene, disguised as Ulysses' friend Mentas, appears to Telemachus, she asks him if he is the son of Ulysses. He replies, "My mother, certaine, sayes I am his sonne" (Homer, *The Iliads of Homer Prince of Poets,* trans. George Chapman [London, 1611?], 1.206–16). The Latin quote is not from the Latin translation of the *Odyssey, Latin and Greek* (trans. Henry Stephano [Cambridge, 1664]).

277. "Everyone loves their own privileges," although Newstead's translation makes more sense in the context.

278. In *Nicomachean Ethics,* Aristotle says that "one does not owe to one's father the same honor as to one's mother, nor yet the honor due to a great philosopher or general, but one owes to one's father the honor appropriate to a father, and to one's mother that appropriate to her" (9.2). <*Mag. in Arist.l.*8.*c.*12> In Aristotle's *Magna Moralia* there is no mention of the honor due one's parents; there is, however, a discussion of why a father loves his son more than a son loves his father (2.12.1). A geometric proportion is a series in which the ratio between successive terms is constant (e.g., 1, 3, 9, 27, 81, . . .) an arithmetic proportion is a series in which the difference between successive terms is constant (e.g., 1, 3, 5, 7, 9, . . .).

279. A loadstone is a magnet. "Obdure" means "obdurate" or "hard-hearted."

280. Whatever I have accomplished, it is worth less than a mother's kindness. <*Sen. de Ben.*> A reference to Seneca's *On Benefits:* "Quidquid praestiti patri, etiam si magnus est, infra aestimationem pars meneris est" ("Whatever I have done for my father, how great soever it be, it is nothing to be esteemed in respect of the benefit he had done for me, for I had not been, had he not begotten me") (3.30.1.2).

281. A ball of thread used to guide oneself (or "thread" one's way) into or out of a labyrinth. This refers figuratively to Newstead's final gathering of the threads of his discourse.

282. Affecting.

283. <*Petrar. de Mater.*> Although Petrarch's best-known poems are in Italian, he wrote two volumes of poetry in Latin: *Bucolicum Carmen* and *Epistolae Metricae.* His fifth eclogue, "The Shepherds' Filial Piety," speaks of the devotion due to mothers.

284. Catastrophe, or a final event or conclusion; used here without its negative connotations.

285. <*Diod. l. Ant.*> See n. 206.

286. According to Diodorus, in Egypt it was "ordained that the queen should have greater power and honour than the king and that among private persons the wife should enjoy authority over her husband, the husbands agreeing in the marriage contract that they will be obedient in all things to their wives" (*The Library of History,* 1.27.2.). According to Herodotus, in Lycia, a mountainous country in the southwest of Asia Minor, "they take their names not from their fathers but from their mothers" (*Herodotus,* 91.173.).

287. Lacedemonian women were considered as courageous as the men. Supposedly, the women would drag all the old bachelors around the altars and beat them with their fists to induce them to marry. Perhaps Newstead is being ironic here. <*Tac. de Mor. Ger.*> In *Germania (Dialogus de Oratoribus)* (Loeb Classical Library, 1963), Tacitus says that among the German tribes the husband, not the wife, provided the dowry of items such as oxen, a horse and bridle, a shield, and a spear or sword. The woman brought a piece of armor to her marriage (18).

288. In *Republic* (Loeb Classical Library, 1946), Plato does not speak of the family but does state that some women, as well as some men, have the qualities to be guardians (or rulers) even though a woman's nature is weaker than a man's (5.5).

289. Musaeus Grammaticus, a Greek epic poet of the (possibly) late fifth century C.E., wrote *On the Love of Hero and Leander,* which influenced Christopher Marlowe's *Hero and Leander.* Hero was a legendary priestess of Aphrodite from Sestos. Her young lover Leander nightly swam the Hellespont—the strait separating Europe from Asia—to be with her. One winter night he drowned in a storm, and after finding his body the following day "flayed by the tiderocks" at the foot of her tower, Hero killed herself by jumping from the tower into the same waters in which he had drowned.

290. On Cato and Scipio, see nn. 49 and 48, respectively. In Virgil's *Aeneid,* Achates is the faithful companion of the hero Aeneas. "Fides Achates" (faithful Achates) was the epitome of friendship and constancy in the early modern period.

291. A sucket (or succade) is a piece of candied fruit. "Marmulade and sucket" probably refers to a sweet style of writing or expression.

292. "Cordial" refers to something that is restorative or comforting to the heart. Nepenthe is a drug of Egyptian origin that was capable of banishing sorrow from the mind of the person who took it.

293. See n. 268.

294. <*Festus hist. Rom. init.*> Rufus Festus was the author of *Breviarum Rerum*

Gestarum Populi Romani (published in English as *The Brevarium of Festus: A Critical Edition with Historical Commentary by J. W. Eadie* [London: Athlone Press, 1967]), an abridged version of Roman history written in ca. 369 C.E. and dedicated to the emperor Valens. The quote is from book 1: "res gestas signado, no eloquar" (p. 45, l. 4). The Latin that appears in Newstead's pamphlet is more precisely translated as, "I have indicated the things that were done, not described them in detail." Perhaps a sexual innuendo?

295. <*Lubin in Juve.*> See n. 229. Aesop is believed to have been a slave in his youth. Many written collections attributed to him were published in the early modern period. Solon (638–558 B.C.E.), the Athenian legislator and poet, rewrote the Athenian constitution and promulgated the Athenian code of law. A version of Aesop's advice to Solon is reported by Plutarch ("Solon," volume 1 in *Plutarch's Lives,* 28.1–4), not by Juvenal. According to Plutarch, Aesop said to Solon, "our converse with kings should be either as rare, or as pleasing as is possible" (28.1).

296. The quote is from Seneca's *Epistles,* 119.7.3. The Latin is more precisely translated as, "That which is adequate is never enough." Self-important critics were sometimes imagined as swelling with pride as a toad or bullfrog swells with air. Pricking a toad was thus used as a metaphor for deflating a pompous speaker.

3 "That it is not lawfull for a husband to beat his wife": William Heale's Pamphlet against Wife Beating

WILLIAM Heale wrote *An Apologie For Women* in response to the statement, made on 11 July 1608 during the Comita disputation required of all candidates for the Doctor of Civil Law degree at Oxford University, that "it was lawfull for husbands to beate their wives." Although the text of the disputation has been lost, the title page of Heale's pamphlet reveals that the disputant was a "Mr. Dr. G.," who was either Thomas Gwin, a doctoral candidate, or William Gager, a well-known Latin playwright.[1] As chaplain-fellow of Exeter College, Heale may have been among those who attended the Comita, and he may have written his rebuttal based on what he heard, rather than his reading of the printed disputation.

An Apologie For Women was published in 1609 by Joseph Barnes, the printer for Oxford University. It is dedicated to "the Ladie M.H.," who, according to Heale, urged him to write quickly on the unlawfulness of wife beating. He assures her, "madam, your commaunde is effected" but claims that her "Honors importunity of hast" and "the shallownes of [his] conceipt" make his treatise weaker than he would have liked. If M.H. was Lady Margaret Hele of Wenbury, in Devon, as Franklin B. Williams believes,[2] then Heale was not the only writer to publish quickly at her insistence. Samuel Hieron's *Life and Death Of Dorcas* (1612) and *Three Sermons, Full of Necessarie Advertisements and Gracious Comforts* (1619) and John Barlow's *Hierons last Fare-well* (1618) were all dedicated to Lady Hele, and Hieron in particular mentions her impatience.[3]

Not much is known of William Heale's life. He was born about 1581 in South Heal in the county of Devon, graduated in 1603 from Exeter College, Oxford, with a B.A., and received an M.A. from Broadgates Hall, Oxford, in 1606. He entered holy orders and was appointed chaplain-fellow of Exeter

College in 1608 but was expelled in 1610 "for absence." He became vicar of Bishopsteignton, Devon, in 1610 and vicar of Rattery, Devon, in 1620, where he served until his death in 1627. There is no record of his being married. Anthony à Wood states that Heale was "a zealous maintainer of the honour of the female sex" and "was always esteemed an ingenious man, but weak, as being too much devoted to the female sex."[4]

Wife beating was not only legal but relatively common in early modern England, although it was discouraged by most writers of marriage conduct books and sermons. In *The Lawes Resolutions of Womens Rights; or, The Lawes Provision for Woemen,* the author (given only as T.E.) quotes Justice Brooke: "if a man beat an out-law, a traitor, a Pagan, his villein [servant], or his wife it is dispunishable, because by the Law Common these persons can have no action: God send Gentle-women better sport, or better companie." But T.E. also cites Anthony Fitzherbert, who claims that a woman may "'sue out of Chancery to compell him [her husband] to finde surety of honest behaviour toward her'" if he threatens to beat or kill her. The chapter, which is entitled "The Baron [husband] may beate his Wife," concludes with the claim that an abused wife is not at a great disadvantage because she can retaliate by beating her husband, and he may take no action against her for doing so.[5] In *Church Courts, Sex, and Marriage in England, 1570–1640,* Martin Ingram states that according to seventeenth-century common law, a husband had the right to beat his wife but an abused wife could seek redress in the church courts if the abuse threatened her well-being or her life. There were, according to Ingram, many cases of "ferocious wife-beating."[6] According to Sara Mendelson and Patricia Crawford in *Women in Early Modern England, 1550–1720,* violence against wives often occurred in public, with neighbors—usually other women—interfering if it became life-threatening. Sometimes husbands castigated their wives in public because they disagreed with their wives' behavior and wanted to gain sympathy for their actions. Such behavior indicated a high tolerance for beating wives who did not submit to their husbands' will.[7]

In early modern marriage conduct books, wives are advised to submit to their husbands, and husbands are advised, as the "lords of the house," to keep order by rebuking and controlling their wives. Most marriage books, however, do not condone wife beating. For example, the *Homily of the State of Matrimony* (1563) states that St. Peter was against wife beating: "'For honest natures will sooner be retained to do their duty rather by gentle words than by stripes.'" In other words, "'I mean not that a man should beat his wife. God forbid that, for that is the greatest shame that can be, not so much to her that is beaten, as to him that doeth the deed.'"[8] William Whately, in *A Bride-Bush; or, A Wedding Sermon,* warns: "If thou be an husband, and wouldest bee regarded, tumble not thy selfe in those foule, dirty and stinking guzzels of passionate rayling, stryking, or the like." In a later edition he adds, "But if necessitie inforce a man to strike, because both the faults committed by his wife, be in their matter hainous and unsufferable, & her manner of committing, presumptuous and wilfull, so that other meanes have in vaine been used to her amendment; yet in such sort also must he strike her, as if he were faine to strike his owne heart."[9] William Gouge, in *Of Domesticall Duties,* advises husbands to seek a magistrate before striking their wives: "If the case so stand as a wife must needs be beaten, it is fitter for an husband to referre the matter to a publike Magistrate (who is as an approved and licensed Chirurgion [surgeon]) and not to doe it with his owne hands."[10]

Moses à Vauts was one of the few who supported wife beating. In *The Husband's Authority Unvail'd; Wherein It is moderately discussed whether it be fit or lawfull for a good Man, to beat his bad Wife,* he states, "If Wives will invent strange new *Fashions* and frisking *strains* of *Disobedience* . . . why should not their *Husbands* suit them with new *Forms* of Discipline?" Vauts also declares, "It were well, and better, the Wife could not deserve Blows; but, if they be due, or needfull, or best for her, why should they be denied her?"[11] Although Vauts was an exception in his support of wife beating, all of the treatises on marriage insist that, in Gouge's words, the wife "acknowledge her husband to be her superior," that he has the right to rule over her, and that she must obey him.[12] However, while it was the duty of husbands to reprove their wives when necessary, they should not do them serious bodily harm.[13]

Violence between husbands and wives is represented in much of early modern popular literature. In Samuel Rowlands's *Whole crew of kind Gossips,* the second gossip tells her assembled women friends that when her husband strikes her, she strikes back: "If he strike me, Ile match him blow for blow; / For though he be my head (as people talke) / about his pate my fists sometimes doth walke." The husband in *A merry Jeste of a shrewde and curste wyfe, lapped in Morrelles skin* (anon., 1580) beats his bride on their wedding night, beats her again in the cellar, and then wraps her bloody body in the salted hide of a horse until she agrees to submit to him. Ballads, too, such as "Hold Your Hands, Honest Men," are sometimes about husband's violence against so-called shrews or about women retaliating against their husbands. In "The Dumb Maid; or, The Young Gallant Trappan'd," the husband's doctor advises him to "'take you the Oyl of Hazel strong; / With it anoint her body round'" when she does not obey.[14] In "Well Met Neighbor" by Martin Parker, the gossips sing,

> "Heard you not lately of Hugh,
> How soundly his wife he bang'd?
> He beat her black and blew—
> *O such a rogue would be hang'd!*"[15]

Contemporary proverbs also illustrate the acceptance of wife beating. Two of the most popular were: "A spaniel, a woman, and a walnut tree, the more they're beaten the better they be"; and "A dead Wife is the best goods in a man's house."[16]

According to Andrew Clark and Mordechai Feingold, the Comita disputations—such as the one that inspired Heale's *Apologie For Women*—were often humorous,[17] so it is possible that in the seventeenth century the topic of wife beating was considered amusing, at least to some men. Joy Wiltenburg suggests that humorous discussions of wife beating may have occurred during a transitional stage in which violent disciplining of wives by husbands was no longer unquestioned but did not arouse revulsion, at least not among men.[18] Heale's tone in his *Apologie* is primarily serious—probably Lady Margaret Hele would not have had it otherwise—but the pamphlet includes moments of levity such as Heale's reference to Publius Sempronius, who divorced his wife for seeing a play, and the bachelor Heale's ironic rhetorical question, "Who can rightly estimate the rites of marriage, who never knew the happines thereof?"

An Apologie is divided into six chapters. In addition to an introduction and a conclusion, Heale opposes wife beating using arguments from nature (chapter 2), rules of morality or civil policy (chapter 3), civil and canon law (chapter 4), and the law of God (chapter 5). To prove his points, he cites numerous authorities in the margins (see the illustration on p. 201). Heale's annotations are the essence of his pamphlet and his method for demonstrating the superiority of his arguments as well as his knowledge of the Bible, classical literature, and civil and canon law. Without marginalia, Heale would not have been able to prove "that it is not lawfull for a husband to beate his wife."

Like Christopher Newstead, Heale had read widely. Among contemporary or near-contemporary writers he cites Philip Sidney, Niccolò Machiavelli, Juan Luis Vives, Jean Bodin, Lorenzo Strozzi, Geoffrey Chaucer, Giglio Giraldi, Guillaume Du Bartas, and Petrarch. His classical references are impressive as well: Seneca, Aristotle, Plutarch, Pliny, Virgil, Ovid, Livy, Cicero, Homer, and Plato are noted most often, but he also cites Isocrates, Herodotus, Tacitus, Ausonius, Stobaeus, Aulus Gellius, Caesar, Arnobius, Xenophon, Martial, Frontinus, Suetonius, Atilius, Lucan, Plautus, Prudentius, Aerodius, Valerius Maximus, Strabo, Lampidius, Varro, and Marcus Aurelius. His knowledge of the church fathers, including Jerome, Augustine, Cyprian, Gregory of Nyssa, Gregory the Great, Origen, Tertullian, and Basil, is thorough, and his knowledge of canon and civil law is dazzling—not to mention curious, since Heale was not trained in law, and the study of canon law had been abolished at Oxford in the sixteenth century.[19] To prove his case, Heale uses Justinian's *Corpus Juris Civilis* (529–33), Gratian's *Decretum* (ca. 1140), and dozens of glossators on each text, such as Accursius, Tiraqueau, Dracontius, Peter of Ancharino, Andreas Alciatus, Tancred, Baldus de Ubaldus, Aretini, Bursati, Ivo, Paulus Liazariis, Joannes Andreae, Donelli, de Baysio, Angilrammis of Metz, Alexander the Great, Deciai, and Andreas Siculus. Whenever possible I have deciphered the abbreviated marginal references to the glossators.

Like Newstead, Heale often cites his sources from memory, and sometimes his references to particular books and chapters are inaccurate (see, e.g., notes 49, 70, and 80). Although less frequently than Newstead, Heale sometimes quotes Latin lines inaccurately from classical texts (see, e.g., notes 27, 80, and 103). More interesting is how Heale, again like Newstead, changes stories to fit his arguments. As an example of a loving husband, Heale cites book 5 of the *Iliad,* which describes Hector bewailing the death of his father, Priam, and his lament for his wife, Andromache, who is still on earth while he is in heaven. This story is fabricated by Heale: in book 22 of the *Iliad,* Hector is slain by Achilles and mourned by his father, Priam; in book 24, Andromache laments the death of her husband, but there is no mention of Hector in heaven grieving for her. One wonders whether any of Heale's seventeenth-century readers recognized his "creative" use of these sources and, if they did, whether they were amused, outraged, or impressed.

Heale introduces *An Apologie* by stating that it has become custom for some men to dispraise women for several reasons: they have been rejected by the women they wooed, they do not know how to love, or they are simply evil. He says that these men have "filled the world with pamphlets, things most idle in themselves, and most disgracefull unto women," and he must offer his response because even Oxford University is calling the name of women into question.

In chapter 2, Heale uses examples from nature to prove the unlawfulness of wife beating. The dove, the swan, the nightingale, and even the viper treat their mates reverently, he argues, and men should not treat their wives with less respect than animals. Even the lion trembles at the sight of a woman and does not do her violence. Other pamphlet literature on women and marriage also uses this appeal to nature to argue for mutuality in marriage. Rachel Speght, in *A Mouzell for Melastomus,* writes of how the male pigeon helps his hen by sitting on their eggs, the cock helps his hen to build their nest, and the cockerel helps his mate defend their chickens. She concludes "that much more should man and woman, which are reasonable creatures, be helpers each to other in all things Lawfull."[20] Similarly, Heale states that if law is "an artificial collection of naturall precepts," and if in nature male animals treat female animals respectfully, then it is "unnatural" for a husband to beat his wife. He refers to the selectivity of examples cited by his opponent, Dr. G., of the ancients' treating their wives badly—such as Faunus, who killed his wife for drinking a cup of wine—and contends that Dr. G. omitted examples of loving husbands, such as Hector and Tygranes. In addition, he argues that Dr. G. omitted the many examples of wives who killed themselves out of love after their husbands' deaths, a familiar convention in male-authored treatises on women (such as Chaucer's *Legend of Good Women* and Boccaccio's *Concerning Famous Women*). Interwoven throughout Heale's argument are ten rhetorical questions that reach a crescendo by the end of the chapter and that, within the context of the chapter, can only be answered by denouncing wife beating.

In chapter 3, Heale marshals arguments from morality or civil society to prove the incivility of wife beating. Men choose their wives, Heale states, so why should they quarrel with their own choices? To beat one's wife is not virtuous because the combatants are not physically equal and, in addition, a husband has no purpose in beating his wife. If one's wife is "gentle," she does not deserve it; if she is "perverse," it will not work. Besides, it may be dangerous to beat one's wife because she may retaliate with blows.

Heale's next argument uses the analogy of the family and the common-wealth: If a man cannot manage his household, how can he be fit to manage the affairs of the commonwealth? He declares that wife beating sets a bad example for one's children, one's servants, and one's neighbors and is "dangerous" to the state. Heale continues with a rapturous description of the mutuality of marriage: "They themselves should bee as *Virgils* vine and elme, the tendernes of the one supported by the others strength. Their hearts as *Leda's* twins both interchangeably imbracing each other." He further argues that the souls of men and women have the "same essence" and that if either man or woman were superior, it would be the woman, whose "complexion is purer, which argues a richer wit." Heale then cites examples of ancients who were against wife beating and asks if Christians will behave worse than heathens. In addition, he points out that wife beating violates the laws of hospitality. Once again, Heale asks his readers many rhetorical questions—at least thirty—that may be answered in only one way. He also uses the device of repetition, working up to a feverish intensity in describing women as "Infortunat in their birth. . . . Infortunate in their education. . . . Infortunate in their estate. . . . Infortunat in their credit, infortunate in al."

In chapter 4, Heale turns to canon and civil law to argue against wife beating. He states that the severity and double standard in the civil and canon laws concerning women have been caused by the ignorance of the canonists, who were unmarried men and did not understand the "estate and mysterie of marriage." There is nothing in the original law, Heale contends, that states directly *"That it is lawfull for a husbande to beate his wife."* The real culprit, according to Heale, is not the law but its interpretation. He divides the interpreters, or glossators, into four groups: those who hold wife beating to be lawful but not convenient; those who say a husband may beat his wife as much as he wishes and may even imprison her; those who are against wife beating, given women's "weaknesse, and imbecillitie" (another word for weakness); and those who say nothing. In his marginalia, Heale cites a long list of glossators who support wife beating and a shorter list of those who oppose it.

Having proven that there is no certainty concerning wife beating in canon or civil law, Heale says he will "compare reason unto reason, oppose Lawyer unto Lawyer, conferre opinion with opinion" to decide the case against wife beating. First, he states that God has given husbands superiority over their wives: a husband should provide "roial protection" and a wife, "loial subjection." Second, husbands have power over their wives' persons (though Heale says he will not discuss the controversies over dowries). And third, husbands have the right to correct their wives according to the seriousness of the fault. When a wife commits adultery or threatens her husband's life, punishments include separation from marriage and other measures determined by the courts, and Heale insists that a wife is not guilty until she is proven to be so by the court. Also, he warns against jealousy and allows that husbands should reprehend their wives for lesser faults, such as managing their households carelessly or being lax in their religion—although he criticizes "too holy women-gospellers, who weare their testament at their apron-springs, and wil weekely catechize their husbands." It is better for women to be silent, Heale says, as silence is their "chiefest eloquence." Furthermore, a husband's reprehension should be given tenderly, and he should realize that sometimes he may have misinterpreted his wife's behavior. Finally, Heale lists a wife's trivial faults that her husband should either ignore or only mildly admonish, such as the "nimblenesse" of her tongue or her "curiositie" of apparel.

The remainder of chapter 4 refutes arguments raised by Dr. G. in his defense of wife beating. Heale takes on the tragedians and cynics who dispraise women, labeling their invectives "the froath of an apish invention." As evidence, he counters their attacks with accounts of men who supposedly praise women, such as Chaucer, Plutarch, Jerome, and Cyprian. He also quotes Marcus Aurelius: "'A wife . . . is often to be admonished, to be reprehended but seldome, never to be dealth withal with violent handes.'" Heale contends that a husband should rule by good example: his wife should learn to speak "At his tongue" and "by his carriage she should compose her behavior." He names countries in which only the husbands are punished for the faults of their wives and includes a reference to a husband in Paris who was made to ride in disgrace through the city. In parts of England, Heale says, he has seen a similar custom (this appears to be a reference to skimmington, in which a cuckolded husband is made to ride backward on a horse). The name "wife," according to Heale, is "a name of dignity," and it is not dignified to beat one's wife; correction by beating is "servile," but wives are not servile. Heale suppports his argument by echoing Hic Mulier: that wives are "in the law free burgesses of the same citie whereof their husbands are free, and free denisons in the same land wherin their husbandes are free: both participating the same rightes, both injoying the same liberties." From this Heale radically argues that wives may leave their husbands if they are beaten and, further, that wives should obtain "sufficient mainetenaunce" until they have security that they will not be beaten again. Although the law allowed wives who were beaten unreasonably to obtain protection, there is no stipulation in *The Lawes Resolutions of Womens Rights* for a wife to leave her abusive husband and receive maintenance until he changes his behavior.[21] In conclusion, Heale states that wife beating is a sin no matter what the law says and that he will continue his apology based on his "own profession" as a minister, with arguments from the law of God.

Chapter 5 begins with an ecstatic description of the creation of Adam and Eve, who was made not from clay but from one of Adam's ribs, near his heart, so that "shee might appeare his equal, and be taken as his fellow-helper." Heale contends that if the city "deride[s] us" or the court does "not smile upon us," we have the "refuge" of home where "wee are sure to finde love waiting at the gate to welcome us, and true contentment within to entertaine us." An extended passage follows from Ovid's *Metamorphosis,* describing the Golden Age. The chapter concludes with an account of Adam and Eve succumbing to the temptation of the serpent, for which Heale claims that Adam was more to blame because, unlike Eve, Adam did not resist. Also, only Adam was given by God the general prohibition against eating the fruit. In the commandment "Thou shalt not eate of the tree of knowledge of good and evill," "thou," according to Heale, refers only to Adam. If Adam had not eaten the fruit, "wee had not tasted of death." Heale also points out that in the creation story Satan sows dissension between husbands and wives; therefore, men who act "rigorous" toward their wives are "apprentices in the Devil's trade." Heale ends his *Apologie* with an exhortation to husbands to love their wives and a desire that his short treatise would serve as a means to remove dissension between husbands and wives.

Modern interpretations of Heale's pamphlet necessarily suffer because we do not have the treatise to which he is responding. Nevertheless, *An Apologie For Women* is a tour de force in its compilation of arguments, its passion, its rhetorical energy, and its radical position that abused wives have the right to leave their husbands and be maintained by them. Although ostensibly an apology for, or defense of, women, Heale's pamphlet fits into the tradition of marriage sermons that insist on a husband's duty to reprehend and admonish his wife but not to beat her. In its marshaling of so many arguments, *An Apologie* is an important treatise both in seventeenth-century disputation and in the history of marriage.

Textual Introduction

William Heale's *Apologie For Women; or, An Opposition to Mr. Dr. G. his assertion. Who held in the Act at Oxforde. Anno. 1608. "That it was lawfull for husbands to beate their wives* (*STC* 13014), printed by Joseph Barnes in 1609, was not entered in the Stationers Register until 12 April 1619, by Barnes's son John, a freeman of the Company of Stationers and a bookseller in London from 1600 to 1621. *An Apologie* was assigned to Richard Redmer, a London bookseller, from 1610 to 1632.

Only one edition of *An Apologie* was printed in 1609, although a significantly revised edition entitled *The Great Advocate and Oratour* was printed in 1682, many years after Heale's death.[22] Copies of the 1609 edition are at the Folger, Huntington, and Bodleian libraries, at Harvard University's Houghton Library, at Cambridge University, at the National Library of Scotland at Edinburgh, at the University of Glasgow, and at the British Library, among others. The copy text for this edition of *An Apologie For Women* is the British Library's copy. It has been collated with the Huntington Library's copy, which is essentially identical, and with the 1682 revised edition, which is very different. In the endnotes I have only commented on differences in the marginalia that might help to locate Heale's citations.

The marginalia has been moved to the endnotes and enclosed in angle brackets; an example of its original presentation can be seen in the photograph of one page of the pamphlet (p. 201). The lettered note callouts in the text have been changed to numbers and moved from the beginning of the borrowed material to the end, as is now customary. Spacing within the text has been silently regularized.

There are no modern editions of Heale's *Apologie,* but there are two facsimile editions: one published by Theatrum Orbis Terrarum (Amsterdam) and reprinted by W. J. Johnson (Norwood, N.J.) in 1974 and the other published by Garland (New York) in 1978. Lloyd Davis has included, without marginalia, chapters 3, 4, and 6 (the conclusion) in *Sexuality and Gender in the English Renaissance,* and Maria Roy has excerpted sections of *An Apologie,* without marginalia, as introductions to the chapters of her edited volume *Battered Women: A Psychosociological Study of Domestic Violence.*[23]

NOTES

1. Nicholas Tyacke and Andrew Clark name Gwin as the defender of wife beating. Tucker Brooke, an entry in the *Dictionary of National Biography,* and Anthony à Wood believe Dr. G. was William Gager. Falconer Madan says Gager was neither "inceptor nor respondent." See Nicholas Tyacke, *Seventeenth-Century Oxford,* volume 4 in *The History of the University of Oxford* (Oxford: Clarendon Press, 1997), 20; Andrew Clark, ed., *Register of the University of Oxford,* vol. 2 (Oxford: Clarendon Press, 1887), 186 ("Dr. Thomas Gwin of All So. was the respondent in the Comita, although incepting. The statutes required that each inceptor in the Comita should oppose; but Convocation on 27 June 1608 granted a dispensation that Gwin might respond, there being no one else to do so"); Tucker Brooke, "The Life and Times of William Gager, 1555–1622," *Proceedings of the American Philosophical Society* 95.4 (Aug. 1951): 429; *Dictionary of National Biography* (1959–60), 9:331, 7:798 (hereafter cited as *DNB*); Anthony à Wood, *Athenae Oxonienses,* vol. 2, ed. Philip Bliss (Hildesheim: Georg Olms Verlagsbuchhandlung, 1969), 89; Falconer Madan, *Oxford Books,* vol. 1 (Oxford: Clarendon Press, 1895), 75.

William Gager (1555–1622) was elected to Christ Church, Oxford, in 1574 and received a B.A. in 1577, an M.A. in 1580, and a B.C.L. and D.C.L. in 1589. He is considered one of the best Latin playwrights of the Tudor period. His plays, which were presented at Christ Church, include *Meleager* (1582), a Latin tragedy, performed in 1585 in the presence of Sir Philip Sidney and the earls of Leicester and Pembroke; the comedy *Rivales* and the tragedy *Dido,* both first staged in 1583 for the visit of Albert Alasco, Prince Palatine of Poland; and *Ulysses Redux,* a tragicomedy. According to Raphael Holinshed, *Rivales* was performed for Queen Elizabeth when she visited Oxford in 1592 (cited in *DNB* 7:797). Dr. John Rainolds of Queen's College was asked in 1592 to attend the Christ Church Shrovetide drama productions that featured three of Gager's plays. Rainolds attacked the theater instead, stating that "'it was wrong for men to dress in women's clothing, that plays are a waste of time and money, that plays are a bad moral influence, that actors were considered infamous even by the Romans, that it is a profanation of the Sabbath to act plays on Sunday'" (quoted in vol. 2 of *William Gager: The Complete Works,* ed. Dana F. Sutton [New York: Garland, 1994], vii).

Note that Gager's name is written in ink in the Bodleian Library copy of Heale's pamphlet, and Dana F. Sutton states that Gager probably did participate, pointing to Gager's poem "Pyramis," written in 1608: "'no law allows a wife to strike a husband, or a son his father. But on the contrary, from time to time a parent may beat his son, a husband his wife. A king is the husband, and the father of his subjects, and so inviolable to his people'" (*William Gager: The Complete Works,* 1:xviii). According to Sutton, Gager often wrote poetic answers to questions posed at disputations (3:xxv).

2. Franklin B. Williams, *Index of Dedications and Commendatory Verses in English Books Before 1641* (London: Bibliographical Society, 1962), 84. William Heale's name is often spelled Hele, so it is possible that Margaret Hele was a relation. But consider John Burke's statement that the ancient family of Hele in Devon was "one of the most

eminent, the most widely spread, and the most affluent which even that quarter of England could boast of" (*A Genealogical and Heraldic History of the Commoners of Great Britain and Ireland,* vol. 4 [London: Henry Colburn, 1838], 505). The Heale family of Devon, while widely respected, was comprised of commoners.

3. Hieron writes: "It hath pleased you sometime, to crave of me the notes of some things which I have (in your hearing) taught in publique" (*The Life and Death of Dorcas* [London, 1612], A3r).

4. Wood, *Athenae Oxonienses,* 2:89. Biographical information about Heale comes from Joseph Foster, *Alumni Oxoniensis: The Members of the University of Oxford, 1500–1714,* vol. 1 (Nendeln, Lichtenstein: Kraus Reprint, 1968), 690; Charles William Boase, *Register of the Rectors, Fellows, and Other Members on the Foundation of Exeter College, Oxford* (Oxford: Clarendon Press, 1894), 93; *Dictionary of National Biography,* 9:331.

5. T.E., *The Lawes Resolutions of Womens Rights; or, The Lawes Provision for Woemen* (London, 1632), 128, 129.

6. Martin Ingram, *Church Courts, Sex, and Marriage in England, 1570–1640* (Cambridge: Cambridge University Press, 1987), 183, quote on 144. For a fascinating discussion of women banding together to ward off male violence and get even, see Pamela Brown, *Better a Shrew Than a Sheep: Women, Drama, and the Culture of Jest in Early Modern England* (Ithaca, N.Y.: Cornell University Press, 2003), 138–49.

7. Sara Mendelson and Patricia Crawford, *Women in Early Modern England, 1550–1720* (Oxford: Clarendon Press, 1998), 140, 216. See also Susan Amussen's important article, "'Being Stirred to Much Unquietness': Violence and Domestic Violence in Early Modern England," *Journal of Women's History* 6.2 (Summer 1994): 70–89; Margaret R. Sommerville, *Second Subjection: Attitudes to Women in Early Modern Society* (London: Arnold, 1995); Margaret Hunt, "Wife Beating, Domesticity, and Women's Independence in Eighteenth-Century London," *Gender and History* 4.1 (Spring 1992): 10–33; G. R. Quaife, *Wanton Wenches and Wayward Wives: Peasants and Illicit Sex in Early Seventeenth-Century England* (New Brunswick, N.J.: Rutgers University Press, 1979), 26. Roderick Phillips says that spouse beating was a crime in Calvin's Geneva and that sixty-one men and two women were convicted and excommunicated for this offense between 1564 and 1560 (*Putting Asunder: A History of Divorce in Western Society* [Cambridge: Cambridge University Press, 1988], 323–30).

8. Quoted in *Daughters, Wives, and Widows: Writings by Men about Women and Marriage in England, 1500–1640,* ed. Joan Larsen Klein (Urbana: University of Illinois Press, 1992), 16, 21.

9. William Whately, *A Bride-Bush; or, A Wedding Sermon* (London, 1617), 20; ibid. (London, 1623), 171–72.

10. William Gouge, *Of Domesticall Duties Eight Treatises* (London, 1622), 391. See also Robert Cleaver, *A Godly Form of Householde Government: For the Ordering of Private Families* (London, 1598), 162–68; Henry Smith, "A Preparative to Marriage," in *The Sermons of Master Henry Smith* (London, 1601), 31; R. Abbot, *A Wedding Sermon* (London, 1608), 58; William Perkins, *Christian Oeconomie; or, A Short Survey of the Right Manner of erecting and ordering a Familie, according to the Scriptures* (London, 1607), 127; John Wing,

The Crowne Conjugall; or, The Spouse Royall. A Discovery of the true honor and happines of Christian Matrimony (Middleburgh, 1620), 136; Thomas Taylor, *A Good Husband and A Good Wife* (London, 1625), 25; William Ames, *Conscience with the Power and Cases Thereof* (London, 1639), bk. 4, p. 156.

11. Moses à Vauts, *The Husband's Authority Unvail'd; Wherein It is moderately discussed whether it be fit or lawfull for a good Man, to beat his bad Wife* (London, 1650), 57, 60.

12. Gouge, *Of Domesticall Duties,* 269, 285.

13. In *Disorderly Women and Female Power in Early Modern England and Germany* (Charlottesville: University Press of Virginia, 1992), Joy Wiltenberg states that "men of both countries are shown readily using violence to subdue their wives, though the German husbands are more unrestrained and more successful in this venture" (107). See also the section entitled "Violence against Women" in Elizabeth A. Foyster's *Manhood in Early Modern England: Honour, Sex, and Marriage* (New York: Longman, 1999), 181–93.

14. Quoted in Wiltenberg, *Disorderly Women,* 109–10.

15. Quoted in Brown, *Better a Shrew Than a Sheep,* 147.

16. Morris Palmer Tilley, *Dictionary of Proverbs in England in the Sixteenth and Seventeenth Centuries* (Ann Arbor: University of Michigan Press, 1950), W644, W347.

17. Clark, *Register,* 83–84; Mordecai Feingold, "The Humanities," in *History of the University of Oxford,* 4:302–5.

18. Wiltenberg, *Disorderly Women,* 108.

19. See R. H. Helmholz, *Roman Canon Law in Reformation England* (Cambridge: Cambridge University Press, 1990), 151–54.

20. Rachel Speght, *A Mouzell for Melastomus* (London, 1617), D3r.

21. See Constance Jordan, *Renaissance Feminism: Literary Texts and Political Models* (Ithaca, N.Y.: Cornell University Press, 1990), 296–97; T.E., *The Lawes Resolutions of Womens Rights,* 128; Amussen, "Being Stirred," 71. Hunt states that "a woman did not technically possess the right to leave her husband, even if he beat her, without his consent" ("Wife Beating," 19).

22. Hunt suggests that the publication of *The Great Advocate and Oratour* in 1682 marked a shift in the discourse on wife beating in that violence against women, previously often committed publicly, was demonized in this pamphlet and, therefore, became more shameful and secret. She compares this shift to Michel Foucault's description in *Discipline and Punish: The Birth of the Prison* (trans. Alan Sheridan [New York: Vintage Books, 1979], 73–131) of the transformation of state-sponsored violence away from public spectacle ("Wife Beating," 25).

23. Lloyd Davis, *Sexuality and Gender in the English Renaissance* (New York: Garland, 1998); Maria Roy, ed., *Battered Women: A Psychosociological Study of Domestic Violence* (New York: Van Nostrand Reinhold, 1972).

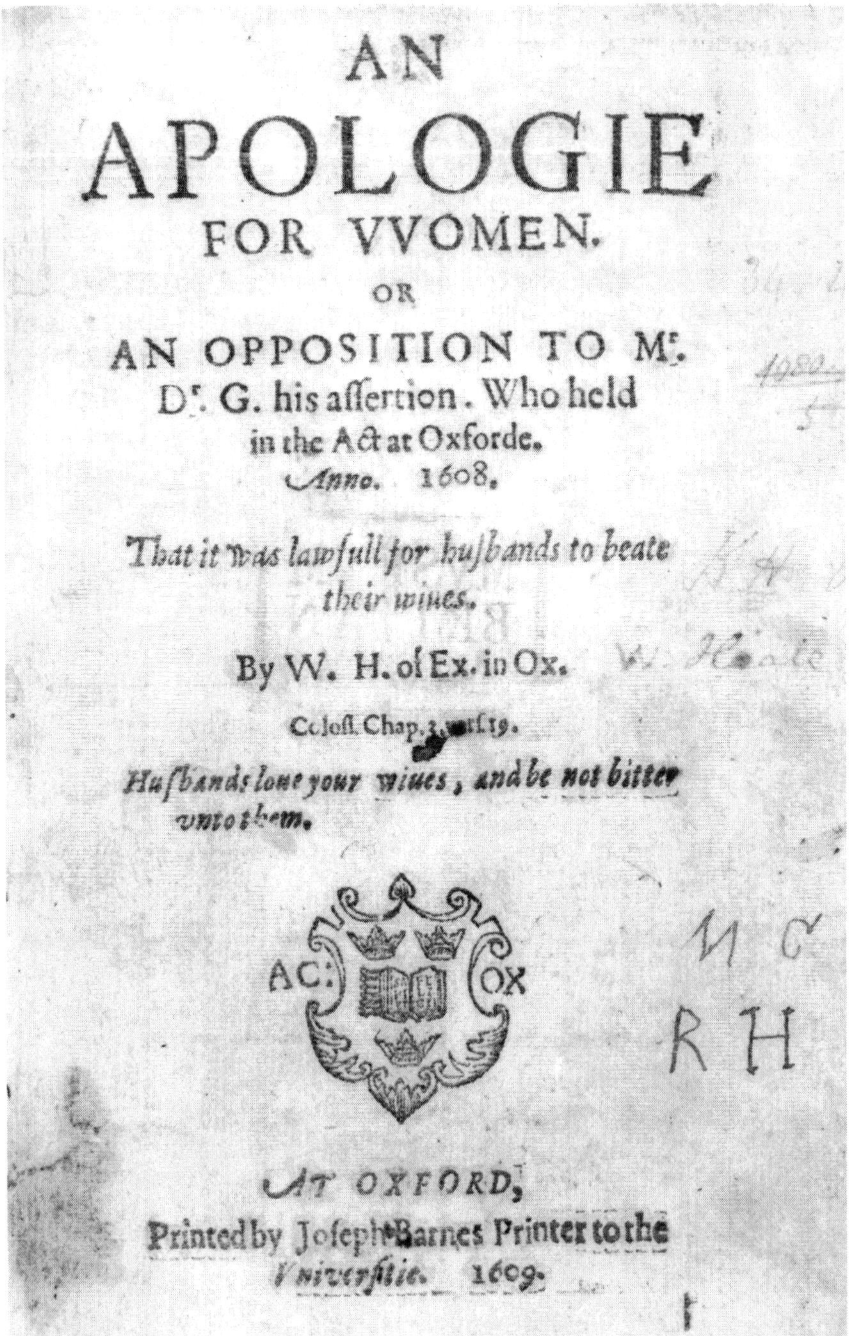

AN
APOLOGIE
FOR VVOMEN.
OR
AN OPPOSITION TO M^r.
D^r. G. his assertion. Who held
in the Act at Oxforde.
Anno. 1608.

*That it was lawfull for husbands to beate
their wiues.*

By W. H. of Ex. in Ox.

Coloss. Chap. 3. vers. 19.

*Husbands loue your wiues, and be not bitter
vnto them.*

AT OXFORD,
Printed by Joseph Barnes Printer to the
Vniversitie. 1609.

An Apologie For Women. Or An Opposition to Mr. Dr. G.[1] his assertion. Who held in the Act at Oxforde. *Anno.* 1608. *That it was lawfull for husbands to beate their wives.*[2] By W.H. of Ex. in Ox.[3] Coloss. Chap.3 vers.19.[4] *Husbands love your wives, and be not bitter unto them.* At Oxford, Printed by Joseph Barnes Printer to the *Universitie.*[5] 1609.

TO THE HONOURABLE AND RIGHT-VERTUOUS *Ladie, the Ladie* M.H.[6] all happinesse.

Madam, your commaunde is effected: And this short discourse (the cause of whose being you are) attends your view. In regard whereof, obsequiously to begge your kinde acceptance, importes a wronge unto your courtesie: utterly to neglect your favourable censure, presumes an overprizing of my labour. To your selfe therefore I leave it: Expecting from your selfe, no other interpretation then as your selfe, faire *and* courteous. *What pleaseth you not, displeaseth me. The harsh lines you may teach a better language. If anie thing delight, let it satisfie for the manie that may chance to dislike. If ought offend, let it weare the blacke liverie of your pennes dash in token of sorrow.*[7] *If al through the weaknesse of argument, debilitate the strenght of so good a cause, then let all suffer for it. For I know that this little body of my apologie is not so artificially featured, nor the limbs thereof so naturallie jointed, that (as it should) it can seeme a naturall art, or an artificial nature. But your Honors importunity of hast,*[8] *must beare a part of the blame, together with the shallownes of my conceipt. And being joined so sweet a yoake ile easily spurne at Detraction it self. The truth is, had not your Ls [Ladies] prefixed time dealt somewhat niggardlie with me, I had dealt more liberallie with it. And those things which now are but sleight lie plaide withall, might have beene more exactlie handled.*[9] *How soever it is, yours it is: and so shall be ever be from whom it is.*

W.H.

THE CONTENTS OF THIS *APOLOGIE.*

An Apologie for women.

Chap. 1.
An Introduction to the discourse following.

If in all reason it hath alwaies beene granted, that courtesie may followe after with defence, where discourtesie with offence hath gone before: I cannot then but imagine this my one only Apologie for women, shall passe your gentle censures, after so many Invectives[10] framed against them, by their disgracefull adversaries. For although we all know that unto womankinde the world oweth halfe of its life, and man is indebted the whole of his love, yet it is a custome growne so common to under.valew their worth, as everie rymer hath a libell to impeach their modestie; everie phantastike a poeme to plaine[11] their unfaithfulnesse; The Courtier though he weare his Mistresse favour, yet stickes not to sing his Mistresse shame; The Cobler though in himselfe most disgracefull,[12] yet wants[13] hee not a ballade for their disgrace. And as this course is usuall with most men, so the cause hereof is manifest unto all. The fairest marke (you know) is most often aymed at; & the goodliest starre is most of all gazed upon: so woman the beautifulst creature of al, is most of al observed.[14] And observation as it is sometimes the guide unto honor, so often also it is the mother of disgrace.[15] Particular reasons hereof, many may be collected, out of the many particular humours of such, who stand out in disloialty with them. For some man wil dispraise that woman whom before he adored, because her modestie hath repelled his unchaste desires. Some will turne their amarous termes of woing into a barbarous stile of rayling, because for want of desert they obtaine not love. Many love not women, because they knowe not how to love them. And most of all men being evil themselves, love but few things that are good, and so perchance hate women also. Some likewise to make ostentation of their wit unto the stage. Few upon anie shew of reason. None (I dare avouch) upon anie just cause, have yet filled the world with pamphlets, things most idle in themselves, and most disgracefull unto women. But oh unmanlike men, and staine of your sexe! Is this a point of your manhood, or anie ornament of your valour, to busie your selves for disgrace of women, whom nature hath disarmed of corporal strenght, and education disabled[16] of mental courage for revenge? Is this the thankful tribute you repaie unto the author of your being? Is this the sweete imbracement you bestow on the paps that gave you sucke? Is this the grateful allowance you afforde them for their sorrow and paines at your birth, for their care and diligence in your youth, for their love and carefulnesse through.out your life? All such courtesies (me seemes) should not be so ungratefullie forgotten, much lesse injuriouslie remembred.[17] But why talke I with these men of gratitude the greatest of vertues, who never were acquainted with anie vertue at al? And therfore had it beene the highest of womens misfortune, to have beene traduced[18] by this infamous crew, they might easilie have smil'd it out; counting no dishonour to be evil-spoken of by them, who never learn'd to speake well of anie. But nowe this bad cause hath gotten better patrones: especially when in the Universitie, in the open Act,[19] in publike disputation their names are called in question, their capacitie thought unfit for learning, themselves adjudged worthie of blowes. To let passe the rest; what more strange and prodigious paradoxe? What opinion more unnaturall and uncivill then this of theirs, *That it is lawfull for a husband to beate his wife?*

Most impure hart which did first conceive, & more then most barbarous tongue,[20] which did afterward bring forth such a monster of opinion.[21] Had I but one word to speake, (save onlie my orizons;)[22] but one onlie line to write, I woulde both speake and write them in defiance hereof.

Chapt. 2.
That it is not lawful for a husband to beat his wife, is proved by reasons drawne from Nature.

And to begin first, whence we al began, from *Nature* her selfe. Her eternal law stampt from the worldes beginning in all her creatures, witnesseth such a soveraigne union of male and female, that in al kindes betweene them there is found no unkindnesse.

No Lions rage against the Lionesse:
The Tygre to the Tygresse is not fierce:
No Eagles doe their fellow birds oppresse:
The hauke doth not the hauke with talents pierce:
All couples live in love by natures lore,
Why should not man & wife do this, & more?[23]

Man the great creators greatest creature indued with *Remembrance* a register to recount former events: with *wisdome* a glasse to behold the present estate of things; with *Providence* an oracle to conjecture of future accidents:

above al with *Reason* a ballance to weigh out al his actions: must now become more cruell and tyranous, nay more savage & barbarous, then verie beasts, who neither have remembrance of things past,[24] wisedome in thinges present, providence of things to come, nor reason in anie thing at al. The *Doves* are observed to be most exquisite in their love, and at the fatal departure of one, the other pines to death with sorrow. The *Nightingall* makes pleasant melody in his loves wel-fare, but in her distresse he mournes in sadder tunes. The *Swanne* is of a nature sutable to his feather, white and faire, and al his feare is, to keepe his mate from feare. Go therefore into the fields, & the *Doves* wil read thee a lecture of love: returne into the woodes, and the *Nightingals* wil sing thee madrigals of love: walke by the river, & the *Swannes* wil schoole thee the art of love: every where such loving couples in brutish beasts will shame the disagreeing matches in reasonable creatures.[25] For shal the bare instinct of a sensible nature worke so powerfully in this case with beasts, as none are found so beastly to infringe it; and shal the helpe of a purer essence take none effect in man and he not adjudged worse then a beast? The *Lion* that spareth no creature, is said to tremble at a woman, and hardly proffereth her that violence, which usually he doth to man:[26] as though *Nature* had taught him a more gentle behaviour towards so faire a personage, or his owne heroicke spirit to scorne of so base a victorie.

For never gotten was immortal fame,
By working of a silly womans shame.[27]

The *Viper* a beast more vile then the vilest, poisonous by nature, and spitefull, odious to be seene and hatefull; Yet when the time of his breeding approacheth, withdrawes himselfe unto the sea or rivers side, and by the gentle murmurre of his knowne hisse calleth fourth the Lamprey with whom his nature is to ingender. The Lamprey being so kindly invited, doth as kindly repaire unto him. Whom when he perceiveth comming to accept of his love, vomiteth forth al his poison; doing reverence (as it were) unto his nuptial rightes: and casting away his natural corruption, meeteth his spouse in his cleanest perfection.[28] Man would take scorne to be thought worse then a *Viper,* and why then scorneth he not to cast out of his hart, all his cancred poison of anger, of strife, of fighting, of quarrelling, when he commeth into his Mistresse presence? To be plaine a dogge wil not so much as bite his mate, & shall a husband beat his wife, and be not therein worse then a dogge? If not, then unhappy is the people, and infortunate the common wealth;

where the liberty shal be more large, and more licentious the laws of men then of beasts.

It may wel be the worlds motto, *All thinges have Nature for their guide.*[29] And of this al, especily Man the worlds commaunder: which we may observe, as in the common course of life; in ordering his diet, in wearing his apparell, in taking his rest: so likewise in the perfit habite of sciences; in his smoothing Rhetoricke, in his sollide disputation, in his profound Philosophy. In al which the greatest preheminence, *Art* can challenge, is to adde perfection where *Nature* hath laid a foundation.[30] The law then being an artificial collection of naturall precepts, how can it dispense with so unnatural an action; as for a husband to beate his wife, the one part of himselfe, nay his otherselfe, or his better halfe? No man did ever willingly hurt himselfe;[31] or if any man hath, certainely he maie justlie of all men bee helde a madde man: and therefore what mutual blowes can lawfully passe betweene man & wife; who are one and the selfesame? Their mindes inseparably one in their love & amity: their bodies individually the same in their children & posteritie.

Indeed some ancient ages of barbarisme (before either civillity was fully imbraced, or christianitie firmely established) seemed to draw from *nature* the practise of some such tyrannie. So *Aristotle* reportes of the Scythians:[32] *Tacitus* of the Germans:[33] *Gellius* of the Romaines:[34] *Caesar* of the French:[35] with whom it was a received custome to dispose of their wives both life and libertie, according to their pleasure. And hence it was that Mr. Doctor[36] seemed to alleadge his history of *Publius Sempronius* who divorced his wife for seeing a play.[37] Of *Egnatius Mecennius* who beate his wife for being found in his cellar.[38] Of *Faunus* who killed his wife for drinking a cup of wine.[39] Fit proofes for confirmation of such a truth. Recount the time, it was in paganisme and a barbarous age: Observe the persons, they lived as mirrors of rigour & cruelty, & are registred as the monuments of murther and tyrannie. Weigh the reasons that moved them thereunto, they wil sooner cast you into laughter, then perswade you of imitation. Lastly judge of al and all is but as though a Physition should go into an Apothecaries shop, where is variety of wholesome medicines, yet prescribes hee some poyson some drudge[40] to strengthen his sicke patient. Right so Mr. Doctor travailed over divers histories where was diversity of good examples, yet produceth he the worse of all to shoulder up his weake opinion. Farre better befitting the place, more plausible to your auditory,[41] and no lesse gracious for your selfe, had beene the famous examples of loving husbands towardes their wives, of loving wives towardes their husbandes, or of either loving towards the other. How welcome would have bin the very name of *Hector*? who in the destruction of *Troie*, did indeed bewaile the death of *Priamus*, the sacking of so great a city, the spoile of so many deare and valiant brethren, the funerals of so faire & large an Empire: but exceeded all excesse in lamenting *Andromache* his wife,[42] and desired (saith *Homer*) to forsake heaven being already seated among the Gods, to defend *Andromache* distressed here on earth. How pleasant had been the rehearsal of *Tygranes* love, who with his beloved Queen being taken prisoner by *Cyrus*, made a free and liberal promise of his life, to purchase her ransome?[43] What good entertainment had the storie of *Calenus* had, who thought he lived no longer, then when he looked on his beloved wife?[44] In how faire a language woulde *Livie* have spoken for you, of *Augustus*, of *Antonius*, of *Scaevola*, of *Aruntius*, of *Scipio*, of *Marius*,[45] and other histories of infinite other, whom for this cause, posteritie hath advanced above men, if not honoured as Gods?[46]

And howbeit in women the sexe be weaker, yet not their love. Witnesse *Cornelia* who so dearely affected her *Pompey*, that she would not suffer him to go into the warres (though he were the worldes terrour) unlesse her selfe in presence might waite upon him.[47] Witnesse *Demotia*, who having lost her *Leosthenes* could not finde her selfe, and therefore through solitarinesse made a speedy voyage unto death after him.[48] Witnesse *Sulpitia*, who being adjudged to stay, and watched that she should stay at *Rome*, when her husband *Lentulus* was banished from *Rome*, yet (notwithstanding the *Senates* commande, her princely fathers charge, the love of her citie and country, the losse of friends & family) shee alone exposed her selfe unto the danger of the night, beguiled the watchfull eies of her stricte guarde, brake forth of the city, and lackied him along the fields, until shee became the joieful companion of his woful banishment. So little she esteemed all the worldes felicity in regarde of one *Lentulus*, and for one *Lentulus* so willingly she incurred whatsoever misery.[49] Witnesse *Panthea, Rhodogune, Laodemia, Martia, Valeria, Portia, Lucretia*,[50] *Penelope*,[51] *Alcinoe*.[52] Millions of like, whose singular fame herein, as it hath caused antiquity to invest them in the eternal shrines of honour: so might likewise their rehearsall enforced posteritie to receive them as the fruitful patternes of imitation.

But to returne to your alleadged histories: who imagines it not a simple house, that is built on such rotten posts? And who sees it not a weake defence (God wot) that hath so unworthy props? Graunt your writers relation to be true: yet how thence prove you the action to bee lawful? Since al was done unadvisedly without discussing of the matter, wrongfully without the hearing of a judge, wilfully without any giving of sentence, al which the law requires.[53] These then being savage & heathenish murders both against *Nature,* and the law of *Nations,* let me demaunde who received the greater soile, either the tyranous husbands which rashly abused, or the modest wives which patiently endured? If you saie the latter, where is your judgement? If the former, of what force then is your argument? But not to trace you too farre in your owne field: Give me leave to remove your case into the court of Morallity, or civil Pollicie; where if the Jurie passe with you, you shall have cause stil to imbrace it: if not, you have no reason longer to fancie it.

Chap. 3.
The same confirmed by the rules of Morallity or Civill Pollicie.

Marriage of al humane actions is the one & only weightiest. It is the present disposall of the whole life of man: it is a *Gordian* knot[54] that may not bee loosed but by the sworde of death: it is the ring of union whose poesie is *Pure* and *endlesse.* In a word it is that state which either imparadizeth a man in the Eden of felicitie, or els exposeth him unto a world of miserie. Hence it is that so mature deliberation is required, before such an eternal bond be united.[55] The mutual affection of each partie, the consent of parents, the approbation of friends, the trial of acquaintance: besides the especial observance of disposition, of kindred, of education, of behaviour. Now then if a man solemnize marriage upon these due respects, he can hardly make his choice amisse, because hee is guided by vertue which never faileth her followers. But if not, he maie well bee styled a foole, because he is carried awaie with passion, which easilie impoisoneth the best designes. The man therefore that is truely wise cannot but choose a vertuous wife, and so by consequent live quietly with her. And if any take a vicious woman, it argues his owne folly, and so by good reason may patientlie endure her. For now he hath, but that which before he desired, and he desired that which then he fancied; though indeede not from the informance of a true judgement, but by the inducement of a giddy affection.

And yet in this infortunate case, it is the greatest folly of al follies, for a man to aggrandize his owne misfortunes by quarreling with his owne choise. For that dissention taketh away the very end and use of marriage, debarreth from all comfort and utility thereof, banisheth its joy and felicity, no man is so ignorant but he may wel knowe, none so obstinat but he must needs acknowledge. What wife is there so absolutely void of all psssionate spleen, who wil so lovingly performe her marriage-rites, so carefully bring up her children, so providently order her house, so diligently direct her servants, for a disagreeing as for a loving husband? Who wil buy blowes as deare as shee will pay for love?[56] Or what husband is there so cleare without gal, that wil so intentively augment his patrimonie, so warily imploie his stocke, so heedylie follow his affaires, so wel in al things use al his diligence, for a wife whom he loatheth, as for her whom he loveth? Who wil be as devout a beadsman to the Saint he fansieth not, as to him whom he chiefly adoreth?[57] So that indeed neither (as they shoulde) caring for the other, both receive an infinite damage to themselves; and for their posterity leave it most infortunat. Infortunat in their birth, for feare their dissentious parents derived to them their dissentious, spirites. Infortunate in their education, for feare their backward parents hindered their instruction. Infortunate in their estate for feare their carelesse parents diminished their portions. Infortunat in their credit, infortunate in al, for feare least al their parents faults redound unto the childrens paine. When as in agreeing matches, where man and wife make up the sweet harmonie of mutual love, in a reciprocal consent and union; yee may observe a heaven of government, the husband intent on his businesse, the wife imploied in her house, their children brought up religiously, their attendants, their servants, every one (as *Virgils* common-wealth of Bees)[58] busied in his place. Whence towardes the autumne of their yeeres, they gather in the fruitfull harvest of true friendshippe, of competent riches, of good estimation, of selfe-content.

But let us discarde those utilities a while. And suppose thy wife not as thy wife, but as a woman only. Tel me then I praie (since everie action of man must bee tutored by some vertue or other)[59] what appearaunce of vertue can it be for a man to beate a woman? It is not *valour,* because that demands equallitie of combatants. It is not *wisdome,* because that depends on a staide carriage. It is not *Justice,* because that requires a serious deliberation: not *Temperance,* because that wants unsettled passion. And if none of these, then no vertue at all: for all other vertues are comprised under them, as some lesser dignitie under a more ample stile.[60] Tel me likewise to what end should men attempt such violence? If a woman be perverse, shee thereby amendeth not; if gentle, shee deserves it not: if you seeke praise thereby, you shal merit laughter: if rewarde, you shal be sure of shame. Whereas therefore you are guided by no vertue, nor directed unto anie end, who but stonie hearts wil laie their violent hands on a woman the patterne of innocencie, the Queene of love, the picture of beauty, the Mistresse of delight? who could with blows deface those rich ornaments of nature? Who could quarrel with her cheekes so purely mixt with Lillies and Roses?[61] Who could violate those eies the spheares of light and loadstars of affection?[62] Who could wrong those lips such rubies of value, and rivers of delight? Who would not imagine those ivorie armes fitter for imbracing then buffeting? And who but thinke those snowy hands more apt for a seamsters needle, then a fencers chudggle.[63]

Beauty must not acquaint her with the warres;
And therefore hates such men, as love such jars.[64]

And howbeit al women are not beautiful, neither hath nature bestowed al perfections on every wife: yet a true-loving husband must imagine them al in his truly beloved wife. For love esteemes not a thing beloved, as in it selfe it is; but as it appeares in the lovers eie.[65] And therfore a woman that is not faire, may yet make a faire wife, in regard of her husbande; as if shee be only faire in her husbandes thought. For he sees her with his owne (not with others) eies: loves her only with his owne hart; injoies her only to his own content; in her then whom need he to please but himselfe? So that if thy wife bee not fairer to thy-selfe then other women are, thou lovest her not truelie. And if thou lovest her not, why diddest thou accept a loathed companion? Why diddest thou dissemble with God before whom thou professedst love? Why diddest thou lie unto Man, in whose presence thou promisedst love? Or if shee be, (as indeed shee should be) fairer in thine owne eie, because dearer to thine own heart, with what art canst thou turne rebel unto love, & whom before thou lovedst, presently hate her: or remaining constant with what face canst thou looke upon thy beloved, and instantlie beate her? No, no: heaven may assoone sinke into hel as perfect love turne into hatred: and whole rivers of water may aswel spring out of flames of fires, as violent blowes proceede from fervent love. In a word therefore, if thou lovest not thy wife, thou haste plaide the hypocrite, and so with shame maist beate her. But if thou lovest her, thou haste performed thy vow, and so with due respect must honour her.

Neither may it be thought a smal reason to deter al husbands from such violence, to forecast the dangers that may ensue thereof. For diverse women being of a diverse stature, strength, complexion and disposition, there must needes fal out a diverse event[66] of such an action. As for other men I dare not speake: and for Mr. Dr.[67] I know not what may befall: but if I shoulde chaunce to marrie with a stoute and valiant woman, such as either *Pentheselaea* was amongst the *Amazons,*[68] or the Lady *Parthenia* of *Greece,*[69] or the Empresse *Livia* in *Rome,*[70] or some other of farre lesse valour: & after a while from *Cupids* warres fal unto Martial armes, I doubt my learning woulde not save mee from some unlearned blowes. If I shoulde accept of a weake and feeble wife, such an one whose courage is daunted with a worde, whose Innocence is her defence, whose yeelding her resistance, and yet play the Tyrant stil, and so dispatch her; I am sure my law wil not free mee from the tribunall of heaven, howsoever it cleare mee from the judgement of man. Suppose I shoulde marrie a modest matrone, whose speech, gate,[71] carriage, and behaviour are as cleare as Christall,[72] all without blemish, and yet al please mee not without some civil warres,[73] howe shoulde I live offensive to my friendes, upbraided by mine enemies, of most men hated, beloved of none. Lastly if I should light on a light hus-wife,[74] who yet being civilly entreated, might civilly demaine her selfe,[75] but being trodden upon (as everie worme) wil turne againe:[76] how justly might I weare *Vulcans* nightcappe[77] on *fooles holydaies,*[78] and in sad devotion do perpetual homage unto the new moone.[79] Now therefore a farre safer course it is for us, to lay aside our weapons, and rest in tearmes of love, then to venture our selves in so doubtful a jeopardy. And let our wives bee what they be, it is our wisdome now to love them, since it was our fortune first to have them.

And as the private event of this action must needs be inconvenient unto our selves, so the publike example thereof is dangerous unto the commonwealth. For whatsoever in this kinde is committed within our own family, is acted (as it were) on an open theater, where wee have store of spectators: our children, our servants, our neighbors, sometimes our nearest kindred, oft times our dearest friends. Who perchance (as most men are) being ready to followe the ill example of others,[80] may prove by little and little the verie abstracts[81] of impietie. Especially when in this case we have experience of so many cruel & execrable murders. Some through open tyranie, as of *Pompeia* by *Nero;*[82] some through secret villanie, as of *Apronia* by *Sylvanus:*[83] some through strangling: some through poisoning: some through false accusing:

too too manie through pining awaie at their husbands unkindnes. With al which kindes I could have wished that this our white *Albion*[84] had never beene bespotted. Now in those hainous crimes though thy selfe perchance abhorrest to bee an actor, yet to teach the principles which breed these conclusions, or to be the exemplarie cause[85] which bringeth forth these effects, wil appale anie morall man, and touch a christians conscience. For faultie is he that gives the occasion, as wel as he who commits the action; seeing men are as greedy to catch at opportunity, as a fish to leape at the hooke, especiallie when the one hath a pretence of law, as the other a shew of baite.

Besides it is a maine hinderance to anie publike preferment, for how can he be thought fit to manage the affaires of a common wealth, who is not able to keepe orders in his owne house?[86] How can he wel preserve peace among the unconstant many, who is at daily strife in his owne family? *Gordias* the Rhetoritian made an oration unto the *Grecians* being then in some civil broiles, to perswade them unto concord; and having generally wonne the harts of both sides, *Melantius* his adversarie replied. O yee foolish *Grecians,* is this fellow fit to perswade you concorde, who lives himselfe in perpetual dissention? Can he rule the whole cittie (thinke you) in peace, where are so many diverse mindes, as there are divers men; and was yet never able to governe his house in quiet, where are none but his wife and himselfe? Which speech of his to this effect, so possessed the people, that what before they were fully perswaded of, they now but faintly believed, & so by degrees falling into a perfit relapse of discorde; whereas at the beginning they entertained him with good applause, in the end they hissed him from the barre with this acclamation. *Gordias rule thy selfe first at home, then after rule us at Olympia.*[87] Neither was this *Gordias* his fortune only, but it is a common brand of infamie to al his followers; who alwaies by their il private carriage draw unto them suspition of their like publike government.

Wherefore antiquity hath beene verie provident herein. When as the chiefe guests at their marriage-feasts, used to offer sacrifice; for those that were married. But before they came unto the altar, they purified their oblation from its gal, and spiced it with fragrant odours.[88] A custome in my sense not so ceremonious, as judicious, whose moral is given by the best moralist to pretend a duety of man and wife, that in them should bee no gal or bitternes, but the sweete relish of pleasing love.[89] They themselves should bee as *Virgils* vine and elme,[90] the tendernes of the one supported by the others strenght. Their hearts as *Leda's* twins[91] both interchangeably imbracing each other. Their house as *Plato's* citty, wherein nothing must bee called *mine* or *thine;* but all things common unto them both: nothing peculiar to the husband, nothing propper to the wife, which upon eithers occasion is not to be imparted to the other.[92] And if those singular pares and paralels of friends[93] (whose fame with golden wings flies throughout the world,) nothing was singular, al things mutual: in prosperity mutual joy; mutual sorrow in adversity: in adventures mutual aide; mutual triumph in victories: in al things mutual love the mother of al this mutuallity?[94] What lesse can we expect in mariage, a stronger bond then friendship, where to the present fruition of a friendly mate, is added the hopeful expectation of future issue? Now we never read nor heard of any of those friends who gave a blow unto his friend, either moved thereunto on violent passion, or otherwise induced by any occasion. Why then should husbands sue for a toleration to beate their wives, to whom as they are in society more nearely linked, so in love more dearely engaged then to their dearest friend? Many are the friendly offices of thy friend; many more of thy wife. Shee sits at thy table: shee lies in thy bosome: she shares of thy grievances and lessens the burden: shee participates thy pleasures and augments the joy: in matters of doubt shee is thy counseller; in case of distresse thy comforter: shee is a co-partner with thee in al the accidents of life. *Neither is there any* sweeter taste of friendship, then the coupling of soules in this mutuallity either of condoling or comforting:[95] where the oppressed minde findes it selfe not altogither miserable, since it is sure of one which is feelingly sorry for his misery. And the joiful spends not his joy either alone, or there where it may be envied: but freely sends it to such a wel grounded object, from whence he shal be sure to receive a sweet reflexion of the same joie. And as in a cleare mirrour of sincere goodwil see a lively picture of his owne gladnes. For which cause especially (as I conceive) *Isocrates* condemnes him for most lewdly disposed, who by his faire speech and close demainour hath wooed a virgin, & in pomp & Joviality married her his wife, will yet through anger or folly live at variance with her.[96] *Seneca* termes the brawls in marriage worse then divorce from marriage.[97] *Cato* plainely cals it sacriledge for a husband to beat his wife.[98] Such as is the soule (saith *Plutarch*) in regard of the body, such is the husband in respect of his wife, both do live in union, in disjunction both doe perish.[99] True love is the best amatorie or chiefest medicine to breede true love:[100] And therefore if thou looke truely to be beloved of thy wife, first love her truely: for els howe canst thou require that for thy selfe of her, which thou affordest not from thy selfe unto her.[101] She may in this case answere thee as *L. Crassus* the Senator replied on *L. Philippus* the Consul; how should I shew my selfe a Senator unto you, whereas you behave your selfe not as a Consull towardes mee?[102] How should a wife prove loving unto her husband when as her husband proves not loving unto her? For both in love and friendship the demaunde of *Martial* unto his *Marcus* stands with good reason.

If Pylades thou wilt me have,
Then (Marke) *Ile thee Orestes crave.*
And not in words thou must it prove;
Wilt be belov'd then thou must love.[103]

Love is a relation, and must have two subjects for its residence, as wel the husband as the wife: if it finde not good intertainment with one, it departs from both. Both therefore must be like *Crateres* and *Hyparchia,* who were said to see with double eies, because in mutual love they acquainted one the other with passage of al things that concerned them.[104] So that as the Prophets in *Israell* were sacredly intitled *Seers,* because they had a double sight, of nature and from God:[105] so was *Crateres* in Athens jestingly tearmed a *Seer,* because he used a double sight, his wives and his owne.

And howsoever we exclaime against women, that they are unworthy of such respect by reason of the multiplicitie of their supposed infirmities: Such words often flash forth indeed, but from the pregnancie of wit,[106] not from the soundnes of judgment: spoken either from a prejudicate[107] opinion, which ever miscarieth, or from particular example, which never concludeth.[108] For instance we may hold them unconstant in their resolutions, shallow in their judgment, lavish of their tongue, and with so many weaknesses beweaken this weake sexe, as that we may revive that old theorem hissed long agoe from of the stage of vertue,

Of women-kinde found good ther's none:
And if perchance there be found one;
I know not how it comes to passe,
The things made good that evill was.[109]

A flat impiety against the al Creators al sufficiencie. Who when hee had built this worlds faire house, lookt in every corner therof, & saw that al was good, yet they in the fairest roome of all, have found that al is naught. And if you flie from their first unspotted creation unto their now corrupted disposition, what priviledge have men beyond women? They are both made of one mettal: cast both in the same mould: al are not good, nor the most best. But if any might challendge preheminence[110] it should seeme the woman might, whose complexion is purer, which argues a richer wit;[111] whose passions are weaker, which pretend a more vertuous disposition. In fine therfore dislike of them we cannot, whom nature hath every way so curiously framed, unlesse we more dislike of our selves, who are the monuments of her rougher workmanship.[112]

Yet for your pleasures sake, suppose women to be as bad as you would have them. Say they are past al vertuous modesty: sweare they are beyonde al hopeful recovery. Be it so. I demand them, wherfore should they be beaten? None but final punishment is there to be inflicted, where the person punished cannot be amended.[113] Women (say you) are past amendment, and therefore (say I) they are past punishment. It is an axiome in Philosophy, that where the cause is taken awaie, the effect perisheth,[114] and it is againe as firme a position in humanitie, that amendment is the chiefe (if not sole) cause of everie such punishment.[115] There being then no hope of the one, there ought likewise be no exaction of the other. Now that women wil never be amended it is as common a phrase in our adversaries mouth, as *what lacke yee* in the *Exchange.*[116] So that it was growne long since unto a proverbe.

They wash a jeat
To make it white as snow:
Who women beat
To make them vice forgoe.[117]

Lastly *Aristotle* (whose words are maximes in Philosophy, & his *Ipse dixit* an authentical proofe)[118] seemeth herein to soare above himselfe, & leaving his wonted schoole of humanity, to speake from out the sacred chaire of divinity. *The divine providence,* (saith he) so framed man & woman, that they of necessity must be of one society, otherwise how could they perpetuate the worlde by their offsprings succession, since neither man without woman, nor woman without man can have any issue? Wherefore they were made both like, & yet dislike.[119] Like in specifical nature, their bodies of the like feature, their soules of the same essence. Dislike in the Individual, the one hotter and drier, th'other colder & moister, that out of this disagreeing concord of a divers temper, should proceed the sweet harmony of agreeing love. The one stronger, the other weaker, that the stronger in love should demaine himselfe[120] more roially; the weaker for feare should behave her.selfe more curteously. The one valiant & laborious in the fields; the other milde & diligent within the dores: that what the one had painfully gotten abroad, the other might carefully conserve at home. The one fairer, & as a delightsome picture of beauty: the other more sterne, & as a perfit mirror of manhood. The one more deepely wise, the other of a more pregnant wit.[121] Both which being by the sacred power of mariage made but one, the first condition of their *Union* is, *That no wrong should be done by either to the other.*[122] For by the *Pythagorians* law of hospitalitie it was decreed, that *None who enteres into an others house, should for the time of his aboad there, suffer any kind of injury upon any occasion.*[123] A husband taketh his wife from her friends, disacquainteth her with her kindsfolkes, debarreth her her parents sight, and estrangeth her from whomsoever was dearest unto her; he takes her into his own hospitality; receives her into his own protection, & himselfe becomes her sole Guardian. Wherefore then to beate and abuse her, is the greatest injury that can be against the law of *hospitalitie.* This law (we read) was so religiously observed of Antiquitie, that had anie one come under their roofe (though he were their mortal enemy) yet dared they do no other, but entertaine him with faire language, and send him away with safe conduct. And hence it was that *Themistocles* being banished from Athens, and pursued by the Athenians, was forced to flie for rescue unto the house of that citizen, who had ever beene his mortal enemy, & at that present the present cause of his banishment. Whereinto neverthelesse being entered, he was curteously received, and delivered foorth in friendly manner.[124] Should then a Christian deale more roughly with his wife, then the heathen would with their enimy? Surely the world wil condemne us for men of litle wisedome, or els it would never have commended them for their laudable custome.

Let me joine unto Aristotle a follower of his, a worthy philosopher and famous Doctor: whose opinion is, that wives are to be perswaded by reason, not compelled by authoritie: led on by perswasion, not drawne by compulsion, induced by lenity, not constrained by severitie.[125] For they are one flesh, one minde togither with us: howbeit then this minde bee troubled with perturbations, and this flesh be wounded with affections, yet should we seeke some cordial[126] to heale them, not a Corrosive to afflict them, for by afflicting them we afflict our selves. But to passe this easier combat, & to enter the lists[127] with you in your owne schoole, give me leave to aske counseil of the *Law* in this case.

Chapt. 4.
The same discussed by the Civill and Canon law.[128]

And as the law in general is generally held the ground.work & foundation of a common.wealth, in whose bosome justice is seated the sole preserver of good governement: so the *Canon* and *Civill* of al other the *species* are by most approved (yet how justlie I cannot tel) the chiefest formes thereof. Whether it bee for its largenesse and universalitie, because observed in almost al our christian world: or for its plainenesse and perspicuitie, because applied wel neare to each particular case of each several estate. Neverthelesse in these also by my slender observation I have found a certaine kinde of stricknesse and obduritie, against no condition more then against the estate of wives. For instance. It decrees, a wife shal loose her dowrie for giving a lascivious kisse.[129] That a wife is legally bound to follow her husband wandring at his pleasure from citty to citty.[130] Be it, from one land into another region.[131] Be it, from her owne country into banishment itself.[132] Especially if it be in pilgrimage unto the holy land.[133] That the wife is onlie dignified by the husband, and not any waies the husband graced by the wife.[134] That the husbands suspition of his wifes lightnes may bee the wives expulsion from her husbands company.[135] Lastly, if a wife play the Adulteresse (a fault indeed deserving no excuse,) her husband may then produce her into publike judgment, deprive her of her promised dowry and expose her to perpetual divorcement.[136] But if the husband commit the like offence, though it were as open as the sun, & as odious as hate it selfe, yet the wife may not in publike as much as open her mouth against it.[137] Infinite such other. Hard impositions in my weake sense for so weake a sexe. And such also as long since have beene deplored by *Syrae* in the Comedian

Alas we women live in servile awe,
But men injoie a freedome of the lawe.
For if a husband serve in Venus pay
Apparantly, the wife must nothing saie.
Yet if a wife chance steale her wantonnesse,
The law is open for the mans redresse.
But were the lawes equall to both the same,
We soone should see who most deserveth blame.[138]

If the adultery of a wife be a wrong unto the husband, why not the adultery of an husband an injury unto the wife? Or if suspition only may discharge a man of his wife, who is more happy then the jealous husband, who as often as his minde changeth may therwithal change his wife? Or if al the lustre and glory of wedlocke descend only from the husband unto the wife, and none reflexe againe from the wife unto the husband, it is hard to be conceived how there can be a true society, or a fit match? The like may be said of the rest. But al are so palpably against reason, that there is no reasonable man who wil seeme to reason for them.

Nowe the rigour & severity of these & the like laws against women, are supposed by some to have proceeded from the lawgivers, not hate but ignorance.[139] Who for the most part (altogither the Canonists)[140] being single and unmarried men, knew not so wel the estate and mysterie of marriage. And so conceiving perchance no better of a wife, then as a mans best servant, ranked them in a degree of two low servility. Neither is their reason unprobable. For who can discerne the suns brightnes that never sawe the light? Who can judge of a pure scarlet who never was acquainted with difference of colours? who can give a true censure in schollership, who never was so much as baptized at the Muses font?[141] Right so who can rightly estimate the rites of marriage, who never knew the happines thereof?

But I accuse not the law: for these former positions are for the most parte but deductions from thence. Neither reprehend I these Law-givers; for they were ancient trophees of yet living glory. Yet needs must I finde some fault with some Interpreters of the law, who fit the square unto the timber, not the timber unto the square:[142] working the law as a waxen nose[143] hither and thither, as the tide & tempest of their braine-sicke fancie drives them. Which no where is more apparently seene, then in the case we have now in hand. For in the whole body of either Law, Canon or Civil, I have not yet found (neither, as I thinke, hath any man els) set downe in these or equivalent termes, or otherwise past by any positive sentence or verdit *That it is lawfull for a husbande to beate his wife.* But whatsoever is cited thence are either far fetcht conclusions, or unfriendly sequels, which hang as wel togither being toucht in judicious trial, as the joints of a rotten carcasse engibbited,[144] being tossed with a violent winde.

There being nothing then directly against us in the substance of the law, let us see what the shadowes thereof I meane the Interpreters please to determine. Whose opinions I finde as various, as they make the subject of their opinion unconstant. And therefore I must place them in their severall rankes.

In the first such who peremptorily hold it lawful.[145] But finding themselves oreprest with contrary reasons; as men altogither desperate use such turnings and windings; such evasions, and contradictions; such poore shifts and trivial sophismes,[146] as the learned may wel laugh at, the ignoraunt perchance admire. If you have seene a mill-horse pasing his circle,[147] or a spannel[148] turning round after his taile, you may justly conceive how those men tread the maze of their uncertaine opinion. Some of them, and amongst this bad the best: hold it lawful but not convenient. Sillie men, not knowing that good lawes are never the direct authors of inconvenience. Some a little more fronticke[149] then the first, thinke it lawful & convenient too, but it must bee but a little forsooth,[150] slightly, and but seldome. Having indeed forgotten, or els having never learned, that circumstances can but lessen a fault, never of an action absolutly evil convert it into good. Some other there are the overgrowne monsters of tiranie, who proclaime it from out the top of follie; That a husband may beate his wife much or litle according to his pleasure, and as the occasion is. Nay more that he may publikely shame her, and if he lists[151] imprison her too. Men who seeme to have banished al humanity; of an yron hart; of a brasen brow, and both so cankered with vice, that vertue can get no impression. For what is it that letteth loose the raines[152] unto furie, and gives madnesse its whole scope? What is it that violats the holy rites of marriage? What is it that infringeth the sacred bonds of love? What is it that breeds horride and domestical massakers? What is that abolisheth all vertuous and matrimonial societie, if this do not?

In the second ranke are those, who out of a staid judgment and upright minde, hold it not only unlawful, but an odious, unmanly, and unseemelie thing.[153] Odious in respect of the breach of their faith given in wedlocke. Unmanly in regarde of woman weaknesse, and imbecillitie.[154] Unseemely for examples sake. And therefore in consideration of all is altogither unlawfull. Learned & vertuous men

Whose praise the sacred Goddesse of eternitie
Keepes hallowed in the eternall shryne of fame:
Vertue doth build them trophees: Dignitie
Crownes their desert; & waites upon their name.
And worthy are they of a marble stone,
Made blessed by an Homers pen, or none.[155]

In the third are such, who though they have written whole tractes and large volumes concerning the estate of wives, of their dowries, of their inheritance, of their portions,[156] of their vows, of their divorcements, and like infinite

In the second ranke are those, [b] who out of a staid iudgment and vpright minde, hold it not only vnlawful, but an odious, vnmanly, and vnseemelie thing. Odious in respect of the breach of their faith given in wedlocke. Vnmanly in regarde of woman weaknesse, and imbecilitie. Vnseemely for examples sake. And therefore in consideration of all is altogither vnlawfull. Learned & vertuous men

VVhose praise the sacred Goddesse of eternitie
[a] *Keepes hallowed in the eternall shryne of fame:*
Vertue doth build them trophees: Dignitie
Crownes their desert; & waites vpō their name.
And worthy are they of a marble stone,
Made blessed by an Homers pen, or none.

In the third are such, [b] who though they haue written whole tractes and large volumes concerning the estate of wiues, of their dowries, of their inheritance, of their portions, of their vows, of their diuorcements, and like infinite circumstances. Yet haue not a word of this question, nor vouchsafe to grace it with a graceful terme. Perchance because they thought it so hainous & ougly a paradoxe as vnfit to be matched with so many honest & goodly precepts of the law; or els so vile a position as vnworthy to be affirmed by a Lawyer.

These are the opinions. So disagreeing you see and altogither contrary, that whosoever waigheth them in the true scales of an vpright iudgmēt, can by them, but hardly rest satisfied in them. For

[b] Donellus de iure ciuili l 13. c. 21. Decianus. leg. 9. c 11. num. 17. And. Tyraquillus de legib. connub. aureū opus. Anchar. Cons. 408. n. 3. Iason. Luppus Angelus Aretinus. pleriq; alij. Tar. vid gl 1. de leg. con.

[a] Transl è Sta. vbi incip Quorū sacra tenet sacris redimita, &c.

[b] Bursatus, eq. aur. imperialis aulæ Com. Palestin. in mag. op. Guido a Bayso. Val Fost. Barbat. Bolognet. D. de Rota Decius, & maxima sane pars in vtroq; iure periti.

where

circumstances. Yet have not a word of this question, nor vouchsafe to grace it with a graceful terme.[157] Perchance because they thought it so hainous & ougly[158] a paradoxe as unfit to be matched with so many honest & goodly precepts of the law; or els so vile a position as unworthy to be affirmed by a Lawyer.

These are the opinions. So disagreeing you see and altogither contrary, that whosoever waigheth them in the true scales of an upright judgment, can by them, but hardly rest satisfied in them. For where trueth seemeth to have taken up her seate, there authority disguiseth her; and where she cannot be found there fancie would needs discrie[159] her. Everie man making an Idol of his owne conceite, and partially impairing an other mans judgment. Not finding therefore in them the certainety wee seeke for: let us compare reason unto reason, oppose Lawyer unto Lawyer, conferre opinion with opinion. And drawing from the law it selfe certaine grounds and foundations in this point, by the ful clearing of them, we shal give a faire light unto our intended purpose.

My first ground shalbe the superiority of husbandes over their wives:[160] whereunto answereth the reverence of wives towardes their husbandes.[161] This superioritie appeareth first in the manner of their first wedlocke, wherein the woman was made of man, and for man, and given in tuition by God unto man. Secondly in the difference of their sexe, because *Nature,* and the God of *Nature* in everie kinde hath given preheminence unto the male. Thirdly in mans universal soveraignetie, which he received over al creatures when God installed him his vice-roy over all the world.[162] And howsoever it was not so absolute a prerogative in regard of his fellow-woman, as it was in respect of others, because she was join'd in commission with him. Yet such it was as might wel beare the title of superioritie for the man:[163] and of the woman require a duty of reverence. But neither is the one so predominant, nor the other so servile, as that from them should proceede any other fruits but of a roial protection, and loial subjection.

My second ground shalbe the power or commande of husbands over their wives:[164] whereunto answeareth the obedience of wives towards their husbands.[165] And here I neede not to wearie out my pen, in deciding the controversies touching the authoritie of husbands concerning their wives goods: possessions, lands, dowries and the like. Only pertaining to my purpose is the commande over their persons. Which the law determines to consist, partely in imposing on them convenient labours for the supportance of their estate; chiefly in exacting the rightes of marriage for the procreation of children, and avoidance of lust.[166] To the former as much as in her lieth the wife must yeeld obedience. To the latter (unlesse on some restrictions which modesty refers unto my margents)[167] she is legally bound to give contentment. Neverthelesse in both, harde it is to bee judged whether the husband should commande with greater obeysance,[168] or the wife obey with greater commande. Both so unitely strife to expresse the effects of so perfit a union: both so interchangeably labour for the building up of the *Temple* of *love.*

My third ground shalbe, The correction lawfully used by husbands against their wives; whereunto answereth the submission required of wives unto their husbands.[169] This correction being a punishment, must (according to the rule of law) bee proportioned unto the fault punished. The faults of wives towards their husbands, are al comprised under three several degrees; and therefore the punishments likewise must be of three several sorts.

In the first and highest degree are faults altogither unexcusable, never committed by anie vertuous or modest wife: never endured by anie loving or honest husband. Such are the defiling of his marriage bed: or against his life & person any trecherous exploite. For these the law sets downe direct punishments. For the former divorce from the bond of marriage:[170] for the second expulsion from the community of wedlocke.[171] And in neither case are the husbands ingaged for payment of their dowry; or any waies bound for reliefe of their poverty. Mistake me not. I only intend that the prosequution[172] hereof lieth in the husbands power not the execution. For that must be consummate in lawful manner: the fact proved by lawful witnesse: the verdit given by a lawful judge. So that the jealousie of husbandes touching their wives incontinencie, or suspition otherwise concerning their disloialty, before they come into actual proofe are no actual faults of the wife, but to be adjudged as the braine-sicke fancies of their fond husbands. Be the suspition of the one vehement, it beareth indeed the better colour, and deserveth the sharper trial.[173] But for the jealosie of the other it is a common ill humour, and therefore in wisedome nothing at all to bee esteemed. Jealousie is a childe conceived of selfe-unworthines, and of anothers worth, at whose birth feare made it an abortive in nature, and a monster in love. For the jealous man unworthily loving a worthily beloved object, stands in feare of communicating his good, unto an other more worthy. So that neither is his love perfit, because mixt with feare which love abhorreth, nor his feare medicinable, because conjoind with love which feare impoisoneth. But of both ariseth this *mungrel* kinde of jealousie,[174] a loving feare, or a fear full love. Wherein (contrary to al other actions of man) we bend al our diligence, and carefulnesse to obtaine the full sight and perfit assuraunce of our owne misery. We would needs forsooth, know our selves to be such Becoes,[175] as we feare to be. For of prevention there is no hope. Our English worthie can tell us.

Sure tis no jealousie can that prevent,
Whereto two persons once be full content.[176]

Being then that these imaginations of husbandes, are not in law the faults of a wife: and when it chanceth that such great faults are, they are determined of their lawful punishments: whatsoever other corrections are added in this case, are done besides the law.

In the second degree are faultes of another nature, farre inferiour to the former, and yet of some moment also. Such may be their backwardnesse in the religious service of God. Carelesnesse in mannaging their houshold-affaires: Ill behaviour towards their neighbours and friends: misdemainour in regard of themselves and husbands. These I confesse to be as so many rootes of weede planted in the faire garden-plot of a womans minde; spreading into many crooked branches & bearing much bitter fruit. In these therfore the law alloweth husbands to use reprehension either sharper or milder, according as the qualitie of the fault requireth and as their owne modest discretion findeth convenience.[177] Yet neverthelesse these faults are not so absolutely evill, but that they might admit some kinde of excuse: Insomuch as they may therby be somewhat extenuated, though perchance not peremptorily defended.[178]

For the first, there is no man so irreligious, but commends a religious woman: especially a religious wife, in whom religion is especially needfull, both for instruction of her family and education of her children. But if in such, an imagination of religion fal into some peevish zeale through ignorance, or through some smal measure of knoweledge amount unto a womannish[179] resolution; it had beene better they had been lesse studious in those pointes, where the best fruit of their labours is a plentiful sheife of errours.[180] Wherfore for my part I could never approve those too too holy women-gospellers, who weare their testament at their apron-strings, and wil weekely catechize their husbands, citing places, clearing difficulties, & preaching holy sermons too, if the spirit of their devotion move them. For sure I am, antiquity helde silence to be a womans chiefest eloquence, & thought it their part to heare more then to speake, to learne rather then to teach. Aswel then too much curiositie of religion, as too much neglect is a fault in women. So that if their frailty lead them into either extreame, the husband hath the bit of reprehension in his power to keepe them in the golden maine.[181]

Againe if a wife be over frugall, it may bee supposed it is for the augmenting of her husbandes estate, and benefit of his children. If shee be very bountiful, it may be thought she intends her husbandes credit,[182] and supportance of his estimation. Likewise if others mislike her carriage, it maie bee her modesty seemeth pride unto them, or her familiaritie otherwise breedeth contempt. Lastlie if through infirmity she fal into any inconvenience, some things are to be given to the weaknes of her sexe, some matter of excuse there is in the rarenes of such offence. In al or either of these aggreivances, the husband hath alwaies the raines in his own direction. And what more soveraigne medicine, then a husbands tender reprehension? What is there that can more effectually move then a word from his mouth? What sooner inforce alleagance then a frowne of his countenance?

In the last and lowest degree are some smal and trivial faults. Indeed vertues in their owne nature, but in their practise perchance are tainted with some favour of vice. Such may be the nimblenesse of womens tongues,[183] which although may sometimes be imploied to their husbands disturbance, yet for the most part are busied in their good. In marchandizing[184] for their profit, in refreshing their wearied spirites, ofttimes in entertaining their friends with curteous complement: commonly in the usual performance of other such offices, as usually belong to such a quality. Of this sort likewise are womens affected curiositie of apparel: their over-nice standing on preheminence:[185] their womannish dislikings, and their fond longings, with other such slender errours; obliquities[186] rather of nature, then faults in manners. Al which a husband might easily reforme, either in his wisdome not stouping so low, as to take notice of them, or from out his love mildly to touch them. Howsoever, his allowance in these points is only admonition.[187] Which as it is the fairest kinde of correction, so it taketh the best effect in any good nature. You know that many sorts of soft waters will pierce deeper then the dint of hardest steele. And many thinges by mildnes have bin accomplished, which through violence could never. Pollicy goeth beyond force in martial actions; wisedome beyond rigour in domestical affaires. And far safer is the obedience yeelded up on faire termes, then that which is constrained on foule conditions: for the one proceeds from love, & is even filiall, the other commeth of feare, and is only servile.[188]

Now that there cannot be thought any misdemainour of a wife towards her husband, not comprised under one of these three, is by discourse plainly manifest. And that there ought not to bee used by a husband towards his wife any other correction besides these three shal evidently be proved[.]

Concerning the former. Our haters of women have indeede well imitated the olde Tragedians, whose use it was, when they would set forth anie odious scene, to plucke the eares of their auditors downe into hell, to invocate the furies, to muster up cursed spirits, and whatsoever was most oughly[189] to the eie of their understanding: to the end they might make their expression more vehement, & leave a deeper impression behinde them. They likewise are well skill'd in this excellent art of railing. They conjure up whole catalogues of vices, they number out numberlesse obliquities, and rake togither as many sins as the world is guilty of: fastning them on women, as on the authors & actors of them al. Pride (say they) and greater then an other pride, the pride of selfe-worth in unworthinesse: Avarice, anger, luxury, gluttonie, slouthfulnesse, envy, are the usual inhabitants of a womans minde.[190] It much offendeth not, that they are ungrateful to their friends, impatient in their coller,[191] babblers of their tongue, witty in their deceipts, wilful in their resolutions, ambitions, flattering, lustful, dissembling: but that they will needes also prove, the cut-throats of friendship, & yet seeme to be our friends. A punishment for man, and yet an inevitable punishment: a tentation[192] of man and yet a natural tentation: a calamitie to man, and yet a desired calamitie: an absolute, and yet a necessarie evil. Infinit are their reproaches. And I should forget the nature of an apology, if I spake any farther in their foule language.

First then let mee give these *Cynickes*[193] to understand, that their trade is not now so good as they could wish it were: for their chiefe ware *detraction* is helde but for childrens rhetoricke. And *Invectives*[194] are counted the poorest share in learning. They are but the froath of an apish invention: the purge of an idle braine; the falling-sicknes of a giddy wit, flat heresies in true schollership. For when you have spoken al that mallice can speake against woman, what yet have you spoken that may not be applied unto men? Sin (you may remember) is of the neuter gender, and therefore neither hateth the one sexe, nor cleaveth unto the other, but is too familiarly acquainted with both masculine and foeminine. Was *Lais* a whore?[195] she was but one: many men in Athens were her minions; but I straine not the comparison.

All women (you saie) are altogither evil: of men you are sure there are some good. And are they evil all? Why, then (oh grave *Plutarch*) how came it to passe thy wisdome so failed thee?[196] ancient *Hesiode,* who corrupted thy mature judgement?[197] *Caelius* who beguiled thy wit?[198] *Chaucer,* how miscaried thy golden pen?[199] Learned and most holy Saints, *S. Hierom,*[200] *S. Gregory,*[201] *S. Cyprian,*[202] *S. Chrysostome,*[203] who deceived you al? for deceived you al are (if this position be received) who have severally written several tracts in honor of honorable women. Are they al evil? How came the whole world then to be so besotted, as to recorde a famous memorie of manie millions of them? Of Cannonized Saints, of constant Martyrs, of grave matrons, of chast virgins, of most vertuous and unspotted wives? Neither are such as I speake of *Phoenices,*[204] rare and but seldome found. Search all histories; travell with the sun round about the earth; recall the former daies even from the worlds minority, & compare them with the latter times unto this present age; you shal finde that the number of vertuous women may wel equallize the number of men that have beene vertuous. And howbeit I cannot say that there is any woman such an absolute paragon of vertue, who is voide of al vice: *Venus* had her mole,[205] the brightest sun suffers an eclipse, the purest golde is not without some drosse, nor the best of women free from al reproofe. Yet thus I say, to object all vices whatsoever have been in al women in general, unto every woman in particular, is most injurious. Were such a conclusion of any force, I would thus dispute. *Catiline* was a Traitor;[206] *Verres* a thiefe;[207] *Nero* a murderer;[208] *AEgistus* an adulterer;[209] *Machivell* atheistical;[210] *Jovianus* heretical;[211] *Battus* a foole,[212] others, other such. These all were men. *Misogynes* is a man; therefore *Mysogynes*[213] is a traitor, a thiefe, a murderer, an adulterer, hee is atheistical, hee is heretical, he is a foole, or what els you please. The forme of argumentation is your owne. Which if you dislike, you cleare women of whatsoever is here spoken against them: If approve, you have al this while travelled with the *Pellican,* & the birth of your owne childe, wil be your own (if not distruction) yet discredit.[214]

By this time perchance your heat is qualified, & you think them not as before you did *absolute evils:* but refining your phrase terme then in the last edition *Necessary evils.*[215] This indeed is the common tenure, and most men thinke they have judiciouslie spoken, when thus they have defined the case. That they are necessarie therefore I wil easilie graunt, since hee that made man saw it was not good that man should be without them. That they are evils I utterly deny, since he that made woman sawe that al he made was good. Is woman good then in the judgement of God, and in your conceit also necessarie? then once againe you must alter your stile & hence forth write her a *Necessary good.* For these very termes *Necessary* and *evill* are incompetent,[216] they are at dissention amongst themselves, they cannot stand peaceably togither. All things that are necessary for man are good; food is necessarie, it is good. Apparel necessary, it is good. The fire, the aire, the earth, the water necessary, they are good: women necessary, and therefore good. For els if wee suppose that God hath bound man in so hard a condition, that some thinges are left necessarie for him, yet evil, we both impaire the wisdom of God, and detract from his goodnesse. But to satisfie some chiefe authours of this received opinion: I answere that some women are lesse good then other and thence they incurre the name of evill: & nature requiring a necessity of them, thence they receive that title of necessarie: & from both they are branded with the infamie of *Necessarie evils.* An attribute yet not appropriat unto them, but usually also applied unto men. *Alexander Severus* an Emperour of *Rome,* called his counsellours necessarie evils: his provincials necessary evils; the officers in his court necessary evils.[217] *Hybicus* in like sort called *Euthidamus* his friend his necessary evil.[218] *Varro* his testie brother his necessarie evill,[219] *Martiall* his angry companion his necessarie evill. With whom (saith he) I can neither live wel, nor yet live without him.[220]

But to break of this idle cavillation, which hath too long withhelde me from my purposed course. Let *Mysogynes* steepe his quill in the gall of Invection, let him speak with as open a mouth as ever Satyre did; yet al that can be alleadged, as offences of wives against their husbands, are only such as either are expresly mentioned, or els directly may be reduced unto my three former heads.

Secondly then that the corrections lawfully used by a husband unto his wife, ought to be no other then I have prescribed, remaines as yet to be more amply proved. For the first, that *divorcements* in cases prefixed are the sole & only lawful punishment, the law it selfe affords so faire testimonies, & the practise of all Lawyers hetherunto have given so ful confirmation, that now it is too late either to be denied, or gaine.said.[221] For the two other *M. Aurelius* a Consull sometimes and Councellour shal speake for me. *A wife* (saith he) *is often to be admonished, to be reprehended but seldome, never to be dealt withal with violent handes.*[222] Where you see not only a flat denial of any rigorous sort of correcting wives; but withall a plaine assertion of my prescribed punishmentes, *admonition* and *reprehension.*

Admonition it is, that with a tender hande bendeth up[223] the wound of a friend, and therefore most needful in marriage the nearest of any friendship. Hence the law injoines[224] us to deale with our wives in milde termes, in loving talke, in gentle and faire speech. That whereas by nature women are milde, loving, gentle & faire, they might not choose but best accept that from others, which is most like unto themselves. *Mercurie* (saith *Plutarch*) was seated the next God unto *Venus,* because in marriage there is alwaies neede of settled reason, and a faire language: *Mars* was then ushering of *Jupiter* in a place remote, because that warres are only fit for kings and states.[225]

Reprehension we have added in the second place, that where admonition with its smooth carriage prevailed not, there reprehension with sharper intreaty might take effect. Hence the law councelleth that overmuch lenity is to be mixt with some few graines of severity, and of them both to be made a third temperature, or golden compound, called Mediocritie.[226] By which in al our reproofes we shal be so guided, as neither using too much exasperation or indulgence, we may soone reforme whatsoever offence. God comwanded [commanded] that in the Arke of the *Tabernacle,* directly over his two *Statute tables* should be *Manna* preserved, but togither with *Moses* rodde.[227] Papirius set up before the Senate house in *Rome* the image of *Mercie,* but placed *Justice* therewithal.[228]

Jupiter *To his intreatie, and his faire perswasion,*
Adjoined threatnings in his princely fashion,[229]

What God himselfe prescribed in matters legall, *Papirius* in civil, *Jupiter* in Imperial: the like maie we likwise follow in mannaging of domestical and uxorial[230] affaires. If the Manna allured not, the rod should constraine; if commiseration prevailed not; justice shoulde succeede, if praiers were rejected, threatnings should terrifie; and if an husbands admonitions be not esteemed, his reprehension then should not be spared.[231]

In both which kinds of correction our successe shalbe the farre more effectual, if we lead the waie before by our example, which by our wordes wee perswade our wives to follow. For the abbreviarie[232] of an husbands words and actions, is as it were the chamber.glasse[233] whereby a wife shoulde addresse herselfe. At his tongue she should learne to speak, by his carriage she should compose her behavior. And a thousand times safer way it is (as in a case not much different *Pacatus* told *Theodosius.*)[234] to governe by example, then by severity. Every good example is a most pleasing ivitation [invitation] unto vertue, where the eie is guided unto present action, not the eare fed with fained speculation. And hereupon was *Petrarch* his opinion grounded, that a mimical husband wil make a lascivious wife, a riotous husband a voluptuous wife, a prowde husband a prowde wife, a modest and honest husband a modest and honest wife.[235] Wherefore it is S. *Austens* counsel, that such as we woulde have our wives appeare unto us, the same wee shoulde first approve our selves unto them.[236] Would wee have them chast of their bodie, civil in their carriage, pure & unspotted of the world? we then must walke before them as the patternes of chastitie, of civillitie, of irreprehension.[237] For what reason have we to expect more of them, then we can performe of our selves? It is a silly master that offendeth in those faults, for which he is offended with his pupil. So is it an impudent and impious fellow (saith *Seneca*) who of his wife requireth an undefiled bed, yet he himselfe defiles it.[238] By our vertuous demainour then wee must direct them in the way of vertue; for there are none of them vicious who wil sticke to tel us that we are their masters. It is reported by esteemed authors, that in some places the husbands are punished only for the faults of their wives. In *Catalonia,* whosoever is cuckoled paieth a summe of mony: in *Parrice* he rideth in disgrace through the citty, the crier proclaiming these wordes before him, *so do, so have.* In some parts of England I have seene a custome not much different.[239] All which though they now are wel neare worne out of date, yet there primary intent was vertuous, being to restraine husbandes to the loving and living with their owne wives, so that neither should need any other company, but by their mutual example one should bee a president[240] unto the other of true chastitie.

Thus then (to draw my selfe unto an end) & only thus may an husband lawfully correct his wife. *Admonition* is his first degree for smallest faults; this must proceed from a patient love, or a loving patience. The next is *reprehension* in greater offences; this must aime at the amendment of the fault, not offending of the faulty. Both of these must bee seconded by our good example, that the worlde may see us do those things which wee would have done by others. Lastly in the last & highest degree is *Divorce* in such cases as before are alleadged. Now for farther satisfaction, to prove that the laws allowe not any verberall correction[241] I have added these few reasons.

First. If a husband may lawfully beate his wife, then is the wife legally bounde to indure his beating. For the lawe gives not authoritie to the punisher, but therewithal injoines obedience on the punished. But the lawe bindes not a wife to such blockish patience. For in such a case it allows her to depart from her husband;[242] and of her husbande in time of her absence to obtaine sufficient mainetenaunce.[243] Neither doeth it limitte her anie time to returne if shee feare his tyrannie:[244] nor yet constraines her to live againe with him, unlesse for her good usage bee given her good securitie.[245]

In answere whereof that shift will not serve, to saie the *Law* authorizeth a man to beate his wife but slightlie, and not in such sorte as may cause her departure. This is too course a salve for such a soare.[246] For a little beating unto some women, is more then much unto others; and therefore in them it wil breede the same or worse effectes: & how little so ever it bee they are not bound to take it.

Secondlie the lawe decrees that he lesse grievouslie offendeth who killeth his mother, then he who killeth his wife,[247] though both be most hainous and execrable sinnes. Hence by rule of disputation I conclude, therefore also hee lesse grievouslie offendeth that beates his mother, then hee who beates his wife. But what a horride and barbarous fact it is for a man to beate his mother judge you, & then also judge what the other is which is worse then that.

And whatsoever is saide amongst Lawyers of the first proposition, some plainelie affirming it, others mincing[248] it with distinction, availeth nothing. For if (as manie doe) you holde the offence onlie greater in respect of the greater punishment allotted it by the law, but lesse in it selfe, and of his owne nature: I would demaunde you whether the lawe doe not proportionate everie punishment to the qualitie of everie offence? To smal offences light punishments; to the greater, punishments of greater torture; to those that are most hainous most exquisite torments? Which if you grant you must necessarily acknowledge the truth of the first proposition: if you deny you accuse the law of injustice. Or otherwise if your reply be (as most mens is) that herein the law was especiallie heedful: and because men are more prone to injure their wives then their parents (as lamentable accidents most usually do testifie) therfore for greater terrour to such offenders, & more evident example to other spectators, the law more severely punished the one then the other. If thus you pleade I then joine hands with you: & in the present case give the same sentence. Because men are more prone to beat their wives then their parents, therfore in law the act should bee held more hainous, because by lawe the punishmente must bee more grivous.

Thirdly the name of a wife is a name of dignity. The law stiles her thy familiar friend: thine equal associate: the Mistresse of thy house: to speake at once, the same person and *Individuum*[249] (as it were) togither with thee. If therfore she beare the name of dignity, shee is to be respected: If thy familiar friend shee is to be imbraced: if thy equal associat, shee is equally to be regarded: If thy Mistresse, she is to be honoured: if thy verie selfe, shee is dearelie to be beloved. All which duties of an husband are necessarily intended by the law; and are as contrarie to the rough and unkinde usage of a wife, as fire unto water, heaven unto earth.

And for the mittigation[250] which is here by some men interposed in way of answere unto this objection: (which is, that in the stricknesse of law, for a husband to beate his wife is lawful, but it is unconvenient in the decencie of manners:) It is a plaine and peevish contradiction, & injuriously robbeth the law of the end of the law. For the end of the law is the happy government of a common-wealth which happinesse is in nothing more eminentlie seene then in the decent conformitie of manners, and orderly behaviour in al estates. And hence it is that the Lawyer as a laborious travellour goeth through al estates, to bring al unto decencie. Hee ordereth the estate of Monarches and princes: of peires[251] and nobles: of Magistrates and subjectes: of parents and children, of husbands & wives: of Masters and servants. And in the whole body of a common-weale whatsoever is out of decent temper must by the law be ordered, as a sicke part in a body natural by physicke cured.[252] So that then an absolute *indecorum* in manners (as they confesse the beating of a wife to be) is an absolute breach of the law.

Lastly correction by way of beating (say the best you can say of it) is meerely servile: and in manie mens judgements so inhumane, as that a wise man whose actions flow from discreet premeditation, will not exercise it upon his slaves or swaines.[253] But servilitie is only to be imposed on such as are servile; and therefore not on wives who are in the law free burgesses of the same citie whereof their husbands are free, and free denisons in the same land wherin their husbandes are free: both participating the same rightes, both injoying the same liberties.[254]

But here againe ariseth a cavil touching the precepts of the law,[255] and permissions of the law. They answere, that though indeed the law commandeth not a man yet it permitteth him to beate his wife. Their reason is because it setteth down no precise penalty in such a case: & whatsoever the law doth tollerate is not unlawful, and therefore this action also is lawful, though not by precept of the lawe yet by permission of the law. Whereunto my reply is, first, to saie that the law setteth downe no precise punishment in this case is a proposition not simply true, for the reasons before in my first reason alleaged. Againe that whatsoever the law doth tollerate is lawful, I hold it to bee a position absolutly false. The law herein shalbe judge of the law; which saith that those things are not without vice (therefore unlawfull) which are permitted or pardoned by the law and not commanded. The law omitteth some things in some good respects: And those things which we omit (saith S. *Chrysostome,*)[256] we unwillingly permit, & what wee unwillingly permit, we by no meanes would have committed, but this only we do because we cannot as we would restraine the unbridled affections of the many. Many things therfore are permitted by the law upon necessitie: many things pardoned by the law upon indulgency, which yet are directly against good manners, and simply sins in themselves. I wil instance the cause. A widdow that remarrieth within her yeere of mourning, is by the law free from infamie, but by the lawe also adjudged unworthie of matrimonial dignity. A virgin that espouseth her selfe without her parentes consent, is by the lawe lawfully; yet by the law also unhonestly espoused.[257] A husband taking his wife in adultery might lawefully kill her, yet not without the guilte of hainous offence. Lastly the Jewes might lawfully crave a bill of divorce, and put away their wives upon any mislike: But Christ tels them it was granted by *Moses* for the hardnes of their hart; being yet a thing most unlawful, and therfore not so from the beginning. In which, and al other cases of like nature, though an evil custome or a peculiar permission may save a man from the punishment of the law, yet it can never cleare him from the unlawful act.

And here I purposely omit many eminent and pregnant[258] proofes which hereafter upon occasion may be added. For what neede I to light so manie torches to the noone day; or propose such multiplicity of reasons to prove a truth so manifest? Let it suffice that hitherto I have made plea in mine adversaries faculty,[259] & through the firmnes of the cause confirmed mine assertion. It is now time to remove the tents,[260] and gather my selfe within the confines of mine own profession. Not fearing to be tried herein by any trial; especially this the highest of al trials; where God is the judge: his worde the law: his Saints & Angels the witnesses, & eternall verity which never doth deceive, nor can ever be deceived attends upon the sentence.

Chap. 5.
The same evinced by the law of God.

Now here towards the evening of the day & end of my jorney I must crave leave to rest my selfe a while and entertaine my reader with historicall discourse: to sit me downe in the bloomy shade of *Paradise,* & contemplate the monuments both of womans first creation, & first institution of her marriage. For in the infancie of al things, when God had framed the worlds compasse, and bespangled it with glittering starres: when he had fastened the center of the earth, and girte it about with chrystal flowds,[261] when hee had finished his glorious worke, and deputed man his last creature,[262] to be the commander of his new-made world. At length he took a general surview of his labors, and founde them al the fit remainders of so perfit a workeman. Only man was excepted: who was yet but a lone creature, without any companion to whom he might communicate his joies, or impart his sorrow;[263] or of whom he could either hope for comfort in his life, or expect continuance of his posterity.[264] So that Man seemed not more happy in his ample dominion, then unfortunate in his solitarie estate.[265] For what could the subjection of al things profit him?[266] Wherein could the pleasures of paradise delight him? What joy could hee take in his angelical perfection, when hee had none to converse withal, but with beasts and trees, & stones, or such, who could nether understand his reports, or returne him contented answeres? Wherefore he who before saw al his works were good, sawe now that it was not good for man to be alone: but said *Let us make him a helper like unto himselfe.*[267] Where the all-eternal creator, who created all other things in a trice of time, for he but spake the word and they were made,[268] doth take a deliberation as it were, and calleth to councel the heavenly trinity:[269] to shew that he had in hand a more divine worke, and was to frame a creature of higher dignitie.[270] He taketh reason to his assistance and wisdome,[271] to manifest that now he was in travel of[272] a reasonable essence, and such an one who was capable of wisdome. And look in what glorious sort as he before proceeded in the creation of man, the same likewise he now followeth in the creation of woman; whom he made as an equal associat and fellow helper for man. For so indeed God pleased to cal her name who best knew her nature.[273]

Poore and forlorned Adam, let the world now judge whether thou then needest not a helper, when being the sole heire unto the worlds diadem, thou haddest not so much as a friend to speake unto,[274] or a servant to commande.

> *No bended knee did do thee homage then,*
> *Nor creeping courtier fawne upon thy state:*
> *Beasts were thy savage guarde insteed of men,*
> *Whose sensles sense could neither love nor hate.*[275]

Yet againe most blessed and fortunate *Adam:* God out of thee created a helper for thee, more dutiful then any servant, more deare then any friend. That whatsoever was yet deficient to the perfection of thy felicitie, might in this last addition be fully accomplished.[276] That insteede of solitarinesse thou mightest injoy a joyful companion, and in lewe of barrennesse thou mightest eternally be honoured for the worlds grandsire. This was thy last, but thy greatest of any mortal indowment. Neither was it without cause that shee was last of al made.[277] For as a princesse preparing to come unto her imperial citie, hath her herbingers[278] sent before, her house adorned & beautified, her courte replenished, her attendants ready, and al things for her entertainement prepared: So it was convenient that before the Queene of the world was created, the world should first be perfited, Paradice the Metropolitan citie of her residence finished,[279] and al things els ready furnished to her hands.

Thus God vouchsafed to honour the first birth of his fairest creature, nothing at all lesse then that of man: and in some things also farre beyond him. *Adam* was moulded out of the dusty clay of the earth:[280] she was framed out of the purified body of man.[281] Neither was shee made of the lowest part, that so shee might seeme his inferiour: nor out of the highest, that therein she might challendge superioritie: but out of the middle of his bodie, of a ribbe of his side, that thereby shee might appeare his equal, and be taken as his fellow-helper.[282] Of a ribbe also from his left side,[283] where the heart as in his privie chamber resteth it selfe, & which the arme as his beloved darling naturally imbraceth: to teach obdurate man, that woman is the Goddes to whom he ought to sacrifice the love of his hart: That shee the Saint on whom he should bestow the chast imbracements of his armes. Or thus much els to intimate, that as it is woman only whose love should inherit the hart of man: so it is especially woman whose defence should merit the arme of man.[284]

Woman therefore by the divine power of creation was made of man: and man by a strange kinde of *Metamorphosis* converted into woman.[285] For when that dead sleepe had seized on *Adam,* and God had taken fourth his ribbe, he closed up the breach with tender flesh insteede of the harde bone:[286] To the end that as his heart had now a more soft pillowe to recline it selfe upon, so his minde should become more mollified:[287] and insteede of its natural fiercenesse begin to assume a natural mildnesse. Which speedily tooke effect. For assoone as he was awaked, hee acknowledged himselfe devided, & turning unto this new creature perceived himselfe imparted unto her. Wherefore his first words and morning-song, were words of amity, & a song of love. *This now is bone of my bone, & flesh of my flesh.*[288]

For God so lively grav'd upon this bone
All Adams beauties; that but hardly one
Could have the lover from his love discride,
Or known the bridegrome from his gentle bride;
Saving that shee had a more smiling eie,
A smoother chinne, a cheeke of deeper die:
A fainter voice: a more enticing face:
A deeper tresse: a more delighting grace:
And in her bosom more then Lilly white,
Two swelling mounts of Ivorie panting light.
Source of al joies: sweet he shee-coupled one
Thy sacred birth I never thinke upon
But (ravisht) I admire how God did then
Make two of one, and one of two againe.[289]

For no sooner were these of one divided into two, and made distinct and personal: but streight waie againe they were of two contracted into one, and made the same and Individuall. Their creation was presently accompanied with institution of their marriage; wherein *Adam* received his owne againe with rich advantage. Hee lost (as far as we read) but a bare bone:[290] He received it againe branched into many bones, bewrapped up in tender flesh, twisted on curious joints, ful of lively spirits, flowing with youthful bloud, characteriz'd with azure veines, in proportion absolute, beautiful in colour, lovely to be seene, lovely to be talk'd withal, like in al things.[291] He lost it without any sense of paine;[292] he receiv'd it againe with an extasie of joy. In regard of which his happy fortunes, he established for himselfe & al succeeding ages an eternall law. *Therefore shall man leave his father and mother, and cleave unto his wife, and they two shall bee one flesh.*[293] This was his Hymineal song, this was the first statute of *Adam* made here in Paradise when hee was yet in the state of innocency: when he was fresh and pure from his creation: and (as the Angels themselves) in Christal perfection. Then was not his reason over cast with any clowds of sensuality:[294] his judgment not tainted of errour: his conscience not stained with sin: the eie of his understanding clear: the propension[295] of his wil free: and therefore then was his law most exquisite, and his words the true oracles of fidelity. In this so absolute and Angelical an estate, which now the nature of man can no waies reach unto, see how the protoplast[296] and first venturer on marriage ratifieth the amiable bond, and indissulable knot, the firme conjunction, and perfit union of Man and wife. *Man shall leave his father and mother and cleave unto his wife.* Parents (there is no man doubts) are to be regarded with al filial and reverential duty: They should be the second Gods in our honour, as they are the seconde causes of our being.[297] Yet as though there were a *nescio quid*[298] in marriage, some higher mysterie, and a relation more essential, wee are authorized to relinquish them, (and therfore much more al other friends and acquaintance, or whatsoever love, the love of God only excepted) to live unto our companion who is our second selfe. An absolute law you see for *Adam* and man his posteritie; without condition with *Eve* and woman her succession. It may be, his prophetical soule sawe that the future obduritie of man would prove to bee so stony, as it might stand in need of lawes to mollifie it: But womans nature to be so gentle, that her loving affection woulde easilie prevent any lawe of love.

And in this the nearest of all neare affinities if *Concorde* be our protector, though we live not in the glory of the world; though we bee as poore as imagination can conceive; though fortune doe in al things the worst she can do: Notwithstanding yet we have an *Asylum* at home or refuge, wherunto when we retire our selves, wee are sure to finde love waiting at the gate to welcome us, and true contentment within to entertaine us.[299] The counsel-house[300] may prove distastful unto us: The citie may chance deride us: the court peradventure not smile upon us: the fields through solitarines may breede our melancholy: the streetes through popularity may displease us:[301] al things abroade may not relish so wel with us. Yet our comfort may be, at home wee have soveraigne[302] physicke for every disease of the minde, a present medicine for every maladie, which is *love,* and *contentment.*

But where *Discorde* raignes, though thy possessions were limited with the bounds of the worlde;[303] though thy attendantes as numberles as *Xerxes* armie; & thy house as glorious as *Salomons* temple,[304] yet al this is but beggarly riches, or a rich beggarie, whereas thy minde which is the seat of true peace and content, is inhabited by the outragious spirit of strife & contention. Suppose *fortune* were thy Minion,[305] and gave thee the whole world at commande: let the rich *Indies* guilde thee with gold, & the sweet *Arabia* perfume thee with odours:[306] let the sea, and aire, and land, bring delicates unto thy table; & let Ivory beds inshrine thee from the dismall night. Yet when thou returnest home unto thine owne bosome, there shalt thou finde a hel of torments, and that bitter roote of the *Colliquintida*[307] of strife which impoisons al the rest.

Farre from the example of this first institution was any such enormity. It was here decreed *They two shalbe one flesh.*[308] Here was an union proclaim'd, their bodies are one flesh, their soules one spirite: themselves no more distinctly two, but perfectly one. And if we may be so bold to draw the comparison with al reverence to mortal man from the immortal God: As their Creator is devided in the trinitie of persons,[309] yet stil remaineth one only God in essence: so these his creatures were distinguished in the duallity of persons, yet stil should they abide as only *Individuum* in nature. On this bargaine our first parents agreed, and this bargaine they truelie performed. For as then the soule of man as the garden of paradice was enameled only with the flowers of *vertue:* no thissels were then growing, no thornes were planted: *Passion* the mother was not yet borne, nor *vice* her daughter hitherto begotten. This was the age whereof we have read

The first, & best of times were pure: a golden age:
Next to the Gods: & fardest[310] *from tempestuous rage*
Of vice. No other Empres of the world was known
As yet, but sacred vertue: shee then rul'd alone.
Then was eternall spring: the earth with richest flowers
Was alwaies richly clad: which (when the christall showers
Perform'd their morning sacrifices) gave such breath,
As though the Gods had daiely new perfum'd the earth.
The sister aire a virgin for the piercing gunne:
The mother earth not yet was wounded by her sonne
The iron instrument: The rugged Oceans backe
Not sadled with the Pine to beare the Marchant packe.[311]
Yet then the earth, the sea, the aire, untouch'd did yeeld
More fruits then labour'd now doth aire, or sea, or field.
Rivers of milke & wine from out each fountaine ran;
The herbes and trees drop'd hony for the foode of man.
Bellona *had not yet in sanguine field displaide*
Her sable armes: nor Vulcan *on his anvill plaide*
Musicke unto the Gods,[312] *whiles forged was the sword*
Which now with sharpe revenge seconds each hasty word.
No bended trumpet yet had taught the furious steede

To keepe his circle, and the crackling speare to guide
Against his adverse crest.[313] *No warres were then, no strife*
But in this golden age, they liv'd a golden life.[314]

And paralel also unto the purity of this golden age was the perfection of mans & womans soule. For when their bodies were first framed as a picture of wrought waxe, or an image of hewen stone, God breathed thereunto a lively soule, which he stiled the breath of life. And that spirit being of an aëreal substance[315] & (as it were) angelical essence, diffused it selfe into each part, giving motion, sense and reason unto the whole. Now in this naturall marriage of soule and body, the soule actuated the body, the body supported the soule. The soule brought with her a rich dowry for the body, quick apprehension, deepe understanding, and a treasury frought[316] with memory. The body, a faire possession for the soule: he received her[317] within the strong wals of his house, seated her in the warlike castel of his heart; fortified her with the thicke bulworke of his breast; attended her with waiting faculties as a family of so many servants; made his eies her watch men; his tongue her orator; his hands her champions; his feet her lackies;[318] his common parts her common vassals: some for admitting of nourishment, the mouth to receive it, the teeth to grinde it, the pallate to rellish it, the fornace[319] of the stomacke to concoct it, the fan of the liver to purifie it, the ferry of the vaines to warfe it[320] through the whole continent of this litle world. Some againe for avoidance of excrement, the eies as conducts of the head, the nostrils as the sluices of the braine, the eares as channels of other ordure, & the hidden members as fit organs for such hidden offices.

Now whomsoever it pleaseth with the eie of judgment to take review of my travels hitherto in this part; Of womans first creation, equal unto mans, having the same maker, the same manner of making: better then mans, because formed of a better substance, in a place more excellent, & at a more sacred time. Of the original of marriage; equal to both, in asmuch as both were one flesh, one nature: more expresly binding the man, because the law was expresly confirmed by the man unto the woman, not expresly reconfirmed by the woman unto the man. Lastly of the purity of this age, from whence all these testimonies are drawn: He wil easily conclude what I have labored to confirme; That man & wife here lived a peaceable life, they injoied a loving union, they lived in pure amity. If ever there were made an absolute law, if ever statute of such perfection, as neither errour coulde corrupte it, nor vice deprave it, this (we are sure) was it, where God at the first creation was the lawgiver, and man in his first perfection the lawe-receiver. Whereas therefore our imitation is to bee drawne from the best patternes, here may wee rest our selves at the mouth of God, and drawe from out the verie fountaine of truth, the true precepts of this mutuall duetie, both of husbandes towardes their wives, and wives againe towardes their husbandes. Beeing indeede all Injunctions of mutual love, and perfit amitie: No wordes of rigorous predomination, no thoughte of unkinde preheminence.[321] It was only (saith *Saint Augustine*) a mysterie of union, a sacrament of love, a bonde of fidelitie, a paradise of content, it was the truce of peace for terme of this present life, and the way unto perfection in that better life to come.[322]

But man (you will saie) by occasion of the woman fell from this integritie, and therefore woman was not afterwardes to expecte from man such dueties of amitie. True it is, the *Serpent* by long perswasions induced her to a delightful sinne of eating the forbidden apple, yet shee shewed a maine resistance; To the Serpents cunning demaunde, *Why hath God forbidden you to eate of the fruite of the garden?*[323] Shee made a short and sharpe answere, implying a plaine falsification in his close assertion. *Wee eate of the fruite of the garden, but of the fruit of the tree in the middest of Paradise God commaunded us not to eate, least we shoulde die the death.*[324] From hence shee drave[325] him to his naturall trade of open lying. *You shall not die the death.*[326] Adding therwithal a vaine hope of shamefull knowledge. Thus in a faire combate, for a faire time shee stoode out at staves end with him;[327] till through his stratagems at length he got the glory of the day.

But *Adam* assoone as the apple was proffered unto him, did never cast anie doubt, never made question, never demurred on the matter, but streight way tasted the sweetnesse thereof, whose bitter rellish remaines in us until this day. I see no reason then, but in this cause Man was more in fault to bee so suddenlie deceived, then woman who was more hardly drawne thereunto. Especially when that general prohibition of eating this forbidden fruite, was not given unto woman, *Thou* (saith GOD unto man) *shalt not eate of the tree of knowledge of good and evill.*[328] And howsoever S. *Gregorie* hath it, *you shall not eate,* as though it were spoken to both man & woman, yet the original reades it in the singular number:[329] And S. *Austen* taketh awaie the doubt, and telleth us that by tradition the woman received this commandement from the man, not by deliverie from God.[330] This I willingly do grant, & thence also conclude, that by reason thereof, the woman might chaunce more easilie to breake this lawe, then the man; since the al-glorious Majesty of God that commanded should take deeper effect in man, then the equallity of person that related could in the woman, the roaring of a Lyon is more trembled at, then the scritching of an Owle; the commands of a King more powerful then the words of a silly subject. And whereas al the fault of our first fall is commonly laid unto womans charge. *Evah* was but in parte the occasion thereof; *Adam* was the sole cause thereof.[331] For had hee observed the commande of God, though shee ten thousand times had broken it, wee had not tasted of death.[332] Wee had never for her fault beene punished, for his only we were. The reason is because he was our first roote, *Evah* and we his after branches, the one being once corrupted, through him only the other withered.

Howsoever yet the case stood betweene *Adam* & *Eve,* I verily perswade my selfe, that the same serpent, who was the perswader of their first fall, was likewise the first sower of dissention betweene man & wife. Doubtlesse it never proceeded from God, who bound them in so strong a bond of love. It never proceeded from man, who so strongly established his love. If neither from God nor from man, from whom then I pray you, but from the Devil, that grand hater of love, and lover of hatred? Neither is this position a childe of mine own fancie, or the conceite only of some other far better learned.[333] *S. Chrysostome* is the author, Satan (saith he) cunningly insinuated himselfe into the companie of man and wife, & craftily disjoined their harts whom God before had joined, whereby strife and contention do now oftentimes reigne with them insteed of love & contentment.[334] May it please you therefore that are rigorous husbands unto your wives, or such as are maintainers of this conceited opinion, to take some notice of the author therof.[335] A worthy patron (beleeve it) for so unworthy a practise, a famous founder of so impious a sect. Heaven abhorres it, the earth was not so base to invent it: hel must bee sought, and the Devil founde out for the first broaker[336] thereof. I thinke there is no man so shamelesse but woulde bee ashamed to take his practise from a notorious wicked man. How can you then be contented to be apprentices in the Devils trade? Were there no other reason in the worlde to disswade men from this impietie, but only this, that it hath the Devill for its author, what reasonable man is there but would abhorre it? But now many manifest authorities out of the worde of God, and practise of al the godlyest men since the worlde beganne: Manie firme testimonies of the ancient fathers, & latter Divines, I am faine[337] for this present to omit, because time and haste of other occasions deny me the Presse.[338] So that to them it cannot now give light, although I had given them as perfecte life as to anye of the rest.

CHAPT. 6

My conclusion therefore shall only bee an earnest request unto such as are married, that as they are bound by the word of God, and as they have impledged their faith unto the church of God, they seeke to honour this honorable estate. Husbands, that they love their wives, as Christ loveth his church: his love unto his church is the dearest of al deare loves, such shoulde yours be unto your wives. Resolve your consciences of what due authority you have over your wives. Try the utmost of your lawful bounds; never step over into the thorny field of tyranny, to which the world hath proclaimed a shame, & God hath denounced a curse. Wives love your husbands as the church againe loveth Christ. Its love unto Christ, is its greatest glory: so should yours unto your husbands. Be you subject unto them in things lawfully commanded; shew obedience unto them where it is due: Both husbands & wives live togither one in the unity of soules and consents as you are pronounced one in the unity of body and flesh. My last wish is, that this my short treatise may prove such as the temple of the goddest *Viri-placa* in Rome, unto whom (as *Livie* reports) whatsoever man & wife dissentiously living came to sacrifice: They returned home againe in love & amity.[339] If my perswasions worke such effect, my labor is amply requited: and their sacrifice of a little time in [in] reading not idlely bestowed.

FINIS

NOTES

1. Perhaps Thomas Gwin, but probably William Gager (see p. 177, n. 1).

2. One of the statements selected for dispute on 11 July 1608 as part of the Doctor of Civil Law degree at Oxford.

3. William Heale, an Anglican divine (see see pp. 167–68).

4. The Epistle of St. Paul to the Colossians in the New Testament (specifically, Col. 3.19). The preceding verse is, "Wives, submit your selves unto your housband, as it is comelie in the Lord."

5. A bookseller and printer in Oxford, 1573–1618. In 1584, Oxford University lent him two hundred pounds to start a press, and he was appointed printer to the University. More than three hundred books can be traced to his press.

6. Probably Margaret Hele, who may have been a relative of William Heale, whose name was often spelled Hele (see p. 177–78, n. 2).

7. Heale is asking M.H. to use her pen to cross out anything in the pamphlet that offends her.

8. Apparently M.H. urged Heale to complete his pamphlet quickly.

9. Those items that Heale has only touched upon would have been treated more fully. "Plaide" means "played."

10. Violent verbal attacks.

11. Bewail, deplore.

12. Cobblers were objects of derision in the early modern period. "Cobbler" was also used to describe a clumsy workman.

13. Lacks.

14. <Seneca. lib.13. ep. 89> See "On the Parts of Philosophy" in Seneca's *Epistles* (Loeb Classical Library, 1996), which instructs the seeker of wisdom in moral, natural, and rational philosophy (377).

15. <Tacitus hist.3. lib ad princip:> May refer to the disgraceful defeat of Vitellius, the subject of book 3 of Tacitus's *History,* who had been weakened by laziness, greed, and immorality.

16. The disabling of women through lack of education is cited repeatedly in early modern discussions of gender. In "A Treatise of the Nobilitie and excellencye of woman kynde," Cornelius Agrippa writes, "she is permitted to know no farther, than her nedle and her threede" (in *A Treatise of the Nobilitie and excellencye of woman kynde,* trans. David Clapham [London, 1542], F8v).

17. <Ausonius de. grat. action. ad Aug.> A reference to "The Thanksgiving of Ausonius of Bordeaux, the Vasate, for His Consulship, Addressed to the Emperor Gratian." Decimus Magnus Ausonius became the tutor to Gratian, who made him consul in 379 B.C.E. "The Thanksgiving" is Ausonius's extravagant praise and thanks to the emperor Gratian.

18. Slandered, misrepresented.

19. See n. 2.

20. <Diabolus hic fuit, ut opinatur Chry hom 57.in 29. Gen. ubi ait Diabolus subingressus tantum in eis damnum facit, ut quotididianae lites aut pugnae inter eos nascentur> St. Chrysostum (347–407 C.E.) was a renowned pulpit orator (his name means "the golden mouth") and writer of homilies and commentaries on the Bible. This reference is to one of his homilies on Genesis: "once the devil gains entry, he causes such harm to them that fighting and squabbling break out daily and there is no end to their troubles" (Saint John Chrysostum, *Homilies on Genesis,* vol. 2 [Washington, D.C.: Catholic University of America Press, 1992], 120 [homily 56]).

21. <Cyclopes fuerunt illi, ut coniiciunt quidem doctisi viri, ex Hom. lib 9 Odis h c dicto de Cyclop. -lus quisq; ministrat Prognatis ac uxoribus> Homer's *Odyssey* (Loeb Classical Library, 1995): "They were Cyclopes, as learned men conclude at least . . . he tends to his children and wives" (9.113). Heale cites the Cyclopes as an example of barbarians who are insolent and lawless. According to Homer, "Each one is lawgiver to his children and his wives, and they have no regard for one another" (9.114).

22. Orisons are prayers.

23. <Translat. ex Strozio, laur. poet. ubi incipit. Non solet in dominam leo trux saevire leaenam &.> "Translated from Strozzi, a distinguished poet, where he begins: The fierce lion is not accustomed to be savage to his lioness, his mistress, etc." Lorenzo Strozzi (1482–1551), a poet who lived in Florence, wrote *Commedia in versi* (1535).

24. This phrase appears in Shakespeare's Sonnet 30. The sonnets were entered in the Stationers Register on 20 May 1609, while Heale's *Apologie* was not entered until 1619, even though it was printed in 1609 (see p. 176 for further details). It is impossible to determine whether Heale's pamphlet was printed before Shakespeare's sonnets or whether Heale had read Sonnet 30.

25. <Plin. nat. hist. li.10.c.24, c.29, ca.23> In book 10 of his *Natural History* (Loeb Classical Library, 1947), Pliny speaks of pigeons (52), nightingales (43), and swans (32), but his pigeons "possess the greatest modesty, and adultery is unknown to either sex; they do not violate the faith of wedlock, and they keep house in company—unless unmated or widowed a pigeon does not leave its nest" (52). The terms *pigeon* and *dove* can be used interchangeably. His nightingale, which sings without stopping for fifteen days and nights as the trees begin to bud, is worth as much or more than a bondslave. Swans, according to Pliny, fly in a pointed squadron and "place their necks on the birds in front of them" (32). Rachel Speght (in *A Mouzell for Melastomus* [London, 1617]) writes of how the male pigeon helps his hen by sitting on their eggs, the cock helps his hen to build their nest, and the cockerel helps his mate defend their chickens. She concludes "that much more should man and woman, which are reasonable creatures, be helpers each to other in all things Lawfull" (D3r). <Stobeus ut recitat Patricius> Stobeus when the Patrician recites. Joannes Stobaeus (fifth century C.E.) compiled extracts from Greek authors (*Four Books of Extracts, Sayings, and Precepts*) for his son Septimius. Much of the original has been lost. To him we owe many of the most important fragments of the dramatists, particularly Euripides. It was translated into Latin in 1529.

26. <Plin.li.8. natur.hist.> In book 8 of his *Natural History,* Pliny speaks of a captive woman of Getulia who pacified the rage of many lions in the forest by her gentle speech. She told them that she was a foolish woman, not worthy to be preyed upon by a glorious lion (8.16).

27. <Translat. è Virgil. Aenead. 2. Nulilum memorabile nomen foemineam in poenam est.> Misquoted from Virgil's *Aeneid* (Loeb Classical Library, 1999): "namque etsi nullum memorabile nomen / feminea in poena est" ("For though there is no glorious renown in punishing a woman") (583–84).

28. <S. Ambrosius. tom.I.lib.5.cap.7 Hexam. & Arist. de hist. anim.> St. Ambrose (ca. 340–97 C.E.), bishop of Milan, was an eminent church father. St. Ambrose's *Hexaemeron* (vol. 42 in *The Fathers of the Church,* trans. John J. Savage [New York: Fathers of the Church, 1961]) consists of nine sermons on the six days of the Creation, delivered to the people of Milan in the last week of Lent, ca. 389 C.E. The fifth day's sermon mentions the viper: "When the viper, the deadliest kind of animal and the most cunning of the whole species of serpents, evinces a desire for copulation, he searches for a sea-murena already known to him or he seeks for a new mate. Proceed-

ing toward the shore, he makes his presence known by a hissing sound, whereby he invites conjugal embrace. The sea-murena does not repulse the appeal and yields to the poisonous serpent the desired enjoyment of their conjugal bond" (173).

Aristotle does not discuss the lamprey in *The History of Animals* (Loeb Classical Libary, 1993), but he does discuss the birth of the viper young. The mother viper "produces them all at once on the same day, more than twenty in number" (5.34) inside a membrane from which the young at times have to eat their way. The lamprey is a fish that resembles an eel in shape and lacks scales. It has a mouth like a sucker, pouchlike gills, seven apertures on each side of its head, and an opening on the top of its head. I can find no evidence that the viper and the lamprey breed together. Andrew Marvell, in *The Rehearsal Transpros'd,* distinguishes between the viper and the lamprey: "'He hath been fed all his life with vipers instead of lampres, and scorpions for cray fish'" (cited in the *Oxford English Dictionary* [1989], s.v. "lamprey" [hereafter *OED*]).

29. <Plato in Phaedon & M.T. Cicero in Lelio Natura optima recte vivendi dux.> The saying, Nature is the best leader in living right, is neither in Plato's *Phaedo,* a dialogue on the immortality of the soul and the death of Socrates, nor in his *Phaedrus,* a dialogue on the art of speaking. The line from Cicero's *Laelius De Amicitia* (Laelius on Friendship) (Loeb Classical Library, 1996) reads, "Naturam optinam bene vivendi ducem" ("Nature, the best guide to good living") (19.7).

30. <Aristot. Phy.2.> Aristotle discusses the relation of nature and art in book 2 of *Physics.*

31. <Arist. Eth. lib.5.> In *Nicomachean Ethics* (Loeb Classical Library, 1994), Aristotle argues that it is not possible for a man to act unjustly toward himself (5.9, 5.10).

32. <Arist. I. lib Pol. cap.1> In book 7 of *Politics,* Aristotle says that among the Scythians a man who had not killed another man was not allowed to drink from the cup handed around at certain feasts.

33. <Cornel. Tac. lib. de moribus German.> In *Germania* (Loeb Classical Library, 1996), written in 98 C.E., Cornelius Tacitus speaks well of how German men treat their wives: "they conceive that in woman is a certain uncanny and prophetic sense: and so they neither scorn to consult them nor slight their answers" (8); punishment for adultery, however, is severe: "her hair close-cropped, stripped of her clothes, her husband drives her from his horse in presence of his relatives and pursues her with a lash through the length of the village" (19).

34. <Aul. Gell. lib. 10. c.2. de Roman. antiquit.> Aulus Gellius (ca. 130–80 C.E.) wrote *Attic Nights* (Loeb Classical Library, 1982), in which he recorded everything of unusual interest that he heard or read. Perhaps Heale is referring to the passage where Gellius quotes Marcus Cato: "If you should take your wife in adultery, you may with impunity put her to death without a trial; but if you should commit adultery or indecency, she must not presume to lay a finger on you, nor does the law allow it" (10.23).

35. <Cesar comment lib. de bello Gallic> In his *Commentaries on the Gallic War* (Loeb Classical Library, 1997), Caesar says that "Men [the Gauls, here referring to the French] have the power of life and death over their wives, as over their children" (6.19).

36. A reference to Gager, who, according to Heale, asserted that it was lawful for husbands to beat their wives.

37. <Stobaeus ex quo recitat Patr. lib 4. tit 3. & Bodin. de rep.1.> See n. 25; Jean Bodin (1530–96) was a French political philosopher and the author of *Six Livres de la République* (Paris, 1576), the first modern attempt to construct an elaborate system of political science (translated by R. Knolles as *Six Lives: The Six Bookes of a Commonweale* [London, 1603]). There is no mention of Sempronius divorcing his wife for seeing a play, although Bodin does say that plays are a "most pernitious plague to a commonweale" (645) and that according to Roman law a husband could put his wife to death for drinking wine, because wine led to drunkenness and adultery (17).

38. <Plinius li. 14 cap 13.> <Metellus ut alii.> Women, according to Pliny in *Natural History,* were not allowed to drink wine in Rome. The "cellar" probably refers to a wine cellar. According to Pliny, Egnatius Maetennus's wife was clubbed to death by her husband for drinking wine from the wine vat (14.14.89). Romulus later acquitted him on the charge of murder. "Metellus" may refer to Censor Quintus Metellus, who in book 59 of Livy's *Ab Urba Condita* (From the founding of the city) (Loeb Classical Library, 1987) proposes that everyone should be forced to marry to produce children; or to Quintus Caecilius Metellus Celer, legate of Pompey in Asia (65 B.C.E.) and praetor (63 B.C.E.), who was believed to have been poisoned by his wife, Clodia.

39. <Arnobius lib. 5. contra gentes.> Arnobius the Elder wrote *Adversus Gentes* (Against the heathen) in ca. 303 C.E. (vol. 6 of the Ante-Nicene Christian Library, ed. Alexander Roberts and James Donaldson [Edinburg: T. and T. Clark, 1993]). In book 5, Faunus Fatua was said to have been scourged to death with rods of myrtle because she drank a whole jar of wine without her husband's knowledge.

40. This could be a play on "drug" as medicine. "Drudge" might be spelled "drug," but "drug" was not spelled "drudge," except as the past tense of "to drag."

41. Audience.

42. <Hom. *Ill* 5> Heale's memory is faulty here. In book 24 of Homer's *Iliad* (Loeb Classical Library, 1999), Priam claims the dead body of his son Hector from Achilles, and Andromache laments the death of Hector, who does not speak of forsaking heaven to defend his wife.

43. <Zenoph. in Cyro suo.> In *Cyropaedia* (Loeb Classical Library, 1994), Xenophon speaks of Tigranes, king of Armenia, who tells Cyrus that he would give his life to keep his wife from slavery (3.1.36).

44. <Martial in epigram. illo O molles tibi quin decim Calene, &c.> Marcus Valerius Martial's *Epigrams* (Loeb Classical Library, 1993): "O molles tibi quindecim, Calene" ("O gentle fifteen years, [years of wedlock with your Sulpicia] Calenus") (10.38.1).

45. <Tit. Livius in diver lo cis hist. ab urbe condita.> Livy, in *Ab Urba Condita,* does not speak of Augustus, Antonius, Scaevola, Aruntius, Scipio, or Marius praising their wives. He mentions in book 26.50 that Scipio Africanus treats women prisoners with great respect; and in books 127 and 130 he writes that Antonius treats his wife Octavia with great disrespect when he falls in love with Cleopatra.

46. "This cause" refers to the advancement of women. <Frontinus in 4 l strat.de P.

Serv. Suet. in Tiberio de C. Attilio. Zonaras de T. Sempronio. Polib. in 3. lib. de M. Pomponi &c.> Sextus Julius Frontinus (ca. 40–103 C.E.), a Roman soldier, wrote *The Strategems* (trans. Richard Morysine [London, 1539]), a collection of examples of military strategy for offices taken from Greek and Roman history; it does not contain any relevant discussion on women. Gaius Suetonius Tranquillus (69? C.E.–first half of second century) wrote *Lives of the Caesars* and *Lives of the Illustrious Men,* fragments of which survive. Suetonius mentions C. Atilius, an early Roman writer, in his chapter on Terence (in *Lives of the Illustrious Men*). Atilius translated Sophocles' *Electra,* part of which was sung at Julius Caesar's funeral games. Joannes Zonares was a Byzantine chronicler and theologian who lived in Constantinople in the twelfth century. Giulio Pomponio Leto (1428–97) wrote on military strategy.

47. <Lucan ubise pellicem luliae vocantem inducit.> Where Lucan introduces her calling her the mistress of lilies. Lucan (C.E. 39–65) mentions Cornelia only once in *The Civil War* ([Loeb Classical Library, 1997], 2.349). Marcia, who was once married to Cato, cites Cornelia, who followed her husband, Pompey, into war, as part of her successful plea to remarry Cato.

48. <D Hieronim. in Iov.> St. Jerome (Hieronymus) wrote *Adversus Jovinianum,* a treatise against Jovinian, a monk who argued that "virgins, widows, and married women who have been once passed through the laver of Christ, if they are on a par in other respects, are of equal merit" (in *The Principal Works of Jerome,* trans. W. H. Freemantle [Oxford: James Parker and Co., 1893], p. 348, l. 3). Jerome praises Demotia, whom he identifies as the virgin daughter of Demotion, for killing herself when Leosthenes, her bethrothed, is slain. (Customarily, only wives killed themselves when their husbands were killed; but Demotia considered herself married to Leosthenes in her heart.)

49. <E Plin. lib 10.c.3. recitat D. Hieron. ibid.> Jerome does not mention Sulpitia, wife of Fulvius Flaccus; but Pliny says that Sulpitia received the prize for continency and was elected to consecrate the image of Venus (*Natural History* 7.35).

50. <De quibus D. Hierom. to. 2. lib.1. contra Jovianum.> Jerome praises a number of women in *Adversus Jovinianum:* Panthea, because when her husband, Abradates, was slain, she stabbed herself and let her blood run into her husband's wounds (bk. 1.45, 382); Rhodogune, because she killed the nurse who was trying to persuade her to remarry after her husband's death (ibid.); Laodemia, because when her husband, Protesilaus, died at Troy, she died with him (ibid.); Marcia (Martia), Cato's youngest daughter, because when she was asked why she did not marry again after the death of her husband she said that "she could not find a man who wanted her more than her money" and that her last day of mourning would be the last day of her life (bk. 1.46, 382); Valeria, because she refused to remarry after her husband's death, insisting that he was "ever alive" (bk. 1.46, 382–83); Portia, because she stated that she could not live without Brutus (bk. 1.46, 382); and Lucretia, because she could not bear her violated chastity and killed herself.

51. <Ovid. in ep. Pen. ad ulis.> In Ovid's *Heroides* (Loeb Classical Library, 1996), Penelope writes to Ulysses of her love and faithfulness to him, despite his long absence, and begs him to return (1).

52. <Ovid Metemorph. li.11.fa.10.> In *Metamorphoses* ([Loeb Classical Library, 1994], bk. 11, 384–748), Ovid tells the story of Alcyone, daughter of Aeolus and wife of Ceyrx, who entreats her husband to take her if he must go on a sea journey. He refuses, is shipwrecked, and dies with Alcyone's name on his lips. The gods change Alcyone and Ceyrx into birds, and they meet and rear their young together.

53. <Justin. instit lib.4.tit. de Jud.> Justinian I, emperor of Eastern Rome (483–565), codified the laws of Rome in the *Corpus Juris Civilis,* which includes the *Institutes.* Book 4.17, "De Officio Judicis," is on the powers and duties of judges.

54. <Boindus de rep.li I.> In *La Republica,* book 1 of *Six Livres de la Rėpublique,* Bodin discusses the obedience a wife owes her husband. He says that "*Cato* commonly reputed to be a sworne enemie unto women, did never beat his wife, reputing that to be as it were a sacrilege" (C4r). Bodin supports divorce: "Yet nothing seemeth unto me more pernitious, than to constraine the parties so in dislike to live together (except they will) to declare the cause of the divorcement they desire, & also wel prove the same before the Judge" (bk. 1.3, C3v). See also n. 37. A Gordian knot is an indissoluble bond. According to the oracle, the knot of Gordius, the ancient king of Phrygia, could only be undone by the future ruler of Asia. Alexander the Great cut the knot with his sword.

55. <Dr. Casus observat. ex veteribus in com. in Oecon Arist. lib 2.>. Dr. Case pays attention from the ancients onwards in his commentary on Aristotle's *Oeconomica.* John Case (d. 1600), a scholar and physician, wrote commentaries on Aristotle's treatises. Book 2 of Aristotle's *Oeconomica* (Loeb Classical Library, 1997) is a collection of anecdotes on how various rulers filled their coffers; books 1 and 3 discuss marriage. Aristotle states that there are "rules that should govern a man's treatment of his wife. And the first of these forbids him to do her wrong" (1.4). Book 3, a homily on married life, does not speak of choosing a wife but does advise a husband to "approach his wife in honorable wise, full of self-restraint and awe" (3.3).

56. <Plautus in Pseudolo.> In *Pseudolo,* a comedy by Plautus, Calidorus and a courtesan, Phoenicium, are infatuated with each other. Phoenicium is due to be sold by her pimp to a soldier who has left sixty pounds and his token and says he will return to claim her when he has the remaining twenty pounds. With the help of his slave Pseudolus, Calidorus tricks the soldier's orderly, gets the soldier's token, borrows twenty pounds, and buys Phoenicium for himself. We know that Phoenicium is infatuated with Calidorus because of a letter she wrote to him.

57. <Tacit annalium l.2.> The reference is confusing since book 2 of Tacitus's *Annals* is concerned with the reign of Tiberius. A beadsman is a man of prayer.

58. <Virg., Aenead lib.1.> In book 1 of the *Aeneid,* Virgil uses the metaphor of the bees to illustrate industry and good order: "Even as bees in early summer, amid flowery fields, ply their task in sunshine, when they lead forth the full-grown young of their race, or pack the fluid honey and strain their cells to bursting with sweet nectar, or receive the burdens of incomers, or martial array drive from their folds the drones, a lazy herd; all aglow is the work and the fragrant honey is sweet with thyme" (430–36).

59. <Arist.li.3.Eth. cap.I.> In *Nicomachean Ethics,* Aristotle discusses voluntary and involuntary actions, not the necessity of tutoring for virtue. He does write that it is "probably a mistake to say that acts caused by anger or by desire are involuntary" (3.1).

60. <Cicero in officiis lib. 1.c. de fortitud. Idem lib. 2. offic. ad princip. Idcm. li.I. offic. circ. medium. Idem. l.2. officicium. Idem offic lib.1. tract. de fortti.> In book 1 of *De Officiis* (On duties) (Loeb Classical Library, 1997), Cicero tells his son Marcus that moral goodness comes from four sources: "it is concerned either (1) with the full perception and intelligent development of the true [wisdom]; or (2) with the conservation of organized society, with rendering to every man his due, and with the faithful discharge of obligations consumed [justice]; or (3) with the greatness and strength of a noble and invincible spirit [valor]; or (4) with the orderliness and moderation of everything that is said and done, wherein consist temperance and self-control [temperance]" (15). Cicero discusses wisdom at the beginning (*ad. princip.*) and justice near the middle (*circ. medium*). He speaks of temperance as "complete subjection of all the passions, and moderation in all things" (93).

61. In his sonnets, the fourteenth-century Italian poet Petrarch often describes his Laura as having cheeks of lilies and roses.

62. "Lodestar" is that on which one's attentions are fixed. See Shakespeare's *Midsummer's Night's Dream* (1595–96): "Your eyes are lodestars" (1.1.183).

63. The needle of a seamstress (one who sews), not a cudgel or club ("chudggle" is not listed as a variant form in the *OED*).

64. <Translat. è Petron. ubi incipit Non amat. arma venus, &c.> Where he begins Venus does not love arms. Petronius, a favorite of the emperor Nero, who lived a life of debauchery, states in one of his poems: "Doves have made a nest in the soldier's helmet: see how Venus loveth Mars" (poem 23 in *Petronius* [Loeb Classical Library, 1987], 425).

65. <S Phillip Syd. Arcad lib.2.> In book 1, chapter 5 of Philip Sidney's *Countess of Pembroke's Arcadia (The Old Arcadia)* (ed. Albert Feuillerat [Cambridge: Cambridge University Press, 1963]), Argalus remains true to Parthenia even though his rival, Demargoras, had rubbed poison over her face, making her as ugly as (or uglier than) a leper.

66. Outcome.

67. Gager was probably Heale's opponent in the debate. See p. 177, n. 1.

68. <Virg. Aenead lib.I.> Virgil writes, "Penthesilea in fury leads the crescent-shielded ranks of the Amazons and blazes amid her thousands; a golden belt she binds below her naked breast, and, as a warrior queen, dares battle, a maid clashing with men" (*Aeneid,* bk. 1.491–93). Penthesilea, daughter of Mars by Otrera or Orithya and queen of the Amazons, fought against the Greeks in the Trojan War. Achilles was struck by her beauty but killed her nonetheless.

69. <Sr Phil. Syd. Arch. lib. 3.> In book 3 of *The Countess of Pembroke's Arcadia,* Sidney writes that Parthenia disguises herself as the Knight of the Tomb to do combat with Amphialus, who has slain her husband, Argalus. Amphialus kills her, but Parthenia is the moral victor.

70. <Aerodius rerum iudi. catarum li.8.cap.8.> Aerodius's *Discourse for Parents honour and authoritie* (trans. John Budden [London, 1614]) does not mention Livia. In book 48 of *Dio's Roman History* (Loeb Classical Library, 1989), Cassius Dio Cocceianus describes Livia as "destined to hold in her lap even Caesar's power and to dominate him in everything" (52.4). Livia was the second wife of Julius Caesar, the first Roman emperor.

71. "Gait" refers to a manner of walking.

72. Clear as crystal. Philip Stubbes, the author of *An Anatomy of Abuses* (1583), also wrote *A christal glasse for christian women. Contayning an excellent discourse of the life and death of Katherine Stubbes, his wife* (1591). Katherine Stubbes died at the age of nineteen after giving birth. "Christ" is also implied in "Christall."

73. Domestic quarrels.

74. An unchaste woman.

75. Behave or conduct oneself properly. Note the play on "civil."

76. "Tread on a worm and it will turn" (Morris Palmer Tilley, *Dictionary of Proverbs in England in the Sixteenth and Seventeenth Centuries* [Ann Arbor: University of Michigan Press, 1950], W909). In other words, even the humblest will resent extreme treatment. See Shakespeare's *3 Henry VI* (1592): "The smallest worm will turn, being trodden on" (2.2.17).

77. <Vide Heroditum in Melpomone.> Herodotus, known as the father of history, recited Greek history at the Olympic Games in 445 B.C.E. His recitation was received so favorably that each of the nine books in his *History* was named for a muse. Melpomone (book 4) is the muse of tragedy. Vulcan, an early Roman deity, was the god of fire. "Nightcap" may refer to a small round cap that Vulcan is often represented as wearing or to the horns of a cuckold. Vulcan's wife was Venus, known for her infidelity.

78. <Vide T. Livium lib.45. hist. ab urbe cond. ad finem.> Livy writes in *Ab Urba Condita* that Lucius Aemilius Paulus conquered Perseus and all Macedonia, but the sons of the captive Perseus lived while Aemilius's two sons died (45.40). Heale is arguing that arms should be put aside.

79. <Vide Ovid. Amorum 2.> In a passage on the efficacy of song in causing peace, Ovid refers to the "horns of the blood-red moon," which is pacified by song (*Amores* [Loeb Classical Library, 1996], 2.1.23).

80. <Ut habet Juven. Sat. 13. Velocius & ci.ius [citius HN] nos corrumpunt vitiorum exempla domestica, magnis cum subant animos authoribus.> Misquoted from Juvenal's *Satire* (Loeb Classical Library, 1958): "velocius et citius nos corrumpunt vitiorum exempla domestica, magnis cum subeant animos auctoribus" ("no evil example corrupts us so soon and so rapidly as one that has been set at home, since it comes into the mind on high authority") (14.31–33).

81. Epitomes.

82. <Plutarch. in lib. Connub.> There is no mention of Nero, the notorious Roman emperor, or his wife, Pompeia, in Plutarch's *Conjugalia Praecepta* (Advice to bride and groom), one of the books of his *Moralia*. Pompeia, died after Nero kicked her when she was pregnant.

83. <Vives ita recitat in l. de off. mar ex Stabe.> Juan Luis Vives wrote *De officiis mariti* (1528), a moral treatise in which he advises against having sexual relations except "in rare occasions and with extreme moderation, more as a compensation for their fatigue and hard work than as a concession to their passions" (Carl G. Noreña, *Juan Luis Vives* [The Hague: Martinus Nijhoff, 1970], 211). Silvanus was said to have murdered his wife, Apronia, by throwing her from the window of his room.

84. England. "White" refers to the cliffs of Dover, which are visible when sailing to England from France. *Albus* is Latin for "white." There may be a racial implication here: white Albion as opposed to black Africa.

85. That which serves as a model or precedent.

86. In early modern literature the family, or "house," is often seen as a micocosm of the government, or "commonwealth." Heale uses this analogy to argue for women's ability to govern.

87. <S Hieronimus li I. contra Juli, anum tom.2.> In *Adversus Jovinianum,* Jerome reports: "Gorgias the Rhetorician recited his excellent treatise on Concord to the Greeks, then at variance among themselves, at Olympia. Whereupon Melanthius his enemy observed: 'Here is a man who teaches us concord, and yet could not make concord between himself, his wife, and maid-servant, three persons in one house.' The truth was that his wife envied the beauty of the girl, and drove the purest of men wild with daily quarrels" (bk. 1.48, 385).

88. <Heroditus in Clio.> See n. 77. Book 1 of Herodotus's *History* is named for Clio, the muse of history.

89. <Plutar. in Connubial.> In "Conjugalia Praecepts" (in vol. 2 of *Moralia* [Loeb Classical Library, 1992]), Plutarch writes: "In the beginning, especially, married people ought to be on their guard against disagreements and clashes, for they see that such household vessels as are made of sections joined together are at the outset easily pulled apart by any fortuitous cause, but after a time, when their joints have become set, they can hardly be separated by fire and steel" (3).

90. <Virgilii Egloga 5. vitis ut, arboribus decus est, &c.> In Virgil's fifth ecologue, Mopsus laments the death of Daphnis and compares him to the vine that "gives glory to its trees, as the grape to the vines, as the bull to the herd, as the corn to rich fields, you alone give glory to your people" (*Ecologues* [Loeb Classical Library, 1999], 30).

91. <Ovidius lib. 6 Met.> Ovid writes in *Metamorphoses* that Arachne, in a weaving contest with Pallas Athene, weaves "Leda, beneath the swan's wings" (6.109). Leda, pregnant by her husband, Tyndarus, is raped by Jupiter (in the form of a swan). She gives birth to two sets of twins: Pollux and Helena, the offspring of Jupiter and therefore, immortal; and Castor and Clytemnestra, the children of Tyndarus and therefore mortal. When Castor is killed, the immortal Pollux begs Jupiter to make his beloved brother immortal. Jupiter agrees and makes the brothers into constellations called Gemini, which never appear together; when one rises the other sets.

92. <Plat. in I. lib. de repub. sive de iusto.> Plato does not speak of common ownership in book 1 of *The Republic* (Loeb Classical Library, 1946); however, in book 5 he states that women in the guardian or ruler class "shall all be common to all these men, and that none shall cohabit with any privately; and that the children shall be com-

mon, and that no parent shall know its own offspring nor any child its parent" (5.7). Perhaps Heale was thinking of Plutarch's *Conjugalia Praecepta:* "Plato asserts that the state is prosperous and happy in which the people hear 'mine' and 'not mine' most rarely uttered, the reason being that the citizens, so far as in them lies, treat all things of real importance as common property. Much more should such expressions be eliminated from the married state" (20). "Peculiar . . . propper" means "belonging to . . . belonging to."

93. Pairs and friends equal in worth.

94. See "The Husband is the Wives head" in William Whately's *A Bride-Bush; or, A Wedding Sermon* (London, 1617): "That there is a mutuall bond of duty standing betwixt man and wife. That they are indebted each to other in a reciprocall debt" (1).

95. <S. Phill. Sydn. Arcad lib.3.> In Sidney's *Countess of Pembroke's Arcadia,* the marriage of Parthenia and Argalus is given as an example of mutuality: "A happy couple, he joying in her, she joying in her selfe, but in her selfe, because she enjoyed him: both encreasing their riches by giving to each other; each making one life double, because they made a double life; one, where desire never wanted satisfaction, nor satisfaction never bred sacietie; he ruling, because she would obey: or rather because she would obey, she therein ruling" (3.12).

96. <Isocrates in Symma.> Isocrates, a celebrated orator who lived from 436 to 338 B.C.E., wrote in "Nicocles or the Cyprians," a treatise addressed to the subjects of King Nicocles: "Furthermore, I had no patience with the perversity of men who take women in marriage and make them partners in all of the relations of life, and then are not satisfied with the compacts which they have made but by their own lawless pleasures bring pain to those whom they expect never to cause *them* pain; and who, though honest in all other partnerships, are without conscience in the partnership of marriage, when they ought to cherish this relationship the more faithfully inasmuch as it is more intimate and more precious than all others. . . . if kings are to rule well, they must try to preserve harmony, not only in the states over which they hold dominion, but also in their own households and in their places of abodes" (in *Isocrates* [Loeb Classical Library, 1991], 40–41).

97. <Sen. li. ad Gallionem de remediis fort.> In epistotle 104, "On Care of Health and Peace of Mind" (in *Epistles* [Loeb Classical Library, 1914]), Seneca mentions his older brother Gallio, who believed in immediately leaving any place where he became ill. Later in the epistle Seneca writes, "for what is sweeter than to be so valued by one's wife that one becomes more valuable to oneself for this reason?" (5).

98. <Plu. in vita Censorii Cat.> According to Plutarch in "Marcus Cato" (in vol. 2 of *Plutarch's Lives* [Loeb Classical Library, 1992]), Marcus Porcius Cato, known as the Elder, who held the office of censor in the second century B.C.E., said "the man who struck his wife or child, laid violent hands on the holiest of holy things. Also that he thought it more praiseworthy to be a good husband than a great senator, nay, there was nothing else to admire in Socrates of old except that he was always kind and gentle in his intercourse with a shrewish wife and stupid sons" (20.2).

99. <Plut. li de praeceptis connubial.> See n. 89.

100. <Lodo Vives in li de offic mar.> See n. 83. An "amatorie" is a love potion.

101. <Sen. ep. 9 ad Lucilium> In the epistle entitled "On Philosophy and Friendship," written two years before his death in ca. 65 C.E. and addressed to his friend Lucilius, Seneca speaks of the importance of men having friendships with men, not with their wives: "As long as he is allowed to order his affairs according to his judgment, he is self-sufficient and marries a wife; he is self-sufficient—and brings up children; he is self-sufficient—and yet could not live without the society of man" (*Epistles,* 9.17).

102. <Valerius lib.6. cap 2.> From *Dictorum Factorum* (Loeb Classical Library, 2000), bk. 6.2., a handbook of examples for rhetoricians by Valerius Maximus, a Roman historian who lived in the first century C.E.

103. <Martia. epig. lib.6. Translatio cius ut prae stem Pyladen aliquis mihi praestet orestes Hoc non fit verbis, Marceut amerisama.> Martial mentions Pylades and Orestes in his *Epigrams,* but the Latin is different from that quoted by Heale. Martial asks Marcus, "Do you wonder that there is no Pylades today, no Orestes? Pylades, Marcus, drank the same wine, nor was Orestes given better bread or thrush; dinner was equal and the identical for the pair." He says that Marcus "devour[s] Lucrine oysters" and wears fancy clothes while he has plainer food and clothes. He concludes: "If I am to play Pylades, somebody must play Orestes to me. Words don't do it, Marcus. To be loved, love" (6.11).

104. <Vide Lodovicum Vivem de off mar.> Heale is citing Vives's *Office and Duty of a Husband* (1538). Crates (ca. 365–285 B.C.E.), a Cynic philosopher, and his wife, Hipparchia, spent their lives wandering, preaching voluntary poverty, reconciling enemies, and comforting people in distress. <θυπε. . . ποίκτης> The Greek means "door-opener." Diogenes Laertius says Crates was "the caller to whom all doors fly open—from his habit of entering every house and admonishing those within" (*Lives of the Eminent Philosophers* [Loeb Classical Library, 1995], 6.86). Plutarch says Crates "had entry to every house and the friendly esteem of his hosts" ("Table-Talk," in *Moralia,* 2.632e).

105. <Sam. 9.6> 1 Sam. 9.9: "Beforetime in Israel when a man went to seke an answer of God, thus he spake, Come, & let us go to the Seer; for *he that is called* now a Prophet, was in the olde time called a Seer."

106. "Pregnancy" refers to imagination or fertility of mind. See Thomas Heywood's *Pleasant comedy called A mayden-head well lost* (1634): "Come, come, I know you have a pregnant wit" (1.4.106).

107. Prejudiced, preconceived.

108. Exclamations against women or generalizations about women should not be concluded or drawn from one example.

109. <Transl. veteris car. Foemina nulla bona est, vel si bona contigit uni. Nescioque pacto res mala facta bona est.> The poem Heale includes is a loose translation of his Latin marginalia. See Juvenal's *Satire:* "Can our arcades show you one woman worthy of your vows?" (6.60–61).

110. Lay claim to superiority or precedence.

111. The marginalia in the 1682 edition reads, "Contrary to that Proverb, faire and foolish." See Tilley's *Dictionary of Proverbs:* "Fair and foolish, black and proud, long and lazy, little and loud" (F28).

112. Heale assumes that his audience is male.

113. <S. Aug li.19 de civitate Dei.> In book 19 of *The City of God* (Loeb Classical Library, 1969), in chapter 28, entitled "What end awaits the wicked," Augustine states that "those who do not belong to that city of God will receive everlasting wretchedness, which is called also the second death, because neither the soul that is alienated from God's life can be said to live there, nor the body, which will be subjected to everlasting torments; and this second death will be all the harder to bear in that it cannot find an end in death" (243).

114. <Arist in I. lib. physic.> Aristotle's *Physics* (Loeb Classical Library, 1996): "everything really has a definite cause" (2.5).

115. <Sen lib I. de Clementia" Et Gell. noct. Attic. lib.6.c.14 (1682 c.4.)> In the moral essay "On Mercy," dedicated to the nineteen-year-old Nero, Seneca says that one of the aims of punishment is "to reform the man that is punished" (in *Moral Essays* [Loeb Classical Library, 1998], 1.22.1). Chapter 6 in Aulus Gellius's *Attic Nights* is about three literary styles (C.14); chapter 4 is about putting caps on the heads of slaves for whom the seller assumed no responsibility.

116. The Exchange, a place where merchants transacted business, was built by Thomas Gresham in 1566 and renamed the Royal Exchange by Queen Elizabeth.

117. <Transl. prove. car. ille lavat la terem qui castigat mulie rem.> The poem Heale includes is a loose translation of the Latin marginalia. A more literal translation is, "That one wastes effort who beats a woman." A "jeat" is black marble. In the 1609 edition, the last line of the proverb is immediately followed by the text.

118. An *ip se dixit* is a dogmatic statement or an unproved assertion resting on the authority of the speaker. An authentic proof is a legally valid, authoritative proof. Heale is affirming the validity of Aristotle's statements.

119. Unlike.

120. Behave or conduct oneself properly. See Shakespeare's *Comedy of Errors* (1588–93): "Now out of doubt Antipholus is mad, / Else would he never so demean himself" (4.3.81–82).

121. <Arist. in Oecon. lib.I.C 3.&4.> Aristotle's *Oeconomica:* "Nature [not Divine Providence] is intent on multiplying severally her types; and this is true of every animal in particular. Neither the female, however, can effect this without the male, nor the male without the female; whence the union of the sexes has of necessity arisen. . . . For Providence made man stronger and woman weaker, so that he in virtue of his manly prowess may be more ready to defend the home, and she, by reason of her timid nature, more ready to keep watch over it; and while he brings in fresh supplies from without, she may keep safe what lies within. In handicrafts again, woman was given a sedentary patience, though denied stamina for endurance of exposure; while man, though inferior to her in quiet employments, is endowed with vigour for every active occupation. In the production of children both share alike; but each makes a differ-

ent contribution to their upbringing. It is the mother who nurtures, and the father who educates" (1.3). For a discussion of the cold and dry nature of women, see Newstead's *Apology for Women,* n. 87.

122. <Idem. ibid c 4 ubileges mariti erga uxores constituit. (1682 Arist. in Oecon.c.4 ubi leges mariti erga uxorem constituit.> Translated when he established laws of the husband against the wife. Aristotle's *Oeconomica:* "We begin then with the rules that should govern a man's treatment of his wife. And the first of these forbids him to do her wrong" (1.4).

123. <Ut memiait. Plat. in Gorgia. & Arist hoc in loco.> Aristotle's *Oeconomica:* "As the Pythagoreans declare, even the common rule or custom of mankind thus ordains, forbidding all wrong to a wife as stringently as though she were a suppliant whom one has raised from the hearthstone" (1.4). "Gorgias" refers to a dialogue Plato named after the famous rhetorician (see n. 87).

124. <Arist ibiedui. (1682 Aristot. Ibid.)> Another citation to Aristotle's *Oeconomica.* Plutarch relates that when Themistocles, an Athenian statesman (527–460 B.C.E.), was banished from Athens, he fled to Epirus and took refuge with his enemy, Admetus, who protected him: "Themistocles was more afraid of kindred and recent jealousy than of an anger that was of long standing and royal, and promptly cast himself upon the king's mercy" ("Themistocles," in *Plutarch's Lives,* 24.2).

125. <Vir orna. tiss. D.Dr. Casus in Comment. suis in hunc locum.> John Case (d. 1600), a scholar and physician, wrote commentaries on treatises by Aristotle. He was forced to resign his position at St. John's College, Oxford, because of his Catholic sympathies. Subsequently, he opened a philosophical school in Oxford, which was widely attended (see n. 55).

126. A medicine that invigorates the heart.

127. The area in which tilting matches or tournaments were held.

128. In this context, "civil law" refers to Roman law, codified by Justinian in the sixth century B.C.E. Civil law was taught at Cambridge and Oxford, where Heale studied, as opposed to common law, which was taught to lawyers in training at the Inns of Court (four London societies: Lincoln's Inn, Inner Temple, Middle Temple, and Gray's Inn). Canon law was ecclesiastical law comprised of decrees by the pope and statutes of councils. Canon law was not taught at Cambridge or Oxford after the Reformation, but students were familiar with Roman canon law, probably because they were familiar with Roman law. Any study of civil law entailed some knowledge of canon law. See R. H. Helmholz, *Roman Canon Law in Reformation England* (Cambridge: Cambridge University Press, 1990).

129. <Auth. const. Neop lib.3 rubrica. 46. Idem. Aur. quaest per Io. Acar q. 34 nu. 2. (1682 32)> A reference to Justinian's *Authenticum,* a collection of laws promulgated in the sixth century. "Rubric" refers to a chapter heading in a law book. "Quaest" means "quaestio," a gloss consisting of a dialectical examination of a question arising out of a decretum. "Io. Acar" may refer to Accursius, a thirteenth-century glossator from Bologne.

130. <Jason in l. de Att. ff. Idem Duacon. in tit. soluto matrimonio. (1682 Dracon)>

"Tit." means "title." "Soluto matrimonio" means "dissolution of marriage." "Dracon" may refer to Blossius Aemilius Dracontius, a fifth-century Latin poet and lawyer who wrote *Romulea,* which has a section on Medea, Jason's wife.

131. <Petr. de Ancha. super decret in c. num.16. (1682 Patr.)> Probably a reference to Petrus de Ancharano (Peter of Ancharino), the early fifteenth-century lay canonist who wrote *Commentaria in Decretales.* "Decret." means "decretal," a letter containing a papal ruling.

132. <Alcit. t a.>. "Alcit." probably refers to Andrea Alciati, the fifteenth-century Italian jurist who published many legal works. He was one of the first to use classical history and literature to interpret civil law and to substitute original research for the more standard interpretations of glossators. Glosses were explanations of words and phrases in a text by way of discussions of possible applications and cross-references to relevant passages in the law.

133. <D. Aloysius. de le in l.5. ad L. Jul. vol 4. (1682 Alcius)>. "Le" probably stands for "lex" or "law."

134. <Com op. lib. 5.tit.de nupt. 2.> "Com" may refer to the fifth *compilatione* (compilation) of canon law (1226), composed by Tancred, another Bolognese law professor. Each book of the compilation was divided into sections that treated different aspects of a subject; for example, book 4 focuses on marriage, while book 5 focuses on crime.

135. <De (1682 Dec) eis Vi-vii. lib.2. de ci.241. nu 4> Probably Gratian's *Decretum* (ca. 1140), the standard text of canon law in schools and the standard reference book in law courts. Gratian's systematization of canon law allowed it to take its place beside Justinian's Roman civil law.

136. <Bald. & Ang. Aret. in L. Imp. ff. de statu hominis.> Baldus de Ubaldis (ca. 1327–1406) wrote extensively on civil and canon law. Among his students were Pierre Roger de Beaufort, who became Pope Gregory XI, and Peter of Ancharino (see n. 131). He wrote a commentary on the *Liber extra,* known as *The Decretales Gregorii.* "Aret." may refer to Angeli Gambilioni Aretini, who wrote a commentary on Justinian in 1568. "Ff." usually refers to Justinian's *Digest.* "De statu hominis" means "of the condition of man."

137. <Cod lib 9 co.7. ad le. Jul. de adul & stupr.> The *Codex* is the section on statutory law in Justinian's *Corpus Juris Civilis.* The other sections are the *Digest* (or *Pandects*), containing extracts of outstanding jurists; the *Institutes,* a student textbook; and the *Novellae,* containing new laws. Justinian promulgated his *Codex* as the law of the eastern Roman Empire in 529. "Ad legam Julian de adulteriis et de stupro" (dealing with adultery and rape) is section 9.9 in Justinian's *Codex.*

138. <Transl. ex Plauto in Com. Mer.sicastor (inquit) lege dura vivunt mulieres. Multoq; inquiore miserae, quam viri, &c.> The Latin is from Plautus's comedy *Mercator; or, The Merchant* (Loeb Classical Library, 1995): "Ecastor lege dura vivont mulieres / multoque iniquiore miserae quam viri" (4.6.817–18). The lines are spoken by Syra, an old slave, when she suspects her master of having a mistress. (He is actually just taking care of the woman for a neighbor who is infatuated with her.) See

Emilia's speech in Shakespeare's *Othello* (1603–4) (4.3.86–103) and Adriana's speech in Shakespeare's *Comedy of Errors* (2.1.104–15).

139. <Vide Tyraquillum de legibus connub.> Andre Tiraqueau (1488–1558), a friend of Rabelais, was known as the "matrimonial lawgiver." He wrote *De legibus connubialibus* (Paris, 1513), a treatise on marriage law. "Vide" means "namely." Although Tiraqueau believed that a wife should be obedient to her husband, he states that his authority must not become abusive: "Vir potest uxorem moderatem castigare" ("A man may castigate his wife with moderation") (1.1.22). He then gives the names of earlier lawgivers who believed that wife beating was ignorant (1.1.23).

140. Experts in canon or ecclesiastical law, here referring to unmarried priests.

141. See Newstead's *Apology,* n. 11. Many fountains, such as Pindus, Helicon, and Parnassus, were sacred to the Muses.

142. Trying to fit a square into a circle rather than a circle into a square, the first of which is impossible (assuming the diameter of the circle and the sides of the square remain unchanged).

143. That is, shaping the law to their purposes as if it were made of wax.

144. Hung from a gibbet, or an upright post with a projecting arm from which executed bodies were suspended for public viewing. In other words, the interpretations of the law that argue for wife beating do not hold up under public scrutiny.

145. <Glos. in l. & si quemcunque parag. vl in fi. ff. ad l. Aqu.> What follows is a list of citations of writers who hold wife beating to be legal. "Ff. ad l. Aqu." refers to "Ad Legem Aquilam" in Justinian's *Digest:* "Sed et si quemcunque" (9.2.5). <Alb. Grand in tract ma l. fic. (malefic HN) tit. de pae. reo. col ult.> "Maleficium" could mean "witchcraft"; "Col ult." means "last column." Albertus Magnus, or Alexander the Great (ca. 1200–1280), the teacher of Thomas Aquinas, wrote on theology, scripture, logic, metaphysics, and natural and moral sciences. <Lucas Pen in lib quicunq; Col.2. & 3. C de Mil. lib.12. Io And. &c (1682 Andr.)> Lucus de Penna, a fourteenth-century law professor, wrote *Commentarium ad Tres Libros Codicis.* "Jo And." refers to Joannes Andreae (ca. 1270–1348), professor of decretals at Bologna. His glosses on the *Liber Sextus* and the *Clementine Constitutions on the Decretals of Gregory IX* were adopted as the *glossa ordinaria,* the best selection of commentaries. He also wrote a *summa,* or summary treatise, on marriage problems and another on consanguinity. Christine de Pizan maintained that Novella, Johannes's youngest daughter, lectured in her father's place when he was busy (*The Book of the City of Ladies* [New York: Persea Books, 1982], 2.36.3). <Panor. in d c lit. ille col.2. in v. incertis. hic col. penul vers.> "Incertis" means "uncertain." "Panor." refers to *Panormia,* an abridgment of Ivo's *Decretum,* an encyclopedia of canon law produced at the end of the eleventh century that is known for its brevity, order, and the legal accuracy of its summaries. "Penul vers." means "penultimate column." <A. Aureae (1682 Acturea) quaest lib 3 quaest. 18. nu 9 & 10.> "Quaest" is short for "quaestione," a question on a situation in a case in *The Decretum of Gratian* (see n. 129). "Nu" means "number." "Aureae" may describe "summae," which are celebrated in the history of canon law. <Alexander Consil 113 (1682 123) Col 1. & 2. v.3.> Pope Alexander III (ca. 1105–81) wrote *Summa Magistri Rolandia,* a com-

mentary on Gratian's *Decretum.* Before he became pope, Alexander's name was Rolando Bandinelli. "Consil" is short for "consilia," or debate. Alexander compiled an important book of marriage decretals. <Bald. Consil. 176.> See n. 136. Baldus wrote a number of *consilia.* <Bouhic. super 2 decr. de jure julando. (1682 Bontl. sup Dec.2. de inrejurando.)> A reference to book 2 of the *Decretals of Gregory IX,* "De iureiurando" (On oathtaking), in the *Corpus Juris Canonici.* <Plures si velis quore A Taraquellam. de legib. connubial. in gl.1.> See n. 139. Tiraqueau lists proponents of wife beating in gloss 1.1.23 of *De legibus connubialibus.*

146. Fallacious arguments used to deceive.

147. A horse walking in circles and turning a millstone to operate a mill.

148. Spaniel (breed of dog).

149. Frantic, although this spelling is not in the *OED.*

150. In truth.

151. Pleases.

152. Reins.

153. <Donellus de jure civili l 13.c.21.> What follows is a list of citations of writers who hold wife beating to be unlawful, unmanly, and odious. Hugonis Donelli, or Huges Doneau, was a sixteenth-century lawyer who wrote *De jure civili.* Book 13, chapter 21 concerns marriage law; 13.21.16 states that neither divine nor civil law permits wife beating. <Decianus. leg.9.c 11. num. 17.> Tiberio Deciani was a sixteenth-century lawyer. <And. Tyraquillus de legib. connub. aureum opus.> See nn. 139 and 145. Tiraqueau lists lawgivers who are against wife beating. <Anchar. Conf. 408.n.3. Jason. Luppus Angelus Aretinus. pleriq; alii. Tar.vid gl 1. de leg. con.> "Anchar." may refer to Peter of Ancharino (see n. 131). For Jason, see n. 130. "Aretinus." may refer to Angelo Gambilioni Aretini (see n. 136). "Tar." probably refers to Tiraqueau and his treatise on marriage laws (see n. 139).

154. Weakness.

155. <Transl è Sta. ubi incip Quorum sacra tenet sacris redimita, &.> The Roman poet Statius (ca. 40–96 C.E.) wrote *Silvae, Thebais,* and *Achilleis,* but this quote does not come from any of those texts.

156. A portion was a woman's dowry, or property given to a woman and/or her husband upon marriage, usually by her family. This is not to be confused with a dower, which was the common-law right of a widow to a share (usually one-third) of her late husband's estate.

157. <Bursatus, cq. aur. imperialis aulae Com. Palestin. in mag. op. Guido a Bayso. Val Fost. Barbat. Bolognet. D. de Rota Decius, & maxima sane pars in utroq; jure periti.> Francesco Bursati wrote a *Concilia* in 1573. In 1300 Guido de Baysio wrote *Rosarium,* a scholarly commentary on Gratian's *Decretum.* Among his pupils was Johannes Andreae (see n. 145). Andreas de Barbatia, or Andreas Siculus (1400–1479), was a renowned teacher and lay canon lawyer who wrote several tracts on canon law. "Utroq" means "to both sides" and "periti." means "experienced."

158. Heinous (hateful) and ugly (dreadful).

159. Reveal, make known.

160. <Cod.li.6. tit 46 lege 5. & plerisq, aliis locis.> Book 6.46.5 and elsewhere in Justinian's *Codex.*

161. <Ibidem subsequent verbis.> This translates as, "Words follow the previous reference."

162. Heale quotes from Genesis four times (*The Geneva Bible: A Facsimile of the 1560 Edition* [Madison: University of Wisconsin Press, 1969]): "And the rybbe which the Lord God had taken from the man, made he a woman, and broght her to the man" (2.22); "The man therefore gave names unto all cattel, and to the foule of the heaven, and to everie beast of the field: but for Adam founde he not an helpe mete for him" (2.20); "Then the man said, This now is bone of my bones, and flesh of my flesh. She shalbe called woman, because she was taken out of man" (2.23); and "And God blessed them, and God said to them, Bring forthe frute and multiplie, and fil the earth, and subdue it, and rule over the fish of the sea and over the foule of the heaven, & over everie beast that moveth upon the earth" (1.28).

163. <S. Chrysost. hom.9. in Gen. Ruper. li.2 de Trinitate.> St. John Chrysostum (347–407) wrote about six hundred commentaries and homilies in addition to treatises, orations, letters, and liturgy. The name "Chrysostum," which means "golden mouth," was given to him because of his oratorial ability. In volume 1 of *Homilies on Genesis* (Washington, D.C.: Catholic University of America Press, 1986), Chrysostum writes, "One is in command, the other is subordinate, just as God had also said to woman from the beginning 'your yeaning will be for your husband, and he will be your master'" (111; note that this is homily 8, not 9). "Ruper." refers to Rupert of Deutz (1075–1129), who wrote *De Sancta Trinitate et Operibus Eius* (ed. Hrabanus Haacke [Turnholti: Typographi Brepols Editores Pontificii, 1971]. The creation of Adam and Eve is described in book 2 (p. 7).

164. <Digest. li. 38. tit. I. lege.8. (1682 leg. 48), Cod. loco superius citato. & Inst 2.> In Justinian's *Digest* (3.1.48), *Codex,* and *Institutes* ("De Nuptiis," bk. 2, title 10). See n. 137.

165. <Ibidem. ut jure etiam bald in C. I tit. An mariti suc. uxor.> "Bald" refers to Baldus, who comments on marriage and wives (see n. 136).

166. <Ang. Aretin. Inst. d.SC. Bar. in d. li.j. parag j. ff. de iniur: & caeteri.> "Ang." may refer to Angilrammus of Metz (d. 791), bishop and canonist, as well as the named author of the pseudo-Isidorian decretals *Capitula Angilramni.* For "Aretin.," see n. 136. "Inst." refers to Justinian's *Institutes.* "Bar." may refer to Bartholomaeus Brixiensis (d. 1258), whose *Glossa ordinaria* on Gratian's *Decretum* was widely reproduced. "Ff." may refer to Justinian's *Digest.* "Iniur." means "injuries." "Caeteri" means "the remaining."

167. <Viz. In tempore menstr. praegnantie. Immunditiae egritudinis Infantiae. sacrae abstinentiae. Uti habet. Pau Ca. in d l. rei jud. iuncta l seq ff. Anto. a Prat. & alii> A wife may abstain from sexual intercourse during menstruation, pregnancy, and childbirth. "Pau" refers to Paulus De Liazariis, a fourteenth-century canonist who wrote *Casus Summarii,* often cited by later writers. "Anto." may refer to Antonius de Butrio, a fourteenth-century lay canonist, decretalist, and teacher; or it may refer to the thirteenth-century saint Anthony of Padua, a famous preacher who wrote sermons. "Margents" means "margins."

168. Obedience.

169. <Gl. in leg si quencunq; parag. vl. in fi. ff ad L.Aquil. Gl. in auth. ut lic. matr: & aviae parag. Quia vero quaedam mulieres in ver. sufficere. Caeteri, vide Tiraquil. I. lib. Connub. gl. I. parte. I.> "Gl." means "gloss," of which "si quencunq" are the opening lines (para. 5 of "Ad Legem Aquilam" in Justinian's *Digest;* see n. 145). "Auth." refers to Authenticum, the new laws of Justinian, of which "ut lic. matr." may be the opening lines. For Tiraquil (Tiraqueau), see n. 139.

170. <Reg. glos. TVae de procurato. Cod. lib 9. ad I Jul. de adul. & stupr.> See n. 137. "Procurato" means "taking care of."

171. <Syntagma communium opin. vide.1.752. n.23.> "Syntagma" may refer to the *Syntagma Canonum Antochenum,* a chronological collection of canons representing one of the main documentary sources of Byzantine law. The distinction is between the annulment of a marriage and legal separation "from bed and board." An annulment could only be granted if impediments to the marriage, such as a prior contract of marriage, impotence, or an underage partner, could be proven. In an annulment the children were declared bastards and the woman lost her dower rights but both parties could remarry. A legal separation was granted for proof of adultery or extreme cruelty, though the parties could not marry as long as their former spouse was living. The woman, however, kept her dower rights.

172. Prosecution.

173. If the suspicion is very strong, then it is more likely and should have a more vigilant trial.

174. That is, "mongrel," because it is jealousy mixed with love.

175. Cuckolds.

176. <S. Phil. Sydn. Arc. lib 3.> In the third ecologue of Sidney's *Countess of Pembroke's Arcadia,* Nico sings a song against jealousy:

Thus may you see the jealous wretch was made
The pander of the thing he most did fear.
Take heed, therefore, how you ensue that trade,
Lest that some marks of jealousy you bear;
  For sure no jealousy can that prevent
  Whereto two parties once be full content. (253)

177. <Tex. in parag. necesse est. 47 dist. & facit C. indignantur in fine. 32.q.6. Glos. in I. si quemcunq; parag. vl. in f.ff. ad 1. Aquil. Tyraquil. 1.l.con. gl. I. par. I.> See n. 145 for "ff." and "Aquil." See n. 139 for Tiraqueau. In *De legibus connubialibus,* Tiraqueau states that the husband may moderately castigate his wife (1.1.22).

178. Diminished though perhaps not positively defended.

179. That is, weak.

180. A sheaf or a large number. Heale is implying that women who labor in the study of religion may bear only errors.

181. The husband may reprehend his wife ("bit" may refer to the mouthpiece of a horse's bridle) to keep her within the golden mean, that is, within moderation.

182. If she is generous and spends a lot of money, she may be furthering her husband's reputation.

183. See Joseph Swetnam's *Araignment Of Lewde, idle, froward, and unconstant women* (London, 1615): "for they have delicate tongues which will ravish and tickle the itching eares of giddy headed youngmen" (32).

184. Trading.

185. Preeminence or priority of place; superiority.

186. Aberrations or errors.

187. <Juriscent. in l.ult. ff. si quis aliq. test prohib S. Bernard in ep ad Rayn und. de re fam. Vide Tyraq. I.l. connub. gl I. par I.> See nn. 145 and 177. In Justinian's *Digest* this is rendered as, "Si quis aliquem testari prohibuerit vel coegerit" (29.6). St. Bernard (ca. 1090–1153) was a Cistercian monk and abbot of Clairvaux who wrote many epistles, a few of which were addressed to Rainaldus. For "Tyraq." (Tiraqueau), see nn. 139 and 177.

188. <Plutarch. in prec connubialibus.> See n. 89 and Plutarch's *Conjugalia Praecepta:* "And control ought to be exercised by the man over the woman, not as the owner has control of a piece of property, but, as the soul controls the body, by entering into her feelings and being knit to her through goodwill" (33). "Filiall" means "like a daughter." A wife was treated as a daughter in Roman law.

189. Ugly.

190. <Myogynes quidam cuius totam spurcam & impuram declamationem recitat Tyraq. I.l con gl. I. par. I. (1682 2.l.con gl. par. I.)> A certain Myogynes [misogynist] reads aloud a totally foul and vile declamation. Swetnam's name in the play *Swetnam, The Woman-hater, Arraigned by Women* (1620) is Misogynos, or woman-hater. For Tiraqueau, see nn. 139 and 177.

191. Choler.

192. Temptation.

193. People who are inclined to find fault.

194. Violent denunciations.

195. Lais was a celebrated courtesan whom many famous Greek men frequented. She was assassinated by their wives in the Temple of Venus ca. 340 B.C.E.

196. <Plutarch. lib. de clar. foem.> Plutarch wrote on the bravery of women in *Moralia* (see nn. 89 and 188).

197. <Hesiodus lib. de mulier heroid> Hesiod (ca. 900 B.C.E.) wrote a series of genealogies entitled *Catalogs of Women* that trace the Hellenic peoples from a common ancestor. Because each family claimed to be descended from a god, he traced each family to a mortal woman beloved by that god—hence the prominence of women.

198. <Caelius li. lection. antiquarum.> May refer to Marcus Caelius Rufus, who wrote letters to Cicero containing the latest news; or to Caelius Aurelianus, a (possibly) fourth-century Greek physician who translated medical texts by Soranus.

199. <Chaucer. lib. faeminarum encomion. I. & alterum, de laudib. bonarum faeminar.> A reference to Geoffrey Chaucer's *Legend of Good Women* (1386), nine stories of women who were all victims of the ideal of chaste love.

200. The lettered notes are mixed up in the 1609 edition. "S. Hieron." has the letter "e" before it, but the note refers to "S. Greg." and there is no note on "S. Hieron" (St. Jerome). In *Adversus Jovinianum,* St. Jerome praises virginal women in his refutation of Jovinian's claim that God views chaste married people as equal to virgins (see n. 48). It has been argued that Jerome's work is satirical and reveals a horror of female sexuality.

201. <S. Greg. Syntagm. de musis.> The Italian poet and scholar Giglio Gregorio Giraldi (1479–1552), not a saint by that name, wrote *Syntagma de Musis* (A Treatise on the Muses). St. Gregory Nazianzen wrote letters, poems, and *Moral Orations,* which includes "On the Indissolubility of Marriage" and a funeral oration addressed to his sister Gorgonia, who died ca. 369–74, whom he praises as a model Christian woman.

202. <S. Cyprian. lib. de singularitate faeminarum.> St. Cyprian (d. 258) was bishop of Carthage and provided material for Gratian's *Decretum.* In epistle 80 Cyprian writes, "Blessed women also, who are established with you in the same glory of confession, who, maintaining the Lord's faith, and braver than their sex, not only themselves are near to the crown of glory, but have afforded an example to other women by their constancy!" (*The Epistles of Cyprian,* in the Ante-Nicene Christian Library, ed. Alexander Roberts and James Donaldson [Edinburgh: T. and T. Clark, 1990], 407).

203. A lettered note is missing. <S. Chrysostom. in hom. decol lat. 10. Baptistae.> See n. 163. Chrysostom's homily 10 speaks of the creation of man and woman in God's image.

204. Phoenixes.

205. That is, her imperfections.

206. Cataline conspired to ruin Rome by doing away with the Senate, plundering its treasury, and setting Rome on fire.

207. The Roman C. Verres was notorious for his misgovernment of Sicily. He stole from the Sicilians, who brought charges against him. Cicero, who defended the Sicilians, wrote *The Verrine Orations* (Loeb Classical Library, 1989) about this incident.

208. Nero murdered his mother and his wife as well as Seneca, Lucan, and Petronius.

209. Aegisthus, king of Argos, murdered Agamemnon and Clytemnestra, Agamemnon's wife, because they had fallen in love. Aeschylus dramatizes the death of Agamemnon in his tragedy *Agamemnon.*

210. Niccolò Machiavelli, author of *The Prince* (1513), was often described as an atheist. *The Prince* was translated into English in 1602.

211. See n. 200. Jovinian's heresy was believing that God viewed chaste married people as equal to virgins. It is interesting that Heale, a Protestant cleric, would consider this heretical.

212. Battus was Caesar's buffoon.

213. That is, a woman hater. See n. 190.

214. Heale uses a faulty syllogism in his attempt to prove that the faults found in some men and women are not in all. If the reader approves of the faulty logic, he or she has "travelled with the Pellican," which could be a symbol of dullness and indo-

lence, as well as migration (Gertrude Jobes, *Dictionary of Mythology, Folklore, and Symbols,* 3 vols. [New York: Scarecrow Press, 1961–62], 2:1250).

215. <Quod vetus apud Graecos proverb ἀναγκαῖον κακὸν = necessary evil> With regard to an old saying in the writings of the Greeks. In *An Araignment Of Lewde, idle, froward, and unconstant women,* Swetnam states: "If God had not made them only to be a plague to men, he would never have called them necessary evils" (31).

216. Insufficient.

217. <Ita (1682 Lex) de eo narrat Aelius Lampidius.> Aelius Lampridius, one of the six biographers of *Historia Augusta.* Alexander Severus, emperor of Rome from 222 to 235 C.E., had some members of his council elected. He was murdered by his soldiers in 235.

218. <Stra. l.14.> In volume 6 of *The Geography of Strabo* (Loeb Classical Library, 1989), Hybreas says of Euthydemus: "You are an evil necessary to the city, for we can live neither with you nor without you" (14.2.24).

219. <Varro.> Varro (d. 25 B.C.E.), a great Roman scholar, wrote prolifically on science, history, rhetoric, music, jurisprudence, medicine, and architecture. One satire was entitled "On the Duty of a Husband."

220. <Martial. de scipsis uarrant. (HD narrant)> Martial speaks about his writings. See n. 44.

221. Opposed, contradicted.

222. Marcus Aurelius, Roman emperor from 161 to 80 C.E., wrote *Meditations* as well as letters to his tutor Fronto.

223. Binds up.

224. <Juriscons in l.ult.ff. siquis aliq. test. proh.> See n. 187.

225. <Plut. li. de praec. connub.> See n. 89.

226. <Vide Tyraquil I.li. connub. gl. I. par.1. & Greg. M. Moral. lib. 20 par. 20. par. 4.c.11.> On "Tyraquil" (Tiraqueau), see nn. 139 and 177. St. Gregory of Nyssa wrote a treatise entitled "On Virginity" in which he states "that all virtue is found in moderation, and that any declension to either side of it becomes a vice" (in *Dogmatic Treatises, etc.* [Grand Rapids, Mich.: Wm. B. Erdmans, 1892], chap. 8, 352). "Mediocritie" is a mean or a condition of being intermediate between two extremes (not to be read negatively). See Sir Thomas Elyot's *Book Named the Governor* (London, 1531): "Fortitude . . . is a Mediocritie or meane betwene two extremities" (3.8)

227. God ordered that, along with the two tablets inscribed with the ten commandments, the tabernacle should contain both "manna," or the Eucharist, representing mercy, and Moses' rod, representing justice (Exod. 4.27).

228. <Liv. vide l. 8. hist. ab urb. cond. Ovid. Met. lib.2.> Perhaps this refers to Lucius Papirius Cursor, fourth century B.C.E. dictator, who was determined to punish Quintus Fabius, his master of the horse, after he had successfully fought the Samnites against Papirius's orders. When the Roman people intervened, Papirius let him go free, as described in Book 8 of Livy's *Ab Urba Condita.* The reference to Ovid's *Metamorphosis* probably belongs to the following note, as book 2 is about Jupiter's rape of Callisto and Europa.

229. <Blanditiis precibusq; minas rega liter addit.> Loosely translated in following text. "Adjoined" means joined, united.

230. Wifely (first *OED* usage is in 1800).

231. Heale is arguing that husbands should treat their wives with mercy and justice, goodness and threats but should not beat them. This paragraph is omitted in the 1682 edition.

232. Epitome.

233. Mirror.

234. <Vide Tytaq. loco supr. citato> In 389 C.E. Latinus Pacatus Drepanius, described by Ausonius as the greatest Latin poet after Virgil, delivered a speech in praise of Theodosius I in the Roman Senate: "You wished the moral reform to begin with yourself, lest anyone consider that he was suffering an injustice. . . . For who could . . . be grieved that something was being subtracted from his private luxury, when he saw his emperor, ruler of the world, master of lands and men, living frugally and contentedly" (*Pacatus Panegyric to the Emperor Theodosius,* trans. C. E. V. Nixon [Liverpool: Liverpool University Press, 1987], 13.1).

235. <Petrarch. lib. de rem. adver. fort.> In Petrarch's "Remedies for Adversity," Reason answers Sorrow's lament that his wife has been unfaithful by stating that he should make certain that he too is chaste: "In marriage, duties should be alike, love equal, and trust mutual. I do not excuse the wives, but I accuse their men and assign to them the major part of the blame. Many times the man has been the guide to prurient conduct and the example for his wife, and the evil started where the remedy ought to have been" (dialogue 21 in vol. 3, bk. 2 of *Petrarch's Remedies for Fortune Fair and Foul: A Modern English Translation of "De remediis utriusque fortune," with a Commentary,* by Conrad H. Rawski [Bloomington: Indiana University Press, 1999], 68). "Mimical" is scoffing, apish, or counterfeit.

236. <S. Aug. in. C. si dictum 23.q.6.> St. Augustine wrote treatises entitled "The Good of Marriage" and "Adulterous Marriage."

237. Blamelessness.

238. <Senec. ad Lucil. epist. 94.> In his epistle 94, "On the Value of Advice," Seneca writes, "Indeed, the persons who take the greatest pains to proffer such advice [conduct proper for a man and for a woman] are themselves unable to put it into practice" (*Epistles* [Loeb Classical Library, 1989], 94.9).

239. <Guil de Monte laud in Cl. cum ex eo. Cardinal. Flor m I. oppo. de sent. exon.> Heale refers to a "skimmington," an English custom in which a cuckolded man was forced to ride backward on a horse while being mocked by the cries and pot banging of the crowd.

240. Precedent (i.e., an example).

241. The *OED* quotes T. Blount's *Glossographia* (1656): "*Verberable,* that which may be, or is worthy to be beaten."

242. <Vide Aegidium in curia Par. Praes.v.2 q 195. n.7. (1682 117)> Probably Giles Aegidius (ca. 1243–1316), archbishop of Bourges.

243. <Vincen. de Franc. decis. 144.n.4.> Probably Vincent of Beauvais (1190?–

1264?), who was close to the king of France and wrote *Speculum Doctrinale* (ca. 1254), books 7–9 of which summarize canonical, civil, and criminal law statutes.

244. <Petr. de Ferrar. in aur pr. p. 624. n.4.>

245. <Durandus in spec. juris. lib.I.de off. iud parag. 2.n.8.> William Duranti (ca. 1230–96), bishop of Mende, wrote *Speculum Juriciale* (ca. 1271–76), a comprehensive treatment of canon law that remained a standard reference work for centuries. It was enlarged in the fourteenth century by the *Additiones* of Joannes Andreae and Baldus. Duranti believed that marriage was not a sacrament but an institution of natural law.

246. Coarse . . . sore.

247. <S. Bonavent lib. 4. dist. 38. art. 2. quest 2.> St. Bonaventure (ca. 1217–74), cardinal of Albano, was a scholastic theologian and the author of *Collations on the Six Days* (1273).

248. Minimizing or suppressing.

249. That which cannot be divided.

250. Qualification.

251. Peers.

252. <Plat lib. I. de justo. finem legis dicit convenientem servare ordinem, odisse mala (1682 malum)> He says culminating law to observe order, to hate evil. This is probably a reference to book 1 of Plato's *Laws* (Loeb Classical Library, 1994): "The highest good, however, is . . . peace one with another and friendly feeling. . . . For imagine a man supposing that a human body was best off when it was sick and purged with physic, while never giving a thought to the case of the body that needs no physic at all!" (1.629.17, 19).

253. Servants.

254. See Rowlands's *Tis Merry*, n. 76. In *Description of England* (N.p., 1577), William Harrison divides people into four groups: gentlemen; burgesses (or citizens), defined by their occupations and possessing the freedoms of the cities in which they resided; yeoman; and laborers. See Keith Wrightson's *English Society, 1580–1680* (New Brunswick, N.J.: Rutgers University Press, 1982), 17, 19–21.

255. Heale states that the "cavil" or frivolous objection concerning the rules of the law is that the law allows a husband to beat his wife because there is no punishment in the law against it. In *The Lawes Resolutions of Womens Rights; or, The Lawes Provision for Woemen* (London, 1632), the author (listed only as T.E.) states: "Justice Brooke 12.H.8.fo 4. affirmeth plainly, that if a man beat an out-law, a traitor, a Pagan, his villein, or his wife it is dispunishable. Because by the Law Common these persons can have no action" (128). However, T.E. says that Fitzherbert has a writ that a wife threatened with abuse may sue "out of Chancery" or may beat her husband in retaliation.

256. See nn. 163 and 203.

257. Keith Wrightson claims that widows often married within a year of their spouses' death and that although parents' approval of their child's marriage was valued, it was not insisted upon (*English Society, 1580–1680* [New Brunswick, N.J.: Rutgers University Press, 1982], 103, 75).

258. Weighty, compelling.

259. That is, Gager's colleagues at Christ Church.

260. To close down or finish up.

261. Clear floods.

262. <Gen. I.28.> "And God blessed them, and God said to them, Bring forthe frute and multiplie, and fil the earth, and subdue it, and rule over the fish of the sea and over the foule of the heaven, & over everie beast that moveth upon the earth" (Gen. 1.28).

263. <Ruper in I. l. de Trin & eius operibus. (1682 Trinit ei.9. openb. 9.)> See n. 163.

264. <S. Tertul. lib. 2. adver. Marcion.> Tertullian (ca. 155–ca. 222), an eminent jurist, is know as the father of Latin theology. In *Against Marcion,* Tertullian writes: "The self-same Goodness provided also a help meet for him, that there might be nothing in his lot that was not good. For, said He, that the man be alone is not good. He knew full well what a blessing to him would be the sex of Mary" (in vol. 3 of the Ante-Nicene Christian Library, ed. Alexander Roberts and James Donaldson [Edinburgh: T. and T. Clark, 1993], 2.4).

265. <Vide sequenti pagina.> This translates as, "See following pages."

266. <Josephus Antiq. lib. I cap.2.> In ca. 93 C.E. Josephus wrote *Jewish Antiquities* (Loeb Classical Library, 1991), a history of the Jews from the creation to the outbreak of war with Rome, intended to glorify the Jewish nation in the eyes of the Romans. Josephus writes: "And God brought before Adam the living creatures after their kinds, exhibiting both male and female, and gave them the names by which they are still called to this day. Then seeing Adam to be without female partner and consort (for indeed there was none), and looking with astonishment at the other creatures who had their mates, He extracted one of his ribs while he slept and from it formed woman" (1.2). Thomas Lodge translated *Jewish Antiquities* in 1609.

267. <S. Basilius hom. ll. in Gene sin.> St. Basil (ca. 329–70), bishop of Caesarea, wrote and delivered nine Lenten homilies on Hexaemeron, the narrative of the six days of creation based on Genesis 1.1–26. Homily 2 is on the creation of light. See n. 28.

268. <Gen. 2.18.> "Also the Lord God said, 'It is not good that the man shulde be him selfe alone: I wil make him an helpe mete for him'" (Gen. 2.18)

269. <Gen.I.> In chapter 1 of Genesis, God creates man; in chapter 2, woman. There is no mention of the "heavenly trinity."

270. <S. Greg. mor li.9.c.27.> May refer to Gregory of Nyssa's *De opificio hominis,* an anthropological and physiological explanation of Genesis 1.26, to his *Sermones de Creatione,* or to Gregory the Great's *Moralia in Job.* See n. 226.

271. <S. Basil. hom. 9. in Gen.> See n. 267. Homily 9 is on the creation of animals and man, but Eve is not mentioned.

272. In travail of or in labor of.

273. <Orig. hom I. in Gen.> Origen (ca. 185–ca. 254), one of the most influential of all theologians of the ancient church, wrote homilies on the Old and New Testaments. In "Genesis Homily 1," Origen discusses how God could have said, "Male and female he made them" before he created Eve (in *Homilies on Genesis and Exodus,* trans. Ronald E. Heine [Washington, D.C.: Catholic University of America Press, 1982], 1.14).

274. <Gen. 2.18> There is no corresponding note in the text. See n. 269.

275. <Translat. ex Prud. Nullus adorabat flexo tum poplite regem, &c.> This is loosely translated in the text that follows. Prudentius (348–410 C.E.) was a Latin poet who wrote many theological poems.

276. <Hugo de S. V. in Gen 2.> Hugh of Saint-Victor (eleventh–twelfth centuries), the leading teacher at the school of Saint-Victor, wrote commentaries on Genesis that read the text literally.

277. <S. Chryso. hom. 8. in Gen. Damascen. in 2.l. de Gen.12.> See nn. 163 and 203. In *Homilies on Genesis,* Chrysostum discusses the creation of Eve after the creation of the animals: "So, from man's rib God creates this rational being, and in his inventive wisdom he makes it complete and perfect, like man in every detail—rational, capable of rendering him what would be of assistance in times of need and the pressing necessities of life" (1.15.200 [not homily 8, as Heale refers to it]). "Damascen." could refer to Damascenus the Studite, one of the most popular writers of the sixteenth-century Greek church, who wrote *Treasury,* a collection of saints' lives and thirty-six homilies based upon biblical texts. "Damascen." could also refer to the seventh- to eighth-century saint John of Damascus, who wrote in book 2.12 of *The Orthodox Faith* (in *Writings,* trans. Frederic H. Chase Jr. [New York: Fathers of the Church, 1958]) on the creation of man but does not specifically discuss the creation of Eve.

278. Harbingers (i.e., Adam).

279. <Joseph. li. I antiq.c.2 Tertullianus lib.2. adversus Marcionem.> See nn. 264 and 266. "Metropolitan citie" means "principal city" (indeed, the only city).

280. <Gen.2.7.> "The Lord God also made the man of the dust of the grounde, and breathed in his face breath of life, and the man was a living soule" (Gen. 2.7).

281. <Gen.2.22.> See n. 162.

282. <P. (1682 Petr.) Lomba. 8. dis. 18.> May refer to Peter Lombard (ca. 1095–1160), a celebrated theologian and bishop of Paris who wrote *Book of Sentences* (ca. 1157–58).

283. <S. Aug. 12 de Civitat. Dei. ca. 21. & 26.> St. Augustine writes in *The City of God* (Loeb Classical Library, 1995): "But he who is joined in marriage . . . considers the things of the world, how he may please his wife" (21.26).

284. <S. Basil. hom. 12. in Gen.> See nn. 267 and 272. St. Basil wrote only nine homilies on the Hexaemeron.

285. <Gil. ant. Interp. in Gen. I> May refer to Gilbert of Holland, a twelfth-century Cistercian abbot and the author of *48 Sermons* who is often cited as a source of medieval exegesis; or to Gilbert de la Porree (ca. 1075–1154), a scholastic theologian who wrote commentaries on the Bible and on Boethius.

286. <Idem ibid. & Brunus in I. Gen.> May refer to Bruno of Segni (ca. 1040–1123), who wrote commentaries on scripture.

287. Less angry, calmer.

288. <Gen.2. 23.> See n. 162.

289. <Transl. ex Bart. per. I. Silvest in opere dici.6.> From "The Sixth Day of the First Weeke" by Guillaume de Saluste sieur Du Bartas (in *The Divine Weeks and Works of Guillaume de Saluste, Sieur du Bartas,* trans. Joshuah Sylvester, ed. Susan Snyder [Oxford: Clarendon Press, 1979], ll. 1033–54). Heale omits eight lines and changes the first

line (which is “Graving so lively on the living Bone” in the original). He also changes “purer” to “deeper” (l. 1291). “Grav’d” (l. 1286) means “engraved”; “deeper” (l. 1293) means “longer.” The original French of “shee-coupled one” (l. 1296) is *amoureux Androgyne.*

290. <Gen 2.21> “Therefore the Lord God caused an heavie slepe to fall upon the man: & whiles he slept, he toke one of his rybbes and closed up the flesh in steade thereof” (Gen. 2.21).

291. <S. Damasenus in l.2 ad Gen.> See n. 277.

292. <Pererius in hunc locum & Brunus (1682 Erunus) ibid.> “Pererius” means “wandering.” See n. 286.

293. <Gen. 2.24> “Therefore shal man leave his father and his mother, and shal cleave to his wife, and they shalbe one flesh” (Gen. 2.24).

294. <Damasen. in lib 2. ad Gen.> See n. 277.

295. Propensity, inclination.

296. That is, first created thing.

297. <Exod. 20.> “Honour thy father and thy mother, that thy daies maie be prolonged upon the land, which the Lord thy God giveth thee” (Exod. 20.12).

298. Knowing nothing about an unspecified thing.

299. <S. Chryso. c. I: hom. 38 in Genes.> See nn. 163 and 277. In volume 2 of *Homilies on Genesis,* Chrysostum states: “let us learn to be restrained and gentle with everyone, especially our wives . . . make it our sole concern to remove the cause of sadness and bring about a deep sense of peace at home so that the wife’s attention may be devoted to her husband and he may be able to find refuge in a haven from external confusion and disturbance and find their utter consolation” (371–72).

300. Meeting place of councillors.

301. That is, because they are crowded with people.

302. That is, the husband as sovereign.

303. Although you had everything you desired in the world.

304. The army of Xerxes (fifth century B.C.E.) was reputed to number no less than 5,283,220. Solomon, king of the ancient Hebrews, built a magnificent temple in Jerusalem in the tenth century B.C.E.

305. Darling.

306. Many early modern explorers sailed to the West Indies in search of gold. Arabia was thought of as exotic.

307. “Coloquintida” refers to the colocynth or bitter apple. See Shakespeare’s *Othello:* “The food . . . as [acerb] as [the] coloquintida” (1.3.347–49).

308. <Gen. 2.24.> See n. 293.

309. God was believed to be a trinity consisting of the Father, the Son, and the Holy Ghost. Similarly, Heale argues, Adam and Eve were two people in one being.

310. Farthest.

311. No merchant ships sailed on the ocean in the Golden Age.

312. Bellona was the goddess of war. Vulcan, son of Juno, wife of Venus, and father of Cupid, was the Greek god who presided over fire and was often represented holding a hammer, ready to strike his anvil.

313. A plume or ornament worn on top of a helmet for identification.

314. <Desciptio aurei seculi translata ex Ovid. & aliisq per authorem.> In *Metamorphoses,* Ovid describes the Golden Age, the first and best age in which people lived in a state of happiness free from all trouble (1.89–112). The translation is by Heale.

315. <Arist. li.I: de anima cap.6.> In *On the Soul* (Loeb Classical Library, 1995), Aristotle writes, "The soul is the cause and first principle of the living body. . . . all natural bodies are instruments of the soul" (2.4 [not 1.6, as Heale refers to it])."

316. Fraught, laden.

317. Note the feminization of the soul.

318. Footman.

319. Furnace.

320. The passage of the veins to discharge it.

321. Predominance, ascendancy, preeminence.

322. <August. li. de cont.t.4> See n. 236.

323. <Gen.3.I.> "Now the serpent was more subtil then anie beast of the field, which the Lord God had made: and he said to the woman, Yea, hathe God in dede said, Ye shal not eat of everie tre of the garden?" (Gen. 3.1).

324. <Gen.3.14. (HN 3.2.3.)> "And the woman said unto the serpent, We eat of the frute of the trees of the garden, But of the frute of the tre, which is in the middes of the garden, God hathe said, Ye shal not eat of it, nether shal ye touche it, lest ye dye" (3.2–3).

325. Drove.

326. <Ibid.v.4.> "Then the serpent said to the woman, Ye shal not dye at all" (Gen. 3.4).

327. That is, at pole's length.

328. <Gen.2.17> "But as touching the tre of knowledge of good and evil, thou shalt not eat of it: for whensoever thou eatest thereof, thou shalt dye the death" (Gen. 2.17).

329. <Greg. l. 39 Moral.c.16> St. Gregory of Nazianzen discusses the tree of knowledge in his oration 38, "On the Theophany, or Birthday of Christ," in which Adam, not Eve, was given the commandment "as to what plants he might partake of, and which one he might not touch" (in *Select Orations of Saint Gregory Nazianzen,* trans. Charles Gordon Browne and James Edward Swallow [Grand Rapids, Mich.: Wm. B. Erdmans, 1893], 348). See also n. 201.

330. <Aug. li. 8. Ge n. ad literam c. 17.> In *The Literal Meaning of Genesis,* St. Augustine writes: "Or was it that knowing he was going to make the woman for the man, he gave the command most appropriately in this way, so that the Lord's command would reach the woman through the man? This is a discipline that the apostle maintains in the Church: *But if they wish to learn anything, let them question their husbands at home* (1 Cor. 13:35)" (in *On Genesis: The Works of Saint Augustine,* vol. 1, trans. Edmund Hill [Hyde Park, N.Y.: New City Press, 2002], no. 13).

331. <(1682 Rom. 5.v.12.14.-19.)> The marginalia of the 1682 edition cites the New Testament Romans 5.12, 14–19, in which the sin of one man (Adam, but not Eve) and the redemption of man by Christ are emphasized.

332. <Communis haec sententia Interpretum & Scholasticorum.> This opinion is universally held by interpreters and scholars.

333. <Hoc enim acutissimè observavit generosissima & doct. foemina I. O dovena in oratione su a apologetica pro foeminis.> This was most acutely noted by the most noble and learned women. O dovena in treatises his defense for women.

334. <S. Chrys. hom. 57. in 29. Gen.> In Chrysostum's homily 17 (not 57), Adam tells God that Eve gave him the fruit and he ate it. God replies, "put the blame on no one but yourself and your own neglect; after all, if you had not been willing, your wife would have been unable to bring you to this disastrous state" (*Homilies on Genesis,* 1.17.231).

335. That is, Satan.

336. Broker.

337. Glad.

338. Printing press or printing house.

339. <Liv. hist. ab urb. cond. li. ult.> Viriplace is the Roman goddess who presided over the peace of families. If a husband and wife were quarreling, they would go to the temple on Mount Palatine and return reconciled. Valerius Maximus, not Livy, mentions this in book 2.1.

4 "*Custome* is an Idiot": Cross-Dressing and Custom

THE PAMPHLETS *Hic Mulier; or, The Man-Woman* and *Haec-Vir; or, The Womanish-Man* were printed in 1620, the second in response to the first. They are dominated by two themes: men's conflicting feelings of horror and desire occasioned by the cross-dressed Queen Omphale's effect on Heracles; and the tension between custom and reason. In the myth of Omphale, Heracles, who has been sold into slavery, is bought by Omphale. He becomes so infatuated with her that he dresses in her clothes and trades his club for her distaff so he can be with her. Omphale dons Heracles' lion skin and wields his club. When Haec-Vir asks Hic-Mulier what his/her name is, he describes her as a "couragious counterfeit of *Heracles* and his Distaffe." Heracles' behavior points to the question that permeates both pamphlets: When is custom warranted and when does it obscure reason?

Hic Mulier was entered in the Stationers Register on 9 February 1620 to the bookseller John Trundle, who was known for publishing popular pamphlets. It is a diatribe against women who dress like men. The joke in the title is grammatical: *mulier,* the Latin word for "woman," should be modified by the feminine *haec,* not the masculine *hic.* When *hic* modifies *mulier,* a possible third gender—a man-woman—is formed, but when *haec* modifies *vir* (Latin for "man") the man simply becomes "womanish."

On 25 January 1620, just a few weeks before *Hic Mulier* was registered, John Chamberlain wrote in a letter to Sir Dudley Carleton:

> Yesterday the bishop of London [John King] called together all his Clergie about this towne, and told them he had expresse commaundment from the King to will them to inveigh vehemently and bitterly in theyre sermons against the insolencie of our women, and theyre wearing of brode brimd hats, pointed dublets, theyre haire cut short or shorne, and some of them stillettaes

> or poinards, and such other trinckets of like moment, adding withall that if pulpit admonitions will not reforme them he wold proceed by another course; the truth is the world is very far out of order, but whether this will mend it God knowes.[1]

Whether or not *Hic Mulier* was written because of Bishop King's sermon, it is clear that anxiety about cross-dressing women and men existed for many years. On 3 January 1556, John Calvin preached a sermon based on Deuteronomy 22:5: "A woman shal not weere the apparel of a man: neither shal a man put on the garments of a woman. For whosoever doth so, is an abomination to the Lord thy God." Calvin addressed fears related to women who cut their hair ("For if a woman were polled, durst she shew her head abroade"), women whose cross-dressing could lead to sexual enticement ("such disguisings are but inticements of baudry, as experience prooveth"), and women who would rather have a "hackebutte [gun] on their shoulder than a distaffe [for spinning] in their hand."[2]

Among other references to cross-dressing in sixteenth-century pamphlet literature are George Gascoigne's *Steele Glas,* which asks if women masking in men's "weedes," including "dutchkin dublets" and "high copt hattes" with feathers, are really women; Phillip Stubbes's *Anatomie of Abuses,* which berates men and women for dressing extravagantly and terms women who cut their hair and wear doublets "*Hermaphroditi,* that is Monsters of both kindes, half women, half men;" and the anonymous *Mervailous combat of contrarieties,* which reaffirms Stubbes by stating that women who wear men's apparel are "neither men nor women, but plaine Monsters."[3]

References to cross-dressing are even more frequent in early seventeenth-century literature. For example, William Parkes, in *The Curtaine-Drawer of the World,* questions both women who "(as it were) transformed into men, by degenerating from their sex, and from the vertue, modesty, and civility thereof, by their mannish complements, and ruffianly attires" and men who are "(as it were) transformed into women, by their lascivious, effeminate, and wanton imitations, none being content with their owne estates and conditions."[4] In *Mysticall Bedlam; or, The World of Mad-Men,* Thomas Adams proclaims that "*Hic Mulier* will shortly bee good latine, if this transmigration [cross-dressing] hold: For whether on horsebacke, or on foot, there is no great difference: but not discernable out of a Coach"[5]—in other words, Adams is disconcerted because when he rides in a coach and looks out the window, he cannot always determine the gender of the people he passes. In 1619, John

Williams, one of King James's chaplains, preached a sermon before James and his son Prince Charles lamenting "the *prodigious* apparition of our *women*" who come into church "halfe male, and halfe female . . . as if it were a Play-house," with short hair, feathers in their hats, and carrying daggers.[6]

Curiously, if we look at the woodcuts in *Hic Mulier* and *Haec-Vir,* we would not say that the women represented are dressed as men because they wear skirts, not breeches. We might say that they look mannish because of their widespread stance and the lack of a narrowed waist, but we would not mistake them for men. (Contrast them, for example, to the women represented in the woodcuts that illustrate the gossip pamphlets, pp. 22 and 67.) Still, one of the women in the *Hic Mulier* woodcut is getting her hair cut and the other women in both woodcuts already have short hair. Also, one of the women is wearing a broad-brimmed hat with a large feather and another is trying on such a hat, the very sort decried by George Gascoigne and John Williams. The woman in the *Haec-Vir* woodcut wears spurs and carries a sword and a pistol, all markers of masculinity. The fear, apparently, was that when women donned these male attributes, they became men. The men in the woodcuts are also represented as much smaller than the women. There is no possibility that Hic Mulier and Haec Vir could exchange clothes, as occurs at the end of *Haec-Vir,* because the womanish man's clothes would be too small for the man-woman. Haec Vir has ribbons hanging from his breeches and wears no spurs. His weapons are reduced to a racquet and battledores for shuttlecock, a game Hic Mulier refers to as "only a female invention" played primarily by women, and scissors to cut women's hair.

The anonymous author of *Hic Mulier* may have been a Puritan man who disliked the city, the theater, and the changing customs of women's behavior in both of these places. In seventeenth-century London, women of any status might have bought the latest fashions, often foreign-made or above their class, in defiance of the sumptuary laws that stated what clothes were appropriate to their status. The author describes these women as the "Apes of the City" who have "inticed forraine Nations to their Cels" and committed "grosse adultery with their Gewgawes." Cross-dressed women are also described as "the gilt durt, which imbroders Play-houses"—in other words, these women are all about appearance and deception. Readers of the pamphlet are also warned of the Devil's lures to ensnare women when they attend the playhouse.

But not all women are the objects of attack in *Hic Mulier.* According to the author, those women who are "the complements of mens excellencies," who "support mankinde" with modesty and chastity, and who marry, have children, and stay at home are worthy of praise. Those who do otherwise are "monstrous" or "deformed," adjectives used repeatedly in the pamphlet to describe the majority of women of the city. A woman's social status does not matter, for this "infection" is like the plague: it affects "women of all degrees, all deserts, and all ages."

The author of *Hic Mulier* posits that women who adopt mannish fashions begin acting like men "by aptnesse to anger," "by pursuing revenge," and by wearing and using weapons. Such behavior is unnatural for women and defies custom, and therefore must be stopped. It is "base" in that it offends God "in the most unnaturall use" and "barbarous" in that it is "an *Antithesis* to kinde." If society does not condemn Hic Mulier's behavior as "barbarous," then it might as well let "the rude *Scithian,* the untamed *Moore,* the naked *Indian,* or the wilde *Irishe,*" four groups considered barbarous in early modern England, rule its cities. The author exhorts all men who are fathers, husbands, or in any other way "sustainers" of these mannish women to "close your liberall hands" and stop funding "these deformities." It is likely that the men who "sustained" these cross-dressed women were the intended audience of this pamphlet.

An underlying anxiety in *Hic Mulier*—perhaps experienced by the author himself—is the sexual provocation of mannish women, who are characterized as "Harlots" with French doublets "all unbutton'd to entice" (though this is hardly the way they are represented in the woodcut). The author admonishes these women to "keepe those parts concealed from the eyes, that may not bee toucht with the hands" so that "a wandring and lascivious thought" may not be provoked by "the contents of an unchaste volume." To strengthen his argument, he quotes Edmund Spenser's *Faerie Queene,* in which Artegall is compared to Heracles, who replaces his club for a "distaffe vile to hold." The Amazon Radigund, after having broken Artegall's sword, dresses him in women's clothes and places a distaff for spinning in his hand (5.5.25).[7] In Spenser's retelling of the myth, it is Radigund who lusts after Artegall, ostensibly proving that women violate reason and nature when they "purchase a licentious libertie" by assuming men's clothes and weapons, not understanding that they were "borne to milde humilitie."

Haec-Vir; or, The Womanish-Man, printed a week after *Hic Mulier* by the same publisher, was probably written by a different person—perhaps a well-read, impudent law student at the Inns of Court. Although the authors of both pamphlets refer to some of the same writers—Virgil, Ariosto, Spenser—the author of *Haec-Vir* includes an impassioned attack on custom, much of which is lifted from John Florio's translation of Michel de Montaigne's essay "Of Ancient Custom," published in 1603 and reprinted in 1613. Today's readers might look on this as plagiarism, but I think the borrowing is intended both for convenience and for the reader's pleasure. Those seventeenth-century readers who were familiar with Montaigne's essays would have recognized it, while those who were not—many of whom were probably women—would not have understood the intended humor.

Haec-Vir is a dialogue between Hic Mulier and Haec Vir, who initially mistake each other's gender. Haec Vir addresses Hic Mulier as "most redoubted and worthy Sir," and Hic Mulier addresses Haec Vir as "most rare and excellent lady." After they clarify who they are, Haec Vir attacks Hic Mulier by describing her as a "most couragious counterfet of *Heracles* and his Distaffe," that is, a man dressed as a woman. Haec Vir proceeds to analyze Hic Mulier's dress, from the "most prophane Feather" in her hat to the "beastly Leaden gilt Spurre" fastened to her "base sale Boote." He berates her "naked, lascivious, bawdy Bosome," again emphasizing the sexual provocation of cross-dressing, and her masculine weapons of "a *Leaden-Hall* Dagger" and "a High-way Pistoll." He builds his argument on the points made in *Hic Mulier* by describing Hic Mulier's coat of arms as consisting of baseness, unnaturalness, shamelessness, and foolishness.

Hic Mulier refutes each of Haec Vir's charges. She contends that she is not base or "a Slave to Novelty" because the whole world is "a very shop or warehouse of change," and she asks whether only women will be deprived of the benefit of delighting in the variety of the world. Many readings of *Haec-Vir* have focused on Hic Mulier's answer to the charge of unnaturalness, with some critics arguing that her masculine garb enables her to make assertive statements of equality.[8] After listing examples of customs that vary according to different nationalities, Hic Mulier proclaims, "*Custome* is an Idiot." Among her examples are five taken directly from Montaigne's essay: (1) the Romans oiling their bodies instead of washing their hands, with a quote from Martial about Thais's oiling her body; (2) the Ancients lying upon "stately and soft beds" to receive ambassadors, with a quote from Virgil's *Aeneid;* (3) Cato Junior eating only while sitting on the ground; (4) the Venetians kissing one another when they meet, unlike the English, who greet one another by asking and answering questions; and (5) the Argian and Roman ladies, who wear white instead of black when in mourning.[9]

Why does the author of *Haec-Vir* fail to cite Montaigne, given that he borrows extensively from the French author? The answer may be found in the material that surrounds what he has borrowed: references to ass wiping and bodily smells. In Montaigne's essay, immediately after the passage about differing customs of greeting people, a discussion of how people "were wont to wipe their tailes" with either sponges or perfumed wool is followed by a description of Roman tubs placed "for passengers to make water in." The Martial epigram cited refers to how badly Thais, covered with a plaster of vinegar and chalk, smelled before her bath. Perhaps the author of *Haec-Vir* was counting on the fact that, in the midst of a speech on liberty and the tyranny of custom made by a cross-dressed woman, his well-read (probably male) readers would understand that the uncited borrowings undercut her impassioned plea—an inside joke, as it were. But even in light of this possibility, the pamphlet does allow a reading that is sympathetic to Hic Mulier's *Custome* is an Idiot. In his essay Montaigne interprets custom as fashion that causes people to narrow-mindedly condemn others who have differing fashions and to giddily change fashions to suit the times. He advocates not for changing custom but for critiquing and not being blinded by it.[10]

To Haec Vir's charge of shamelessness—that Hic Mulier "runne[s] wilde through a wildernesse of opinions"—Hic Mulier proclaims that women are "as free-borne as Men, have as free election, and as free spirits" and, furthermore, that men and women are "compounded of like parts." She says she will not act like the dolls sold at the Bartholomew Fair, whose bodies cannot move. Instead, she will be free to "heare the Wise, and bee deafe to Ideots" and to "move swiftly to do good offices." At the end of her defense, Hic Mulier invokes the city: if living "free-borne" is "barbarous," then "let me leave the Citie, and live with creatures of like simplicity." Unlike Haec Vir, Hic Mulier is pro-London.

To the final charge of foolishness, or "infinite folly and indiscretion," Hic Mulier asks that she and other *hic muliers* not be bound to custom. She quotes two contemporary poets, G.C. (George Chapman) and Guillaume de Salluste (translated by Josuah Sylvester), Du Bartas, who affirm that blind loyalty to custom often leads to vice. This section is part of a seventeenth-century debate on the possible dangers of custom. In a dedication to the 1613 edition of Montaigne's essays, Samuel Daniel praises Montaigne because he has made

> such bolde sallies out upon
> Custome, the mightie tyrant of the earth,
> In whose Seraglio of subjection
> Wee all seeme bred-up, from our tender birth.

For his part, in "Of Ancient Customes" Montaigne criticizes people who are tied to the latest fashions and then lists some ancient customs in various countries to show that customs are arbitrary. In "Of Custome, and How a Received Law Should Not Be Easily Changed," Montaigne states, "Custome is a violent and deceiving schoole-mistris."[11] Once again he lists varying customs from different nations, but here he warns against defying the established customs of "outward matters." Custom and law, which Montaigne equates with custom, are to be critiqued and understood but not necessarily changed.

In borrowing examples from Montaigne, the author of *Haec-Vir* was participating in a continuing debate about the constructedness of custom—in other words, the idea that there is no universal way of doing things. This concern was reflected in the early modern popularity of travel literature that records how different peoples lived and in books such as *The Manners, Lawes, and Customes Of All Nations,* collected by Joannes Boemus Aubanus and translated from the Latin by Edward Aston. The discussion is continued in Meric Casaubon's *Treatise of Use and Custome,* which argues that custom may be an impediment to truth but should be maintained if "just and reasonable"; and in John Milton's *To The Parliament of England, with the Assembly,* in which he states that "Error supports Custome, Custome count'nances Error."[12]

Haec Vir counters Hic Mulier's condemnation of custom by saying that no one will listen to her because by cross-dressing she has announced that she is a slave to custom or fashion. Haec Vir notes the Bible's declaration that a woman may put on men's clothes only to escape persecution. Further, he argues that women (Hic Mulier in particular) who exchange their "light skirts and French doublets" for "shapt, comely and close Gownes," their pistols for samplers, and their spurs for prayer books will stop being the subject of ballads and will no longer be described as base, unnatural, shameless, and foolish. To conclude his argument, Haec Vir quotes the poet C.M., who states that "A stronger hand restraines our wilfull powers"; in other words, Hic Mulier should follow the teachings of God.

Admitting that Haec Vir's argument has "raysd" her "eielids up," Hic Mulier cleverly, and perhaps disappointingly, turns the argument against him. If, according to nature, religion, and "the Customes of all civill Nations," a distinct difference must be maintained between men and women, then why, Hic Mulier asks, does Haec Vir "curle, frizell and powder" his hair, wear ruffs and French bodices, and sport fans and cosmetics? His behavior blurs social distinctions so that there is not "any difference between the fayre Mistris & the foolish Servant." Gone are the old days of "Tilts and Tournies and loftie Gallyards," when men danced like men; now men strut like puppets and show themselves off at the playhouse. Hic Mulier concludes by quoting Ariosto's description of the effeminate Rogero.

Haec Vir responds by saying that Hic Mulier has "rais'd" his "eye-lids" and "cleered" his sight and that he will immediately exchange clothes with her and correct his name to Hic Vir—if she will become Haec Mulier. "From henceforth," Haec Vir proclaims, "deformitie shall packe to Hell." The renamed Haec Mulier and Hic Vir will be filled with "heavenly and divine love," as expressed by the lines of Spenser's "Colin Clout's Come Home Again," which look to a simple pastoral life removed from the city and which conclude the pamphlet.

Much has been written by modern scholars on *Hic Mulier* and *Haec-Vir* because of the fascination with Hic Mulier's condemnation of custom and her plea for women's equality. In *Middle-Class Culture in Elizabethan England,* Louis Wright describes *Haec-Vir* as "the *Areopagitica* of the London woman." Linda Woodbridge, in *Women and the English Renaissance,* asserts that *Haec-Vir* "falls very little short of being a flaming manifesto of liberty for women," while Mary Beth Rose, in *The Expense of Spirit,* writes that "the debate shows female independence and equality between the sexes as desireable and just, but also as impossible for a hierarchical society to absorb without unacceptable disruption." Bryan Reynolds, in "The Devil's House, 'or Worse,'" argues that Hic Mulier's lament that cross-dressing is "an enemie to Custome" anticipates Judith Butler's conclusion "that the transvestite 'effectively mocks both the expressive model of gender and the notion of a true gender identity.'"[13]

Although *Haec-Vir* ends with traditional gender roles being reinscribed, Hic Mulier does announce that "*Custome* is an Idiot" and "we [women] are as free-borne as Men, have as free election, and as free spirits, we are compounded of like parts." Surely some people—women especially—read or heard these words as offering some possibility of agency. The potential subversiveness of an idea depends on the context of its articulation and its reception.[14] Like the gossips' independence and good talk in Rowlands's pamphlets, to which women may have responded positively, women reading or hearing Hic Mulier's words may have identified with or been inspired by her plea for equality. This may be quite different from the intentions of the publisher and the anonymous author, given that the pamphlet was written so soon after King James's command that sermons against cross-dressing be preached from all pulpits. Certainly, many of today's readers will interpret Hic Mulier's words as a call for equality.

Textual Introduction

The copy text for *Hic Mulier* (*STC* 13375.5), printed in 1620, is located at the Huntington Library. This is the final corrected version that incorporates errors, primarily in spelling and punctuation, made in earlier impressions of the 1620 edition of the pamphlet.[15] Signatures A3r–4v and most of B1r and B3v–4v are reset, with the rest being reimposed. The first impression (*STC* 13374), located at the Bodleian Library in Oxford, the Beinecke Library at Yale University, and the Houghton Library at Harvard University, is imperfectly cropped. Two copies of the second impression (*STC* 13375) exist; they are housed at the British Library and at the Houghton Library. The title page of the former is cropped on the bottom right-hand side, eliminating the date of publication; the latter copy has a clearly marked date. There are no later editions of *Hic Mulier.*[16]

Haec-Vir was registered by John Trundle on 20 February 1620, eleven days after he registered *Hic Mulier.* Trundle was a publisher of popular literature. In addition to these two pamphlets, in 1620 he printed *Westward for Smelts; or, The water-mans fare of mad-merry western wenches;* the ballad "Good Sir, you wrong your britches, pleasantly discoursed by a witty youth, and a wily wench"; and Thomas Middleton and William Rowley's *Courtly Masque: The Device Called The World Tost At Tennis,* in which "*hic mulier*" and "*haec vir,*" in addition to "fashions, fictions, felonies, [and] fooleries," are mentioned as subjects for the ballad writer.[17]

The copy text for *Haec-Vir* (*STC* 12599) is located at the Huntington Library. This is the only edition of the pamphlet. Other copies are owned by the Folger Library, Queen's College at Oxford, the British Library, and the Houghton Library. The title pages of the Houghton Library and British Library copies are cropped.

According to Edward Hodnett, the woodcuts that appear in *Hic Mulier* and *Haec-Vir* were designed especially for the pamphlets by an unknown artist whose style was characteristic of illustrations of contemporary ballads and broadsides.[18]

On 29 April 1620, an answer to *Hic Mulier,* entitled *Muld sacke; or, The apologie of Hic Mulier: to the late declamation against her,* was published by R. Meighen. Although the pamphlet begins with a poem to Hic Mulier and continues with a description of Hic Mulier, it is more concerned with vice than with cross-dressing.

NOTES

1. *The Letters of John Chamberlain,* vol. 2, ed. Norman Egbert McClure (Philadelphia: American Philosophical Society, 1939), 286–87.

2. *The Sermons of John Calvin Upon the Fifth Booke of Moses called Deuteronomie,* trans. Arthur Golding (London, 1583), 772–73.

3. George Gascoigne, *The Steele Glas* (London, 1576), I.i.v; Phillip Stubbes, *The Anatomie of Abuses,* ed. Margaret Jane Kidnie (Tempe: Arizona Center for Medieval and Renaissance Studies/Renaissance English Text Society, 2002), 118; Anonymous, *A mervailous combat of contrarieties* (London, 1588), Bv.

4. William Parkes, *The Curtaine-Drawer of the World* (London, 1612), 29.

5. Thomas Adams, *Mysticall Bedlam; or, The World of Mad-Men* (London, 1615), 50.

6. John Williams, *A sermon of apparell* (London, 1620), 20–22.

7. See also Philip Sidney, *The Countess of Pembroke's Arcadia (The Old Arcadia),* ed. Jean Robertson (Oxford: Clarendon Press, 1973): "And this effeminate love of a woman doth so womanize a man that, if you yield to it, it will not only make you a famous Amazon, but a launder, a distaff-spinner, or whatsoever vile occupation their idle heads can imagine and their weak hands perform" (20).

8. See, for example, Jonathan Dollimore, "Shakespeare Understudies: The Sodomite, the Prostitute, the Transvestite, and Their Critics," in *Political Shakespeare: Essays in Cultural Materialism,* ed. Jonathan Dollimore and Alan Sinfield, 2d ed. (Ithaca, N.Y.: Cornell University Press, 1994), 144; and Mark Breitenberg, *Anxious Masculinity in Early Modern England* (New York: Cambridge University Press, 1996), 168.

Other articles and sections of books that discuss *Hic Mulier* and *Haec-Vir* include: Vern L. Bullough and Bonnie Bullough, *Cross Dressing, Sex, and Gender* (Philadelphia: University of Pennsylvania Press, 1993); Sandra Clark, "*Hic Mulier, Haec Vir,* and the Controversy over Masculine Women," *Studies in Philology* 82.3 (Spring 1985): 157–83; Jonathan Dollimore, *Sexual Dissidence: Augustine to Wilde, Freud to Foucault* (Oxford: Clarendon Press, 1991); Elizabeth D. Harvey, *Ventriloquized Voices: Feminist Theory and English Renaissance Texts* (London: Routledge, 1992); Constance Jordan, *Renaissance Feminism* (Ithaca, N.Y.: Cornell University Press, 1990); R. Valerie Lucas, "*Hic Mulier:*

The Female Transvestite in Early Modern England," *Renaissance and Reformation,* n.s., 12.1 (Winter 1988): 65–84; Bryan Reynolds, "The Devil's House, 'or Worse': Transversal Power and Antitheatrical Discourse in Early Modern England," *Theatre Journal* 49 (1997): 143–67; Mary Beth Rose, *The Expense of Spirit* (Ithaca, N.Y.: Cornell University Press, 1988); Simon Shepherd, *Amazons and Warrior Women* (Brighton: Harvester Press, 1981); Linda Woodbridge, "*Hic Mulier* and *Haec-Vir,*" in *Women and the English Renaissance: Literature and the Nature of Womankind, 1540–1620* (Urbana: University of Illinois Press, 1984), 139–51; Louis B. Wright, *Middle-Class Culture* (Chapel Hill: University of North Carolina Press, 1935).

9. Michel de Montaigne, *Essayes,* trans. John Florio (London, 1613), 161–63. These examples appear in all editions of Montaigne's essays. I used the 1613 edition because it was probably the one read by the anonymous authors of *Hic Mulier* and *Haec-Vir.*

10. See Montaigne, "Of Customs, and how a received Law should not be changed," in *Essayes,* 46–55; and Ulrich Langer, "Montaigne's Customs," *Montaigne Studies* 4.1–2 (Sept. 1992): 81–96.

11. Montaigne, "Of Custome," 46.

12. Joannes Boemus Aubanus, *The Manners, Lawes, and Customes Of All Nations,* trans. Edward Aston (London, 1611); Meric Casaubon, *A Treatise of Use and Custome* (London, 1658), 138, 164; John Milton, *Complete Prose Works,* gen. ed. Don M. Wolfe (New Haven, Conn.: Yale University Press, 1959), 223.

13. Wright, *Middle-Class Culture,* 497; Woodbridge, *Women and the English Renaissance,* 148; Rose, *Expense of Spirit,* 77; Reynolds, "Devil's House," 162, 163 (quoting Judith Butler, *Gender Trouble: Feminism and the Subversion of Identity* [New York: Routledge, 1990]). *Areopagitica: A Speech of Mr. John Milton for the Liberty of Unlicenc'd Printing, to the Paliament of England* was a pamphlet published in 1644 that protested Parliament's order that all published books must be approved and licensed. Areopagus was the site of the high court of Athens that imposed censorship.

14. Dollimore discusses this in "Shakespeare, Cultural Materialism, and the New Historicism," in *Political Shakespeare,* 13.

15. *"Hic Mulier; or, The Man-Woman" and "Haec-Vir; or, The Womanish-Man"* (University of Exeter: Rota, 1973), i–ii.

16. See A. W. Pollard and G. R. Redgrave, eds., *A Short-Title Catalogue of Books Printed in England, Scotland, and Ireland and of English Books Printed Abroad, 1475–1640,* 2d ed. revised and enlarged by W. A. Jackson and F. S. Ferguson, completed by Katharine F. Pantzer (London: Bibliographical Society, 1976), 1:583.

17. Thomas Middleton and William Rowley, *A Courtly Masque: The Device Called The World Tost At Tennis* (London, 1620), B4v.

18. *"Hic Mulier" . . . "Haec Vir,"* ii.

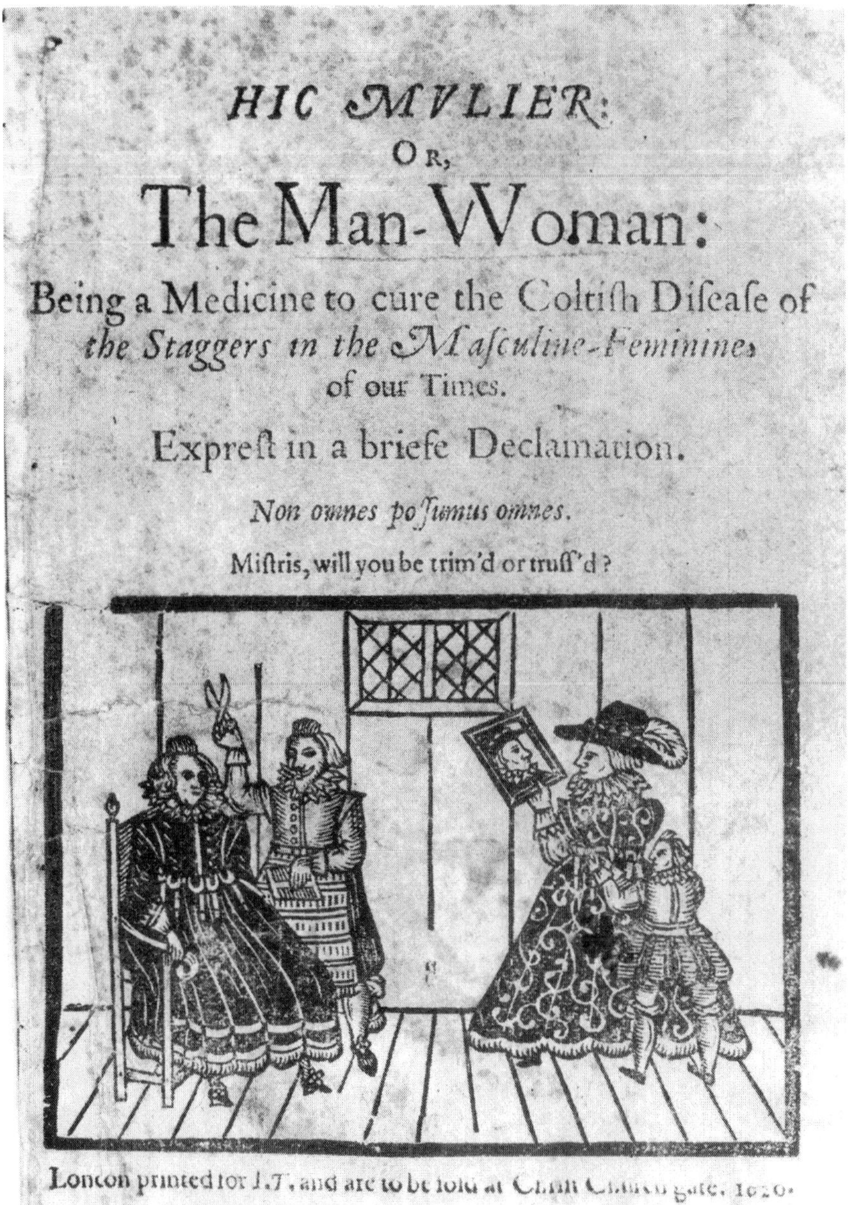

HIC MVLIER:
OR,
The Man-Woman:
Being a Medicine to cure the Coltish Disease of *the Staggers in the Masculine-Feminines* of our Times.
Exprest in a briefe Declamation.
Non omnes possumus omnes.
Mistris, will you be trim'd or truss'd?

London printed for J.T. and are to be sold at Christ Church gate. 1620.

Hic Mulier:[1] Or, The Man-Woman: Being a Medicine to cure the Coltish[2] Disease of *the Staggers*[3] *in the Masculine-Feminine,* of our Times. Exprest in a briefe Declamation. *Non omnes possumus omnes.*[4] Mistris, will you be trim'd[5] or truss'd[6]? London printed for J.T.[7] and are to be sold at Christ Church gate. 1620.

HIC MULIER.

HIC MULIER; How now? Breake *Friscians* head[8] at the first encounter? but two words, and they false Latine? Pardon mee good Signior *Construction;*[9] for I will not answere thee as the Pope did, that I will doe it in despight of the Grammar: but I will mainetaine, if it bee not the truest Latine in our Kingdome, yet it is the commonest. For since the daies of *Adam* women were never so Masculine; Masculine in their genders and whole generations, from the Mother, to the youngest daughter; Masculine in Number,[10] from one to multitudes; Masculine in Case,[11] even from the head to the foot; Masculine in Moode,[12] from bold speech, to impudent action; and Masculine in Tense:[13] for (without redresse)[14] they were, are, and will be still most Masculine, most mankinde, and most monstrous. Are all women then turn'd Masculine? No, God forbid, there are a world full of holy thoughts, modest carriage,[15] and severe chastitie; to these let mee fall on my knees, and say; You, O you women; you good women; you that are in the fulnesse of perfection, you that are the crownes of natures worke, the complements of mens excellencies, and the Seminaries of propagation;[16] you that maintaine the world, support mankinde, and give life to societie; you, that armed with the infinite power of Vertue, are Castles impregnable,[17] Rivers unsaileble, Seas immoveable, infinit treasures, and invincible armies; that are helpers most trustie, Centinels most carefull,[18] signes deceitlesse, plaine wayes failelesse, true guides dangerlesse; Balmes that instantly cure, and honours that never perish: O doe not looke to finde your names in this Declamation, but with all honour and reverence doe I speake to you: You are *Seneca's* Graces,[19] women, good women, modest women, true women: ever yong, because ever vertuous, ever chast, ever glorious: when I write of you, I will write with a golden pen, on leaves of golden paper; now I write with a rough quill, and blacke Inke, on iron sheetes,[20] the iron deeds of an iron generation.

A Petition to good women.

*Sen. de Benef.l.*I.

Of whom the Author writes.

Come then, you Masculine-women, for you are my Subject, you that have made Admiration an Asse, and fool'd him with a deformitie never before dream'd of, that have made your selves stranger things then ever *Noahs* Arke unladed,[21] or *Nyle* ingendred;[22] whom to name, hee that named all things, might study an Age to give you a right attribute, whose like are not found in any Antiquaries[23] study, in any Sea-mans travell, nor in any Painters cunning; you that are stranger then strangenesse it selfe, whom Wisemen wonder at; Boyes shoute at, and Goblins themselves start at; You that are the gilt durt, which imbroders Play-houses;[24] the painted Statues which adorne Caroches,[25] and the perfumed Carrion that bad men feede on in Brothels: 'Tis of you, I intreat, and of your monstrous deformitie; You that have made your bodies like anticke Boscadge, or Crotesco worke,[26] not halfe man, halfe woman; halfe fish, halfe flesh; halfe beast, halfe Monster: but all Ody ous, all Divell, that have cast off the ornaments of your sexes, to put on the garments of Shame; that have laid by the bashfulnesse of your natures, to gather the impudence of Harlots; that have buried silence, to revive slander; that are all things but that which you should be, and nothing lesse then friends to vertue and goodnesse; that have made the foundation of your highest detested worke, from the lowest despised creatures that Record can give testimonie of; the one cut from the Common-wealth at the Gallowes; the other is well knowne[.] From the first you got the false armoury of yellow Starch (for to weare yellow on white, or white upon yellow, is by the rules of Heraldry basenesse, bastardie, and indignitie) the folly of imitation, the deceitfulnesse of flatterie, and the grosest basenesse of all basenesse, to do whatsoever a greater power will command you. From the other, you have taken the monstrousnesse of your deformitie in apparell,[27] exchanging the modest attire of the comely Hood, Cawle, Coyfe,[28] handsome Dresse or Kerchiefe, to the cloudy Ruffianly broad-brim'd Hatte, and wanton Feather,[29] the modest upper parts of a concealing straight gowne, to the loose, lascivious civill embracement of a French doublet,[30] being all unbutton'd to entice, all of one shape to hide deformitie, and extreme short wasted to give a most easie way to every luxurious action: the glory of a faire large hayre, to the shame of most ruffianly short lockes; the side, thicke gather'd, and close guarding Savegards,[31] to the short, weake, thinne, loose, and every hand-entertaining short basses;[32] for Needles, Swords; for Prayer bookes, bawdy Jigs; for modest gestures, gyant-like[33] behaviours, and for womens modestie, all Mimicke and apish incivilitie: These are your founders,[34] from these you tooke your copies, and (without amendment) with these you shall come to perdition.

Sophocles being asked, why he presented no women in his Tragedies but good ones? and *Euripides* none but bad ones? answered, he presented women as they should be; but *Euripides* women as they were.[35] So I present these Masculine women in the deformities as they are, that I may call them backe to the modest comelinesse in which they were.

Why the Author writ thus.

The modest comelinesse in which they were? Why did ever these *Mearemaids,*[36] or rather *Meare-Monsters,* that weare the Car-mans blocke,[37] the Dutchmans feather *Upse-van-muffe,*[38] the poore mans pate poul'd by a Treene dish,[39] the French doublet truss'd with points,[40] to *Mary Anbries*[41] light nether skirts, the Fooles Baudrike,[42] and the Divels Ponyard.[43] Did they ever know comelinesse, or modestie? Fie, no, they never walkt in those pathes; for these at the best are sure but ragges of Gentry, torne from better pieces for their foule staines, or else the adulterate branches of rich Stocks, that taking too much sap from the roote, are cut away, and imploy'd in base uses;[44] or, if not so, they are the stinking vapours drawne from dunghils, which nourisht in the higher Regions of the ayre, become Meteors[45] and false fires blazing and flashing therein, and amazing mens mindes with their strange proportions, till the substance of their pride being spent, they drop down

The description of a Masculine Feminine.

againe to the place from whence they came, and there rot and consume unpittied, and un-remembred.

And questionlesse it is true, that such were the first beginners of these last deformities, for from any purer bloud would have issued a purer birth: there would have beene some sparke of vertue: some excuse for imitation: but this deformitie hath no agreement with goodnesse, nor no difference against the weakest reason: it is all base, all barbarous. Base, in respect it offends man in the example, and God in the most unnaturall use: Barbarous, in that it is exorbitant from Nature, and an *Antithesis* to kinde;[46] going astray (with ill-favoured affectation) both in attire, in speech, in manners, and (it is to bee feared) in the whole courses and stories of their actions. What can bee more barbarous, then with the glosse of mumming Art,[47] to disguise the beauty of their creations? To mould their bodies to every deformed fashion: their tongues to vile and horrible prophanations,[48] and their hands to ruffianly and uncivill actions; To have their gestures as pye-bald, and as motley-various[49] as their disguises; their soules fuller of infirmities then a horse or prostitute, and their mindes languishing in those infirmities: If this bee not barbarous, make the rude *Scithian,* the untamed *Moore,* the naked *Indian,* or the wilde *Irish,*[50] Lords and Rulers of well governed Cities.

Deformitie is base and barbarous.

But rests this deformitie then onely in the baser? in none but such as are the beggery of desert?[51] that have in them nothing but skyttishnesse, & peevishnesse? that are living graves, unwholesome Sinkes?[52] quartan Fevers for intolerable cumber,[53] and the extreme injury and wrong of nature? are these, and none else guilty of this high Treason to God, and nature?

O yes, a world of other, many knowne great; thought good, wisht happy, much loved, and most admired, are so foulely branded with this infamie of disguise, and the markes sticke so deepe on their naked faces, and more naked bodies, that not all the painting in *Rome* or *Fauna*

Of the better sort guilty of this disguise.

can conceale them,[54] but every eye discovers them almost as low as their middles.

Where the best painting is sold.

It is an infection that emulates the plague,[55] and throwes it selfe amongst women of all degrees,[56] all deserts, and all ages; from the Capitoll[57] to the Cottage, are some spots or swellings of this disease, yet evermore the greater the person is, the greater is the rage of this sicknesse, and the more they have to support the eminence of their Fortunes, the more they bestowe in the augmentation of their deformities: not onely such as will not worke to get bread, will finde time to weave her selfe points to trusse her loose Breeches:[58] and shee that hath pawned her credit to get a Hat,[59] will sell her Smocke[60] to buy a Feather; Shee that hath given kisses to have her hayre shorne, will give her honestie to have her upper parts put into a French doublet:[61] To conclude, she that will give her body to have her bodie deformed, will not sticke to give her soule to have her minde satisfied.

What women will doe for their pleasures.

But such as are able to buy all at their owne charges, they swimme in the excesse of these vanities, and will bee man-like not onely from the head to the waste,[62] but to the very foot, & in every condition:[63] man in body by attyre, man in behaviour by rude complement,[64] man in nature by aptnesse to anger, man in action by pursuing revenge, man in wearing weapons, man in using weapons: And in briefe, so much man in all things, that they are neither men, nor women, but just good for nothing.

The excesse of the great persons.

And can Greatnesse and great Birth; great beauty, great bringing up, and great riches, stoope to the basenesse of these monstrous imitations? Why, what are all they when the face of vertue is disguised, more then as silver Bels on a Jacke an Apes coate[65] that shew faire, and chyme sweet; but save not poore Jacke from one lash of the whip, when his knaverie[66] requires it? no more shall their greatnesse or wealth save them from one particle of disgrace, which these monstrous disguises have cast upon them.

What a woman is when her vertue is lost.

Oh you that are the great rich builders of this huge

frame or Masse of disguises, remember what the Poet[67] saith;

S.T.O.

As for the (oddes of sexes)[68] *portion,*
Nor will I shunne it, nor my ayme it make,
Birth, Beauty, wealth are nothing worth alone,
All these I could for good additions take:
Not for good parts, those two are ill combin'd
Whom any third thing from themselves hath joind.

Rather then these the object of my love,
Let it be good; when these with vertue goe,
They (in themselves indifferent) vertues prove,
For good like fire turnes all things to be so:
Gods Image in her soule, O let me place
My love upon; not Adams *in her face.*

That from the first there was difference in attire.

Remember how your Maker made for our first Parents coates,[69] not one coat, but a coat for the man, and a coat for the woman; coates of severall fashions, severall formes, and for severall uses: the mans coat fit for his labour, the womans fit for her modestie: and will you lose the modell left by this great Work-master of Heaven?

Of beauty and deformitie.

The long hayre of a woman is the ornament of her sexe, and bashfull shamefastnesse her chiefe honour: the long haire of a man, the vizard[70] for a theevish or murderous disposition: and will you cut off that beauty, to weare the others villany? The Vestals in *Rome*[71] wore comly garments of one piece from the neck to the heele; and the Swordplayers motley doublets, with gaudy points: the first begot reverence; the later laughter: and will you lose that honor, for the others scorne? the weapon of a vertuous woman was her teares, which every good man pitied, and every valiant man honoured: the weapon of a cruell man is his sword, which neither Law allowes, nor reason defends: and will you leave the excellent shield of innocence for this deformed instrument of disgrace? Even for goodnesse sake (that can ever pay her owne with her owne merits) looke to your reputations, which are undermined with your owne Follies, and doe not become the idle Sisters of foolish *Don Quixote*,[72] to beleeve every vaine Fable which you reade, or to think you may bee attired like *Bradamant*, who was often taken for *Ricardetto* her brother; that you may fight like *Marfiza*, and winne husbands with conquest, or ride astryde like *Claridiana*,[73] and make Gyants fall at your stirrops, (the Morals will give you better meanings) which if you shunne, and take the grosse imitations, the first will deprive you of all good societie; the second, of noble affections; and the third, of all beloved modestie: you shall lose all the charmes of womens naturall perfections, have no presence to winne respect, no beauty to inchaunt mens hearts, nor no bashfulnesse to excuse the vildest imputations.[74]

Women compared to *Don Quixote*.

Arist. Cant. I.13.

The fayrest face covered with a foule vizard, begets nothing but affright or scorne, and the noblest person, in an ignoble disguise, attaines to nothing but reproch, and scandall: Away then with these disguises, and foule vizards; these unnaturall paintings,[75] and immodest discoveries; keepe those parts concealed from the eyes, that may not bee toucht with the hands: Let not a wandring and lascivious thought read in an intising Index[76] the contents of an unchaste volume. Imitate nature: and as shee hath plac't on the surface and superficies of the earth, all things needfull for mans sustenance, and necessarie use; as Hearbs, Plants, Fruits, Corne[77] and such like, but lockt up close in the hidden caverns of the earth, all things which appertaine to his delight and pleasure: as gold, silver, rich Mynerals and precious Stones: so doe you discover[78] unto men all things that are fit for them to understand from you: as bashfulnesse in your cheekes, chastitie in your eyes, wisedome in your words, sweetnesse in your conversation, pitie in your hearts, and a generall and severe modestie in the whole structure or frame of your universall composition:[79] But for those things which belong to this wanton and lascivious delight and pleasure: as eyes wandring, lips bylling,[80] tongue inticing, bared brests seducing, and naked armes imbracing: O hide them,

How women should imitate nature.

for shame hide them in the closest prisons of your strictest government: shield them with modest and comely garments, such as are warme and wholesome, having every window closed with a strong Casement,[81] and every Loope-hole furnisht with such strong Ordnance,[82] that no unchaste eye may come neere to assayle them; no lascivious tongue wooe a forbidden passage, nor no prophane hand touch reliques so pure and religious. Guard them about with counter-scarfes[83] of Innocence, Trenches[84] of humane Reason, and impregnable walles of sacred Divinitie: not with Anticke disguise,[85] and Mimicke fantastickenesse,[86] where every window stands open like the *Saburra,* and every window a Curtizan with an instrument,[87] like so many *Syrens,* to inchant the weake passenger to shipwracke and destruction.[88] Thus shall you be your selves againe, and live the most excellentest creatures upon earth, things past example, past all imitation.

A street where the Curtizans dwelt in *Rome.*

Remember, that God in your first creation did not forme you of slyme and earth, like man, but of a more pure and refined metall;[89] a substance much more worthy: you in whom are all the harmonies of life, the perfection of Symetry, the true and curious consent of the most fayrest colours and the wealthy Gardens which fils the world with living Plants. Doe but you receive vertuous In-mates (as what Palaces are more rich to receive heavenly messengers?) and you shall draw mens soules unto you with that severe, devout, and holy adoration, that you shal never want praise, never love, never reverence.

But now mee thinkes I heare the witty-offending great Ones reply in excuse of their deformities: What, is there no difference amongst Women? no distinction of places, no respect of Honours, nor no regard of bloud, or allyance? Must but a bare payre of sheeres passe betweene Noble and ignoble,[90] betweene the generous spirit and the base Mechannick;[91] shall we be all co-heires of one honor, one estate and one habit?[92] O Men, you are then too tyrannous, and not onely injure Nature, but also breake the

The excuse of great persons.

Lawes and customes of the wisest Princes. Are no Bishops knowne by their Myters,[93] Princes by their Crownes, Judges by their Robes, and Knights by their Spurres? but poore Women have nothing (how great soever they bee) to divide themselves from the intising shewes or mooving Images which do furnish most shops in the City.[94] What is it that eyther the Lawes have allowed to the greatest Ladies, custome found convenient, or their bloods or places challenged, which hath not beene ingrost into the Citie with as great greedinesse, and pretence of true tytle; as if the surcease from the Imitation were the utter breach of their Charter everlastingly.[95]

The Cities accused.

The Cities Pride.

For this cause, these Apes of the City have inticed forraine Nations to their Cels,[96] and there committing grosse adultery with their Gewgawes,[97] have brought out such unnaturall conceptions,[98] that the whole world is not able to make a *Democritus*[99] big inough to laugh at their foolish ambitions. Nay, the very Art of Painting[100] (which to the last Age shall ever be held in detestation) they have so cunningly stoln and hidden amongst their husbands hoords of treasure, that the decayed stock of Prostitution (having little other revenues) are howerly in bringing their action of *Detinue* against them.[101] Hence (beeing thus troubled with these *Popenjays,*[102] & loth still to march in one ranke with fooles and *Zanyes*)[103] have proceeded these disguised deformities, not to offend the eyes of goodnesse, but to tyer with ridiculous contempt the never to be satisfied appetites of these grosse and unmanerly intruders: nay, look if this very last edition of disguise, this which is so full of faults, corruptions and false quotations,[104] this bayt which the Divel hath layd to catch the soules of wanton Women, be not as frequent in the demy-Palaces of Burgars and Citizens,[105] as it is either at Maske, Tryumph, Tilt-yard,[106] or Play-house: call but to account the Taylors that are contained within the Circumference of the Walles of the City, and let but their Hels[107] and their hard reckonings[108] be justly summed together, and it will bee found

Bringing in of forraine fashions.

Citizens blamed for painting.

Citizens got into this new disguise.

they have raised more new foundations of this new disguise,[109] and metamorphosed more modest old garments, to this new manner of short base and French doublet (onely for the use of Freemens wives and their children)[110] in one moneth, then hath beene worne in Court, Suburbs, or Countrey, since the unfortunate beginning of the first divellish invention.

Let therefore the powerfull Statute of apparell[111] but lift up his Battle-Axe, and crush the offenders in pieces, so as every one may bee knowne by the true badge of their bloud, or Fortune: and then these *Chymera's*[112] of deformitie will bee sent backe to hell, and there burne to Cynders in the flames of their owne malice.

Thus, mee thinkes, I heare the best offenders argue, nor can I blame a hye[113] bloud to swell when it is coupled and counter-checkt with basenes and corruption; yet this shewes an anger passing neere a kinne to envy, and alludes much to the saying of an excellent Poet:

Women never,
Love beauty in their Sexe, but envy ever.[114]

They have *Caesars* ambition,[115] and desire to bee one and alone, but yet to offend themselves, to grieve others, is a revenge dissonant to Reason; & as *Euripides* faith, a woman of that malicious nature is a fierce Beast, and most pernicious to the Common-wealth, for she hath power by example to doe it a world of injury.[116] But farre bee such cruelty from the softnesse of their gentle dispositions: O let them remember what the Poet saith: Eur. in Trag.

Women be
Fram'd with the same parts of the minde as we:
Nay Nature triumpht in their beauties birth,
And women made the glory of the earth,
The life of beauty, in whose simple brests,
(As in her fairest lodging) Vertue rests:
Whose towring thoughts attended with remorce,
Doe make their fairenesse be of greater force.[117]

But when they thrust vertue out of doores, and give a shamelesse libertie to every loose passion, that either their weake thoughts ingenders,[118] or the discourse of wicked tongues can charme into their yeelding bosomes (much too apt to bee opened with any pick-locke of flattering and deceitfull insinuation)[119] then they turne Maskers, Mummers, nay Monsters in their disguises, and so they may catch the bridle in their teeth, and runne away with their Rulers,[120] they care not into what dangers they plunge either their Fortunes or Reputations, the disgrace of the whole Sexe, or the blot and obloquy[121] of their private Families, according to the saying of the Poet:

What makes Women to deforme themselves.

Such is the cruelty of women-kinde,
When they have shaken off the shamefac't band
With which wise nature did them strongly binde,
T'obey the hests of mans well-ruling hand;
That then all Rule and Reason they withstand
To purchase a licentious libertie;
But vertuous women wisely understand,
That they were borne to milde humilitie,
Unlesse the heavens them lift to lawfull soveraintie.[122]

E.S.

To you therefore that are Fathers, Husbands, or Sustainers of these new *Hermophrodites,*[123] belongs the cure of this Impostume;[124] it is you that give fuell to the flames of their wilde indiscretion. You adde the oyle which makes their stinking Lamps defile the whole house with filthy smoke, and your purses purchase these deformities at rates, both deare and unreasonable. Doe you but hold close your liberall hands, or take a strict account of the imployment of the treasure you give to their necessarie maintenance, and these excesses will either cease, or else dye smothered in prison in the Taylors Trunkes for want of Redemption.

A warning to Husbands and Fathers.

Seneca (speaking of liberalitie) will by no meanes allow that any man should bestowe either on friend, wife or children, any treasure to be spent upon ignoble uses, for

Stu. de Ben.l.2.

it not onely robs the party of the honour of bounty, and takes from the deed the name of a Benefit; but also makes him conscious, & guiltie of the crimes which are purchast by such a gratuitie.[125] Bee therefore the Schollers of *Seneca;* and your Wives, Sisters and Daughters, will be the Co-heires of modestie.

Licurgus the law-giver made it death in one of his Statutes, to bring in any new custome into his Commonwealth.[126] Doe you make it the utter losse of your favour and bounty, to have brought into your Family, any new fashion or disguise, that might either deforme Nature, or bee an injury to modestie: so shall shamefastnes and comelinesse ever live under your roofe, and your Wives and Daughters like Vines and faire Olives, ever spread with beauty round about your Tables.

Lycurgus Law against novelties.

The *Lacedemonians*[127] seeing that their children were better taught by examples, then precepts; had hanging in their houses in faire painted tables[128] all the Vertues and Vices that were in those dayes raigning, with their rewards, and punishments. O have you but in your houses the fashions of all attires constantly, and without change held and still followed through all the parts of Christendom. Let them but see the modest Dutch, the stately Italian, the rich Spaniard, and the courtly French, with the rest, according to their climates, and they will blush, that in a full fourth part of the world there cannot be found one piece of a Character, to compare or liken with the absurditie of their Masculine Invention; nay, they shall see, that their naked Countreyman, which had liberty with his Sheeres to cut from every Nation of the World, one piece or patch to make up his garment,[129] yet amongst them all could not find this *Misselanie*[130] or mixture of deformities, which onely by those (which whilst they retained any sparke of womanhood, were both loved and admired:) is loosely, indiscreetly, wantonly and most unchastely invented.

The custome of the Lacedemonians.

And therefore to knit up this imperfect Declamation,[131] let every Female-Masculine that by her ill example is guilty of Lust, or Imitation; cast off her deformities, and cloath her selfe in the rich garments which the Poet bestowes upon her in these Verses following.

Those Vertues that in women merit praise
Are sober shewes without, chast thoughts within,
True Faith and due obedience to their mate,
And of their children honest care to take.[132]

FINIS

NOTES

1. The title of the pamphlet combines *hic,* the male form of the Latin word for "this," with *mulier,* the Latin word for "woman," playing on the gender confusion that the writer claims results from women wearing men's clothes.

2. Wild, frisky, or untamed; wanton or lustful. See the *Oxford English Dictionary* (1989; hereafter *OED*), s.v. "coltish," citing James Shirley's *School of complement* (1631): "A parson's wife that was coltish once" (3.5).

3. Various diseases that affect domestic animals, including horses, manifesting themselves in a staggering or unsteady gait. See Shakespeare's *Taming of the Shrew* (1593–94): "his horse hipp'd" and "stark spoil'd with the staggers" (3.2.48, 54).

4. Actually, *Non omnia possumus omnes* (Virgil, *Eclogues* [Loeb Classical Library, 1999], eclogue 8, l. 63): "not all things can we all do." In other words, women cannot dress like men.

5. Adorned; to cut off the excrescence of; metaphorically, given a beating to. In the woodcut, Hic Mulier's hair is being cut.

6. Fastened up the hair with ribbon, pins, or combs; fastened the wings or legs of a fowl to the body with skewers in preparation for cooking. Phillip Stubbes comments on what women do to their hair: "Then followeth the trimming and fricking of their heds in laying out their hair to the shewe, which of force must be curled, frisled and crisped, laid out (a World to see) on wreathes & borders from one eare to an other. And least it should fall down it is under propped with forks, wyers & I can not tel what, rather like grime sterne monsters, then chaste christian matrones" (*The Anatomie of Abuses* [London, 1583], F2r).

7. John Trundle, a bookseller in London from 1603 to 1626, was known for publishing ballads, pamphlets, news-books, and plays. With Nicholas Ling he published the first quarto of Shakespeare's *Hamlet.* See Ronald B. McKerrow, gen. ed., *A Dictionary of Printers and Booksellers in England, Scotland, and Ireland, and of foreign printers of English books, 1557–1640* (London: Blades, East, and Blades, 1910), 269.

8. Priscian was a celebrated Roman grammarian, ca. 500–532. "To break Priscian's

head" means to break the rules of grammar. See Shakespeare's *Love's Labour's Lost* (1594–95): "Priscian a little scratch'd, 'twill serve" (5.1.28–29).

9. "Signor" is an Italian term of respect used with a man's name. "Signor Construction" personifies grammatical form or structure. Throughout this passage, the writer uses a series of puns on grammar to indicate that the man-woman not only violates accepted social structures but also confuses grammatical structures that differentiate masculine from feminine.

10. In most Western languages, verbs and pronouns agree in number with their respective nouns; in inflected languages, such as Latin, adjectives must also agree.

11. In inflected languages, "case" is a grammatical term referring to the forms that may be given to nouns, pronouns, and adjectives to indicate relationships among different words in a sentence or phrase. "Case" may also refer to a person's exterior.

12. In most Western languages, "mood" is a grammatical term referring to any of the different groupings in the conjugation of a verb that indicate the function of the verb. Here, the writer puns on "mood" as also referring to a person's frame of mind or natural disposition. Hic Mulier says the mood of contemporary women is bold and impudent.

13. A grammatical term referring to any of the different forms in the conjugation of a verb, indicating when the action of the verb occurred.

14. Remedy. This may be a pun on "dress" as an article of clothing: Without redressing, women will remain dressed as men.

15. How a person carries or holds his/her body.

16. Seedbeds where plants or other living creatures grow. This is a pun on woman's body as the source of life. Hic Mulier is describing women who have not become masculine.

17. Impenetrable castles. The writer is using military terminology, probably with a pun on "pregnancy."

18. Careful sentinels or guards; continues the writer's use of military terminology.

19. In book 1 of *De Beneficiis* (On benefits), in *Moral Essays* (Loeb Classical Library, 1958), Lucius Annaeus Seneca the younger, a Roman writer who lived ca. 4 B.C.E. to 65 C.E., speaks of the three Graces, the beautiful daughters of Jupiter (3.9).

20. The Roman poet Ovid (43 B.C.E.–17 C.E.) describes the four ages of gold, silver, bronze, and iron in book 1 of *Metamorphoses.* He writes that in the iron age "Fayth and Truth were faine / And honest shame to hide their heads" (trans. Arthur Golding [London, 1612], B3r). The English playwright Thomas Heywood wrote a series of plays on each of these ages: *The Golden Age* (1611), *The Silver Age* (1613), *The Brazen Age* (1613), and *The Iron Age* (1632).

21. Noah's ark unloaded. In Gen. 7–8, God commands Noah to load an ark with his family and one pair of every kind of animal on earth so that they might be saved from a flood He will visit on the world for man's sinfulness.

22. Things engendered or begotten in the Nile River in North Africa. The waters of the Nile were supposed to have special powers as a source of life. Ovid describes this in book 1 of *Metamorphoses.*

23. Belonging to an antiquarian, a person who studies the remains of older cultures.

24. Dirt that has been gilded (i.e., covered with a thin layer of gold) embroiders, or deceptively covers, the walls of the theaters. The Globe Theatre was probably painted in bright colors, occasionally making use of gold leaf. Often one material was painted to look like another. See John Ronayne, "'Totus Mundus Agit Histrionem [The whole world moves the actor]': The Interior Decorative Scheme of the Bankside Globe," in *Shakespeare's Globe Rebuilt,* ed. J. R. Mulryne, Margaret Shewring and Andrew Gurr (New York: Cambridge University Press, 1997), 123–29.

25. Stately or luxurious coaches.

26. A grotesque decorative design of branches and foliage; or *grottesco,* ornamentation composed of loosely connected motifs, including whimsical human figures and fantastic beasts.

27. "The one" refers specifically to Anne Turner, who was hanged for assisting Lady Frances Howard in the murder of Sir Thomas Overbury, who had objected to Howard's adulterous affair with Robert Carr, Earl of Somerset. Anne Turner introduced the fashion of yellow starched cuffs and ruff into England. At her hanging, the executioner wore yellow starched cuffs, which ended the fashion. "The other" refers to Lady Frances Howard, who had her marriage to the Earl of Essex annulled and later married Robert Carr. In a stanza entitled "Equality of Persons" in "Epithalamion," describing their marriage, John Donne writes: "If by that manly courage they be tried, / Which scorns unjust opinion; then the Bride / Becomes a man" (*The Complete Poetry of John Donne,* ed. John T. Shawcross [New York: New York University Press, 1968], 182). In a portrait of Howard by Simon van de Passe, ca. 1618, Turner is wearing a broad-brimmed hat with a feather. See David Lindley, *The Trials of Frances Howard: Fact and Fiction at the Court of King James* (London: Routledge, 1993), following p. 76.

Heraldry is the art of emblazoning arms and tracing the rights of persons to bear arms. A general rule of heraldry is that a colored object may not be laid upon a colored background on a coat of arms because of the difficulty of distinguishing a warrior in the field. Yellow is connected with Turner's yellow starch.

28. A caul is a close-fitting cap or a round cap worn at the back of the head. A coif is a close-fitting hood shaped like a baby's bonnet.

29. As worn by one of the women in the two woodcuts on the title pages of *Hic Mulier* and *Haec-Vir* and by Lady Frances Howard.

30. A popular, close-fitting body garment with or without sleeves, usually belonging to men. Stubbes comments that "the Women also there have dublets & Jerkins as men have . . . & though this be a kinde of attire proper onely to man, yet they blush not to wear it, and if they could as wel chaunge their sex, & put on the kinde of man, as they can weare apparel assigned onely to man, I think they would" (*Anatomie of Abuses,* F5r–F5v). Notice that the author of *Hic Mulier* complains that the doublet women are wearing is too short, whereas Stubbes says it is too long.

31. Petticoats that women wore over their clothes to protect them from dirt. See Thomas Middleton and Thomas Dekker, *The Roaring Girl,* ed. Paul A. Mulholland (Manchester: Manchester University Press, 1987): "Enter Moll in a frieze jerkin and a black safegard" (2.1, stage direction preceding l. 175).

32. Bases; a braided skirt of cloth, either velvet or rich brocade, appended to the doublet and reaching from the waist to the knee.

33. Monstrous.

34. Creators.

35. Euripides and Sophocles were fifth-century B.C.E. Greek writers of tragedy. The comment probably derives from a passage in Aristotle's *Poetics* (Loeb Classical Library, 1932): "Sophocles said that he portrayed people as they ought to be and Euripides portrayed them as they are" (25.11–12).

36. Mermaids (i.e., half women and half fish); prostitutes.

37. The hat of a person who hires out a cart or other vehicle.

38. "Dutchman" was often used to refer to a German. "Upsey" means "extreme" or "in excess." "Muffe" was a derogatory term for a German or a prostitute. The writer is commenting on the foreignness of the masculine women's clothes.

39. "Pate" means "head." "Poll" means to cut one's hair short. "Treen" is the old plural form of "tree" and in this context means "wooden." Perhaps the writer is referring to the women's short hair, a kind of bowl cut.

40. Tied with laces used to attach hose to the doublet.

41. Mary Ambree, an Englishwoman, was renowned for her bravery in battle at the siege of Ghent in 1584, and her name is applied to women of spirit and strength. (A ballad was written about her; see Thomas Percy's *Reliques of Ancient English Poetry,* vol. 2 [London: Swan Sonnenschein and Co., 1891], 231–37.) A nether skirt is worn closest to the skin. By using this term the writer is disparaging Ambree's dress.

42. Baldric; a belt or girdle, usually of leather, worn across the shoulder to support a sword or other weapon.

43. A dagger.

44. That is, these women are like defiled branches from excellent trees (i.e., families) that are being used in corrupt ways.

45. It was believed that meteors were formed in the air by inflammable gases.

46. The opposite of "natural."

47. A disguise. This may also refer to the performance of mummers or dumb shows, dramatic productions without speaking parts, usually with a metaphorical or symbolic meaning.

48. Desecrations.

49. "Pye-bald" means "incongruous." "Motley-various" means "many colored," especially when referring to the multicolored outfits of professional fools.

50. Seventeenth-century English readers would have associated the people listed in this passage with barbarism and warlike, uncivilized living. Scythians were residents of a region north of the Black Sea, formerly called Scythia. The violent and warlike hero of Christopher Marlowe's popular sixteenth-century play *Tamburlaine* is described as a "sturdie Scythian thief (1.1.44). Moors were descendants of the Berber and Arab peoples. They were adherents of the Muslim religion and constituted the bulk of the population of northwestern Africa. (See Rowlands, *A whole crew,* n. 62.) The "naked Indian" probably refers to American Indians. The "wild Irish," according to the *OED,* were the "less civilized Irish." The writer is stating that if these women

dressed as men are not barbarous, then these uncivilized peoples should be allowed to rule well-governed cities.

51. The impoverished, whom the writer thinks are deserving of their lowly status.

52. Pits for waste and sewage. See the *OED*, s.v. "sink," citing Henry Crosse's *Vertues common-wealth* (1603): "A Play is like a Sincke in a Towne, where unto all the filth doth runne."

53. Fevers accompanied by fits that occur every fourth day, causing insufferable distress.

54. That is, all people can see the truth about these women.

55. In 1603 almost one-sixth of the population of London—people of all social classes—died from the plague. Although it continued to kill many people, it did not reach epidemic proportions again until 1625.

56. Women from all social and economic backgrounds.

57. An estate held directly from the king.

58. To weave herself laces or cords of twisted yarn, silk, or leather to fasten her (man's) trousers. See n. 40.

59. To give away her credit as security against a small loan to buy a hat. The "credit" the woman gives away is her reputation. See Rowlands, *Tis Merry,* n. 10.

60. A woman's undergarment.

61. A woman will surrender her honesty, or her reputation, in order to have her upper body dressed in a French jacket. As noted above, the writer is suggesting that women will sell sexual favors, or their "lower parts," to afford fashionable clothing, prostituting their bodies both figuratively and literally. See also n. 30.

62. Waist.

63. In every way.

64. That is, by rude imitation of a man.

65. Bells that decorate the coat of a tame ape or a buffoon. The term "Jacke an Apes" was originally used to refer to the unpopular William de la Pole, Duke of Suffolk, who was murdered in 1450. It was probably coined because de la Pole's coat of arms included a clog and chain such as was used to harness a tame ape. After de la Pole's death, the term came to refer to any ridiculous fellow. See Rowlands, *Tis Merry,* n. 45.

66. Untrustworthy or unruly behavior.

67. S.T.O. in the margin refers to Sir Thomas Overbury (1581–1613), who published a poem entitled "A Wife" (1614) from which these lines are taken. Overbury's father believed that his son wrote the poem to persuade Robert Carr not to marry Lady Frances Turner (see Anne Somerset, *Unnatural Murder* [London: Weidenfeld and Nicolson, 1997], 59). Overbury was poisoned by Anne Turner and Lady Frances Howard (see n. 27 above).

68. Differences; unequal conditions.

69. In Gen. 3.21, the coats for Adam and Eve are not differentiated: "Unto Adam also and to his wife did the Lord God make coates of skinnes, and clothed them."

70. A mask.

71. Chaste priestesses who watched the sacred fire of the temple of Vesta in Rome.

72. Don Quixote, in the eponymous novel by Miguel de Cervantes Saavedra (1547–1616), is driven mad by reading chivalric romances, imagining himself to be a knight errant. *Don Quijote* was first published in Spain in 1605; it was translated into English by Thomas Shelton in 1605 (part 1) and 1620 (part 2).

73. Characters in the Italian epic poem *Orlando Furioso* by Ludovico Ariosto (1475–1535). Bradamant and Marfisa are woman warriors; Ricardet is Bradamante's twin brother. Even Bradamante's lover mistakes her for her brother. Canto 15 of *Orlando Furioso* is cited in the margin of *Hic Mulier,* but none of these characters appear there. *Orlando Furioso* was first printed in England in 1532; it was translated into English by Sir John Harington in 1591 (see n. 132 below). Edmund Spenser (1552–99) based Britomart, the cross-dressed woman warrior in *Faerie Queene,* on Ariosto's Bradamante.

74. Vilest or most depraved accusations.

75. By comparing the cross-dressed women to paintings, the writer is emphasizing the unnaturalness of the women's imitation of men. "Painting" also refers to the wearing of cosmetics, frequently condemned by writers of the period as a sign of vanity and the result of a woman's desire to create an unnatural or "imitation" face.

76. The table of contents.

77. Grain.

78. To reveal.

79. The constitution of mind and body.

80. Kissing; derived from the way birds rub their bills together as a sign of affection.

81. A window frame.

82. A vertical entrance, usually widening inward, cut into a wall to allow for the outward passage of military missiles.

83. Walls (or supports for walls) and towers of a castle. Throughout this passage the writer is using military terms to describe the efforts to which women should go to protect their chastity.

84. Long narrow ditches used for defense and protection against attacks by enemy forces.

85. An incongruous or bizarre disguise (such as, the writer implies, wearing men's clothing).

86. Imitating or copying another person's speech, behavior, or dress in a "fantastic" or perverse way.

87. In the margin the writer notes that the Saburra is a street in Rome where courtesans dwelt. Livy reports a brawl occurring in a street named Suburba (*Ab Urbe Condita* [Loeb Classical Library, 1922], 3.13.2). Prostitutes often displayed their wares by sitting in open windows. English writers claimed that Italy was infamous for its prostitutes, especially its sophisticated "courtesans"—women who frequented the court and who, according to their detractors, offered sexual favors to courtiers.

88. A mythological creature, half woman and half bird, who lured sailors to their destruction with its singing, often confused with mermaids. See Homer's *Odyssey,* book 12.

89. A reference to Gen. 2.21–22, which describes how God made women out of man's rib.

90. That is, must a pair of scissors make us all alike.

91. A manual laborer, here used contemptuously.

92. One rank and one kind of clothing.

93. Miters, or tall hats in the shape of a pointed arch, deeply cleft at the top, worn only by bishops.

94. Poor women or merchants' wives and daughters are known by the cheap London shop goods that copied the fashion of ladies. "Images" is possibly being used disparagingly to refer to Roman Catholic religious icons such as statues of saints.

95. The clothing that once identified "the greatest Ladies" was being sold in London shops. These goods were amassed in large quantity in London, as if ceasing to copy the fashions of ladies would be akin to breaking a legal agreement. The writer is saying that the noblewomen are defending their right to dress as men because the fashions that previously identified them as noblewomen have been taken over by poorer women.

96. Small rooms. "These Apes of the City" are women of low status.

97. Ornaments or pretty things of little value.

98. Outlandish clothes that are the adulterous offspring of foreign fashion and city women in court dress.

99. A fifth-century B.C.E. Greek philosopher known as "the laughing philosopher" because he argued that we should aim to achieve cheerfulness in our lives. In *De tranquillitate animi* (On tranquility of mind), in *Moral Essays* (Loeb Classical Library, 1951), Seneca states: "We ought . . . to imitate Democritus rather than Heraclitus. For the latter, whenever he went forth into public, used to weep, the former to laugh; to the one all human doings seemed to be miseries, to the other follies" (15.2).

100. Wearing cosmetics.

101. A lawful action requiring the defendant to return personal possessions wrongfully taken from their owners. The writer is implying that women who wear the newest fashions paint their faces so heavily that they have, as it were, appropriated prostitutes' wares.

102. Parrots; used figuratively for vain persons, such as those who wear the gaudy colors of the parrot.

103. Servants who act as clowns in Italian commedia dell'arte; laughingstocks.

104. The writer is using a series of puns on printing terminology: "faults," "corruptions," and "false quotations" are terms used for errors in setting type, all of which result in an incorrect or "corrupt" edition. The marginal note indicates that it is the citizens who are disguised.

105. Small palaces or houses belonging to people of middle rank and more modest social and economic standing. "Burghers" and citizens were the freemen of a city or town who had earned civic rights but had no title of honor by birthright.

106. A court entertainment that includes dancing, dumb shows, some dialogue, and richly ornate costumes and settings. Courtiers and even members of the royal family often take part in the production. A "triumph" is a procession or pageant, usu-

ally of the court. A "tilt-yard" is an enclosed space for sporting tournaments, usually between two men of the court on horseback.

107. Places under a tailor's table where pieces of cloth, removed in the process of cutting out clothes, are thrown. Robert Greene writes in *A Quip for an Upstart Courtier* (1592): "He can cast large shreds of such rich stuff into hell, under his shopboard" (cited in the *OED*, s.v. "hell").

108. Accounts of citizens' bills and charges on bills or sums owed, especially high sums. Tailors were frequently accused of cheating customers and being wastrels themselves. Robert Nares comments in *A Glossary* (London: R. Triphook, 1822), that "many were the jests current at all times upon that unfortunate fraternity, owing, doubtless, to the effeminacy of their business, in using needles, thead, thimbles" (505). In Shakespeare's *King Lear* (1605), Kent insults Oswald by stating "a taylor made thee" (2.2.54–55).

109. Created more extravagant new clothes out of old clothes. The writer is saying that cross-dressing is most prevalent in the city of London.

110. Freemen practiced a trade, belonged to one of the city's craft guilds, and had enough wealth to buy themselves the privileges of the city, including the right to vote and hold municipal office.

111. The "sumptuary laws" in early modern England regulated the clothes, especially the quality and color of the cloth, that persons of different social and economic ranks were allowed to wear. The writer is saying that if the sumptuary laws were enforced, cross-dressing would no longer be a problem.

112. A mythological fire-breathing monster said in some accounts to have a lion's head, a goat's belly, and a serpent's tail. See John Williams, *A Sermon of Apparell* (London, 1619): "For a woman therefore to come unto a Church, *Chimaera-like* . . . halfe male, and halfe female" (20).

113. Arrogant.

114. George Chapman. The source of the quote is his "Musaeus: Of Hero and Leander" (in *The Works of George Chapman*, ed. R. H. Shepherd [London: Chatto and Windus, 1875]): "Women for Beauty their owne sex envy" (95).

115. Gaius Julius Caesar (102–44 B.C.E.), a Roman general and statesman known for his ambition and prowess on the battlefield. His detractors saw him as an ambitious demagogue who forced his way to dictatorial power.

116. Probably a reference to Euripides' *Medea* (431 B.C.E.). After Medea's husband, Jason, deserts her, she kills Jason, his new wife, and her children.

117. According to Simon Shepherd's *Amazons and Warrior Women: Varieties of Feminism in Seventeenth-Century Drama* (New York: St. Martin's Press, 1981), 87, the quote is from Sidney's *Arcadia.*

118. Gives birth to, creates.

119. A person, especially a thief, who opens a door by picking the lock. Metaphorically, the thief is using flattery to gain another person's confidence or trust.

120. That is, to act and dress above their social status.

121. Stain and disgrace.

122. The quote is from Spenser's *Faerie Queene* (5.5.25), in which the Amazon

Radigund has subdued Artegall in a battle, forced him to dress as a woman, and replaced his sword with a distaff so that he can spin. However, Radigund is secretly in love with Artegall. The last line refers to Queen Elizabeth, who is an exception among women "born to base humility."

123. Human beings with the physical characteristics of both female and male sexes. These women are called hermaphrodites because they dress like men. According to Stubbes, women who wear men's clothing "may not improperly be called *Hermaphroditi,* that is Monsters of bothe kindes, half women, half men (*Anatomie of Abuse,* F5v).

124. An abscess, swelling, cyst, or ulcer in any part of the body; a moral flaw.

125. Lucius Annaeus Seneca the younger discusses inappropriate gifts: "There are certain gifts that are likely to harm those who obtain them, and, in the case of these, the benefit consists, not in giving, but in withholding, them" (*De Beneficiis,* 2.14.1).

126. A legendary lawmaker and founder of the Spartan constitution whose name became synonymous with harshness. This passage is probably based on Plutarch's *Lives.* According to Plutarch, Lycurgus "did not permit [the people of Sparta] to live abroad at their pleasure and wander in strange lands, assuming foreign habits and imitating the lives of people who were without training and lived under different forms of government. Nay more, he actually drove away from the city the multitudes which streamed in there for no useful purpose. . . . For along with strange people, strange doctrines must come in. . . . Therefore he thought it more necessary to keep bad manners from invading and filling the city than it was to keep out infectious diseases" ("Lyceurgus," in *Plutarch's Parallel Lives* [Loeb Classical Library, 1914], 27.3–4).

127. Inhabitants of Lacedaemon, or Sparta, in Greece.

128. Tablets that were painted upon.

129. That is, if an Englishman took a piece of fabric from each nation of the world, his garment would not be as deformed as the dress of these "female-masculines." For recorded instances of female cross-dressing in early modern Europe, see Rudolf M. Dekker and Lotte C. van de Pol, *The Tradition of Female Transvestism in Early Modern Europe* (New York: St. Martin's Press, 1989), 1–24.

130. Miscellany, a collection of different items.

131. To conclude this pamphlet.

132. Quoted from Ariosto's *Orlando Furioso,* trans. John Harington (London, 1591), bk. 7, ll. 509–12. See also n. 73.

HÆC-VIR:
OR
The Womanish-Man:

Being an Anſwere to a late Booke intituled *Hic-Mulier.*

Expreſt in a briefe Dialogue betweene *Hæc-Vir* the Womaniſh-Man, and *Hic-Mulier* the Man-Woman.

London printed for *I.T.* and are to be ſold at Chriſt Church gate. 1620.

Haec-Vir:[1] Or The Womanish-Man: Being an Answere to a late Booke intituled *Hic-Mulier.*[2] Exprest in a briefe Dialogue betweene *Haec-Vir* the Womanish-Man, and *Hic-Mulier* the Man-Woman. London printed for J.T.[3] and are to be sold at Christ Church gate. 1620.

HAEC-VIR:
Or,
The Womanish-Man.

The Speakers.
Haec-Vir; The Womanish-Man.
Hic-Mulier; The Man-Woman.

Haec-Vir. Most redoubted and worthy Sir (for lesse then a Knight I cannot take you) you are most happily given unto mine imbrace.

Hic-Mul: Is she mad? or doth shee mocke mee? Most rare and excellent Lady, I am the servant of your vertues, and desire to be imployed in your service.

Haec-Vir. Pitie of patience, what doth hee behold in me, to take me for a woman? Valiant and magnanimous Sir, I shal desire to build the Tower of my Fortune upon no stronger foundation then the benefit of your grace and favour.

Hic-Mul: O! proud ever to be your Servant.

Haec-Vir. No, the Servant of your Servant.

Hic-Mul: The Tythe[4] of your friendship (good Lady) is above my merit.

Haec-Vir. You make mee rich beyond expression. But faire *Knight,* the truth is I am a Man, and desire but the obligation of your friendship.

Hic-Mul: It is ready to be sealed and delivered to your use. Yet I would have you understand I am a Woman.

Haec-Vir. Are you a Woman?

Hic-Mul: Are you a Man? O *Juno Lucina*[5] help me.

Haec-Vir. Yes I am.

Hic-Mul: Your name; most tender piece of Masculine.

Haec-Vir. Haec-Vir. No stranger either in Court, Citie, or Countrey. But what is yours, most couragious counterfet of *Heracles*[6] and his Distaffe?

Hic-Mul: Neere a kinne to your goodnes; and compounded of fully as false Latine.[7] The world cals me, *Hic-Mulier.*

Haec-Vir. What, *Hic-Mulier,* the Man-Woman? She that like a Larum-Bell[8] at midnight hath raised the whole Kingdome in Armes[9] against her? Good, stand, and let me take a full survay, both of thee, and all thy dependants.

Hic-Mul: Doe freely: and when thou hast dawbed me over, with the worst colours thy malice can grinde,[10] then give mee leave to answere for my selfe, and I will say thou art an accuser just and indifferent.[11] Which done, I must intreat you to fit as many minutes, that I may likewise take your picture, & then referre to censure, whether[12] of our deformities is most injurious to Nature, or most effeminine to good men, in the notoriousnes of the example.

Haec-Vir. With like condition of freedome to answere. The Articles[13] are agreed on: Therefore stand forth, halfe *Birchen-Lane,*[14] halfe St. *Thomas Apostles:* The first lent thee a doublet, the later a nether-skirt: Halfe *Bridewell,* halfe *Blacke-Friers;* the one for a scurvy Blocke, the other for a most prophane Feather;[15] halfe Mull'd-Sacke the Chimney-sweeper, halfe *Garrat* the Foole at a Tilting; the one for a Yellow Ruffe, the other for a Skarfe able to put a Souldiour out of countenance;[16] halfe *Bedlam,* halfe *Brimendgham,* the one for a base sale Boote, the other for a beastly Leaden gilt Spurre:[17] and to conclude, all Hell, all Damnation. For a shorne, powdered, borrowed Hayre,[18] a naked, lascivious, bawdy Bosome, a *Leaden-Hall* Dagger, a Highway Pistoll,[19] and a mind and behaviour sutable or exceeding every repeated deformitie. To be briefe, I can but in those few lines deliniate your proportion, for the paraphrase or compartment, to set out your uglinesse to the greatest extent of wonder. I can but referre you to your God-child that carries your own name, I meane the Booke of *Hic-Mulier,* there you shall see your character, and feele your shame, with that palpable plainenesse, that no *AEgyptian* darknes[20] can bee more grosse and terrible.

Hic-Mul: My most tender piece of mans flesh, leave this lightening and thunder, and come roundly to the matter, draw mine accusation into heads, and then let me answere.

Haec-Vir. Then thus. In that Booke you are arraigned, and found guilty. First of *Baseness,* in making your selfe a slave to novelty, and the poore invention of every weake Braine that hath but an imbroidered out-side, Next, of *Unnaturalnesse,* to forsake the Creation of God, and Customes of the Kingdome, to be pieced and patched up by a French Tailor, an Italian Baby-maker, and a Dutch Souldiour (beat from the Armie for the ill example of Ruffianly behaviour)[21] then of *Shamelesnesse,* in casting off all modest softnesse, and civilitie, to runne thorow every desart and wildernesse of mens opinions, like carelesse untamed Heyfers, or wilde Savages. Lastly, of *foolishnesse,* in having no moderation or temper, either in passions or affections: But turning all into perturbations and sicknesses of the soule, laugh away the preciousnes of your Time, and at last dye with the flattering sweet malice of an incurable consumption. Thus *Basenesse, Unnaturalnesse, Shamelesnesse, Foolishnesse,* are the maine Hatch-ments, or Coat-Armours,[22] which you have tane[23] as rich spoiles to adorne you in the deformitie of your apparell: which if you can excuse, I can pitie, and thanke *Proserpina*[24] for thy wit; though no good man can allow of the Reasons.

Hic-Mul: Well, then to the purpose: First, you say, I am *Base,* in being a Slave to Novelty. What slavery can there be in freedome of election? or what basenesse, to crowne my delights with those pleasures which are most sutable to mine affections? Bondage or Slavery, is a restraint from those actions, which the minde (of it owne accord) doth most willingly desire: to performe the intents and purposes of anothers disposition, and that not but by mansuetude[25] or sweetnesse of intreatie; but by the force of authoritie and strength of compulsion. Now for mee to follow change, according to the limitation of mine owne will and pleasure, there cannot bee a greater freedome. Nor do I in my delight of change otherwise then as the whole world doth, or as becommeth a daughter of the world to doe. For what is the world, but a very shop or ware-house

Not Base.

What Bondage is.

A defence of change.

of change? Sometimes Winter, sometimes Summer; day and night: they hold sometimes Riches, sometimes Povertie, sometimes Health, sometimes Sicknesse: now Pleasure; presently Anguish; now Honour; then contempt: and to conclude, there is nothing but change, which doth surround and mixe withall our Fortunes. And will you have poore woman such a fixed Starre, that shee shall not so much as move or twinkle in her owne Spheare? That were true Slavery indeed, and a Basenesse beyond the chaines of the worst servitude. Nature to every thing she hath created, hath given a singular delight in change, as to Hearbs, Plants and Trees a time to wither and shead their leaves, a time to budde and bring forth their leaves, and a time for their Fruits and Flowers: To wormes and creeping things a time to hide themselves in the pores and hollowes of the earth, and a time to come abroad and sucke the deaw; To Beasts libertie to chuse their foode, liberty to delight in their food, and liberty to feed and grow fat with their food. The Birds have the ayre to fly in, the waters to bathe in, and the earth to feed on. But to man, both these and all things else, to alter, frame and fashion, according as his will and delight shall rule him. Againe, who will rob the eye of the variety of objects, the eare of the delight of sounds, the nose of smels, the tong of tasts, & the hand of feeling? & shall only woman, excellent woman; so much better in that she is something purer, be onely deprived of this benefit? Shall she bee the Bondslave of Time, the Handmaid of opinion, or the strict observer of every frosty or cold benummed imagination? It were a cruelty beyond the Racke or Strapado.[26]

What noveltie is.

But you will say it is not *Change,* but *Noveltie,* from which you deterre us: a thing that doth evert the good,[27] and erect the evill; preferre the faithlesse, and confound desert;[28] that with the change of Opinions breeds the change of States, and with continuall alterations thrusts headlong forward both Ruine and Subversion. Alas (soft Sir) what can you chrysten by that new imagined Title, when the words of a wiseman are; *that what was done, is but done againe: all things do change, & under the cope of Heaven there is no new thing.*[29] So that whatsoever wee doe or imitate, it is neither slavish, Base, nor a breeder of Novelty.

Next, you condemne me of *Unnaturalnesse,* in forsaking my creation, and contemning[30] custome. How doe I forsake my creation, that doe all the rights and offices due to my Creation? I was created free, born free, and live free: what lets me then so to spinne out my time,[31] that I may dye free?

Not unnaturall.

To alter creation, were to walke on my hands with my heeles upward, to feed my self with my feet, or to forsake the sweet sound of sweet words, for the hissing noise of the Serpent: but I walk with a face erected, with a body cloathed, with a mind busied, & with a heart full of reasonable and devout cogitations;[32] onely offensive in attire, in as much as it is a Stranger to the curiositie of the present times, and an enemie to Custome. Are we then bound to be the Flatterers of Time, or the dependants on Custome? O miserable servitude chained onely to Basenesse and Folly! for then custome, nothing is more absurd, nothing more foolish.

It was a custome amongst the Romanes, that as we wash our hands before meales, so they with curious and sweet oyntments anointed all their armes and legges quite over, and by successe of time grew from these unguents[33] to bathes of rich perfumed and compound waters,[34] in which they bathed their whole bodies: holding it the greatest disgrace that might be, to use or touch any naturall water, as appeares by these Verses.

Foolish Customes.

She shines with oyntments to make hayre to fall,
Or with sowre Chalke she over-covers all.[35]

Mart.l.2.

It was a custome amongst the Ancients to lye upon stately and soft beds, when eyther they delivered Embassages,[36] or entered into any serious discourse or argument, as appeares by these Verses:

Father Æneas thus, gan say,
From stately Couch whereon he lay.[37]

Virg.Aen.l.2.

Cato Junior held it for a custome, never to eat meat but sitting on the ground:[38] the *Venetians* kisse[39] one another ever at the first meeting: and even at this day it is a generall received custome amongst our English, that when we meet or overtake any man in our travell or journeying, to examine him whither hee rides, how farre, to what purpose, and where he lodgeth? nay, and with that unmannerly boldnesse of inquisition, that it is a certaine ground of a most insufficient quarrell,[40] not to receive a full satisfaction of those demands which goe farre astray from good manners, or comely civilitie;[41] and will you have us to marry our selves to these Mymicke[42] and most fantasticke[43] customes? It is a fashion or custome with us to mourne in Blacke: yet the *Argian*[44] and *Romane* Ladies ever mourned in White;[45] and (if we will tye the action upon the signification of colours) I see not but we may mourne in *Greene, Blue, Red* or any simple colour used in *Heraldry*.[46] For us to salute strangers with a kisse, is counted but civilitie, but with forraine Nations immodestie: for you to cut the hayre of your upper lips, familiar heere in England, every where else almost thought unmanly. To ride on Side-Saddles[47] at first was counted heere abominable pride, &c. I might instance in a thousand things that onely Custome and not Reason hath approved. To conclude *Custome* is an Idiot; and whosoever dependeth wholely upon him, without the discourse of Reason, will take from him his pyde coat,[48] and become a slave indeed to contempt and censure.

But you say wee are barbarous and shameles and cast off all softnes, to runne wilde through a wildernesse of opinions. In this you expresse more cruelty then in all the

Not shameles.

rest, because I stand not with my hands on my belly like a baby at *Bartholomew* Fayre, that move not my whole body when I should but onely stirre my head like Jacke of the Clocke house which hath no joynts,[49] that am not dumbe when wantons court mee,[50] as if Asse-like I were ready for all burthens, or because I weep not when injury gripes[51] me, like a woorried Deere in the fangs of many Curres: am I therefore barbarous or shamelesse? He is much injurious that so baptiz'd us: we are as free-borne as Men, have as free election,[52] and as free spirits, we are compounded of like parts, and may with like liberty make benefit of our Creations: my countenance shal smile on the worthy, and frowne on the ignoble, I will heare the Wise, and bee deafe to Ideots, give counsell to my friend, but bee dumbe to flatterers, I have hands that shall bee liberall to reward desert, feete that shall move swiftly to do good offices, and thoughts that shall ever accompany freedome and severity. If this bee barbarous, let me leave the Citie, and live with creatures of like simplicity.

Not foolish.

To conclude, you say wee are all guilty of most infinite folly and indiscretion. I confesse, that *Discretion* is the true salt which seasoneth every excellency, eyther in Man or Woman, and without it nothing is well, nothing is worthy: that want[53] disgraceth our actions, staineth our Vertues, and indeed makes us most prophane and irreligious, yet it is ever found in excesse, as in too much, or too little: and of which of these are wee guilty; do we weare too many cloathes or too few? if too many, wee should oppresse Nature, if too few, we should bring sicknesse to Nature: but neither of these wee do, for what we do weare is warme, thrifty and wholesome, then no excesse, and so no indiscretion: where is then the error? onely in the Fashion, onely in the Custome.[54] Oh for mercy sake bind us not to so hatefull a companion, but remember what one of our famous English Poets says:

Round-headed Custome th'apoplexie is G.C.
Of Bedrid Nature, and lives led amisse,
And takes away all feeling of offence.[55]

Againe, another as excellent in the same Art, saith,
Custome the Worlds Judgement doth blind so farre, D'Bart.
That Vertue is oft arraign'd at Vices Barre.[56]

And will you bee so tyrannous then, to compell poore Woman to bee a mistrisse to so unfaithfull a Servant? Beleeve it, then we must call up our Champions against you, which are *Beauty* and *Frailty,* and what the one cannot compell you to forgive, the other shall inforce you to pitty or excuse: and thus my selfe imagining my selfe free of these foure Imputations,[57] I rest to bee confuted[58] by some better and graver Judgement.

Haec-Vir. You have wrested out some wit, to wrangle forth no reason; since every thing you would make for excuse, approves your guilt still more ougly: what baser bondage, or what more servile basenesse, then for the flattering and soothing of an unbridled appetite, or delight, to take a wilfull libertie to do evill, and to give evill example? this is to bee Hels Prentice, not Heavens Freewoman.[59] It is dispntable [disputable] amongst our Divines, whether upon any occasion a woman may put on mans attyre, or no:[60] all conclude it unfit; and the most indifferent will allow it, but onely to escape persecution. Now you will not onely put it on, but weare it continually; and not weare it; but take pride in it, not for persecution, but wanton pleasure; not to escape danger, but to runne into damnation; not to helpe others, but to confound the whole sexe by the evilnesse of so lewd an example. *Phalaris*[61] (though an extreme tyrant) when he executed the inventer of the Brazen Bull in the Bull) did it not so much for the pleasure he tooke in the torment, as to cut from the earth a braine so divelish and full of uncivill and unnaturall inventions. And sure had the first inventer of your disguise perisht with all her cooplements[62] about her, a world had been preserved from scandall and slander; for from one evill to beget infinites, or to nourish sin with a delight in sinne, is of all habits the lowest, ignoblest and basest.

Now, who knowes not, that to yeeld to basenesse, must needs be folly? (for what Wisedome will bee guilty of its owne injury?) To be foolishly base, how can there bee an action more barbarous? and to bee base, foolish and barbarous, how can there appeare any sparke, twinkle, or but ember of discretion or judgement? So that notwithstanding your elaborat plea for freedome, your severe condemnation of custome, your fayre promise of civill actions, and your temperate avoiding of excesse, whereby you would seeme to hugge and imbrace discretion; yet till you weare hats to defend the Sunne, not to cover shorne locks, Caules to adorne the head, not *Gregorians* to warme idle braines,[63] till you weare innocent white Ruffes, not jealous yellow jaundis'd bands,[64] well shapt, comely and close Gownes, not light skirts[65] and French doublets, for Poniards,[66] Samplers,[67] for Pistols Prayer-bookes, and for ruffled Bootes and Spurres, neate Shooes[68] and cleane-garterd Stockings, you shall never lose the title of *Basenesse, Unnaturalnes, Shamelesnesse,* and *Foolishnesse,* you shall feede *Ballads,*[69] make rich shops, arme contempt, and onely starve and make poore your selves and your reputations. To conclude, if you will walke without difference, you shall live without reverence: if you will contemne order, you must indure the shame of disorder; and if you will have no rulers but your wills, you must have no reward but disdaine and disgrace, according to the saying of an excellent English Poet:

A stronger hand restraines our wilfull powers, C.M.
A Will must rule above this will of ours;
Not following what our vaine desires do woo,
For Vertues sake but what wee ought to doo.[70]

Hic-Mul. Sir, I confesse you have raysd mine eielids up, but you have not cleane taken away the filme that covers the sight: I feele (I confesse) cause of beliefe, and would willingly bend my heart to entertaine beliefe, but when the accuser is guilty of as much or more then that hee accuseth, or that I see you refuse the potion,[71] and are as grievously infected, blame mee not then a little to stagger,[72] and till you will bee pleas'd to be cleans'd of that leprosie which I see apparant in you, give me leave to doubt whether mine infection be so contagious, as your blinde severity would make it.

The descripti-on of a Wo-manish Man.

Therefore to take your proportion in a few lines, (my deare Feminine Masculine) tell me what Charter, prescription or right of claime you have to those things you make our absolute inheritance? why doe you curle, frizell and powder your hayres, bestowing more houres and time in deviding locke from lock, and hayre from hayre, in giving every thread his posture, and every curle his true sence and circumpherence then ever *Caesar* did in marshalling his Army, eyther at *Pharsalia,* in *Spaine,* or *Brittaine?*[73] why doe you rob us of our Ruffes, of our Earerings, Carkanets,[74] and Mamillions,[75] of our Fannes and Feathers, our Busks[76] and French bodies,[77] nay, of our Maskes,[78] Hoods, Shadowes[79] and Shapynas?[80] not so much as the very Art of Painting,[81] but you have so greedily ingrost[82] it, that were it not for that little fantasticall sharp pointed dagger that hangs at your chins, & the crosse hilt which gards your upper lip,[83] hardly would there be any difference between the fayre Mistris & the foolish Servant. But is this theft the uttermost of our Spoyle?[84] Fie, you have gone a world further, and even ravisht from us our speech, our actions, sports and recreations. Goodnesse leave mee, if I have not heard a Man court his Mistris with the same words that *Venus* did *Adonis,* or as neere as the Booke could instruct him;[85] where are the Tilts and Tournies,[86] and loftie Gallyards[87] that were daunst in the daies of old, when men caperd[88] in the ayre like wanton kids on the tops of Mountaines, and turnd above ground as if they had been compact of Fire or a purer element?[89] Tut all's forsaken, all's vanisht, those motions shewed more strength then Art, and more courage then courtship; it was much too robustious,[90] and rather spent the body then prepared it, especially where any defect before raigned; hence you tooke from us poore Women our traverses and tourneys, our modest statelinesse and curious slidings,[91] and left us nothing but the new French garbe of puppet hopping and jetting.[92] Lastly, poore Sheetle-cock that was only a female invention, how have you taken it out of our hands, and made your selves such Lords and Rulers over it, that though it be a very Embleme of us,[93] and our lighter despised fortunes, yet it dare now hardly come neere us; nay, you keepe it so imprisond within your Bedde-Chambers and dyning roomes, amongst your Pages and Panders,[94] that a poore innocent Mayd to give but a kicke with her Battle-dore,[95] were more then halfe way to the ruine of her reputation. For this you have demolish'd the noble schooles of Hors.manship (of which many were in this Citie) hung up your Armes to rust, glued up those swords in their scabberds that would shake all Christendome with the brandish, and entertained into your mindes such softnes, dulnesse and effeminate nicenesse, that it would even make *Heraclitus* himselfe laugh against his nature[96] to see how pulingly[97] you languish in this weake entertained sinne of womanish softnesse: To see one of your gender either shew himselfe (in the midst of his pride or riches) at a Play house, or publique assembly how; (before he dare enter) with the *Jacobs*-Staffe of his owne eyes[98] and his Pages, hee takes a full survay of himselfe, from the highest sprig in his feather, to the lowest spangle that shines in his Shoostring: how he prunes and picks himselfe like a Hawke set a weathering,[99] cals every severall garment to Auricular confession,[100] making them utter both their mortall great staines, and their veniall and lesse blemishes,[101] though the moat bee much lesse then an Attome:[102] Then to see him plucke and tugge every thing into the forme of the newest received fashion; and by *Durers* rules make his legge answerable to his necke; his thigh proportionable with his middle, his foote with his hand,[103] and a world of such idle disdained foppery:[104] To see him thus patcht up with Symetry, make himselfe complete, and even as a circle: and lastly, cast himselfe amongst the eyes of the people (as an object of wonder) with more nicenesse, then a Virgin goes to the sheetes of her first Lover,[105] would make patience her selfe mad with anger, and cry with the Poet:

O Hominum mores, O gens, O Tempora dura,
Quantus in urbe Dolor; Quantus in Orbe Dolus![106]

Now since according to your own Inference, even by the Lawes of Nature, by the rules of Religion, and the Customes of all civill Nations, it is necessary there be a distinct and speciall difference betweene Man and Woman, both in their habit and behaviours: what could we poore weake women doe lesse (being farre too weake by force to fetch backe those spoiles you have unjustly taken from us) then to gather up those garments you have proudly cast away, and therewith to cloath both our bodies and our mindes; since no other meanes was left us to continue our names, and to support a difference? for to have held the way in which our fore-fathers first set us, or to have still imbraced the civill modestie, or gentle sweetnesse of our soft inclinations; why, you had so farre incroacht upon us, and so over-brib'd the world, to be deafe to any grant of Restitution,[107] that as at our creation, our whole sexe was contained in man our first Parent, so we should have had no other beeing, but in you, and your most effeminate qualitie. Hence we have preserved (though to our owne shames) those manly things which you have forsaken, which would you againe accept, and restore to us the Blushes we layd by, when first wee put on your Masculine garments; doubt not but chaste thoughts and bashfulnesse will againe dwell in us, and our Palaces beeing newly gilt, trimmed, and reedified, draw to us all the *Graces,* all the *Muses;*[108] which that you may more willingly doe, and (as wee of yours) growe into detestation of that deformitie you have purloyn'd,[109] to the utter losse of your Honours and Reputations; Marke how the brave Italian Poet, even in the Infancy of your abuses, most lively describes you;

About his necke a Garknet rich he ware[110]
Of precious Stones, all set in gold well tryed;[111]
His armes that earst all warlike weapons bare,
In golden Bracelets wantonly were tyed:
Into his eares two Rings convayed are
Of golden Wyer, at which on either side,
Two Indian Pearles, in making like two Peares,
Of passing price were pendant at his eares.

Ariost.

A description Effeminatenesse.

His Locks bedewed with waters of sweet savour,
Stood curled round in order on his head;
He had such wanton womanish behaviour,
As though in Valor he had ne're been bred:
So chang'd in speech, in manners and in favour,
So from himselfe beyond all reason led,
By these inchantments of this amorous Dame;
He was himselfe in nothing, but in name.

Thus you see your injury to us is of an old and inveterate continuance, having taken such strong root in your bosomes, that it can hardly bee pull'd up, without some offence to the soyle: ours yong and tender, scarce freed from the Swaddling clouts,[112] and therefore may with as much ease bee lost, as it was with little difficulty found. Cast then from you our ornaments, and put on your owne armours: Be men in shape, men in shew, men in words, men in actions, men in counsell, men in example: then will we love and serve you; then will wee heare and obey you; then will wee like rich Jewels hang at your eares to take our Instructions, like true friends follow you through all dangers, and like carefull leeches powre oyle into your wounds:[113] Then shall you finde delight in our words; pleasure in our faces; faith in our hearts; chastitie in our thoughts, and sweetnesse both in our inward & outward inclinations. Comelinesse shall be then our study; feare our Armour, and modestie our practice: Then shall we be all your most excellentest thoughts can desire, and have nothing in us lesse then[114] impudence and deformitie.

Haec-Vir. Inough: You have both rais'd mine eye-lids, cleered my sight, and made my heart entertaine both shame and delight at an instant; shame in my Follies past; delight in our Noble and worthy Conversion. Away then from me these light vanities, the onely Ensignes[115] of a weake and soft nature: and come you grave and solid pieces, which arme a man with Fortitude and Resolution: you are too rough and stubborne for a womans wearing we will heere change our attires, as wee have chang'd our mindes, and with our attires, our names. I will no more be *Haec-Vir,* but *Hic Vir,* nor you *Hic-Mulier,* but *Haec Mulier:* from henceforth deformitie shall packe to Hell: and if at any time hee hide himselfe upon the earth, yet it shall bee with contempt and disgrace. Hee shall have no friend but Poverty; no favourer but Folly, nor no reward but Shame. Henceforth we will live nobly like our selves, ever sober, ever discreet, ever worthy; true men, and true women. We will bee henceforth like well-coupled Doves, full of industry, full of love: I meane, not of sensuall and carnall love, but heavenly and divine love, which proceedes from God; whose unexpressable nature none is able to deliver in words, since it is like his dwelling, high and beyond the reach of humane apprehension; according to the saying of the Poet, in these Verses following:

Of loves perfection perfectly to speake,
Or of his nature rightly to define,
Indeed doth farre surpasse our reasons reach,
And needs his Priest t'expresse his power divine,
For long before the world he was ybore,

And bred above ith hy'st celestiall Spheare,
For by his power the world was made of yore,
And all that therein wondrous doth appeare.[116]

FINIS.

NOTES

1. The writer is combining the feminine form of the Latin pronoun *haec* with *vir,* the Latin word for "man."

2. The writer is combining the masculine form of the Latin pronoun *hic* with *mulier,* the Latin word for "woman." *Haec-Vir,* a pamphlet attacking women who dress in men's clothing, answers *Hic Mulier,* which was printed by the same printer and distributed in the same year. Note that Haec-Vir translates into a man who has become womanish, while Hic Mulier translates into a new gender, a man-woman.

3. See *Hic Mulier,* n. 7.

4. The tenth part, i.e., a very small part.

5. In Roman mythology, the wife of Jupiter, goddess of marriage and childbirth.

6. In *The Defence of Poesy,* ed. Dorothy M. Macardle (London: Macmillan, 1962), Philip Sidney describes Hercules as "painted, with his great beard and furious countenance, in women's attire, spinning at Omphale's commandment . . . [which] breedeth both delight and laughter" (47). Hercules was so in love with Omphale that he spun by her side. She dressed as Hercules and often hit him with her sandals for his lack of skill with the distaff (used in spinning). See *Hic Mulier,* n. 122.

7. Made up of incorrect Latin. The writer is playing on the fact that the characters' names incorrectly apply the masculine pronoun to a woman and the feminine pronoun to a man. See nn. 1 and 2.

8. The obsolete form of "alarm bell," a bell rung to indicate danger or emergency.

9. The whole kingdom is up in arms, ready to fight.

10. Painted me in the most unflattering light. Paints and dyes were given their color by grinding plants or insects.

11. Impartial.

12. Which.

13. The terms or conditions.

14. Birchen Lane was inhabited by drapers or dealers in cloth. See Thomas Middleton's *Blackbook* (in vol. 5 of *The Works of Thomas Middleton,* ed. Alexander Dyce [London: Edward Lumley, 1840]), in which he describes Birchen Lane as "a camp-royal of hose and doublets" (531). For "doublet," see *Hic Mulier,* n. 30. Haec Vir says that Hic-Mulier bought her doublet in Birchen Lane and her nether skirt, or underskirt, near St. Thomas Apostles Church, where hosiers sold hose and woven underwear.

15. Originally a royal palace, Bridewell was given by Edward VI to the city for "a Workehouse for the poore and idle persons of the Citie" (John Stow, *A Survey of Lon-*

don [1603; Oxford: Clarendon Press, 1971], 2:45). Later, it became a prison. Hic Mulier must have bought her hat, or "Blocke," near Bridewell. "Block" may also refer to the block at Bridewell where public floggings took place. "Blacke-Friers," formerly a Dominican monastery, became a playhouse. Feathers were sold near Blackfriars.

16. *Muld Sacke; or, The apologie of Hic Mulier* was printed in 1620 in response to *Hic Mulier.* It was dedicated by Hic Mulier to Muld Sacke, "None of the least of the ancient Societie of Chimney Sweepers." "Mulled sack" was a hot, sweet, white wine imported from Spain. "Sack" could also mean drowning a person in a sack. For "Yellow Ruffe," see *Hic Mulier,* n. 27; Rowlands, *Tis Merry,* n. 20. "Garrat" is a method of capital punishment by strangulation or a cudgel to twist the strangling cord. Here, a scarf is used.

17. Hic Mulier probably bought her "base" boots near Bedlam, or the hospital of St. Mary of Bethlehem, where the insane had been housed since 1402. "Base" may refer to an inferior ready-made boot rather than one made to fit. "Brimendgham" probably refers to Birmingham, in which "a great part of Birmingham's livelihood derives from its smiths" who most likely made spurs (John Leland, *John Leland's Itinerary,* ed. John Chandler [Dover, N.H.: Alan Sutton, 1993],471). Hic Mulier's spurs were made of lead and covered with gold, and therefore were inferior and deceptive.

18. Hair cut short, dusted with cosmetic powder, and filled out with swatches of false hair.

19. Daggers were sold at the market in Leadenhall. According to Stowe, "Artillerie, Guns, and other armors of the said citie" were stored in Leadenhall, which was also where the gear for the city's pageants and processions was kept (*Survey of London,* 1:158). A "highway pistol" was a small gun, easily carried on the public highways in England and fired with one hand. Daggers were sometimes combined with pistols in early modern England.

20. Intense darkness. Exod. 10.22: "Then Moses stretched forthe his hand toward heaven, and there was a blacke darcknes in all the land of Egypt thre dayes."

21. Women's gowns were made by tailors. The writer's use of "French" implies excessiveness; "baby-maker" probably means a maker of puppets. In other words, Hic Mulier is a puppet to foreign fashion and has forsaken the "Customes of the Kingdome." In the English view, the Dutch drank too much, so perhaps Hic Mulier's pistol belonged to a Dutch soldier forced out of the army for excessive drinking.

22. A "hatchment" was the shield on which the "coat-armours," or coat of arms, was displayed. Hic Mulier has baseness, unnaturalness, shamelessness, and foolishness on her coat of arms.

23. Taken.

24. In classical mythology, the queen of the infernal regions, or Hell.

25. Meekness.

26. Instruments of torture. The rack was an iron frame with rollers at each end to which victims were fastened by their wrists and ankles; the rollers were then turned and the victim's joints were stretched, causing extreme pain. The strapado tied the victim's hands across his back and lifted him up and down with a pulley, wrenching the joints.

27. Novelty, or an attraction to useless objects and behaviors, "evert[s]" (i.e., overthrows) the good.

28. To frustrate or otherwise circumvent that which is deserved or merited.

29. Eccles. 1.9: "What is it that hathe bene done? that & what it is which shalbe done: and there *is* no new thing under the sunne."

30. Disdaining.

31. Hinders me from drawing out my time, as cotton is drawn out when being made into thread.

32. Thoughts or ideas.

33. Ointments or salves.

34. Water mixed with perfumes or herbs.

35. This is a reference to epigram 6.93.9 by Marcus Valerius Martial (40–102 C.E.), who was known for his caustic epigrams. Martial is describing how badly Thais, who is hidden behind a plaster of chalk and vinegar, smells before she enters her bath. See also Michel de Montaigne's essay "Of Ancient Customs," in which he describes the Romans washing their entire body with "compounded and perfumed waters" (in *Essayes,* trans. John Florio [London, 1613], 161). Montaigne quotes the Martial epigram and then translates it as "She shines with ointments that make haire to fall, / Or with dry chalke she over-covers all" (161). Montaigne then quotes the same two lines from the *Aeneid* that are quoted in *Haec-Vir.*

36. The sending of ambassadors.

37. This is a translation of section 2.2 in Virgil's *Aeneid,* the national epic of ancient Rome written in the first century B.C.E.

38. Porcius Cato (105–46 B.C.E.), great grandson of Porcius Cato Marcus, "the censor," was a noted Roman stoic who often went to his tribunal without his shoes or tunic. Montaigne writes, "*Cato Junior,* that after the battell of *Pharsalia* . . . he ever eat sitting on the ground" ("Of Ancient Customs," 161).

39. Montaigne writes, "They used to kisse one another, as the Venetians doe at this day" ("Of Ancient Customs," 161). This statement is followed by a discussion of various customs of wiping one's genitals.

40. The foundation of an argument that lacks force or legitimacy.

41. From Montaigne, "Of Ancient Customs," 161.

42. Imitating another person's speech, behavior, or dress. In *Hic Mulier,* "Mimicke fantastickenesse" is used to describe the clothing of women who dress like men.

43. Eccentric, fanciful, or grotesque.

44. Argos was the chief town in eastern Peloponnesus, in Greece. Under the Roman Empire, Argos was a resort of Roman merchants. See Montaigne's "Of Ancient Customes": "The Argian and Romane Ladies, mourned in white, as our dames wont to doe" (163).

45. Although many people dressed in black when in mourning, Greek and Roman women dressed in white.

46. The art of emblazoning arms. See Shakespeare's *Hamlet* (1600–1601): "Pyrrhus, he whose sable arms, / / . . . smear'd / With heraldry more dismal . . . / . . . tricked / With blood" (2.2.452–58). See also *Hic Mulier,* n. 27.

47. Saddles designed to allow women to sit with both feet on one side of the horse so as to preserve their modesty and not dishevel their skirts.

48. A multicolored coat, especially one worn by a professional fool or jester.

49. Bartholomew babies were the dolls sold at Bartholomew fair, which was held in West Smithfield every year on August 24, St. Bartholomew's Day. A Jack of the Clock was a mechanical figure that struck the bell on the outside of a public clock. Apparently both figures moved only their heads.

50. Not silent when lascivious persons court me.

51. Grips.

52. Choice between alternatives.

53. Lack.

54. See Shakespeare's *King Lear* (1605): "If only to go warm were gorgeous, / Why, nature needs not what thou gorgeous wear'st, / Which scarcely keeps thee warm" (2.4.268–70).

55. The "apoplexie," or sudden illness, of impotent nature and of lives lived astray. "Custome" is used as an excuse for offending others. Perhaps "round-headed" refers to wearing the hair cut short, as the term later referred to members of the Parliamentary Party in the English Civil War who wore their hair cut short. G.C. is probably George Chapman (1559?–1634), a poet and playwright best known for his translations of Homer's *Iliad* and *Odyssey*.

56. Custom so blinds judgment that virtue is often arrested by vice. D'Bart. is probably Guillame de Salluste Du Bartas (1544–90), a French poet whose epics were translated into English by Josuah Sylvester in 1608.

57. Accusations, here of baseness, unnaturalness, shamelessness, and foolishness.

58. Proved wrong.

59. An apprentice to Hell or the Devil, not Heaven's citizen or an honorable woman.

60. See pp. 251–52. See also Deut. 22.5: "The woman shal not weare that which perteineth unto the man, nether shal a man put on womans raiment: for all that do so, *are* abominacion unto the Lord thy God."

61. The fabled ruler of Agrigentum, Sicily, known for his cruelty, who lived ca. 570–549 B.C.E. Legend had it that he ordered criminals roasted alive in a bronze bull, beginning with the ingenius inventor of the bull.

62. Things coupled with her.

63. A caul was a close-fitting cap; a gregorian was a kind of wig that was fashionable in the sixteenth and seventeenth centuries, named after its inventor, Gregory, a London barber.

64. Bands were collars that supplanted the ruff in the seventeenth century. Yellow starch was used for stiffening bands, producing a "jaundiced" look. See *Hic Mulier*, n. 27; see also Middleton, *Roaring Girl* (in *Complete Works of Thomas Middleton*): "The falling band succeeded the cumbersome ruff" (1.1 [Mary]), cited in *A Glossary of Tudor and Stuart Words Especially from the Dramatists*, comp. Walter W. Skeat, ed. A. L. Mayhew (Oxford: Clarendon Press, 1914), 24.

65. Close gowns are those with skirts that stay close to the body, neither built out with farthingales nor so light as to be easily lifted or kicked up. The writer uses "light"

to pun on the weight and substance of the skirts and on the slang meaning of "light," a reference to anything immoral or sexually promiscuous.

66. A short dagger.

67. A piece of embroidery, especially one used as a pattern to be copied.

68. Boots with turned-down tops, hanging in a loose manner like the ruffle of a skirt; that is, not plain shoes and stockings. See Ben Jonson's *Every Man Out of Humor* (ed. Helen Ostovich [Manchester: Manchester University Press, 2001]): "not having leisure to put off my silver spurs, one of the rowels catched hold of the ruffle of my boot" (4.3.425–27). "Neat shoes" might refer to clean, trim shoes or to shoes made of neat (i.e., the hide of an ox).

69. You will give writers of penny ballads material to write about.

70. C.M. may be Christopher Marlowe (1564–93), author of the plays *Tamburlaine* (ca. 1587), *The Jew of Malta* (ca. 1589), and *Faustus* (ca. 1588), the narrative poem *Hero and Leander* (1598), and translations of Ovid's *Amores* and Lucan's *Pharsalia*. However, the concordance to Marlowe's works does not include these lines. Another possibility for C.M. is Christopher Middleton, author of *The Historie of Heaven* (1596) and *The First [and Second] Part of the Nature of a Woman* (1596).

71. You refuse the medicine.

72. The title page of *Hic Mulier* suggests that women who dress as men may suffer from the staggers, a disease that causes an unsteady gait in horses.

73. Hic Mulier says that Haec Vir spends more time frizzling his hair into small, crisp curls, dusting it with powder, and arranging every strand than the Roman commander Julius Caesar (100–44 B.C.E.) spent organizing his army to conquer Spain, Britain, or Pharsalia (where he defeated Pompey in 48 B.C.E.). In *The Anatomie of Abuses* (ed. Margaret Jane Kidnie [Tempe: Arizona Center for Medieval and Renaissance Studies/ Renaissance English Text Society, 2002), Philip Stubbes describes how women styled their hair: "their hair . . . which of force must be curled, frizled and crisped, laide out, (a worlde to see) on wreathes and borders, from one eare to another. And least it should fall down it is under-propped with forks, wiers and I can-not tel what, like grim and sterne Monsters, rather than chaste Christian matrones" (111).

74. A carcanet is a collar or necklace of jewels. Later, the writer quotes a passage from Ludovico Ariosto's *Orlando Furioso* (1532) that reads, "About his necke a Carknet rich he ware" (trans. John Harington [London, 1591], C3).

75. Round, protruding objects, especially those shaped like breasts; perhaps padding used to ornament apparel or fill out the curves of the body.

76. A piece of wood or whalebone worn down the front of the corset to keep the body straight. See John Marston's *Scourge of Villanie* (1599): "Her long slit sleeve, stiffe buske, puffe verdingall, / Is all that makes her thus angelicall."

77. Probably French doublets. See *Hic Mulier*, n. 30.

78. Coverings for the face, worn either as a disguise or for protection. Black masks were often worn by ladies in public, particularly at the theater.

79. Any implement for providing shade and protection from the sun, such as a hand screen, parasol, or headdress that shades the face.

80. Perhaps an Anglicized spelling of the French word *chapeau* (hat).

81. The use of cosmetics. See Thomas Tuke's *Treatise Against Painting and Tincturing of Men and Women* (London, 1616): : "Shall we say the painting of haire or face is *juste*? . . . Sure there is wrong done to God, whose workmanship they would seeme to mend, being discontented with it" (2). The writer of *Hic Mulier* also attacks the use of cosmetics (see n. 101).

82. Engrossed; gathered quantities of something for their own.

83. Styles of beards and mustaches.

84. Objects taken by force.

85. This probably refers to Shakespeare's very popular Ovidian poem *Venus and Adonis,* first published in 1593, in which Venus, the goddess of love and beauty, aggressively woos Adonis, a mortal: "He burns with bashful shame, she with her tears / Doth quench the maiden burning of his cheeks /. . . . He saith she is immodest, blames her miss; / What follows more, she murthers with a kiss" (ll. 49–54). Adonis rejects her and dies hunting boar the following day; Venus is bereft.

86. Tournaments; sports or exercises in which combatants practiced their jousting skills.

87. A brisk and lively dance in triple time.

88. Leaped.

89. Composed of fire, one of the four elements (the others are earth, water, and air, the purer element).

90. Robust or boisterous, a common term in the seventeenth century. See Shakespeare's *Hamlet* (1600–1601): "O, it offends me to the soul to hear a robustious periwig-pated fellow tear a passion to totters" (3.2.7–9).

91. No longer are there duels ("traverse" is a fencing term) and tournaments; now men even walk like women, "sliding" or gliding along. "Sliding" may also have connotations of inconstancy.

92. Hopping and strutting, like a puppet.

93. Shuttlecock is similar to badminton, a game initially played by children. It became a fashionable pastime during the reign of James I. When the writer says that shuttlecork was emblematic or symbolic of women, he is probably alluding to a shuttle used in weaving. The man in the woodcut on the title page of *Haec-Vir* is carrying a shuttlecock racquet and a shuttlecock.

94. Boys employed as servants and go-betweens in clandestine love affairs. In Geoffrey Chaucer's *Troilus and Criseyde* (1385–86), Pandarus arranges the secret tryst between the lovers. His name has since been applied to those who arrange a secret meeting between lovers or who procure a prostitute or sexual partner.

95. A racket used in playing shuttlecock; also an instrument used to smooth out clothes or to beat someone or something.

96. Heraclitus of Epheseus (540–475 B.C.E.), a Greek philosopher known as "the weeping philosopher" because he cried over people's frailties and vicissitudes.

97. Whiningly.

98. An instrument for measuring distances and heights.

99. Preens himself and smooths his feathers, like a hawk. In falconry, to weather a hawk is to accustom it to sit unhooded on a block in the open air.

100. A confession heard by the ear; thus, the practice of verbally confessing sins to a priest.

101. Great blemishes, with a pun on the mortal sins that, according to Catholicism, lead to spiritual death; as opposed to venial sins, which are less serious.

102. A mote (i.e., particle of dust) is smaller than an atom, a body Leucippus and Democritus theorized as the smallest building block of matter.

103. Albert Durer (1471–1528), a German painter and engraver, was especially interested in capturing the proportions of the human body. His *Treatise on Proportions* was published in 1528.

104. Foolishness; silly affectation of elegance.

105. With more care than a virgin takes in going to bed with her lover for the first time.

106. "O morals of men, O nation, O harsh times! / How much anguish in the city; how much deceit in the world!" (I was unable to locate the source of this quote.)

107. A restoration of something to its rightful owner (i.e., male clothing to men).

108. In classical mythology, the Graces are the sister goddesses of beauty and charm: Aglaia, Thalia, and Euphrosyne; the Muses (the nine daughters of Mnemosyne) are the goddesses of learning and the arts: Calliope (epic poetry), Clio (history), Thalia (comedy), Melpomene (tragedy), Euterpe (flute playing), Terpsichore (dancing), Erato (lyre), Polyhymnia (sacred song), and Urania (astronomy).

109. Stolen.

110. A description of Rogero, after being enchanted by the witch Alcynas, in Ariosto's *Orlando Furioso* (7.46–47). The marginal note in John Harington's 1591 translation reads: "A description of an effeminate courtier." In the translation, l. 12 reads: "As though in Valence [Valor] he had long beene bred." A "Garknet" is a carcanet (see n. 74 above).

111. Refined, purified.

112. Pieces of cloth used to swaddle a baby. Hic Mulier is saying that women dressing as men is a recent "injury," unlike men's effeminacy.

113. Like conscientious physicians pour oil in wounds to soothe and heal them.

114. Rather be empty than contain.

115. Characteristic marks.

116. Quoted from Edmund Spenser's *Colin Clout's Come Home Again* (1535), ll. 835–42. In the original, l. 837 reads, "Indeed (said Colin) passeth reasons reach" and l. 40, "And bred above in *Venus* bosome deare." Spenser's poem is a pastoral that looks to a simple life removed from the city. "Ybore" means born.

Afterword

Ann Rosalind Jones

Susan Gushee O'Malley's transcription of Samuel Rowlands's 1602 pamphlet *Tis Merry when Gossips meet* includes an exchange between a gentleman and an eager bookseller's apprentice. The gentleman wants a new book, "a prettie / thing come foorth to my humours liking." The apprentice convinces him that Rowlands's three gossips are not only brand new but that he is "in Love, or at least / will be with one of these three"—and, trying an opposite tack, that the time he spends reading the little book will keep him "from Dice, / Taverne, Bawdy-house, and so foorth." This rapidly offered advertisement for a pamphlet voicing women's complaints about marriage typifies the appeal that printed entries in the gender debate had for centuries in England and Europe: the little book is new, it's entertaining, and it's a serious pastime.

As O'Malley's collection of six early seventeenth-century pamphlets demonstrates, writers on the topic of women and marriage performed in a variety of registers. Rowlands's gossip pamphlets, like the anonymous pair *Hic Mulier* and *Haec-Vir,* are clearly aimed at popular readers: the intriguingly detailed woodcuts that illustrate their title pages, their dedications to imagined groups ("London / Gentle-women that are friends to mirth") rather than highly placed individuals mentioned by name, and the colloquial energy of their dialogues set the reader in the midst of angry, street-smart, up-to-the-minute voices. Even the nameless speaker of *Hic Mulier* identifies good and bad women as his addressees and pictures them at length.

William Heale and Christopher Newstead, in contrast, dedicate their treatises to specific noblewomen and write in the Latinate, highly citational mode of university-trained divines. Yet even these learned, leisurely monologues share the argumentative, immediate engagement of the popular pamphlets. Each writer promises something new, responding to a recent entry in the gender debate: Heale to an examination speech he heard delivered by a graduating law student at Oxford, Newstead to a chorus of writers he calls "Hyperbolizing selfe-conceitists, who deeme it their greatest grace, to be able to disgrace women." Both writers, with the rhetorical force of newly trained preachers, throw challenges and questions at their readers. Heale appeals to husbands presumably open to persuasion: explaining that it was the Devil who damned Eve, he asks, "How can you then be contented to be apprentices in the Devils trade?" Newstead sweetly reminds husbands, "who so convenient as a wife to unclaspe the bosome of thy thoughts unto?" One reason to study the gender debate is simply that the writing in it is so often inspired: aggressive, combative, building in face-to-face encounters even when the arguments themselves are abstract or familiar. At the climax of *Haec-Vir,* the second pamphlet on cross-dressing, the reader senses that Hic Mulier's verbal battle with Haec Vir is what has raised her spirits to the pitch at which she can make the exhilaratingly daring claim, "*Custome* is an Idiot"!

For today's readers trained in the formal meters and archaizing or noble diction of canonized writers of the Renaissance, these pamphlets open up a whole new world. O'Malley's careful and abundant notes show how much there is to learn about popular culture: a particular decade's sexual slang, the transformation of French fashion terms into English words, the proverbs and biblical tags through which Londoners of all classes made sense of their lives. We discover, as well, the material realities of London life: the relevance of the landmarks of the city and the location of its markets to common people, the tricks of city innkeepers (their use of "nicks," or false bottoms, to fool their customers into thinking a wine cup or beer can was fuller than it was), the availability of cheap spurs coated with gold but made of lead. As in city comedy, the pamphlets show how saturated with class meanings were certain objects and styles and how keenly people of all ranks observed and judged the possessions of their neighbors as significant forms of public behavior.

A good deal of doubt has been cast on how far the seventeenth-century gender debate furthered the interests of women: whether it wasn't mainly rhetorical, paralyzed in preset categories, more a topic for male writers' virtuosity than a real challenge to power relations among men and women. These texts, in different ways, all justify a more positive view. Rowlands may appear to give the final word to men by finishing *A whole crew of kind Gossips* with the husbands' response to their wives, but the energy and frankness he writes into the speeches of the widow give her real authority as a woman who knows how the world works. As the far greater success of the Wife, the Widow, and the Maid's pamphlet suggests, the Widow's earthy honesty and the accuracy of her attack on marriage far outweigh the often heard complaints written for the less vividly characterized "Six honest HUSBANDS." Heale's careful scrutiny of civil and church law proves that there is no official justification for wife beating, and if we are to believe his dedication, Lady Margaret Hele saw such proof as a genuinely valuable document for women, urging him to write and publish it quickly. Christopher Newstead's *Apology For Women; or, Women's Defense* may be a self-regarding performance, exhibiting his ability to pile up *sententiae* on almost any subject, but he nonetheless works out a new, if contradictory, position: women may have fallen through Eve, but through ensuing history they have evolved to a state superior in many ways to that of men. Newstead energetically attacks the sexual double standard, rephrasing the lines of Alice Countess of Salisbury from Michael Drayton's *England's Heroical Epistles* to address the critique directly to men:

> To men is granted
> priviledge to tempt:
> But in that Charter,
> women be exempt:
> Their fault it selfe
> serves for the fault excuse,
> And makes it ours,
> though yours be the abuse.

And he reverses the common argument that a wife should be a moon to her husband's sun, shining in reflected glory when he is present and invisible when he is absent. Newstead twice turns the metaphor upside down: "She is as the Sunne, and hee the Moone, the beames of her presence is the cause of his shining."

The novel, entertaining, and serious qualities of gender-war pamphlets are most vividly illustrated in the *Hic Mulier* and *Haec-Vir* pair. London women appear to have adopted the style of wearing men's hats, doublets, and swords at several points in the late sixteenth century, but a specifically topical element in the 1620 attack on Hic Mulier is its writer's reference to the Overbury scandal. In 1615 and 1616, two women had been accused of killing the courtier Sir Thomas Overbury: the seamstress Anne Turner, known for having brought the style of yellow starched cuffs and ruffs from France to England, who confessed to providing poison for the murder, and the noblewoman Frances Howard, who was said to have ordered the whole affair. The author of *Hic Mulier* condemns London women as imitators of these two "founders": "From the first you got the false armoury of yellow Starch. . . . From the other, you have taken the monstrousnesse of your deformitie in apparrell." Drawing on a sensational scandal from the recent past to condemn the new resurgence of masculine style, this writer describes what he sees and is enraged by in the streets at the moment. His publisher, John Trundle, like many printers involved in the gender debate, knew a good thing when he saw it; in the same year that this pamphlet went into a second printing, Trundle brought out a response.

Haec-Vir, beginning with each character's misrecognition of the gender of the other, is far funnier than *Hic Mulier,* and the dialogue form allows one character to advertise the famous pamphlet in which the other has appeared: Haec Vir exclaims, "What, *Hic-Mulier,* the Man-Woman? She that like a Larum-Bell at midnight hath raised the whole Kingdome in Armes against her?" The dialogue, even though it is orchestrated finally to convert cross-dressers of both sexes, nonetheless gives us an eloquent, irrepressible, and persuasive female speaker. When Haec Vir repeats the first pamphlet's claim that women in men's clothes are slaves to fashion, he provokes Hic Mulier's serious claim, drawing on centuries of defenses of women, that she, like men, "was created free" and "born free"—and she adds, more radically, that she intends to "live free . . . to spinne out my time, that I may dye free." In the same way, Haec Vir's summary of the earlier pamphlet's charge that women dressed as men follow foolish novelty provokes Hic Mulier's rapid survey of variable ancient, European, and local habits of dress and behavior as evidence of the "thousand things that onely Custome and not Reason hath approved." In fact, it is at her suggestion that each debater agrees to return to conventionally gendered behavior, implying not that they have rediscovered fixed essences but that equal collaborators can redistribute gender habits by choice. If Hic Mulier and Haec Vir can bargain to return to traditional social roles, their pact demonstrates that such roles are man-made—or, as a 1620 punster might have it, man-maid.

It is difficult, as O'Malley concedes, to know for certain whether what we, as modern readers, see as radical new elements in such pamphlets were read the same way at the time. Certainly, as Cis van Heertum has shown, a progressive tract like Rachel Speght's *Mouzell for Melastomus* was read with ferocious hostility by the annotator whose remarks are preserved in the Beinecke Library copy of the pamphlet.[1] By contrast, Albert Rabil has shown that whatever ironies and absurdities Agrippa may have intended in his *Declamation on the Nobility and Preeminence of the Female Sex,* later readers took at face value his claim for absolute equality between the sexes: the jokes disappeared and the new ideas prevailed.[2] O'Malley's argument for a kind of pointillist appropriation, a practice of partial reading by women through which they focused on liberating lines out of context, seizing what they could in their own interests, makes good sense. Such partial readings certainly underlay the widely shared early modern practice of assembling commonplace books by men and women alike. Thanks to O'Malley's appreciative introductions and rich explanatory material, today's readers of both sexes can read these novel, entertaining, and serious pamphlets with the understanding and pleasure they deserve.

NOTES

1. Cis van Heertum, "A Hostile Annotation of Rachel Speght's *A Mouzell for Melastomas* (1617)," *English Studies* 68.6 (1987): 490–96.

2. Albert Rabil Jr., "Agrippa and the Feminist Tradition," in Henricus Cornelius Agrippa's *Declamation on the Nobility and Preeminence of the Female Sex,* trans. Albert Rabil Jr. (Chicago: University of Chicago Press, 1996), 27–29.

Index

SUSAN GUSHEE O'MALLEY is a professor of English at Kingsborough Community College, City University of New York, and a professor of liberal studies at the CUNY Graduate School. She is the editor of *Defences of Women* in *The Early Modern Englishwoman: A Facsimile Library of Essential Works* (Scolar Press, 1996) and has contributed essays to *Debating Gender in Early Modern England, 1500–1700* (Palgrave, 2002) and *Shakespeare Matters* (University of Delaware Press, 2003). Currently she is chair of the nineteen-campus faculty senate of the City University of New York and a trustee *ex-officio* of the University.

ANN ROSALIND JONES, Esther Cloudman Dunn Professor of Comparative Literature at Smith College, has published *The Currency of Eros: Women's Love Lyric in Europe, 1540–1620,* a translation, with Margaret Rosenthal, of *The Poems and Selected Letters of Veronica Franco,* and, with Peter Stallybrass, *Renaissance Clothing and the Materials of Memory.* She teaches a course on the Renaissance gender debate every year at Smith and is now working on printed costume books throughout Europe.

The University of Illinois Press
is a founding member of the
Association of American University Presses.

University of Illinois Press
1325 South Oak Street
Champaign, IL 61820-6903
www.press.uillinois.edu